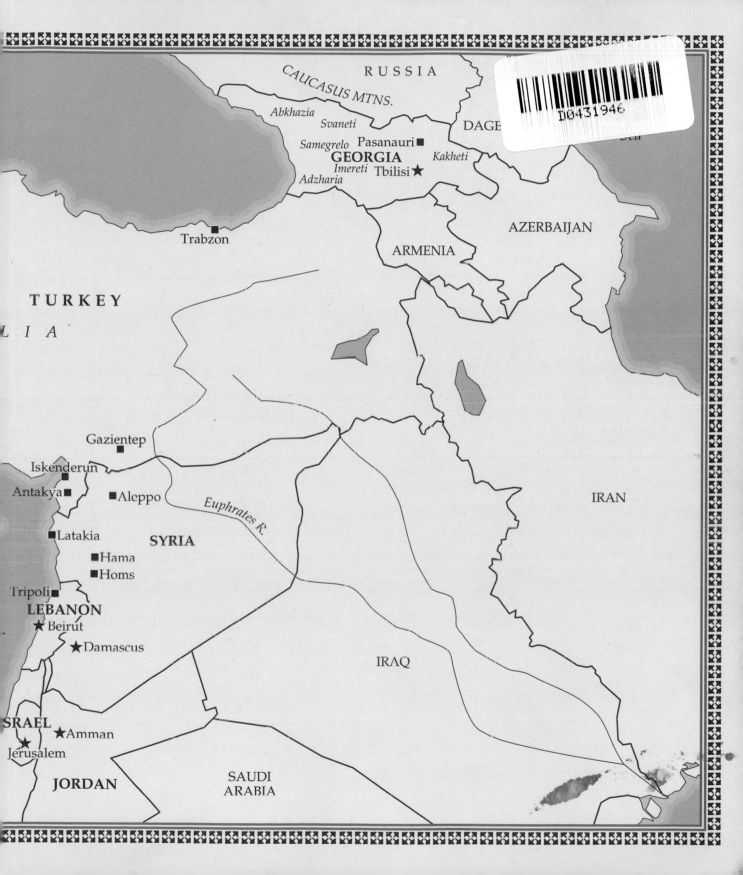

RUSSIA

CAUCASUS MTNS.

Abkhazia

Svaneti

DAGE

Samegrelo Pasanauri ■

GEORGIA *Kakheti*

Imereti Tbilisi ★

Adzharia

AZERBAIJAN

ARMENIA

Trabzon ■

TURKEY

LIA

IRAN

Gazientep ■

Iskenderun

Antakya ■ Aleppo ■

Euphrates R.

SYRIA

Latakia ■

■ Hama

■ Homs

Tripoli ■

LEBANON

★ Beirut

★ Damascus

IRAQ

SRAEL ★ Amman

★ Jerusalem

JORDAN SAUDI ARABIA

THE COOKING
OF THE EASTERN
MEDITERRANEAN

Also by Paula Wolfert

COUSCOUS AND OTHER GOOD FOOD FROM MOROCCO
MEDITERRANEAN COOKING
THE COOKING OF SOUTH-WEST FRANCE
PAULA WOLFERT'S WORLD OF FOOD

THE COOKING
OF THE EASTERN
MEDITERRANEAN

215 Healthy, Vibrant, and Inspired Recipes

PAULA WOLFERT

HarperCollins*Publishers*

Portions of this book have appeared in somewhat different form in
Cuisine; Eating Well; Food & Wine; Gourmet; Modern Maturity;
and the *New York Times.*

HarperCollins books may be purchased for educational, business, or sales
promotional use. For information please write: Special Markets
Department, HarperCollins Publishers, Inc., 10 East 53rd Street,
New York, NY 10022.

FIRST EDITION

DESIGNED BY JOEL AVIROM
PHOTOGRAPHY: PAULA WOLFERT
LINE ART: LAURA HARTMAN MAESTRO
PHOTO ILLUSTRATION: JASON SNYDER

Library of Congress Cataloging-in-Publication Data
Wolfert, Paula.
The cooking of the eastern Mediterranean : 215 healthy, vibrant, and
inspired recipes / Paula Wolfert.—Ist ed.
p.   cm.
Includes bibliographical references and index.
ISBN 0-06-016651-7
I. Cookery, Mediterranean.   2. Cookery, Middle Eastern.
I. Title.
TX725.M35W63   1994   93-44645
641.59182'2—dc20

94 95 96 97 98 DT/RRD 10 9 8 7 6 5 4 3 2 1

For Bill,
Who Walked with Me Through the Souks

CONTENTS

IV
SOUPS

V
SMALL UNCOOKED SALADS

VI
SMALL COOKED VEGETABLE DISHES

XIV
DESSERTS

ACKNOWLEDGMENTS

Many wonderful, generous people helped me with this book, often receiving me in their homes and sharing their food and their recipes. I hope every one of them will find his or her name arranged regionally and alphabetically below.

There were some people who helped me in major ways of whom I would like to make special mention.

My husband, Bill Bayer, who always steered me in the right direction and never complained, even when he had to eat the same dish over and over again.

My editor and friend, Susan Friedland, for her encouraging and brilliant editorial guidance.

My agent, Susan Lescher, for her patience and encouragement.

My dear Greek food-journalist friend and fellow *kalofagaou* ("good eater"), Aglaia Kremezi, who traveled with me through the countryside of Macedonia, Epirus, and Thrace, on our own nonviolent culinary version of *Thelma and Louise.*

Kind and generous Nevin Halici, a Turkish food authority and cookbook author extraordinaire, who took me into her home in Konya, taught me dishes, and answered all my questions.

Kind and generous Ayfer Ünsal, a Turkish journalist and gastronome, who hosted me in her home in Gaziantep, introduced me to the prize-winning cooks in her area, and helped me far beyond the call of duty. She has become my "spiritual sister."

Filiz Hösukolglu, my friend and companion in Gaziantep, who translated almost nonstop for three weeks, and was forever patient with my incessant questioning.

Tamara Kurdashivili, my friend, guide, and companion in the Republic of Georgia, who showed me everything and responded to my endless questions, always with a smile.

Tsino Natsuvlishvili, my hostess in Tbilisi, who marketed with me, cooked with me, and taught me the secrets of the Georgian kitchen.

Ayman Ramadan of Damascus, who escorted me and my husband through his country, taking us wherever we wanted to go, introducing us to some of Syria's best cooks, and acting as interpreter, guide, and friend.

Vefa Alexiadou, for providing me with a wonderful home away from home in Salonika (Thessaloniki), and for sharing some wonderful recipes.

With thanks to Rosa Abdulkarim, Emelie Abdy, Adnan and Maja Abrash, Adnan Al-Jabri, Amal Al-Jabri, Lamya Al-Jabri, Anar Al-Zarzour, Anne-Marie Weiss Armush, Alice Bezjian, Samira Ghorra, Jennifer Hamarneh, Soudiah Hammoudi, Barbara Thomas Isaac, Isam Al-Jabri, Hilweh Malhas, Hayat Mufti, Imam Najjar, Miriam Haj Osmaan, Christine Sahadi, Grace Sasson, William Shallah, Linda Shallah, Elias Shamaz, David Shanah, Hayat Taghi, Soheilia Talas, and Hayat Malhas Yaghi for their hospitality, guidance, recipes, and notes on Armenian, Circassian, Jordanian, Sephardic, and Syrian cooking.

With thanks to Elena Averoff, Mr. and Mrs. Gianni Boutari, Mary Choncoff, Panayiotis Kamanikas, Sotiris Kitrilakis, Bessy Morafeti, Voula Papadapolous, Maria Papadina, Meredith Pilon, Julie Rounds, and Margarita and Charisis Voyiatzis for their hospitality, guidance, recipes, and notes on Greek Macedonian, Epirote, Thracian, and Slavic Macedonian cooking.

With thanks to Zuran Amiransashvilli, Junbar Asatiani, Jerrilyn Brusseau, Laura Dewell, Aishat Gasanguseinova, Gorgy Gorgodze, Dr. Dee Holisky, Timori Huaberidze, Buba Khotoveli, Etheri Nukri, Tsitsi Ratishvili, and Roman Saifullin for their hospitality, recipes, and notes on Georgian and Dagestani cooking.

With thanks to İlhan Arslanyürek, Aysel Budak, Burham Çadğaş, Ismail Demir, Nüket Ersoy, Hilmet Goktekin, Fikriye Gulenler, Sevilay Güllü, Fazilet Igde, Mr. and Mrs. Selim Nazilicam, Mükerrem Özcan, Tuğrul Şavkay, Leman Sezer, Aybek Surdam, Meziyet Telbisoğlu, Medhia Tuzcu, and Emil Yetlin for their hospitality, notes, and recipes on Turkish cooking.

A special thank-you to the following editors for their assignments, guidance, and help: Catherine Bigwood, Patricia Brown, Penelope Green, Jennifer Griffin, Florence Gross, Patricia Jamieson, Richard Kot, Carole Lalli, Kemp Minifie, Scott Mowbry, Warren Picower, Susan Stuck, Susan Taylor, Zanne Zakroff, and Gail Zweigenthal; also to my copy editor, Bitite Vinklers, and to Mary Kurtz, production editor at HarperCollins.

And thanks to my dear friend Dalia Carmel, who helped me amass a library on the various cuisines covered in this book, and who went out of her way to find cooks across America who would answer my questions and check my facts.

I am sincerely grateful to Arlene Wanderman, U.S. representative of the International Olive Oil Council, for giving generously of her time and knowledge.

I lift a glass to the team at Oldways Preservation & Exchange Trust for so generously providing me with extra valuable time in northern Greece and Turkey.

I offer very special thanks to Joel Avirom, Joseph Montebello, and Laura Hartman Maestro for making this book so attractive.

Some food and health professionals were extremely helpful in sharing information: Shirley Corriher, Cara DaSilva, Dr. Adam Drewnowski, Suzanne Hamlin, Nancy Harmon Jenkins, Barbara Kafka, Grace Kirschenbaum, Dr. Barbara Levine, Harold McGee, Molly O'Neill, Charles Perry, Linda Russo, Elizabeth Schneider, Jeffrey Steingarten, Arlene Wanderman, Jan Wiemar, James Villas, and Martha Villas.

INTRODUCTION

This book reflects my travels of the past five years in search of good food and the people who prepare it.

Although I often describe my travels as a quest for recipes, looking back I realize I have always sought more. The recipes are merely the fruits; the joy is the encounters with the people, nearly always women, who prepare the dishes. I recognize these women almost as soon as I meet them, for the eyes of true cooks always light up when they speak about food, and share their methods and secrets. You will meet many of these women in these pages. I hope their lives and enthusiasms will move you as much as they have moved me.

Though I call this book *The Cooking of the Eastern Mediterranean*, it is not a definitive text, nor could it be, since, by my calculations, it would take three lifetimes to compile such a work. Rather, it is a personal selection of dishes from a vast area, diverse in languages, cultures, and traditions. But there are, I believe, unifying threads, which will, I hope, become apparent: clarity of taste, ease of preparation, food that is healthful and honest. And there is something else as well—a certain embracing culinary spirit that I define as generosity. More on this later.

Four principal regions are surveyed here: Slavic Macedonia and northern Greece (Macedonia, Epirus, and Thrace); Turkey (particularly the southeastern part of the country); the Levant (particularly the northern Syrian city Aleppo); and the Republic of Georgia, a country that, although it has no Mediterranean shore, is Mediterranean in spirit and agriculture.

As I traveled and cooked, I began to discover fascinating cross-connections among the regions covered in the pages that follow: the use of red pepper pastes (I often felt I was meandering down a "pepper trail," from the Syrian coastal village of Latakia to the bustling Georgian capital, Tbilisi); emphasis on cooked and raw vegetable dishes; meat treated as a condiment rather than the focus of a dish; the use of pulses, grains, and nuts; rusticity and honesty. Whether in the country pies (*pittas*) of northern Greece, the stuffed peppers of the Balkans, the raw salads of Lebanon, Turkish eggplant dishes, Georgian bedazzlements with spices and herbs, Syrian kibbeh, or the Regional Sampler of Vegetable Stews with meat that I have included here, I found a core simplicity of approach that, in my view, is the mark of culinary sophistication. I'll go out on a limb: you won't find a dishonest dish in this book. Nothing fancy, nothing gussied up by an ambitious chef. The food here is real food, some of it farmhouse, some urban and complex, the real food of real people.

THE REGIONS

Slavic Macedonia is tucked away in the southern part of former Yugoslavia, close to the Albanian, Bulgarian, and Greek frontiers. There has been civilization here for more than two thousand years. A town such as Ohrid was a center of learning when most of Europe was lost in the darkest of the Dark Ages, and the town is filled with Byzantine churches and Turkish mosques. Lake Ohrid is extraordinary—the water is so clear and still that on a calm day you can see to a depth of sixty feet; the surrounding mountains are still capped with snow in summer, and in the mornings the mists rise slowly, revealing a soft, smooth surface that glows from deep within—the scene is altogether hypnotic. The trout from this lake is a spotted, pink-fleshed species found nowhere else. It is at its best simply pan fried.

Slavic Macedonian cuisine is strongly influenced by Greek and Turkish cooking, though there are differences. The desserts are not quite so sweet; phyllo pastry is more likely to enclose brined cabbage or leeks and cheese than nuts. In this part of the Balkans, however, I noticed that sweet and hot paprika was usually applied with a generous touch. There are such dishes as pork stewed with leeks, and a soup of pureed nettles and lamb topped with chopped spinach. Although each Macedonian region has its specialties, there are certain similarities found in all Macedonian food: the lavish use of garlic, paprika, peppermint, black pepper, basil, and a wild oregano called *chambusa.* The Crusaders who passed through on the Via Egnatia brought an unusual hot version of Circassian chicken.

Northern Greece, comprising Macedonia, Epirus, and Thrace, is a green, ravishingly beautiful area, as different from the familiar parched Greece of the

Aegean Islands as night is from day. Sparsely populated, it is a land of majestic mountains, rushing streams, gushing waterfalls, valleys of wildflowers, pristine beaches, and extraordinary rock formations.

In my opinion, the food of the North is a fascinating mélange of dishes— spicy and earthy, more complex and better seasoned than in the South, probably because the area is a genuine crossroads of culinary ideas. Dishes from the western region, Epirus, bear Italian, Romanian, and Slavic influences. Here the cooks use coarse cornmeal, sometimes substituting it for pastry in their pies of wild greens and cheese. They are specialists in edible weeds and innards—all kinds of sheep and goat parts stewed, roasted, or stuffed into cabbage leaves or pork skins—and they produce cheeses of stunning quality.

Macedonian dishes have strong roots in Turkey and the lands invaded by the Crusaders. Sephardic Jews, who settled in Salonika in large numbers after 1492, brought Moorish recipes. And today one finds returning Pontian Greeks (Greeks from Eastern Europe and the Black Sea regions of the former Soviet Union) executing recipes that bear the influence of the Caucasus.

At a dinner party in the penthouse of an elegant Art Deco apartment building on the famous curving waterfront of Salonika, my host, a well-known wine entrepreneur, held forth on the culinary superiority of his region: "Here we are the meeting point of all the influences that have ever touched our country, per- haps, in a sense, the eye of the storm. We share the hospitality and zest for living of our cousins in the South, but I think our food is more interesting, because we live together as so many different races."

I looked toward the terrace. A cool breeze blew off the water. Freighters strung with lights dotted the bay. I thought over my experiences of northern Greek food: the last-minute dustings of black pepper; pickled vegetables served as garnishes; white-wine-based stews; long white leeks, pickled cabbage leaves, and wild herbs used as fillings for phyllo pastry pies. In the pages that follow you will read much about this cuisine. I hope it delights you as much as it did me, giving you a whole new conception of Greek cooking.

If one thinks of the eastern Mediterranean as an arc, Turkey is the keystone, a country that not only synthesized the cooking styles of the many nations it conquered but also reinterpreted and then exported these ideas to the farthest reaches of the greater Mediterranean.

Turkish home cooking is simple to prepare, easy to like, healthy to eat. Although all Turkish regions have their specialties, there are certain culinary constants: the use of yogurt, vegetables (for centuries, it seems, Turkish cooks have had a love affair with the eggplant!), fruits, herbs such as mint and dill, grains, beans, nuts, and spices. In Turkey the word "meat" nearly always means lamb. For pilafs, cooks use cracked wheat, charred green wheat, or hulled wheat berries, as well as rice. If a green leaf or a vegetable is suitable for stuffing, you can be sure a Turkish cook has found a way to stuff it.

You will find recipes here from Istanbul and Izmir, some dating back to the Ottoman period, and recipes too from the holy city Konya, where, in an adjoining village, I learned to make Turkish country breads from an amazing woman named Mukerrem. But my focus is on Gaziantep in the Southeast, where some of the most exciting Turkish food is prepared.

Gaziantep is located on an ancient caravan route, near the Syrian border. Its spectacular spicy, robust food is influenced by the best of Arabic, Armenian, and Kurdish cookery. In the following pages you will find recipes for numerous Gaziantep specialties, among them baklava and various meat dishes, for which the city is justly famous. But there are many less familiar dishes, equally delicious—for instance, a lentil soup with nutritious rich greens, finished with a flourish of herbs and spices; and a dish of creamy eggplant, raw onion slivers, and hot green chili used as a bed for spicy meat grilled over coals. The strong flavors and earthy aromas of these and other Gaziantep recipes will treat and tantalize you.

I had always wanted to go to Aleppo; for years tales of its superb cuisine had reached me, tales too of its huge covered market, or souk, magnificent mosques, and the decaying Baron Hotel, where T. E. Lawrence stayed and Agatha Christie wrote *The Orient Express*.

I was timid at first about traveling to Syria, but when an opportunity arose, I embraced it. Damascus was fascinating, and I adored the ruins of Palmyra, but when I finally reached Aleppo, in the North, I could tell by the aromas in the streets that I had found a culinary paradise. The city, it turned out, was everything

I had dreamed, and its food was as fine as I had heard. More Oriental than Damascus, its cooking is influenced by the rich traditions of its inhabitants—Arabs, Armenians, Assyrians, Jews, and Turks. Though the food of Lebanon, Jordan, and the rest of Syria can be very good indeed, for me Aleppo will always be the Mecca of Middle Eastern cooking.

Famous for its hot red pepper pastes, pistachios, delicious pomegranate-flavored sauces, and dozens of varieties of kibbeh (which I regard as a masterpiece of Middle Eastern cuisine), Aleppo offers a great array of specialties. I most particularly recommend *muhammara*, a delicious rust-colored dip of ground walnuts, tangy tart pomegranates, and hot fleshy peppers; *ormuk*, a wonderful pear-shaped meat dish in which ground meat encases baby eggplant that has been cooked until it reaches a state of pure creaminess; and a remarkable dessert called Syrian Cheese Rags, made of semolina, fresh moist cheese, and sugar syrup. You will not be disappointed!

My wanderlust took me to the Republic of Georgia in the mid-1980s, when it was still part of the Soviet Union. I had heard much about this little country, the size of Ireland, hovering beneath great Mother Russia, and clinging to the eastern coast of the Black Sea and the southern slopes of the Caucasus. Here, I was told, the markets were filled with the produce of abundant harvests, the wine and food were good, the climate and spirit were supremely Mediterranean. Everything I heard was true, but nothing prepared me for the superb quality of Georgian cuisine—its sophisticated spiciness and pungency, and the masterful, lavish use of herbs and spices by its cooks, often producing tastes so exotic they reminded me of Indian food.

Pomegranates, lemons, unripened grapes, vinegars, sour plums, sour cherries, sumac, barberries, and yogurts are used as souring agents; cinnamon, coriander, pepper, fenugreek, caraway, and paprika are the main spices; parsley, coriander, dill, basil, tarragon, mint, and lovage are the principal herbs. I was constantly dazzled by the ingenious ways Georgian cooks combine these condiments, creating sensual, harmonious dishes. I will never forget a mountain preparation of trout cooked with pomegranate and eggplant, then strewn with basil, parsley, green coriander, and scallions, or a deep-tasting blackberry sauce flavored with garlic and coriander, and offered as an accompaniment to the famous Georgian specialty, Chicken *Tabaka*. Indeed, in Georgia one finds a whole new slant on eastern Mediterranean flavors.

John le Carré, in his novel *The Little Drummer Girl*, describes a scene in which an Israeli spy master, recruiting a British girl as a penetration agent, says of Palestinians, with complete sincerity, "You will find them an easy people to love."

This is true of all the cooks I met on my eastern Mediterranean travels—Arabs, Armenians, Georgians, Greeks, Jews, Kurds, Macedonians, and Turks alike. Whatever their views—political, social, or religious—when encountered one-on-one, they consistently treat a visitor with unbounded warmth and kindness. A lot has been written about Middle Eastern hospitality, perhaps so much that the expression has become a cliché. But in all my travels, over the quarter century I have written about food, I have never met such gracious, generous people. For them the sharing of food, as in any culture, is the most important symbol of hospitality.

A little story will, I hope, illustrate the point. During my stay in Georgia, I and a friend, Jerrilyn Brusseau (founder of the Peace Table, an organization that tries to bring people together through cooking), were invited to the tiny autonomous republic of Dagestan, on the Caspian Sea.

When we arrived at the ancient Caucasian village of Khunzakh, nine thousand feet above sea level, we were greeted by the mayor, who bore a striking resemblance to James Mason.

"Guests here are holy," he told us. He then assured us that his villagers were "excellent fighters" and would "protect" us with their lives. "Not one of your hairs will be lost here! You are guests of our entire village. By the end of your stay, all our women and children will have kissed you!" With that he toasted us with tea.

The following morning, at six, seven elderly local women, in black dresses and black head shawls, appeared on our doorstep from the icy air and began to kiss us. They had come, they explained, to teach us to make corn bread. I can still feel the parchment-like texture of their deeply weathered cheeks.

It is for experiences such as this that I travel, my search for recipes being my work and my excuse.

A NOTE ON PREPARING MENUS USING THIS BOOK

Dishes suitable as mezze, or hors d'oeuvres, are scattered throughout this book, marked by an asterisk (*).

The sauces and dips in the first chapter all make good mezze. You will also find mezze or small dishes in the following chapters: "Savory Country Pies and Pastries," "Small Uncooked Salads," "Small Cooked Vegetable Dishes," "Vegetables," "Stuffed Fruits and Vegetables," "Kibbeh," and "Meat." I have scattered them this way because the modern concept of mezze (described below) is basically a restaurant concept, rarely employed in a private home except, perhaps, when giving a large party.

For me, mezze-type dishes constitute some of the very best, most delicious, most wholesome eastern Mediterranean food. One or more of them—such as Georgian Eggplants Stuffed with Walnuts (page 167) or a Turkish Kisir (page 143), a sparkling "poetic" salad of bulgur wheat, chopped parsley, red pepper paste, and cucumber—make excellent main-course dishes. However, if used this way the number of servings given will not apply. As a rule of thumb, the reader should assume that a dish described as serving 6 as part of a mezze will serve only 2 as a main course. Since many of these mezze dishes (there are over one hundred) can be made ahead of time, any leftovers can be served the following day. Finally, there is no need to try and dazzle by presenting a large number of mezze. I will often serve just one or two to excellent effect.

The remaining non-mezze recipes (without an asterisk), such as soups, meat dishes, etc., will fit in well with the normal pattern of eating in the United States.

I

Sauces & Dips

*A*ll sorts of sauces and dips grace the eastern Mediterranean table—some fresh and uncomplicated, others rich and lavishly structured. Once you have the basic ingredients on hand—tahini, yogurt, walnuts, stale bread, garlic, lemons, pomegranate molasses, and olive oil—you can make any number of excellent sauces to offer with vegetables, meat, fish, and poultry or simply to serve up as a course. Think of these thick, chunky dips as side dishes—an approach taken by most eastern Mediterranean cooks.

MEZZE

Imagine a table piled high with tempting salads, plump stuffed grape leaves, roasted peppers, dips, kabobs, spicy sausages, spinach pies, and pickled vegetables. Such a spread would be a popular presentation of mezze, Middle Eastern appetizers. I don't think there is an hors d'oeuvres table in the world that can match one with Middle Eastern mezze at their best. For all its honest simplicity, it is extremely elegant food, full of exotic aromas and vibrant colors, fragrant with sweet spices and pungent with hot. Dishes refreshed by yogurt, soothing creamy purees, and the tantalizing smokiness of grilled eggplant provide a variety of tastes and textures that contrast and entwine like the intricate motifs in a Turkish carpet.

A great Mediterranean mezze table is like a giant *menu dégustation*. One has the opportunity to sample a whole slew of delicious foods at will: rustic red beans simmered in olive oil; grilled chicken with crackling skin, perfumed with the flavors of garlic and lemon; purees enriched with sesame seeds, nuts, and oils; pastries in all shapes and sizes, stuffed with meat, poultry, and cheese, and seasoned with sweet spices such as cinnamon, nutmeg, and allspice or with fresh herbs; crunchy fritters of mussels or fish served with a heady garlic-flavored sauce; mounds of olives in all colors and sizes; sweet-and-sour strips of carrots, onions, or leeks, served cool and garnished with fresh herbs and pickled cabbage. The list goes on and on.

I first discovered the magic of mezze years ago, at an unforgettable meal in an Arab restaurant in East Jerusalem. A profusion of first courses was presented, forty-two in all, served in groups of seven. The desire to show largesse is part of the region's famous hospitality. Moments after we sat down, our table was covered with numerous little dishes, in which very simple ingredients—chickpeas, wild greens, okra, ripe tomatoes, small red onions—were packaged in various enticing ways. Each preparation was distinct, yet the complete assemblage was harmonious.

Such lavish offerings of numerous small dishes began, according to the Lebanese food writer Faez Aoun, in the 1920s in the Lebanese town of Zahle, at cafés competing for the attention of wealthy Lebanese Christians. To attract clients, these cafés began offering larger and larger spreads of small quantities of traditional food, to accompany *arak* and other alcoholic drinks. The fad spread, and soon restaurants in Beirut started doing the same thing. In the meantime, many Islamic people eschewed mezze, associating them with alcohol consumption. Today, at restaurants catering to tourists, one is likely to be served thirty or more mezze, the little dishes completely covering the table to achieve a kind of tour-de-force effect that has grown completely out of hand. This is true in that crescent of countries—including Lebanon, Israel, Cyprus, Jordan, Greece, and the Turkish coast—that makes up part of the eastern coastline of the Mediterranean.

In Syria, inland Turkey, and Georgia there is a tradition of serving various mezze-type salads to accompany, rather than begin, a meal. In these countries, the little dishes stay on the table throughout the meal, thus treated as side dishes.

The bottom line on all this is that virtually any food, hot or cold, can be turned into a mezze, if served in the multiple little-dish mezze form. For example, one of the few meat preparations common to mezze is kibbeh, a blend of ground lean lamb, bulgur, grated onion, and spices that is often broiled like a hamburger and served on a small plate. And finally, one can offer a plate of freshly picked untorn leaves—assorted mints, cress, arugula, radish tops, flat-leaf parsley, dill, and coriander for nibbling.

Most mezze can be prepared in advance. In general, they are extremely healthful, made of whole grains, dried beans, yogurt, olive oil, fish, dark green vegetables, fruits, herbs, garlic, onions, and spices. These fresh, natural dishes are not contemporary inventions, but have been set out on tables for generations. Nearly every food used this way is particularly delicious, as almost all appetizers are (such as Spanish tapas and Italian antipasti), since by definition these dishes arouse a diner's appetite.

TWO WALNUT AND POMEGRANATE SAUCES AND DIPS

*HOT AND SWEET RED PEPPER DIP WITH WALNUTS AND POMEGRANATES (MUHAMMARA)

This is one of the outstanding dips of the eastern Mediterranean, as delicious and striking as the far more famous hummus and *baba ghanoush*. I urge readers to take the time to make it. I promise it will be a revelation.

The dish comes from Aleppo, where a very flavorful hybrid of a hot red pepper is a favorite condiment. The heat in this recipe is tamed by ground walnuts and sweet-and-sour pomegranate molasses. The Arabic name is *muhammara*, which means brick colored—exactly the color of the finished dish.

Some food historians have stated that this dip is unique to Aleppo, but this is not true. *Muhammara* is made in various ways in Lebanon (see my *Mediterranean Cooking* for *mahammara labni*); in Georgia, where the pepper is muted and pomegranates and walnuts dominate (page 15); and in Turkey, where the dip has been imitated with equally delicious Maraş peppers.

Try it with meat or fish kabobs, or simply with crisp pita triangles or warmed floppy *lavash*. The dip will keep well for up to one week in a closed container in the refrigerator, improving a little each day. Remember to return the dip to room temperature before serving.

continued

2½ pounds red bell peppers

I to 2 small hot chili, such as Fresno or hot Hungarian, or
  substitute Turkish red pepper paste to taste (page 389)

1½ cups walnuts, coarsely ground (about 6 ounces)

½ cup wheat crackers, crumbled

I tablespoon fresh lemon juice

2 tablespoons pomegranate molasses (page 404) or more to
  taste

½ teaspoon ground cumin

¾ teaspoon salt

½ teaspoon sugar

2 tablespoons olive oil

2 teaspoons toasted pine nuts or chopped, peeled, and
  unsalted pistachios, a good pinch of ground cumin, and a
  flourish of olive oil for garnish

For best results, make the recipe at least one day in advance.

I. Roast the red bell peppers and the chili either over coals or a gas burner or under an electric broiler, turning frequently until blackened and blistered all over, about 12 minutes. Place in a covered bowl to steam 10 minutes (this loosens the skin). Rub off the skins; slit the peppers open and remove the stems, membranes, and seeds. Spread the bell peppers, smooth side up, on a paper towel and let drain 10 minutes.

2. In a food processor, grind the walnuts, crackers, lemon juice, pomegranate molasses, cumin, salt, and sugar until smooth. Add the bell peppers; process until pureed and creamy. With the machine on, add the olive oil in a thin stream. Add the chili to taste. (If the paste is too thick, thin with I to 2 tablespoons water.) Refrigerate overnight to allow the flavors to mellow.

3. When ready to serve, transfer the dip to a serving dish. Sprinkle the pine nuts or pistachios and cumin on top and drizzle with olive oil.

NOTES TO THE COOK: To make crisp pita triangles: Preheat the oven to 350°F. Split the pitas into rounds. Cut into triangles, lightly film the insides with olive oil spray, and spread out on a baking sheet. Bake until golden brown. Remove from the oven. The pita triangles will crisp when cool.

Peppers, ideally, should be placed directly on a gas flame or over very hot hardwood coals so that their skins quickly blister and char. This method yields a wonderful smoky flavor and a pleasing texture, in contrast to the slimy texture that frequently results from oven cooking.

With thanks to Christine Sahadi for sharing this recipe

*CREAMY WALNUT AND POMEGRANATE SAUCE

ooks in Georgia make literally dozens of walnut sauces (see page 316). Here is a light, quick, easy-to-make sauce that you can keep for several days in the refrigerator. Serve it as a dip or with fish kabobs.

When walnuts and pomegranate juice are used together in Georgian sauces, the acid turns the walnuts an unsightly shocking pink. Georgian cooks remedy this with marigold petals, which turns the color a golden beige. A pinch of saffron or safflower filaments also does the job.

Makes about 1 cup

Place the walnuts, pepper or cayenne, paprika, garlic, marigold petals or saffron, coriander seeds, and salt into the work bowl of a food processor; blend until finely pureed to a smooth sauce, about 45 seconds. With the machine on, add the diluted pomegranate molasses. Scrape into a jar, fold in the crushed fresh coriander, and allow to mellow at least 2 hours.

NOTES TO THE COOK: All nut sauces tend to thicken as they age and need a little thinning with water.

Extremely smooth, creamy sauces can be made in an electric blender. A food processor works well too, but the texture will be a little grittier because of the nuts. Taking an extra step, such as pounding or grating the nuts first, will result in a better sauce.

To crush fresh coriander, pound it to a paste in a mortar.

1¾ cups shelled walnuts (6 ounces), grated or crushed in a mortar (see Notes to the Cook)

½ teaspoon Near East or Aleppo pepper (page 395) or a pinch cayenne and ½ teaspoon sweet Hungarian paprika

2 garlic cloves, peeled and crushed with a pinch of salt

Pinch of crumbled dried marigold petals (page 398) or powdered safflower or powdered saffron filaments

1 teaspoon ground coriander seeds

Pinch of salt

1½ tablespoons pomegranate molasses (page 404), diluted in ½ cup hot water

1 tablespoon crushed fresh coriander (see Notes to the Cook)

Two Garlic
Sauces and Dips

A raw garlic sauce can be delicious or nasty: its pungency depends upon the amount of garlic used, the quality, and the time of year—spring, when garlic is plump, moist, and delicate, or late fall and winter, when it is dry and bitter.

The acidity of a garlic sauce will depend upon whether you choose a strong, assertive vinegar or a fruity, sour lemon. In most cases, I opt for a mild white wine vinegar or lemon. Try to avoid red wine vinegars, for they will discolor your sauce.

The sauces that follow are best served at room temperature and best made at least 2 hours before serving. They will usually keep 1 to 2 days and sometimes longer (see recipes). Return sauces to room temperature before serving. Always adjust the seasoning just before serving.

Garlic-flavored sauces do not freeze well.

SOME NOTES ON EQUIPMENT

In the days before the blender and the food processor, garlic sauces were made entirely by hand in a thick-walled wooden mortar, with a strong solid pestle. Garlic was pounded to a puree along with a little salt, then nuts were added and pounded down to a smooth texture. The resulting sauce had a particularly creamy texture that no machine can totally reproduce.

If you decide to make any of these sauces in the traditional way, you will need to have a large granite* or wooden mortar.

Season a new wooden mortar by filling it up with olive oil and leaving it overnight. (You can use the oil for cooking afterward.) The following day, pour out the oil, rub the outside of the mortar with a little oil, and leave another day. Give the mortar a quick wash and dry it, and it will be ready. Never soak a wooden mortar or pestle in water; simply wash and dry after each use. To remove garlic odors, dust with baking soda, rinse with fresh water, drain, and dry well.

*Oriental and Far Eastern food markets sell large granite mortars and pestles for under $35. These superb, heavy stone mortars are large enough to make 1½ cups sauce.

MACEDONIAN GARLIC AND OIL DIP

A few years ago, while browsing through a musty bookstore in Salonika, Greece's second largest city, I came upon a six-volume set of cookbooks published a dozen years before, and knew I had found something unique. There were descriptions of dishes from all the regions of Greece, as prepared by home cooks, whose names and addresses were given alongside their recipes.

The books were in Greek, of course, but still the possibilities tantalized me. With these books in hand, could I not travel through northern Greece, visiting villages and tracking down and verifying numerous fascinating dishes?

Working with a neighbor and a good dictionary, I was able to decipher enough recipes to gain a feel for the food before leaving on a long-planned exploratory trip.

I soon learned I was not the only person who had this idea. A Greek food journalist and cookbook author, Aglaia Kremezi, had already cross-referenced the six-volume set on her computer to use as a reference for her own book on Greek cuisine.

To make a long story short, Aglaia and I met, and decided to team up on a trip through Macedonia, Thrace, and Epirus. It turned into a wonderful, zany fifteen-hundred-mile culinary adventure.

As it turned out, the volumes were unreliable. Many of the women listed had died or moved away. Also, many of the recipes were not really Greek and others were pure fabrications. But still, when we entered villages and markets, the names and descriptions of the dishes became the basis for informal inquiries, which led us to other hitherto unknown excellent cooks, dishes—and, sometimes, wonderful eating experiences.

In the town of Drama, in eastern Macedonia, Aglaia and I came upon a group of grape pickers sitting under a tree eating *tsioula*, a creamy mixture of crushed garlic, vinegar, and oil thinned with water to a souplike consistency. It was constructed very much like *skordalia:* A thick emulsion was made by pounding cloves of garlic with salt until pureed, then mashed potatoes were added, as well as a few spoonfuls of vinegar and olive oil, drop by drop, always stirred in the same direction (also to keep the emulsion from collapsing) until all the oil was absorbed. The grape pickers ate it with bread for lunch. They told us how to use it as a sauce to serve with crisp fried codfish or boiled beets. It is also delicious with the Creamy Giant White Beans and Greens Casserole (page 257). Here is their recipe.

Makes about ½ cup

I. Cook the whole, unpeeled potato in a saucepan of salted boiling water until tender but not falling apart. Meanwhile, in a wooden or granite mortar, crush the garlic with the salt to a pulp. Pour the oil in a glass measuring cup with a spout. Have the vinegar ready in a small cup. Use a wooden pestle to stir the garlic in the same direction and, at the same time, let the olive oil drip down inside the mortar in

1 very small boiling potato, preferably Yukon Gold
2 plump cloves garlic, peeled, halved, and green shoot removed
Pinch of sea salt
5 tablespoons olive oil
1 tablespoon mild white wine, cider, or rice vinegar or more to taste

a very slow, steady stream. Don't stop stirring. When there is a good emulsion, alternate the olive oil with the vinegar, dribbling them in at the same speed. You should have a thick, mayonnaise-like emulsion. (At this point, you could serve the sauce as is.)

2. To stabilize the sauce: Scrape the contents of the mortar into the glass measuring cup. As soon as the potato is cooked, peel it and then crush it in the mortar to a creamy puree. (Yukon Gold potatoes are best for this.) Discard all but 1 tablespoon of the potato. Add a spoonful of the garlic sauce and stir with a pestle until smooth. Dribble in the remaining garlic sauce while stirring in one direction. The sauce should be smooth, golden, and fluffy. Serve at once or cover and serve within a few days.

*Turkish Tarator with Almonds or Pine Nuts

Nevin Halici, in her comprehensive cookbook on Turkish cooking, *Türk Mutfaği*, describes all the different ways one can use this sensually rich, subtly flavored sauce. She suggests serving it with cooked favas; zucchinis; cauliflower; spinach stems and roots; cooked mottled beans and fresh onions; boiled potatoes; fried eggplants; green beans and savory; shredded salad greens; or, with the addition of some olive oil, on fresh purslane.

The sauce will be more delicate if made with almonds. If made with pine nuts, it will have a resinous flavor.

Makes 1¾ cups

1 cup blanched almonds or pine nuts, chopped (4 ounces)
2 to 3 plump cloves garlic, peeled and crushed with a pinch of sea salt (to make 1 teaspoon)
½ cup water
2 cups cubed stale crustless bread, soaked in water and squeezed dry (to make ½ cup)
3 tablespoons mild cider or rice wine vinegar or lemon juice or more to taste
Salt to taste
2 tablespoons olive oil

In a skillet or oven, heat the nuts for a few minutes to develop aroma. Place in a food processor with the garlic and ⅓ cup of the water; process until smooth. With the machine running, add the bread, vinegar, salt to taste, and the oil; process until well blended. Add the remaining water to loosen the mixture. Let mellow at least 2 hours before serving.

SEVEN
TAHINI-BASED
SAUCES AND DIPS

Dips and sauces based on tahini, or sesame seed paste, are rich and creamy, and excellent on broiled meat, chicken, fish, and shellfish. They are also good over vegetables—such as cooked cauliflower, crisp fried eggplant and zucchini, kibbeh, potatoes, and Swiss chard; hard-boiled eggs; and boiled snails; and they can simply be used as a dip for pita bread.

Tahini, you see, has an uncanny ability to enrich the flavor of almost any food. In collecting recipes for this book, I came across Middle Eastern dips made with tahini and onions, pine nuts, Swiss chard leaves and stalks, pumpkin puree, lentils, radishes, red cabbage, anchovies, and cured herring!

Tahini is very healthy, with plenty of B vitamins, and is an excellent source of calcium, phosphorus, and iron. Because of its unusual antioxidant makeup, it has a long shelf life. Turn the jar upside down from time to time to keep the oil from separating. (When tahini is mixed with garlic, olive oil, water and spices, it loses these keeping qualities.)

You can, of course, just scoop out some tahini from a jar and use it straight, but your dip or sauce will be lighter and creamier if you mix it first with a little lemon juice until the mixture is white and "tight." After mixing, loosen with cold water and then add the remaining ingredients.

continued

*Basic Tahini with Citrus

This tahini dressing is great with raw vegetables. Try it on chopped tomatoes and cucumbers; blend it with grated radishes; put it on sliced red cabbage with plenty of parsley and a bowl of cooked brown lentils; or use it as a base for some of the dips that follow.

Makes about 2 cups

1 cup tahini

1 teaspoon garlic, peeled and crushed with salt

½ teaspoon salt

½ cup fresh lemon juice mixed with fresh grapefruit juice

½ cup cold water

Ground cumin (optional garnish)

In a food processor, blend the tahini with the garlic, salt, and the fruit juices until the mixture is white and "tightens." Add the water and blend until smooth. Serve poured over fish, sprinkled with cumin, or in a small bowl with a drizzle of olive oil. Store in the refrigerator up to 5 days.

*Tahini with Parsley

This is the classic sauce for cauliflowerets or fish.

Makes about 2 cups

Steam one small head of cauliflower, separated into florets. Reserve ½ cup of the cooking liquid and use in making Basic Tahini with Citrus (page 22). Fold ½ cup (or more to taste) chopped flat-leaf parsley into the sauce. Spread the sauce over the cauliflower and garnish with thinly sliced radishes.

*Tahini with Yogurt

This sauce is used for fried, steamed, and baked kibbeh, and with boiled vegetables. Mix 1 cup Basic Tahini with Citrus (page 22) with 1¼ cups drained yogurt (for directions on draining yogurt, see page 410). Correct the seasoning.

*Tahini with Swiss Chard Stalks

Another good sauce for fish.

Makes about 2 cups

Steam, boil, or microwave the Swiss chard stalks until tender; drain well. When cool enough to handle, press out all moisture. Finely chop the stalks. Mix with the tahini sauce. Loosen with cold water. Allow dip to mellow at room temperature for 1 to 2 hours. Turn the mixture into a shallow serving dish and garnish with the nuts.

2 pounds thick Swiss chard stalks, trimmed and stringed

1 cup Basic Tahini with Citrus (page 22)

⅓ cup chopped walnuts or ½ cup pine nuts, browned in butter or oil, for garnish

VARIATION:

TAHINI WITH BOILED GREENS

Use 1½ pounds boiled and chopped Swiss chard leaves, young dandelion leaves, or spinach. Add a good pinch of hot Aleppo pepper.

*Hummus

Of course, the most famous tahini dip of all is hummus, a dish that has begun to lose its charm, for it has turned into a mediocre deli item. A good plate of hummus is never presented undressed. It should be spread on a plate, then smoothed down from the middle outward with the back of a spoon to create a wide well in the center. A sprinkle of ground cumin and a little drizzle of olive oil and lemon is then added. An exceptionally pretty presentation is achieved by heating some hot paprika in olive oil until the oil turns red; strain the oil, then drizzle it over half the hummus while sprinkling the other half with a few dots here and there, finally finishing with a thin line around the dish.

Makes 2 1/2 cups

I cup dried chickpeas

I small onion, peeled

1/4 cup tahini

2 cloves garlic, peeled and crushed with 1/2 teaspoon coarse salt

1/4 cup fresh lemon juice or more to taste

I to 2 tablespoons olive oil

Ground cumin, hot paprika, or pomegranate seeds for garnish

I. Soak the chickpeas overnight in water to cover. Drain; rinse and cook with the onion in water to cover until the chickpeas are very soft. Drain, reserving 1/2 cup cooking liquor for the dip; save the rest for soup. Set aside 1/4 cup chickpeas for the garnish. Discard the onion.

2. Stir up the tahini in its jar with the oil until well blended. Place tahini in blender jar or the work bowl of a food processor and blend the tahini, garlic, and lemon juice until the mixture "whitens." With the machine running, add the reserved cooking liquor. Add 1 3/4 cups chickpeas and process until well blended. Correct the seasoning with salt and lemon juice. Allow dip to mellow at room temperature for 1 to 2 hours. To serve as a dip, spread on a shallow serving dish. Use the back of a spoon to make a well in the center, drizzle with olive oil, and sprinkle with cumin, hot paprika, or pomegranate seeds.

NOTES TO THE COOK: For a smoother and more digestible dip, push it through the fine blade of a food mill and discard the skins of the chickpeas.

*Hummus with Meat Sauce

The nutty flavor of chickpeas matched with the nuttiness of tahini is the base for a stew of ground lamb and pine nuts.

Serves 2

Ten minutes before serving, spread the chickpea puree evenly on a shallow rimmed plate. Heat the butter in an 8-inch skillet. Add the onion and cook over medium heat until softened, 2 minutes. Add the ground lamb and sauté until browned and crumbly. Add the pine nuts, spices, and salt. Cook 2 minutes. Add ¼ cup water or reserved chickpea cooking liquor. Bring to a boil, reduce the heat, cover and cook at a simmer 5 minutes. Pour the meat sauce over the chickpea puree, garnish with the ground allspice, and serve hot or warm surrounded with the pita triangles.

1¼ cups homemade hummus (page 24) or 1¼ cups
  store-bought chickpea puree
1 tablespoon unsalted butter
3 tablespoons minced onion
¼ pound ground lean lamb
3 tablespoons pine nuts, browned in butter
¼ teaspoon freshly ground black pepper
¼ teaspoon ground cinnamon
Salt to taste (about ¼ teaspoon)
¼ cup water or ¼ cup chickpea cooking liquor

GARNISH
Pinch of ground allspice
Pita triangles, toasted

*Baba Ghanoush

Everyone knows this wonderful eggplant dip. To infuse a smoky flavor into eggplants during the winter months, I use a trick that I learned from a Greek cookbook author, Vefa Alexiadou. I wrap a large eggplant in a double thickness of foil and set it over high flames on top of the stove.

Makes about 1 1/3 cups

1 large eggplant (1 1/4 pounds)
4 level tablespoons tahini
1/2 teaspoon garlic, peeled and crushed with salt
3 tablespoons fresh lemon juice or more to taste
3 to 4 tablespoons cold water
1/2 teaspoon salt
Dash of freshly ground black pepper
1 tablespoon olive oil

GARNISH
Aleppo or Near East pepper (page 395) or hot Hungarian
   paprika
2 tablespoons chopped parsley
Diced ripe tomatoes

1. Pierce the eggplant in several places with a toothpick. If you are cooking indoors, wrap the whole eggplant in aluminum foil and set it over a gas grill to cook on all sides until it collapses and begins to release a great deal of steam.

If you are cooking over coals, grill the eggplant until blackened, collapsed, and cooked through. Dump the eggplant into a basin of cold water; peel while still hot and allow to drain in a colander until cool. Squeeze pulp to remove any bitter juices. Mash the eggplant to a puree.

2. In a food processor, mix the tahini with the garlic and lemon juice until the mixture contracts. Thin with the water. With the machine running, add the eggplant and the salt, pepper, and olive oil. Spread out in a shallow dish and garnish with pepper, parsley, and tomatoes.

FOUR YOGURT
SAUCES AND DIPS

*YOGURT-GARLIC SAUCE

I was surprised by the Turkish method of draining yogurt, then replacing the whey with cold water or milk until a desired consistency is obtained. I had never seen drained yogurt reconstituted this way, nor such a sweet and creamy result. Even drained nonfat yogurt benefits from this trick—a lot of the unpleasant, chalky, bitter taste simply disappears.

In winter, when the flavor of garlic is strongest, carefully add it to the yogurt in measured amounts. *The quantity of garlic is the most crucial factor to the success of this sauce; it will make or break the result.*

The sauce is good on hot and cold foods, especially grilled eggplant, batter-fried spinach leaves, stuffed vegetables, meat, stews, rice, and bulgur pilafs.

Makes 2 cups

continued

I quart (32-ounce container) plain, low-fat yogurt, drained
   to 2 cups (see page 410 for directions on draining
   yogurt)
About ½ cup water
2 or more cloves garlic, peeled
¼ teaspoon coarse salt

OPTIONAL ADDITIONS
I tablespoon crumbled dried mint leaves, pressed through a
   fine sieve
2 teaspoons fresh lemon juice if the yogurt is not acidic
   enough
Fresh mint leaves for garnish
or
Pinches of Near East or Aleppo pepper (page 395) or hot
   Hungarian paprika

Finely ground black pepper to taste
2 tablespoons olive oil to drizzle on top

I. Place the yogurt in a shallow bowl. Use a fork to work in the water gradually until creamy and smooth. (This can also be done in a food processor.) Crush the garlic with the salt and add to the yogurt, beating until smooth. If the sauce is acrid, add a pinch of sugar. Let mellow at least I hour before using.

2. Beat in the mint leaves, if using, and sharpen the flavor with lemon juice and/or red pepper, if desired. Adjust the salt and black pepper. Chill well. Just before serving, decorate the yogurt with swirls of olive oil. If not using the mint, dust lightly with Near East pepper.

VARIATIONS:
Omit the mint and substitute any one of the following:
   2 tablespoons finely chopped parsley
   ½ pound raw or lightly steamed, chopped purslane leaves
   4 tablespoons boiled, drained, pressed, and finely chopped Swiss chard leaves
   4 finely chopped inner leaves of romaine lettuce
   2 to 3 grated carrots, previously sautéed in garlic-flavored olive oil, drained,
      and sprinkled with a pinch of sugar

*Cucumber, Garlic, and Yogurt Sauce

Called *cacik* in Turkey, *tzatziki* in Greece, and *khiyar bi lben* in the Arab countries, this saladlike sauce is ubiquitous in the Middle East.

Serve this sauce with sautéed spinach, bulgur pilafs, Roast Chicken Stuffed with Lamb, Rice, and Pine Nuts (page 323), "Split Tummies" of Stuffed Eggplants (page 364), and An Arabian Stew of Chickpeas, Eggplant, and Tomatoes (page 249).

Makes 2½ cups, serving 4 to 6

Finely dice the cucumber. In a medium bowl, combine the yogurt, garlic, and ¾ teaspoon salt. Add the cucumber and the dried mint, and blend well. Cover and refrigerate until well chilled, about 1 hour. Garnish with a drizzle of olive oil and sprigs of fresh mint.

1 long English cucumber, peeled
2 cups plain low-fat yogurt
2 garlic cloves, peeled and crushed with a pinch of salt
Sea salt
3 teaspoons dried mint, crumbled and pressed through a fine sieve
1 teaspoon olive oil
Sprigs of fresh mint for garnish

*SHREDDED BEETS WITH THICK YOGURT

Although the vibrant pink color of this Middle Eastern dip is startling, the flavor is superb. There are many versions. Sometimes the beets are pureed and blended into the yogurt; other times, they are simply sliced or cubed; still other times, a little tahini is blended in for a deeper, richer flavor. In this recipe, the beets are simply grated, with the shredding disk of a food processor, then folded into thick, creamy yogurt. Serve as a dip or an accompaniment to fish.

Serves 6

1 pint plain low-fat yogurt, drained to 1½ cups (see page 410 for directions on draining yogurt)

8 small beets

1 large clove garlic, peeled and crushed with a pinch of salt

2 tablespoons fresh, strained lemon juice

Salt to taste

Freshly ground black pepper to taste

Pinch of sugar (optional)

Sprigs of fresh mint for garnish

1. Drain the yogurt to 1½ cups. Cut off all but 1 inch of the beet stalks and leave the roots intact. Rinse the beets well but do not peel. Cook the beets in boiling salted water until tender, 25 to 35 minutes. Drain, slip off the skins under cold running water, and cut away the root ends and stalks. Coarsely grate the beets, using the shredding disk of a food processor or the large holes of a hand grater. Makes about 2 cups.

2. In a medium bowl, combine the garlic, lemon juice, salt, and pepper. Add the beets and yogurt and blend well. Taste and add a pinch of sugar if desired. Transfer to a serving dish, cover, and refrigerate until well chilled, about 1 hour. Garnish with sprigs of fresh mint just before serving.

*SUMMER SQUASH, TAHINI, AND YOGURT DIP

A small quantity of tahini added to yogurt dips and sauces results in a uniquely nutty flavor, as in this disarming little dip made from the leftover cored pulp of small yellow or pale green squash. This dip is so good, you needn't wait until you core a squash—simply chop up enough summer squash to make 1 cup pulp, follow the recipe, and luxuriate.

Makes 1 cup

1. In a small skillet, heat the olive oil and fry the squash over medium-low heat until all moisture evaporates and there is only oil and vegetable left, 10 minutes. With a slotted spoon press out the oil and discard. Leave the squash to cool to room temperature.

2. Place the tahini, garlic, and lemon juice in a mixing bowl and blend until smooth. Add 1 tablespoon cold water and gradually fold in the yogurt and then the squash. Adjust the seasoning with the salt, pepper, and cumin. Scrape into a shallow serving dish, leave to mellow at least 1 hour, and serve at room temperature with a sprinkling of ground cumin.

1 tablespoon olive oil

1 cup cored pulp of 8 to 10 small yellow squash or 1 cup chopped summer squash, thickly peeled

1½ tablespoons tahini, stirred until well blended

1 small clove garlic, peeled and crushed with ½ teaspoon salt

1 teaspoon fresh lemon juice

⅔ cup plain low-fat yogurt, drained to ⅓ cup (see page 410 for directions on draining yogurt)

Salt and freshly ground black pepper to taste

Ground cumin to taste

*GEORGIAN SOUR PLUM SAUCE

I was once invited to a fabulous meal at the home of a family from Svaneti, a beautiful mountainous region in western Georgia. After lunch, I complimented Etheri, the mother, who had prepared all the dishes. I asked her about her splendid sour plum sauce called *tkemali*—a sauce that, according to connoisseurs, separates ordinary Georgian cooks from great ones. Dark, thick, tart, and spicy, it is the backbone of Georgian gastronomy, accompanying grilled meats, poultry, beans, boiled beans, boiled greens, and bread.

Sitting tall in her chair, Etheri widened her eyes, blew a few stray hairs away from her forehead, and leaned forward as if to impart to me the ultimate truth about Georgian food. "There can be no *satsivi* * without marigold flowers. There can be no lamb *chakapuli* † without tarragon. There can be no *tkemali* without *ombalo*."

Ombalo? What was that? I had never heard of it. Then she fetched a sample. I thought it tasted like musty mint.

Did I really have to put this strange and awful-smelling substance in the sauce? Etheri's culinary pronouncements were so adamantly expressed that I decided to do a little research.

A few days later, I headed over to the Agricultural Institute in Tbilisi to confer with local botanists about the names of all the herbs and spices in Georgia that puzzled me. When I asked about *ombalo*, one of the botanists had to consult three texts (Russian-Georgian, Russian-Latin, and Latin-English. "*Ombalo*," he finally explained, "is *Mentha pulegium*, or European pennyroyal. It says here it is very good if you want to avoid fleas."

Well, I count myself second to no cook in my eagerness to avoid fleas, but with all due respect to Etheri, I've decided not to worry too much about obtaining *ombalo* for the following adaptation of her sour plum sauce.

Satsivi is a creamy cooked walnut sauce served over cold turkey, chicken, fish, or green beans.
†*Chakapuli* is a stew of lamb, herbs, and sour fruits.

Makes about 2½ cups

I. In a 3- or 4-quart non-corrodible saucepan, combine the plums and 2 cups cold water. Bring to a boil and cook, covered, over low heat until the plums fall apart, about 30 minutes.

2. Drain the plums and reserve the cooking juice. When the plums are cool enough to handle, discard the pits, and push the plums through the medium blade of a food mill. Discard any debris that won't go through the holes. Put the mixture into a food processor; add the garlic, herbs, and pepper; and pulse 12 times. Scrape the puree into a saucepan, add the reserved cooking juice, and quickly bring to a boil, stirring. Remove from the heat, adjust the seasoning with salt and sugar or, if the plums are not very sour, lemon juice to taste. Immediately pour into a tall, clean ¾-quart Mason jar. Cover tightly. After 1 to 2 hours place the bottle in the refrigerator. Wait at least 1 day before serving so that the flavors can meld. Keep refrigerated up to 1 month.

2 pounds small sour yellow or red plums
3 cloves garlic, peeled and crushed in a mortar with
 ¾ teaspoon salt
½ cup chopped cilantro
4 tablespoons chopped mint
4 tablespoons chopped dill
¼ teaspoon hot Hungarian pepper
Salt to taste
Sugar to taste or juice of ½ lemon or more to taste

NOTES TO THE COOK: For the best flavor, try to find cilantro that has gone to seed and use all parts except the stems.

For a delicious cold salad of red beans, fold ½ cup of this sauce into 2 cups freshly cooked red beans.

Also excellent as a sauce for fried, grilled, broiled, and baked fish, chicken, and meat.

II

Breads

*B*read (often referred to as esh, meaning "life," in some Arabic dialects) is eaten in huge amounts at every meal in all parts of the eastern Mediterranean—starting in the morning, again at lunch, and still again at dinner. Constructed simply of wheat, water, salt, and heat, sometimes leavened, sometimes not, bread is treated by eastern Mediterranean people with reverence. For them bread equals sustenance, and is thus sacred.

There are simple breads in the Middle East that were first made when man discovered how to pound grain, moisten it, and cook it over hot stones. There are flat breads, thick breads, ridged breads, griddle breads, stuffed breads, crackling breads, barley breads, corn breads, breads that are folded, breads that are scented, and breads that taste of wood smoke and brick. In the villages of the region there are women who make bread fresh for every meal or set aside one morning a week to make bread. And, too, there are women who never make bread at all but buy it daily in the markets. Eastern Mediterranean people are all connoisseurs of bread. For them, life without bread is inconceivable.

Had I written this book a few years back, I would have offered recipes for pita, the region's most famous flat bread, for I could not have imagined my readers eating hummus or baba ghanoush without good pita. But today such recipes are unnecessary. Top-quality pita breads are available at American supermarkets. This trend reached a zenith only months before I finished this book, when my Middle Eastern grocer began selling 12-inch-wide brick-oven flat breads imported daily from Canada—breads that are, in his own words, "as good as it gets." But even if you don't shop at a Middle Eastern store, you will have no trouble finding excellent flat breads. Sheets of tandoori mountain bread, pocketless pitas, and other brick-oven breads are now commonly available at supermarkets.

Store-bought tandoori mountain bread, sold in floppy speckled sheets, is perfect for tearing up for use as the bottom layer for the splendid juices of *musakhan,* chicken cooked with sumac and onions (page 319). And when it finally goes stale, it is perfect for delicious *umaci,* in which stale torn sheets soak up the juice of ripe tomatoes, mixed with grated mozzarella and chilis (page 139).

As for the pocketless pita often sold as "Mediterranean pita," it is so close to Turkish *pide*—an inch-thick, soft, round white-flour bread—as to be indistinguishable. *Pide* is used as a platform for Cumin-Flavored *Köfte* with Two Sauces (page 341) and, when stale, for the cherry dessert on page 371.

My daughter, Leila, who patronizes a Middle Eastern restaurant in Woodstock, New York, taught me how to make almost any store-bought pita bread taste as if it just came out of a brick oven. Place a piece of pita directly over a low stovetop flame, gently toast each side, then serve at once.

☙ STALE BREAD ❧

In the eastern Mediterranean stale bread is never thrown away. Instead, it is used as a base for bread salads such as *umaci,* described above; toasted and blended with a rich array of chopped herbs in *fattoush* (page 140); simply wetted down and blended with ground meat to make *köfte;* or, in the Balkans, blended with pureed olives to make a simple spread for fresh bread.

One of the region's most fascinating assortment of dishes is called *fatta.* In the most lavish version, stuffed eggplants are placed on a bed of stale pita, covered entirely with thick, delicious yogurt, then sprinkled with pomegranate seeds. This is one of the memorable dishes of the Middle East (page 218).

In Macedonia, when thick, firm-textured loaves go stale, they are dried out to make a type of *paximadia*—rusks that, when moistened with water and oil, can be turned into a quick bread soup. *Paximadia* are also dipped into morning coffee or served to accompany a glass of wine or *raki*. And the wonderful Greek sauce *skordalia*, often spread over grilled fish and vegetables, is made of little more than garlic, olive oil, and stale bread.

In the Turkish town of Bolu, which for generations schooled the best chefs of the Ottoman Empire, there is a home dish of stale bread browned in the hearth, cut up, soaked in simmering stock with beaten egg, tomatoes, and garlic, then eaten hot. It is every bit as good as it sounds.

TANDIR BREADS

There is one class of breads, found in Tunisia, Syria, Turkey, and Georgia, for which, unfortunately, I cannot offer authentic recipes, simply because the type of oven required does not exist in North American homes. These are the flat breads created in the equivalent of an Indian tandoor—clay pits fired from below, called *tabouna* in Tunisia, *tone* in Georgia, *tandir* in Turkey, and *tanor* in Syria. When the walls of these ovens become immensely hot, rounds of uncooked dough are slapped against them. The rounds stick, then billow slightly, because of gravity, into enchanting teardrop shapes.

The resulting bread is delicious, with a good rustic texture, a marvelous fragrance, and a golden crust. As the loaves bake, they begin to design themselves, creating a kind of personality. Some slide into the shape of snowshoes, others begin to resemble beanbags. And yet they all have one thing in common: Each seems to wear a happy face.

Though we do not have the correct ovens here, we can simulate the effect. See the recipe for Buba Khotoveli's Crackling Flat Bread (page 46) and the Turkish Ridge-Patterned Bread (page 49).

FLOPPY BREADS MADE ON A GRIDDLE OVER A FIRE

Most flat breads made in the eastern Mediterranean are soft and floppy—good for tearing up and dipping into rich spicy gravies, wrapping around morsels of kabobs, sprinkling with olive oil for breakfast, spreading with one of numerous delicious and nutritious eastern Mediterranean dips, or just rolling up and placing in one's pocket for munching during the day.

These floppy breads are easy to make on an upside-down wok or, in a smaller size, in an ordinary seasoned skillet. I like an upside-down wok for the way it simulates the heavy 30-inch-diameter iron griddle dome used in the countryside of Turkey, Jordan, and Syria. These domes, called *saj* or *sorj*, are set over fires of dried grape vine cuttings, olive wood, or glowing charcoal. The unleavened bread dough is rolled or stretched paper thin, then placed over the hot dome to be cooked into a speckled sheet almost in an instant. So beloved is this type of bread that in central Anatolia, in the windows of appliance shops, I saw gas-fired domes for indoor use, along with washing machines, refrigerators, and electric stoves.

MÜKERREM'S UNLEAVENED
FLAT GRIDDLE BREAD

When I visited the noted Turkish food authority Nevin Halici, in Konya, she offered to take me to some traditional farmhouses so that I could see how country breads are made. One such trip stands out, a visit to the house of Mükerrem Özcan, reputed to be a fine bread maker.

As we approached her house, I peered down narrow paths. There were stones and children everywhere, and very few trees for shade. Mükerrem turned out to be a big, ruddy woman, about forty-five years old, with a face of such vitality and friendliness I felt happy just to meet her. She wore the traditional clothing of a country woman: tight-fitting shawl, baggy wide pants, and brightly printed skirt. After spending some time with her, I understood that her farm-based cooking was directly related to her lifestyle—frugal, generous, and fatalistic.

It always amazes me how little equipment one actually needs to turn out good, simple, wholesome family food. Mükerrem's kitchen contained hardly anything—just a two-burner stove top on a table, and two small round tables about 10 inches high for preparation and assembly. There were some enameled basins, jugs, barrels, three or four jars, and a few assorted pots and pans.

One of the jars contained the seasoning *baharat*, the most popular spice mixture in Konya, used in meats, soups, stews, and everything else. *Baharat* is a mixture of cinnamon, cumin, black pepper, mint, allspice, bay leaf, red pepper, and a pungent wild herb called *kekik*.

We worked in the courtyard, beneath a grape arbor. The two low round tables were brought out for shaping the breads. The various leavened and unleavened doughs, kneaded before we arrived, sat in wide, white enamel bowls covered with gaily colored cloths.

On one side of Mükerrem's house was a six-foot-deep *tandir* pit and also an enormous igloo-shaped oven. A fire was prepared in the pit from a mixture of charcoal, green wood, and dried manure mixed with straw. Meanwhile, Mükerrem chatted about life and her husband as she divided and coaxed the leavened bread dough into flat disks and then pressed their centers down. "I do this so they will cook better," she explained.

She washed down the intensely hot inner walls of the pit with a mop and then slapped some of the dough disks against the walls. She left them for just a few minutes, until they puffed. Then the pit was covered so the bread would "bake" before being fished out with a hook.

When she uncovered the pit, a marvelous aroma arose. The first breads were removed. Each had drooped or puffed and developed its own particular personality, some resembling beanbags, others Frisbees.

"When a loaf falls into the fire, we pull it out and call it 'the sultan,' because it has such a wonderful taste," she said.

Mükerrem retrieved a "sultan" for me and dusted off the ashes. "It won't need any butter," she told me as she offered it.

She was right. The bread had a wonderful and unusual nutty flavor, quite sufficient in itself, and its charred edges gave it an excellent crunchy texture.

When Mükerrem was finished baking the leavened loaves, she added a prepared lentil, chickpea, and bean soup to the pit, in order, she explained, "not to waste the heat." The soup was flavored with dried mint and red and black pepper, and enriched with lamb bones, then sealed. It cooked slowly the rest of the day.

Ballooning her skirt over a squat stool, Mükerrem then prepared to demonstrate some unleavened breads—one nearly identical to Indian chapati. She divided the dough into small balls. Meanwhile, one of her daughters made a fire on the ground with dried grape vine cuttings, to heat up the *saj*.

Mükerrem rolled out the dough to onion-skin thinness, sprinkled it with crumbled cheese and parsley, folded it in half, and then lifted it onto the dome. Since there was no oil in the dough, nor on the dome, the bread had to be constantly turned, with a long, wooden flat sword called a *çevirgeç*. Again a mouth-watering aroma began to rise. The soft bread was splendid, with a unique nutty, wheaty flavor and a rippled, bubbly surface. At Mükerrem's suggestion, I brushed the top with clarified butter, then ate it accompanied by a glass of *ayran*, yogurt mixed with cold water.

It took all morning for Mükerrem to make enough bread for the week. As I talked with her, I came to understand that she devotes her life to preparing food for her family. She tends animals that produce milk, from which she makes fresh cheese and yogurt; grows vegetables to pickle or dry for the winter; and makes pastas and bread. Although it was only May, she told me, "Already I must start preparing for winter. The only products we buy are sugar and wheat. I feel fortunate to have two daughters to help me." And then, having finished making bread for the week, she sighed and recited a melancholy and deeply revealing rhyme. Roughly translated, it went like this: "So many burned loaves, and now I am finished. My husband will be happy, but my life is finished too."

This is my adaptation of Mükerrem's griddle bread. Following the bread recipe, you will find recipe suggestions for using the bread: Filled and Folded Bread Sheets (*Saj Boregi*) and Double-Folded Griddle Sheets.

Makes I pound dough, enough to make 9 16- to 18-inch paper-thin bread sheets, 12 10- to 12-inch paper-thin bread sheets, or 24 6-inch paper-thin bread sheets

I. One day in advance, make the dough. Place the flour and salt in the mixing bowl of a food processor. With the machine running, slowly add just enough warm water to moisten the flour mixture within 10 seconds. Stop the machine, then process the dough with 4 10-second pulses, or until the dough is spongy, soft, and tacky to the touch. Turn out onto a floured work surface, lightly dust with flour, and knead until smooth, about 20 seconds.

9 ounces (approximately 2⅛ cups) chapati flour, preferably the Laxmi brand

I teaspoon salt

¾ cup plus I tablespoon warm water

Plenty of chapati flour for dusting and rolling the bread sheets

Butter or the rich topping from top-quality natural unflavored yogurt for garnish

Place ball of dough in a nonmetallic bowl, cover tightly, and let stand at room temperature overnight or at least 8 hours.

2. Slowly heat a flat iron or nonstick griddle or an upside-down wok over medium heat until hot, about 10 minutes. Reduce the heat to medium low to maintain a steady heat. Meanwhile, on a well-floured surface, divide the dough into 9, 12, or 24 equal parts and roll each into a smooth ball. Cover with plastic or a cloth. Flatten the first ball with the palm of your hand, then use a smooth rolling pin to roll the ball into a thin, even round, flouring lightly between each roll. When the round has been rolled paper thin, dust off excess flour and immediately slip it onto the hot griddle to bake until spotted brown on the underside. Use fingers or tongs to turn the bread over and finish the baking on the second side, about 15 seconds; to avoid hard sheets of bread, do not overcook. Fold in quarters and cover with a cloth or store in a plastic bag. Repeat with the remaining balls of dough. Serve hot with a light brushing of melted butter.

NOTES TO THE COOK: Mükerrem used a whole-meal flour that had been very finely ground. It was so similar to Indian chapati bread flour (finely milled flour that includes the whole grain as well as the husk) that I have chosen to use this Indian flour in my adaptation of her recipe. You can find chapati flour in health-food, Middle Eastern, and Indian stores. Store the bag in the refrigerator to keep the flour fresh. Breads made with this flour are easy to make, especially in a food processor.

Although you can make these breads after just a few hours' mellowing, I have had the best results when I prepared the dough, like Mükerrem, the night before. Less tearing and easier rolling result from a mild overnight fermentation.

If you don't use the dough right away, wrap it in plastic and keep it refrigerated for up to another day. Return to room temperature before rolling out.

Though you will need the curved surface of an upside-down wok to make the 16-inch breads, the smaller ones can be made on any flat, smooth griddle. I am very fond of my non-stick square griddle and use it for many recipes in this book.

Just as when you make French crepes, the griddle bread may take a few tries before you find the right griddle temperature. Although it takes experience to handle this thin dough properly, your confidence and ability will build quickly after you make your first bread.

The cooked sheets of bread, which will cool to the consistency of a cracker, may be stacked and left for weeks in a dry place. Or they can be wrapped well in a kitchen towel to preserve suppleness, ready for serving later in the day. The sheets can also be frozen.

To rehydrate the dried bread: Sprinkle with warm water, then wrap in plastic until the bread becomes supple; reheat just before serving.

Crumbled and broken pieces make a delicious salad with cheese and hot peppers. See *umaci*, page 139.

Dampened and reheated sheets are perfect for wrapping around Georgian *kotelettis* (page 345) and Turkish *köfte* kabobs (pages 335–44). You can also tear them apart, to use in Musakhan (page 319).

FILLED AND FOLDED BREAD SHEETS
(*SAJ BOREGI*)

One of the best things to do with Mükerrem's unleavened flat griddle breads is to fill and fold them. Sprinkle about 2 tablespoons dried, crumbled fresh cheese (pot cheese; *akkawi;* soaked feta, drained and squeezed dry; or crumbled ricotta *salata*) on one half of an unbaked sheet. Then sprinkle a teaspoon of chopped scallions, a pinch of freshly ground black pepper, and a little minced green chili on top of the cheese. Fold over and cook on the griddle until both sides are spotted brown. Brush one side with a little melted butter and serve hot.

Mükerrem made an especially delicious stuffed bread with cooked, peeled, and finely grated waxy potatoes mixed with chopped parsley, chopped scallions, hot paprika, salt, and a drop of olive oil. Prepare as directed above.

She made another quick snack by brushing some beaten egg on the dough, then sprinkling on some salt, black pepper, and flour, before folding over and setting on the griddle. This variation reminded me of a Tunisian *brik.*

She saved the best filling for last: a paste of toasted white poppy seeds. Fresh white poppy seeds are deliciously nutty when toasted in a dry skillet over low heat. As they warm up, they exude oil, in which they fry until golden. They are then crushed to a paste that is spread over an uncooked sheet of dough, which is folded, then placed on the hot griddle.

Mükerrem offered me this delicious bread with a bowl of pure grape molasses and a glass of cold yogurt drink, *ayran.*

DOUBLE-FOLDED GRIDDLE SHEETS

When Mükerrem's griddle sheets are folded twice (with a filling placed inside), the bread is called *katmer boregii.* A typical stuffing might consist of mustard greens, lamb's-quarters, young mallow leaves, nettles, or dandelions, shredded, salted, and squeezed dry. Often the greens are blended with crumbled fresh cheese, scallions, green chili, pepper, and parsley—resulting in a sort of primitive version of Greek spinach-cheese pie.

SYRIAN BROWN-SPECKLED BREAD MADE WITH YEAST (*MARKOUK*)

This soft, spotted, paper-thin Syrian leavened griddle bread has a superb texture, lightness, and aroma. There are numerous versions. My favorite, and the basis of this recipe, was not, however, prepared outdoors on a mountain slope but in the fashionable dining room of the Sheraton Hotel in Damascus, by a chef working at his *saj* behind a glass wall visible to the diners.

I was mesmerized as I watched the chef flip paper-thin sheets of dough back and forth between his arms, making the gossamer sheets thinner and thinner before placing them first on a cushioned paddle and then flipping them over a 30-inch domed metal pan to cook in an instant. As each bread was finished, a waiter would rush it to a table, delivering what looked like a giant soufflé—two feet in diameter and nearly a foot high. By the time it reached a diner's plate, it was collapsing, but this didn't affect the flavor in the least.

Later I was invited to the kitchen and given the recipe, which includes both yeast and baking powder. I asked the food scientist Shirley Corriher if she could explain why both were needed for this particular bread. She told me that the double action gave the dough an extra boost, which created an exceptionally light bread.

Makes 4 14-inch rounds

1. In the work bowl of a food processor, combine the yeast, sugar, and warm water, pulse once, and let proof, covered, for about 10 minutes. Add the flours, salt, and baking powder, and pulse once. With the machine running, add the milk, oil, and water. Process 20 seconds. Turn the dough out onto a lightly floured surface and knead until smooth and springy in texture, 5 minutes. Cover and let stand 2 hours.

I teaspoon active dry yeast
½ teaspoon sugar
2 tablespoons warm water
2½ cups (approximately 12 ounces) unbleached flour
½ cup (2 ounces) sifted whole wheat flour
I teaspoon salt
I teaspoon baking powder
½ cup warm milk
4 tablespoons olive oil
½ cup water

2. Punch the dough down, divide it into 4 equal parts, and, with your hands, form each into a round flattened loaf. Leave on a wooden board, covered with a flour-dusted cloth, in a warm place for about 3 hours. Or refrigerate overnight and return to room temperature.

3. Preheat an upside-down wok or a very large griddle. Roll out each piece of the dough into a 10-inch round. Keep the others covered while preparing the first round. Stretch and flip the dough from one hand to the other to form a thin sheet, 12 to 14 inches in diameter. (This isn't difficult if you emulate a pizza maker working with pizza dough.) Then press the dough out to about 15 inches in diameter. Flip it onto the heated wok or griddle and cook until spotted and swollen on both sides, about 2 minutes. Repeat with the remaining dough. Serve while still warm or let stand until completely cold, sprinkle lightly with water, and fold in triangles before storing in plastic bags in the freezer.

BUBA KHOTOVELI'S CRACKLING FLAT BREAD

Since hardly anyone in North America owns a tandoor-style oven, home cooks have tried numerous methods in an attempt to simulate the extraordinary, tasty crust and delicate crumb of a good pit-oven bread. Here is one clever Georgian émigrés method, which works beautifully.

The following recipe was created by Buba Khotoveli, a mustachioed, ever-smiling restaurateur, who taught me how to make his native Georgian crackling flat bread in the kitchen of his restaurant, Primorski, in the Brighton Beach section of Brooklyn, called Little Odessa.

Buba's method is ingenious and produces excellent loaves. After stretching a round of dough and tossing it from hand to hand, he douses it under cold running water, pats it into a hot stoneware skillet, and places it in the oven to bake. Through the glass oven wall, I watched his breads puff up and make waves—not very differently from the traditional breads of Georgia.

This bread can be extraordinarily flavorful if you have a good starter. The aroma, texture, and flavor are all the result of the sponge, or starter, which simulates the "good bacteria" found in an old-fashioned wooden kneading trough. Later a long, slow rise will cause the dough to ripen, producing a unique flavor and texture.

This bread makes a good accompaniment to stews and soups. Or you can break it apart and dip it into any number of spreads and dips.

Makes 2 large or 4 small rounds

SPONGE

¼ teaspoon active dry yeast

½ cup warm water

5 ounces (approximately 1⅛ cups) bread flour, plus more for dusting

In a deep, thick Ziploc bag, dissolve the yeast in a few tablespoons of the warm water. Add the remaining water, then gradually blend in the flour. Once the starter comes together, dust your hands with flour and gently knead to form a smooth, soft ball. Close the bag without sealing and leave at room temperature until airy, light, and bubbly, about 8 hours or overnight. Stir down the dough and use at once or press out air, seal, and refrigerate until ready to use, within one week. Or freeze the dough; return to room temperature, about 4 hours.

1. In a large mixing bowl, combine the yeast, ¼ cup water, and the sugar. Let stand until foamy. Stir down the starter in the plastic bag; cut into small pieces; add to the mixing bowl. Gradually incorporate 1 cup warm water, oil, 2½ cups bread flour, whole wheat flour and salt to form a kneadable dough. Add more flour if necessary. Turn out onto a lightly floured surface and knead 10 to 15 minutes to achieve the proper consistency—an elastic, soft, and slightly blistered dough. (If you are using a food processor, halve the dough and knead each part for 30 seconds. Turn out and finish kneading by hand.)

Lightly oil a medium bowl and turn the dough to coat on all sides. Cover with plastic wrap and let rise at room temperature until more than doubled in bulk, about 3 hours.

2. Punch down the dough and turn out onto a work surface and briefly knead. Divide dough in half (or quarters); shape each into a smooth flattened mound. Cover with a cloth and let rise at room temperature until puffy, soft, lively, and spongy, about 2 hours.

3. Preheat the oven to 450°F. Place 2 lightly oiled 14- or 16-inch pizza pans or 2 large well-seasoned cast-iron griddles on the upper and lower oven racks.

4. Meanwhile, punch down one ball of dough and flatten with the palm of your hand to form a round disk about 1 inch thick. Lift the dough and drape over floured hands—palms down and fingers bent loosely underneath. Stretch the dough carefully from the center outward to loosen it up. (If the dough starts to snap back to a smaller size, cover with a towel and let it relax for 5 minutes.) Wet your palms and gently press out the dough to make an 11-inch round. Repeat with the remaining dough.

5. Remove the hot pans from the oven and set them on trivets next to the rounds of dough. Be sure to use thick oven mitts when handling the preheated pans. Brush the rounds of bread with cold water and quickly invert each into a preheated pan; brush the top side with more cold water. Use wet fingertips to dimple the center, leaving a good 1½-inch rim.

Immediately return the pans to the oven. Bake about 17 minutes, rotating the pans once or twice.

6. Place the pans on trivets or racks. After 5 minutes use a spatula to remove the breads to wire racks. Wrap in a kitchen towel if serving within 30 minutes. The bread will be crusty at first but then will turn soft. For a crustier bread, bake the breads in advance and reheat in a hot oven just before serving. Serve hot, warm, or reheated.

NOTES TO THE COOK: Your choice of flour will greatly influence your success. For best results, use a flour strong in gluten and enrich it with some whole wheat flour.

Any flat surface that holds heat evenly can be used for baking: quarry tiles, baking stones, 12-inch pizza pans, heavy baking sheets, soapstone or cast-iron griddles. To use unglazed terra-cotta pans, choose 12-inch bulb seed tray pans (available at garden centers) with or without drainage holes. Because they break easily, you must season them first with oil. To season: Brush each pan all over with vegetable or olive oil, place in a cold oven, turn the heat on to 425°F., and leave for 1 hour; allow to cool; lightly oil before using.

To make smaller loaves: Divide the dough into 4 parts and flatten each with the moistened palm of the hand to form a 1-inch-thick oval. Wet your palms and press out to 7 by 3½ inches. (Seven-inch terra-cotta pans can be purchased through mail order. See Appendix C, Pizza Pans and Terra-cotta Pans under Mail-Order Addresses.)

If you are using a heavy-duty mixer to knead the dough, cut up the starter into small pieces and place in the mixing bowl. Add half the flour and slowly beat with a flat paddle until creamy and smooth. Add the oil and salt, then gradually add the remaining flour. Knead for 10 minutes. The dough will be slightly blistery and soft. Knead 1 more minute by hand on a lightly floured board until smooth, then allow to rest. Remember: Every time you handle the dough, you must let the gluten rest a little afterward.

TURKISH RIDGE-PATTERNED BREAD
(*AGIK EKMEK* OR *PIDE*)

Here is the Turkish version of a flat leavened bread baked in a wood-fired igloo-type oven. Although the recipe is similar to Buba Khotoveli's, above, I include it because of the delightful ridged pattern and the addition of black nigella seeds, which impart a unique scent. Sesame seeds may be substituted.

This is one of the best breads of the eastern Mediterranean.

Makes 2 large or 4 small ovals

In a deep, thick Ziploc bag, dissolve the yeast in a few tablespoons of the warm water. Add the remaining water, then gradually blend in the flour. Once the starter comes together, dust your hands with flour and gently knead to form a smooth, soft ball. Close the bag without sealing and leave at room temperature until airy, light, and bubbly, about 8 hours or overnight. Stir down the dough and use at once or press out air, seal, and refrigerate until ready to use, within one week. Or freeze the dough; return to room temperature, about 4 hours.

1. Follow steps 1 and 2 in the recipe for Buba Khotoveli's Crackling Flat Bread on page 46.

2. Preheat the oven to 450°F. Place a heavy baking stone or tiles or baking sheet on oven rack. Lightly sprinkle a wooden pizza paddle or an upside-down baking sheet with cracker crumbs, cornmeal, or white poppy seeds and set aside.

continued

SPONGE
¼ teaspoon active dry yeast

½ cup warm water

5 ounces (approximately 1⅛ cups) bread flour, plus more for dusting

DOUGH
1 teaspoon active dry yeast

1¼ cups warm water

½ teaspoon sugar

1 recipe sponge, at room temperature (see above)

2 tablespoons olive oil

14 ounces (approximately 3 cups) bread flour

2 ounces (½ cup) whole wheat flour

4 teaspoons fine salt

Fine cracker crumbs, coarse cornmeal, or white poppy seeds for rolling out the dough

Flour, a pinch of sugar, and water for glazing the dough

¼ to ½ teaspoon of nigella seeds or a handful of sesame seeds to sprinkle on top

3. Punch down the balls of dough and flatten with the palm of the hand to form an oval about 1-inch thick. To make it easier to coax into long ovals, lift one oval and drape it over your floured hands—palms down and fingers bent loosely underneath; slightly stretch each portion of the dough by carefully rotating your hands one after the other and coaxing the dough from the center outward. If the oval snaps back to a smaller size, cover it with a sheet of plastic and let it relax for 5 minutes. Wet the palms of your hands with water and tamp each oval to stretch to the desired length—approximately 14 inches by 8 inches. Place the first oval on the prepared paddle.

Combine the flour, a pinch of sugar, and enough water to make a thick paste. Dip four fingertips into the thick flour-water mixture and make deep lines down the length of the bread at 1-inch intervals. Lightly sprinkle with nigella seeds and/or sesame seeds and slide the oval(s) onto the heated stone or tiles. Bake 8 to 12 minutes. Repeat with the second half of the dough. Keep warm in a kitchen towel. Repeat with the remaining portions of the dough. Cool the bread on wire racks. Return to the oven for 5 minutes to crisp just before serving.

NOTES TO THE COOK: If necessary, rotate the bread. Timing depends upon the size of the bread and the retained heat of the tiles.

For a soft bread: Leave the oven door open during the latter half of the baking time.

To make smaller ovals: Divide the dough into 4 parts and flatten each with the wet palm of the hand to form a 1-inch-thick oval. Wet palms and press out to 7 inches by 3½ inches.

Two Corn Breads

In many parts of the eastern Mediterranean (Epirus in northern Greece, southern Serbia, Albania, western Georgia, Dagestan, and the Black Sea coast in Turkey) corn is the grain of choice.

I learned some hard truths about corn bread nine thousand feet above sea level in the ancient village of Khunzakh in Dagestan. I have described in the introduction the hospitality my friend and I received from the mayor. After assuring us that we would be protected and even kissed by all his villagers, his wife, Aishat, prepared a local feast dish of boiled mountain lamb, accompanied by disks of bean bread, wheat bread, and corn bread cooked and served in lamb broth.

As we were eating all this, the mayor said to us apologetically, "Actually, very few people love this dish. It is truly our own." He went on to tell a story about the corn bread disks, which were as hard as hockey pucks, despite total immersion in the broth.

"This is the bread we take on trips. Once, when some of our villagers were on a pilgrimage to Mecca, they met up with some friendly bedouins. In the tradition of our people, we shared our food. The trouble was that some of the bedouins started eating our corn bread before it had finished soaking. At first they gagged, then they thought our villagers were trying to poison them. 'Please! Please!' they begged. 'Tell us the antidote!' Our villagers then told them that the antidote was twofold: patience and also more broth."

We watched the local women make flat loaves with homemade yeast and a dough of corn meal blended with a little wheat, which they had previously prepared and then allowed to rise slowly overnight. They patted their dough directly onto long wooden paddles, and then slid them onto the oven floor after pushing the hot coals aside. These loaves came out imbued with the aroma of wood smoke, dense and gritty, and although primitive were exceptionally good to eat.

In the end, the bread-making women were so delighted by our compliments they offered us sniffs of their very strong tobacco. At nine thousand feet, this was a special sensation.

GEORGIAN CORN BREAD CAKES

Everywhere in central and western Georgia I was served cornmeal cakes made simply of stone-ground cornmeal, salt, and water, called *mchadi*. I found them crusty, heavy, and not particularly good-tasting. Furthermore, I noticed that as they cooled down, they turned hard as stones. I really came to despise them until I had a chance to eat the Svaneti province version. Then I understood!

The Svans, a people who live high in the Caucasus, make their corn bread cakes differently. They don't use water, but substitute fresh, unsalted cheese, which they blend with fresh stone-ground cornmeal, then pat out and bake in a hot oven or over hot coals.

These cakes may be prepared in advance, to be baked just before serving. These are especially delicious right from the oven, to accompany a dish such as Georgian Spicy and Sour Beef Soup (page 117) or simply to nibble along with a Georgian *pkhali* of vegetables (pages 176–78), or with Chicken *Tabaka* (page 315).

Makes 4 cakes

3½ ounces fresh, unsalted mozzarella, well chilled
3½ ounces (¾ cup) stone-ground cornmeal
5 ounces (⅔ cup) pot cheese or farmer cheese
Fine salt to taste
1 teaspoon melted butter

1. Preheat the oven to 475°F.

2. Grate the mozzarella to make about ¾ cup. In a shallow mixing bowl, use your hands or a wooden spoon to blend the mozzarella with the cornmeal and the pot cheese until smooth. Salt to taste. Divide into 4 parts and shape each into a flat ½-inch-thick oval about 5 inches long. (Up to this point the cakes can be prepared hours in advance. Wrap each in plastic film and keep refrigerated.)

3. Place the unwrapped cakes on a lightly greased baking sheet and bake until puffed and golden, about 12 to 15 minutes. Serve at once with a light brushing of butter.

BALKAN VILLAGE CORN BREAD

Serve this light, fluffy corn bread with fresh or imitation *kaymak* (page 386) or thin, moist slices of feta and cold cuts, washed down with a glass of *slivovitz*, a potent but delicious plum brandy. This bread goes well with Balkan Stuffed Cabbage (page 224), Mottled Beans with Collard Greens (page 256), and Macedonian Pork Smothered in Leeks (page 356).

These types of bread are traditionally produced at home in the hearth under a preheated domed earthenware or iron cloche called a *gastra*. Live coals are then heaped around and sometimes over the top of the cloche so that the bread will bake slowly and evenly. An earthenware cloche available from Williams-Sonoma (see Appendix C) is a modern version of this very ancient piece of cooking equipment.

Serves 8

I cup ricotta or cottage cheese

I cup sour cream

2 eggs, lightly beaten

2 cups milk

I cup club soda

½ cup corn oil

1½ cups yellow cornmeal, preferably stone ground

I cup regular-cooking "breakfast" farina

1½ teaspoons baking powder

Pinch of salt

Unsalted butter for greasing a baking pan 13 by 9 by 2 inches

I. Combine the cheese and sour cream in a large bowl; stir in the eggs, milk, club soda, and corn oil and stir until smooth. In a separate bowl, stir together the cornmeal, farina, baking powder, and salt until thoroughly combined; add to the cheese mixture and pass through a sieve (to avoid overworking the mixture) into the buttered baking pan. Let stand, covered, at room temperature I to 2 hours.

2. Preheat the oven to 375°F. Bake the bread 45 minutes, or until golden brown and firm to the touch. Turn off the oven and leave to settle 10 minutes. Serve warm, cut into squares.

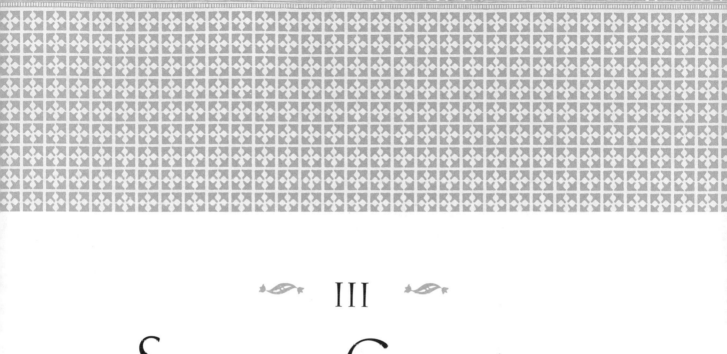

III

Savory Country
Pies & Pastries

*C*rackling or soft, golden brown or snowy white, intricate or plain, delicate or earthy, diminutive or enormous, ethereal or rustic—there is a savory pie for nearly every taste. The eastern Mediterranean repertory comes in a myriad of shapes and sizes—made with paper-thin phyllo, short pie dough, flaky pastry, puff pastry, grape leaves, and bread dough enriched with olive oil. Turkish böreks; Jordanian, Syrian, and Lebanese fatayers; Armenian, Arab, and Anatolian meat pies; northern Greek pittas; and Georgian cheese breads are among the best-loved country dishes in the region. Make them and partake of a great and ancient tradition.

Any of these pies can be part of the mezze table, a first course, or a main dish. Some are served hot, others cold; they are often accompanied by a glass of buttermilk or a yogurt drink, salads, and pickled vegetables.

ALL-PURPOSE PIE DOUGH WITH YEAST

This pie dough, made with yeast and enriched with good, flavorful olive oil, is used to make the next three savory pies—stuffed with ground meat, onions, and spices; mixed herbs and spices; and Swiss chard enriched with tomatoes and tahini.

Two notes on the preparation of this dough: I make it in a food processor not only to cut work time but also because I believe this method produces the best result. Whenever I make this dough, I put aside half to freeze for another time.

Makes about 2 pounds dough

1. In the bowl of a food processor, combine the yeast, sugar, and ¼ cup warm water. Pulse to blend. Cover and let stand until bubbly, about 5 minutes.

2. Add the flour and salt and pulse to combine. With the machine running, add 1⅛ cups water and the oil and process until a soft, tacky dough forms, about 20 seconds. Turn the dough onto a lightly floured board and knead it by hand 1 to 2 minutes. Form it into a ball and place it in a deep bowl; lightly brush with oil, cover the bowl with plastic wrap, and let rise in a warm place until doubled in bulk, 2 to 3 hours.

1 package (about 2½ teaspoons) active dry yeast

½ teaspoon sugar

¼ cup warm water for the yeast

1 pound (about 3¾ cups) all-purpose flour with a high gluten content, plus more for kneading the dough

1½ teaspoons fine sea salt

1⅛ cups warm water for the dough

6 tablespoons olive oil

Coarse cornmeal, bran, or fine-grain bulgur for rolling out the dough (optional)

3. Return the dough to a lightly floured board and knead it again, 1 minute. Form the dough into 2 even balls and use as directed in the recipes below. If desired, wrap and freeze for use at some other time.

*SPICY EASTERN MEDITERRANEAN PIZZA WITH MEAT

In Gaziantep, Turkey, I found the perfect version of this popular Middle Eastern form of pizza. And, to my delight, it turned out to be easy to reproduce. A superb combination of chopped meat, peppers, tomatoes, spices, and a little bit of pomegranate molasses, it "melts" as it cooks into thin, flat dough, which is then rolled up into a tube for easier eating.

These pies actually have very little meat, but the meat taste is strong because of the way the meat fuses with the dough. I pan grill these pies in a nonstick skillet just long enough to cook the bottom layer; then I slip them under the broiler to cook the meat. Finally, I garnish them, Gaziantep style, with strips of peeled eggplant that have been roasted over charcoal or under the broiler. Serve with glasses of *ayran*, a chilled yogurt drink (page 411).

These pies can be frozen and reheated.

Makes 8 pizzas, each about 7½ by 5½ inches

1. Place all the ingredients for the filling in a food processor and process until chunky and well blended. Cover and refrigerate for at least 3 hours for flavors to mellow. Correct the seasoning with salt and pepper, and sharpen with pomegranate molasses or lemon juice. Makes 15 ounces filling.

2. Slowly heat up a flat, non-stick griddle on top of the stove.

3. Punch down the prepared dough, knead for 2 minutes, then divide the dough into 8 even pieces. Flatten each piece into a thin round, cover with a floured cloth, and let rest 10 minutes. Roll each piece on a lightly floured work surface into a thin and even oval, about 7½ by 5½ inches. (See hint for easy rolling in Notes to the Cook below.) Transfer 2 ovals to a pizza paddle dusted with cornmeal or fine bran. Place about 3 tablespoons meat mixture on one oval; moisten fingers with cold water and spread filling evenly in a thin layer to completely cover the surface. Repeat with a second oval. Slip each onto the heated griddle and cook over medium heat for about 8 minutes or until the bottom of each oval is cooked but still soft and pliable, regulating the heat to avoid browning. Slide each oval onto a broiler rack and hold. Repeat with remaining ovals. Broil 1 to 2 minutes and serve hot or warm with the eggplant. These pizzas are at their best when freshly made.

I pound (half recipe) All-Purpose Pie Dough with Yeast (page 57)

FILLING

½ pound ground boneless lamb or beef

¼ cup minced parsley

½ tablespoon red pepper paste (page 389)

½ cup grated onion, rinsed and squeezed dry

I tablespoon tomato paste

¼ cup canned Italian tomatoes, drained and crushed

½ teaspoon ground cumin

Cayenne to taste

Sea salt to taste

¼ teaspoon freshly ground black pepper

¾ teaspoon pomegranate molasses (page 404) or lemon juice to taste

2 large eggplants, grilled, peeled, and gently crushed for garnish

NOTES TO THE COOK: This is an easy way to thin out a round of dough: Flour a flattened round; fold in half; roll once; unfold; flour the round again; fold in half in the other direction; and roll again; unfold and then roll out to a thin, even round or oval.

To keep the pizzas warm, wrap in foil and set in a 225°F. oven. The pizzas can be reheated, uncovered, in a microwave oven. To hold longer, stack the ovals folded with the meat filling inside. Store in plastic bags and reheat at a later time.

If there is any leftover filling, it can be blended with a small amount of moistened fine bulgur, shaped into patties, and grilled to be served as a snack. Serve hot or cold. *continued*

VARIATIONS:

To bake pizzas in the oven: Preheat the oven to its highest setting. Place two heavy, well-seasoned baking sheets, preferably heavy steel, in the oven or set tiles on the racks. Slide the pizzas onto the hot sheets or tiles. Do not close the oven door for 5 minutes. Shift the pizzas so that they bake evenly. Shut the oven door and bake 3 to 5 minutes until the meat and dough are cooked; the dough should be pale golden on the bottom and still soft.

You can make thin breads with the same dough used for the pies. Divide into golf-ball-size balls. Roll, then stretch each ball until paper thin. Bake the rounds on a heated griddle or upside-down wok until lightly brown, about 75 seconds per side. Fold and keep in a plastic bag until dinner. Reheat and serve warm.

You can also stuff each round. Crush 2 tablespoons feta with ½ teaspoon minced hot green chili, a few rings of sliced scallion, and a sprinkling of freshly ground black pepper. Place on half the round, fold over to cover, then place on the heated upside-down wok or griddle to cook. Brush the bread with butter while hot.

*ZA'ATAR PIE

This pie, a kind of bitter and pungent herb and sumac-flavored bread, is eaten by Middle Easterners for breakfast, along with fresh cheese doused with lemon and oil, sliced onions, roasted chickpeas, yogurt, black olives, and perhaps a dish of chopped ripe tomatoes and sweet young cucumbers. It is not, let me make clear, to everyone's taste!

The taste of a *za'atar* mixture can be herbal, nutty, or toasty. In the Middle East there are shops where *za'atar* mix is the only item sold. There are secret blends, some of which are quite wonderful. I purchased one in Aleppo but was never able to duplicate it; you can buy blends at most Middle Eastern markets.

"Israeli" is a pale green blend of pungent herbs that includes the biblical *hyssop,* along with toasted sesame seeds and sumac. The "Syrian" blend, the color of sand, has a decidedly toasty flavor. The "Jordanian" blend is dark green and very herbal, with some turmeric. All three blends can be purchased by mail order (see Appendix C).

Makes 16 5-inch rounds

1. Preheat the oven to its highest setting. Punch down the prepared dough. Turn it out onto a lightly floured work surface and knead 1 minute. Divide into 16 balls. Flatten each and let rest 10 minutes.

2. Combine the *za'atar* mix, oil, and enough warm water to make a medium-thick cream. Roll the balls of dough to make 4-inch rounds and arrange on ungreased heavy baking sheets. Use fingertips to dimple the rounds of dough, then thinly spread about 2 teaspoons mixture on each round. Bake 5 minutes, or until just pale golden around the edges. Serve warm. The bread should be soft enough to fold in half.

1 pound (half recipe) All-Purpose Pie Dough with Yeast (page 57)
4 ounces imported *za'atar* mix (see page 398)
⅔ cup olive oil

NOTES TO THE COOK: Store the baked pies in plastic bags in the refrigerator or freezer. Reheat in a 325°F. oven before serving.

*Mrs. Bezjian's Swiss Chard and Tahini Beureks

*B*eurek, or *börek*, as it is called in Turkey, is an umbrella term for many different kinds of dough: phyllo, piecrust, yeast, and noodle dough. Popular fillings are cheese, meat, poultry, and all sorts of vegetables. *Beureks* can be baked, steamed, fried, or cooked over a *saj*.

This savory *beurek* is my adaptation of a recipe in Mrs. Alice Bezjian's *The Complete Armenian Cookbook*, one of my favorite books on eastern Mediterranean cooking. Mrs. Bezjian is the only other author I know who writes about the food of Aleppo *and* Gaziantep. These pies are wonderfully versatile; serve them warm or at room temperature, as a lunch dish, snack, or part of a large buffet.

Makes 24 *beureks*

I pound (half recipe) All-Purpose Pie Dough with Yeast (page 57)

FILLING
I pound Swiss chard leaves, shredded (8 cups)
Coarse sea salt
I pound onions, chopped (4 cups)
3 tablespoons olive oil
I¼ cups finely chopped walnuts (4 ounces)
¼ cup tomato paste
I cup chopped parsley
⅓ cup fresh lemon juice
½ teaspoon cayenne
I teaspoon garlic, peeled and crushed with salt
I cup tahini
I egg, lightly beaten, for glazing the *beureks*
3 tablespoons sesame seeds

1. In a large bowl, toss the Swiss chard with 2 tablespoons salt; let stand for at least 30 minutes. In a separate bowl, sprinkle the onions with another 2 tablespoons salt and let stand for 30 minutes.

2. Dump the Swiss chard into a colander and set under running water to wash away all the salt; drain and squeeze out all moisture until dry. Repeat with the onions.

3. In a 10-inch skillet, heat the olive oil, add the onions, and cook, covered, 3 minutes. Add the Swiss chard and sauté another 2 minutes. Remove the skillet from the heat. Add the remaining ingredients except the tahini, blending well. When the mixture is cool, fold in the tahini. Adjust the seasoning with more pepper and lemon juice if needed. Makes I quart filling.

4. Preheat the oven to 350°F.

5. Divide the prepared dough into 4 equal parts. Cover 3 parts with a towel. On a lightly floured work surface, divide the remaining ball of dough into 6 equal small balls. Flatten each and allow to rest 10 minutes. Repeat with the remaining balls of dough. Flour the first flattened round and roll out to an even, thin 5- or 6-inch round. (See Spicy Eastern Mediterranean Pizza with Meat, Notes to the Cook on page 59, for suggestions on rolling out the dough.) Place about 2 tablespoons of the filling over half the round and fold the other half over to form a half moon. Seal the edges by crimping with the tines of a fork. Repeat with the remaining rounds. Dust off excess flour, then set on lightly greased baking sheets. Lightly prick the top of each *beurek* with a fork. Brush all with the beaten egg and sprinkle with sesame seeds. Bake until golden brown, about 20 minutes. Cool on a rack.

*GEORGIAN BEEF PIE
IN THE STYLE OF SVANETI

In north-central Georgia there is a beautiful mountainous area, called Svaneti, with some of the highest villages in Europe. While I was in the Georgian capital, Tbilisi, I met a family of Svans who invited me to their home to help prepare a meal of Svaneti food.

The lunch we cooked was proof that authentic mountain food can be both robust and light. We made pork cutlets with red onions and pomegranates; cucumbers and tomatoes sprinkled with Svaneti salt (a pungent mixture of coriander, garlic, caraway, salt, and pepper—see page 393); and the following meat pie, called *kupdari*, seasoned with a blend of Svaneti spices. The surrounding soft and tender dough is made with yogurt, flour, oil, and baking soda.

Serve this delicious pie as a main dish at lunch or in wedges to accompany red wine.

Makes 2 8-inch pies, serving 6 to 8

DOUGH

½ pound (about 1⅔ cups) unbleached all-purpose flour, plus more for dusting

3 tablespoons sunflower or olive oil

¾ cup plain low-fat yogurt

1 tablespoon cornstarch

¼ teaspoon sea salt

¾ teaspoon baking soda

I. In a medium bowl, with a wooden spoon combine 3 tablespoons of the flour with the oil. Stir in the yogurt, mixing thoroughly, then stir in ½ cup of the flour, stirring in one direction. Then stir in another ½ cup of the flour, the cornstarch, the salt, and the baking soda, in that order, and finally the remaining flour, mixing in only enough to form a soft but not sticky dough. Lightly dust the dough with flour, cover with a kitchen towel, and set aside to rest in a warm place 2 hours.

2. In a food processor, combine the steak, the onions, and the garlic. Coarsely chop by pulsing 15 times. Add the spices; pulse 15 more times. Transfer to a bowl and stir in the fresh coriander and salt. Cover and refrigerate until ready to fill the pies, about 1½ hours.

3. About 50 minutes before serving, divide the dough and meat into two portions. Roll the dough into balls; keep one ball covered while shaping the other. Lightly dust your hands and the piece of dough with flour. If you are right-handed, lay the ball in the palm of your left hand. Dust the knuckles of your right hand with flour and gently begin to shape a smooth, even cavity large enough to hold a ball of meat. Be careful not to tear the dough. Put in the meat. Gently pull the edge of the dough up over the filling to enclose it. If necessary, pinch the edges together. Place on a well-floured work surface and pat into a neat, flat, 8-inch round. Repeat with the remaining dough and filling.

4. Heat 2 lightly buttered 8-, 9-, or 10-inch seasoned or non-stick skillets over low heat. Slide a pie into each skillet, seam side up. Reduce the heat to very low, cover, and cook 10 minutes. Uncover the skillets and shake them to loosen the pies. Cover and continue cooking over very low heat 10 minutes. Flip the pies and cook on their second sides, covered, 20 minutes, or until they are deep golden brown. Brush the tops with the butter and slide onto a wooden board. Let stand 5 minutes before serving. Use a serrated knife to cut into wedges; serve warm.

FILLING

I pound rib eye steak, boneless, cut into I-inch cubes (no substitutes)

¼ cup roughly chopped onions

I plump clove garlic, peeled

1¼ teaspoons ground caraway

¼ teaspoon freshly ground black pepper

⅛ teaspoon hot paprika

¼ teaspoon ground fenugreek

¾ teaspoon ground coriander seeds

I tablespoon chopped fresh coriander

½ teaspoon salt

I teaspoon unsalted butter for cooking and glazing the pies

NOTES TO THE COOK: Cornstarch has been added to make the flour more like the kind used in Georgia.

Be sure to cook the pies at the lowest possible heat. If you are using an electric stove, set just above "warm"; if using gas, set a trivet over a low flame.

*Georgian Home-Style Cheese Bread Pie

This bread pie, called *khachapuri,* is the national snack of Georgia, served and eaten at any time of day. In fact, the minute you walk into a Georgian home, someone will scurry off to the kitchen to start putting together the family version. Made quickly, stuffed with cheese, then baked or fried until tender and golden brown, this pie is best eaten warm.

Many doughs can be used for *khachapuri:* yeast, sour cream, yogurt, even phyllo. Fillings vary too. Such boiled greens as nettles, spinach, or Swiss chard are sometimes added to the cheese.

In Mingrelia, in western Georgia, the local people claim they make the best *khachapuri* in the country, because they use a high-quality, moist cheese called *suluguni* rather than the crumbly fresh cow's-milk cheese used elsewhere. When I finally tasted their cheese, I discovered it was the same as the fresh, unsalted mozzarella we know in the United States, but with a deeper flavor.

When I make this pie, I use a fresh, handmade, unsalted mozzarella and add a little feta or Roquefort for tanginess.

I cook these pies very slowly on top of the stove in heavy-bottomed, nonstick skillets. If the pies brown too quickly, use a flame tamer. The mark of a well-made *khachapuri* is this: When you cut into the pie, the middle should be no thicker than the edges.

Makes 2 7-inch round pies, serving 6 to 8

1. In a medium bowl, with a wooden spoon blend 3 tablespoons of the flour with the oil. Add the yogurt, mixing thoroughly, stirring always in the same direction, then gradually stir in 1 cup of the flour. In a small bowl, mix together the cornstarch, baking soda, and salt; stir in the final ½ cup flour. Add this mixture to the bowl, stirring always in the same direction, to form a soft but not sticky dough. Lightly dust the dough with flour, cover with a kitchen towel, and set aside in a warm place to rest 2 hours.

2. If you are using feta, soak it in water 10 minutes, then drain well and crumble. In a medium bowl, with a fork mix the feta or Roquefort and mozzarella with the beaten egg, blending well. Shape into 2 even balls. Set aside until ready to use.

3. Divide the dough into 2 portions and roll into balls. Keep one ball covered while shaping the other. On a floured surface, flatten the ball of dough into a 7-inch round. Generously dust your hands and the dough with flour. Gently rotate and pull the edges of the dough into an even 10-inch circle, about ¼ inch thick. Be careful not to tear the dough.

DOUGH

½ pound (about 1¾ cups) all-purpose flour, plus more for dusting

3 tablespoons sunflower or olive oil

¾ cup plain low-fat yogurt

1 tablespoon cornstarch

¼ teaspoon baking soda

¼ teaspoon salt

FILLING

½ cup imported feta (2 ounces), preferably Bulgarian, or ¼ cup crumbled Roquefort (1 ounce)

4 ounces fresh, unsalted mozzarella (1 cup grated) or a dry farmer cheese

3 tablespoons beaten egg (about ¾ egg or 1 small egg)

1 teaspoon melted unsalted butter for cooking and glazing the pies

4. Flatten one ball of the cheese mixture into a 5-inch circle in the center of the dough. Gently pull the edge of the dough up over the filling, pleating and pinching to seal. Pat into a 7-inch round. Repeat with the second ball of dough and cheese.

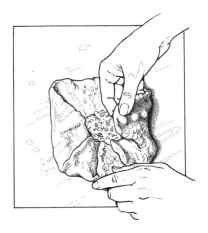 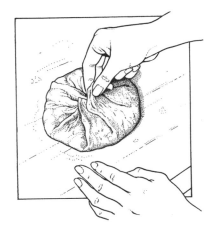

5. Heat 2 8- or 9-inch well-seasoned or non-stick skillets over low heat 2 minutes. Lightly film the skillets with some of the melted butter and slide each of the breads, seam side up, onto the skillets. Cover each and cook over very low heat, shaking the skillets often, until the underside of each is deep golden brown, about 12 minutes.

6. Uncover and flip the breads; cover and continue cooking over very low heat, shaking the skillets from time to time, until the bottom is deep golden brown, about 12 minutes. Lightly brush the tops with butter and slide the breads onto a wooden board. Let stand 5 minutes. Use a serrated knife to cut into wedges; serve warm.

NOTES TO THE COOK: To grate mozzarella easily: Chill in the freezer about 20 minutes.

When you are shaping the dough, it may tear, making it difficult to entirely cover the cheese. Never mind! Simply put the pie, exposed cheese side up, in the skillet, cover, and cook as directed. In 12 minutes, the cheese will form a thin crust. Invert the pie and continue cooking on the other side.

Northern Greek Pies

I had always wanted to learn to make the dense, aromatic pies of northern Greece, reputed to be that region's gastronomic triumph. I had heard about pies baked on hot stones called *conepittas;* pies baked under embers in the fireplace; pies shaped like logs or snakes. I had also heard tales of pies made of bread dough as thin and fine as phyllo; rustic pies of coarse cornmeal sprinkled with water to fashion a primitive crust; pies filled with pumpkin, mushrooms, sauerkraut, meat, chicken, leeks, eggplant, unique regional cheeses, and, most legendary of all, wild and cultivated greens. Well, I finally *did* learn to make these wonderful pies, the process of learning being as enjoyable as the feeling of empowerment that comes with mastering new recipes and techniques.

Macedonian Phyllo Dough

During my stay in Salonika, I met Gianni Boutari, a well-known Greek wine maker and a Vlach. The Vlachs were formerly a nomadic sheep-herding people, and are now celebrated for their business acumen. When I told Gianni of my interest in phyllo doughs and their intricate foldings, he sent me off to his natal village, Nympheon, in northern Macedonia, to learn to make various types of phyllo pastry, as well as some savory pies from a local cook. The fifty-mile journey from Salonika, which took more than two hours, carried me through an incredible wild country of immense heights and furious rivers.

continued

Nympheon was a revelation, one of the most charming villages in all of northern Greece. Set amidst idyllic mountains, with most of its buildings made of crumbling stone, the town is now semi-abandoned, with only thirty-six full-time residents, equally divided between men and women. But wealthy Vlachs have renovated many of the old stone houses, turning them into summer villas. As in every Greek village, no matter how tiny, there were two cafés, one catering to the Socialists, the other to the New Democrats. I found my instructor, Mrs. Nerantso, at the local restaurant, where the village priest was playing cards with about a quarter of the male population.

Mrs. Nerantso took me to a semi-abandoned garden, where we collected *horta*, the generic word for a whole slew of wild greens. A bag in one hand, a knife in the other, she gathered tender, young nettles. (Nettles are one of the most delicious and nutritious of wild greens, but only the young shoots don't sting. Be careful and wear gloves when gathering them.) We also collected some sorrel and incredibly long white leeks.

It was a pleasure to watch the effortless way Mrs. Nerantso made phyllo pastry from scratch, working the dough until it was, in her words, "as soft as an earlobe." She used a long, thin rolling pin called a *plasti* to snap two orange-size chunks of dough into thin rounds, which she lightly greased and then, by an intricate series of folds, turned into small packets. She let these rest 10 minutes while she prepared the filling. She then rolled the first ball of dough into a large sheet. With three deft rolls of the pin, a sheet was ready to line her large, round tinned copper pie pan. After filling the lower sheet with a mixture of wilted nettles and sheep's-milk cheese, she rolled out a second sheet a little larger than the first, and draped the sheet over the pie filling so that it fell naturally into soft wrinkles. She did this, she explained, so that when the filling cooked, the rising steam would have a place to go. Afterward, the dome would fall back into place.

If you like working with dough, you'll enjoy Mrs. Nerantso's phyllo sheets, which bake to a golden brown and crunchy crust. Try the dough with the Dandelion, Swiss Chard, and Cheese Pie (page 75), the Epirote Sorrel, Spinach, and Cheese Pie (page 80), and the Pickled Cabbage Pie (page 91).

Makes approximately 1½ pounds dough, enough for a 14- or 16-inch round pie

I. In a large bowl, combine the flour, salt, egg, oil, and water, blending well. Turn out onto a floured work surface (marble is too cold for this dough) and knead until smooth and soft, 2 to 3 minutes.

2. Divide the dough in half, brush or spray with oil, and set on an oiled plate; cover with an inverted bowl and put in a warm place at least 1 hour.

3. Lightly dust the work surface with flour and cornstarch. Remove one of the rolls from the plate; dust it lightly with the flour and roll, using even strokes, into a large square, about 2 by 2 feet. (Ideally, the dough is rolled out with a 3-foot extra-thin rolling pin—an untreated, plain wooden broomstick or curtain rod will do. The length and thinness of the pin enable you to roll a round of dough into a thin sheet. Once you get used to the thinner rolling pin, you will see that it is actually easier to use than an ordinary pin, and faster too.) Set a dessert plate in the center of the dough. Brush the dough with oil. Make 8 to 10 slits, at equal distances, from the rim of the plate to the outer rim of the pastry.

DOUGH

3 cups (1 pound) all-purpose flour

¾ teaspoon salt

1 egg, lightly beaten

3 tablespoons olive oil

1 cup warm water

Flour mixed with a little cornstarch for rolling out the dough

Olive oil for brushing or spraying the dough

5 to 6 cups prepared filling (pages 75–84)

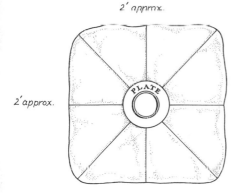

2' approx.

2' approx.

PLATE

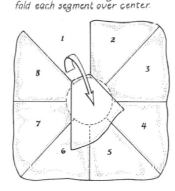

Remove plate. Moving clockwise, fold each segment over center.

1 2 3 4 5 6 7 8

8 7

4. Remove the plate. Brush or spray the dough generously with oil. Fold one of the wedges over the center; working clockwise, repeat with the remaining sections. Brush the top with oil and fold to make a rectangle. Allow to rest 10 minutes. Repeat with the second piece of dough.

5. Preheat the oven to 375°F.

6. Roll out the first dough "packet" to fit into an oiled 15- or 16-inch pizza pan; spread the filling on top, leaving a 1-inch edge. Repeat with the second packet of dough, but roll it out to 18 to 20 inches. Brush the sheet with oil and roll it up around the pin. Cover the filling, allowing the sheet of dough to unfurl into wavy wrinkles.

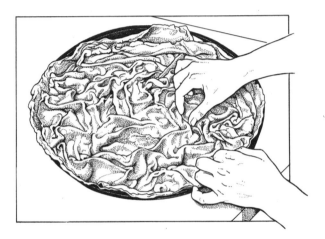

7. Trim the edges of the pie, and set to bake on the center oven rack until golden brown, about 1 hour. Reduce oven temperature to 325°F. and bake 15 minutes longer. Allow to cool 10 minutes before serving.

HOMEMADE PASTRY DOUGH WITH OLIVE OIL

Here is another recipe for homemade dough, scale downed for smaller pies. For the most tender crust, prepare the dough many hours in advance. Use this recipe with any of the following fillings, but remember to halve the filling ingredients for use with this quantity of dough.

Makes I pound dough

1. To make the pastry, place all the ingredients in the work bowl of a food processor. Process 20 seconds. On a lightly floured work surface, knead the dough for an instant, form into a ball, wrap in plastic, and chill at least 4 hours; better, chill overnight.

2. Meanwhile, prepare about 3 to 4 cups filling (see pages 75–84).

3. Divide the dough in 2 parts. Roll out one piece of dough to make a 12-inch round. Brush with olive oil. Place a small ramekin in the center of the dough. Make 8 radiating spokes, at equal distances from the rim of the ramekin to the edge of the pastry. Remove the ramekin. Working clockwise, fold "wedges" one on top of the other to create a small packet. (See illustrations on page 71.) Leave to rest 10 minutes. Meanwhile, repeat with the second round.

4. Roll the first packet of dough to line a 9-inch oiled tart pan or pie plate. Spoon the filling into the shell. Roll out the remaining dough just large enough to fit over the top of the pie shell and place it over the pie. Trim the edges, brush the top with oil, score the surface, and bake in a preheated 375°F. oven until golden brown and well puffed, about 45 minutes.

10½ ounces (2 cups) all-purpose flour with a high gluten content, plus more for kneading the dough
½ cup seltzer or soda water or I cup water and I teaspoon baking powder
½ cup olive oil, plus more for brushing the dough
1½ teaspoons white or cider vinegar
I teaspoon salt
Approximately 3 cups filling

RECIPES FOR NINE NORTHERN ↪ GREEK PIES ↩

Here are nine recipes for a range of pies with greens, including foraged greens or weeds: bitter dandelion, earthy Swiss chard, and lemony sorrel, as well as nettles, leeks, pickled cabbage, dill, mint, scallions, and ordinary fresh spinach. There is also a pie with grape leaves as a wrapping, and one that contains only cheese. You will find these pies easy to make and forgiving, since there is a lot of room for improvisation as well as error.

If you use commercial phyllo pastry, use this trick I learned from the Greek cookbook author Vefa Alexiadou. To simulate the appearance of a homemade dough, brush the top sheet with a batter made with flour, oil, and water. Mix 4 tablespoons flour, 2 tablespoons oil, and enough water to make a loose batter; strain it, if necessary, and brush it all over the surface of the pie just before baking.

*Dandelion, Swiss Chard, and Cheese Pie

This spring dandelion and Swiss chard pie is laced with a little mint and a bit of sugar to take off some of its bitter edge. If your dandelion greens are a little old or tough, steam rather than wilt by salt.

Makes 32 pieces

1. Wash the Swiss chard thoroughly; discard thick stems or use for some other purpose. Shred the leaves and fine stems, toss with salt, and leave to wilt 1 hour. Meanwhile, wilt or steam the dandelion greens, squeeze dry, and chop coarsely. Rinse the chard under running water to remove the salt; drain and squeeze to extract as much moisture as possible.

2. In a 10-inch skillet, heat 1 tablespoon olive oil; add the scallions and cook, covered, over medium heat for 2 minutes, or until soft, and transfer to a side dish. Add another tablespoon oil to the skillet; add the greens and cook, uncovered, about 3 minutes, stirring, or until the oil has been absorbed, and transfer to a mixing bowl to cool. (Up to this point, can be prepared up to 1 day in advance; cool, cover, and refrigerate.)

3. Add the scallions, mint, sugar, black pepper, and cheeses to the mixing bowl; add salt to taste and mix well with hands. Add the eggs to the mixture. *continued*

1 pound Swiss chard leaves

Coarse salt

1 pound cultivated dandelion greens or ½ pound wild dandelion greens

2 tablespoons oil

2 bunches scallions, chopped

3 tablespoons shredded mint

1 to 2 teaspoons sugar or to taste

1 scant teaspoon freshly ground black pepper or more to taste

1 cup grated Asiago, Parmesan, or pecorino

1½ cups (6 ounces) grated fresh top-quality mozzarella or *akkawi*

1½ cups ricotta or cottage cheese

3 to 4 eggs, lightly beaten

1 pound commercial phyllo sheets or 1 recipe Macedonian Phyllo Dough (page 69)

Olive oil (mixed with melted butter, if desired) to brush or spray commercial phyllo sheets

Batter topping if you are using commercial phyllo; see note on page 74

Lemon wedges (optional)

4. Preheat the oven to 400°F. and set oven rack in the center.

5. If you have used the homemade phyllo recipe on page 69, follow the instructions for assembling and baking the dough on pages 71–72.

If you are using commercial phyllo, unroll the pastry sheets. Oil a 14- or 16-inch pizza pan. Arrange half the leaves one on top of the other so that they barely overlap the rim of the pan, quickly and lightly sprinkling or spraying with oil between each layer. Spread the prepared mixture in one even layer over the pastry base to within 1 inch of the sides, then cover with the remaining phyllo, brushing every layer with oil. Trim the thick edges. Use a sharp knife to score the top layers of the phyllo as illustrated. Brush the surface with the flour, oil, and water mixture.

6. Bake 15 minutes. Reduce oven temperature to 350°F. and bake 45 minutes longer, or until golden brown. Remove the pie from the oven, and cool on a rack 10 minutes before cutting and serving with a small spatula. Serve warm or at room temperature with lemon wedges, if desired.

CHEESES FOR NORTHERN GREEK PIES

"You can't make a good pie without a good cheese," a cook from Metsovo told me. How right she was! In northern Greece, particularly in Epirus, cheese making is taken very seriously. Although it has always been a farmhouse activity, an actual industry has recently developed. Delicious cheeses—a smoked mozzarella type (*metsavone*), *kasseri*, and *graviera* (superb for frying)—are all being produced for sale throughout the country.

For the pie recipes that follow, creamy sheep's-milk cheeses are preferred and, when specified, feta. If not available, use cow's-milk fetas. Be careful of goat's-milk cheeses: They sometimes release a pungent odor when heated. For freshness, and to add a certain "bounce" to a pie, use some of the moist curd cheeses, such as ricotta, dry pot cheese, sieved cottage cheese, and dry farmer cheese.

I also add fresh, unsalted mozzarella to many of my pies. (I buy the cheese in quantity and freeze it, grated, in individual packets.) A high-quality mozzarella simulates the buttery taste and texture of the fresh sheep's-milk curds used in pies in northern Greece. Readers who would like to try fresh sheep's-milk curd cheese can buy it by mail order from Hollow Farm; see Appendix C.

One cow's-milk cheese that works very well in all pastries is *akkawi*, which you can find in Middle Eastern shops under the Indo-European label. Though firmer than feta, it melts beautifully, is less salty, and has a milder flavor.

Eastern Mediterranean cooks often combine cheeses to obtain a perfect balance of taste, texture, and "melt-in-the-mouth" quality. The perfect mix may have been discovered in Los Angeles. Linda Burum, writer for the *Los Angeles Times*, reports upon a special blend, created for Middle Eastern cooks, called *börek* cheese, also sold under the Indo-European label. A blend of sharp and mild cheeses, it is richer in flavor and creamier in texture than mixtures one is likely to create on one's own.

I have successfully mixed aged nutty-flavored Asiago, Parmesan, and pecorino. Other good candidates for that "melt-in-the-mouth" effect are medium-grating cheeses such as Gruyère, ricotta, *salata, graviera*, white cheddar, and Monterey Jack. Some types of *haloumi* will provide a sweet, soft, mellow flavor.

LATE-SUMMER PITTA
WITH MIXED GREENS

H ere is a popular Thracian pie, made in late summer when young, tender greens are scarce. The local people use the spinach-like leaf amaranth or pigweed (Greek *vlita*). These greens are a little tasteless in a pie, so I use a combination of tender early-fall kale, Swiss chard, and New Zealand spinach, all easily foraged in the produce section of a supermarket in late summer. My choices of greens and cheeses are only suggestions. When I make a pie like this, I buy and use what looks young and fresh.

Makes 32 pieces

2 pounds mixed greens:
 ½ pound tender kale, trimmed of all yellow leaves and
   roots, or young mustard greens
 I pound Swiss chard leaves, stemmed
 ½ pound spinach or New Zealand spinach, stemmed
I bunch scallions
I½ tablespoons oil
Pinch of sugar
2 tablespoons snipped dill
I cup grated Asiago, Parmesan, or pecorino
I½ cups (6 ounces) grated top-quality fresh unsalted
   mozzarella or *akkawi*
I½ cups ricotta or cottage cheese
3 to 4 eggs, lightly beaten
Freshly ground black pepper to taste
Olive oil (mixed with melted butter, if desired), to brush or
   sprinkle each commercial phyllo sheet
Batter topping if you are using commercial phyllo; see note
   on page 74

Follow the steps on pages 75–76.

NOTES TO THE COOK: If young, tender kale is unavailable, substitute another tender green. Mature leaves, especially those of the mustard and cabbage families, should not be used in these pies, for two reasons: Salting will intensify their bitterness; these vegetables remain too aggressive in flavor even after blanching.

Leaf amaranth seeds can be purchased by mail order from Johnny's Selected Seeds, Foss Hill Road, Albion, Maine 04910–9731.

A nice idea for flavoring mixed-green pies, taught me by Diane Kochilas, the author of *The Food and Wines of Greece,* is to thinly slice a fresh fennel bulb, blanch for I minute, then spread the slices among the greens. The anise flavor goes particularly well with spinach and beet greens.

WILD AND CULTIVATED GREENS FOR
NORTHERN GREEK PIES

Ralph Waldo Emerson described a weed as a "plant whose virtues have not yet been discovered."

The people of northern Greece, Macedonians and Epirotes, are specialists in edible weeds and nutritious wild greens. They will often blend as many as eight different varieties to use as fillings for their rustic pies.

For me, the use of nettles, sorrel, dandelion greens, beet greens, lamb's-quarters, Swiss chard, alone or in combination inside pastries, was a revelation. I was simply not prepared for the extraordinary quality and variety of the pies with greens, or *hortapittas*, of northern Greece. But cooking there is a zealous affair. A fur trader in Kastoria told me, "We have different tastes from the southerners and islanders. We know and understand what flavor is. When we make pies, we can put anything in them, and make them sing." They do!

Northern Greek pies are much thinner than the familiar plump, butter rich, and oil rich pies served in other parts of the country. The greens provide the pies with special "tones"; the pies are crisper and lighter but deeply aromatic. Combined with just the right amount of cheese, these pies with greens are bold in flavor and nutritious too.

*EPIROTE SORREL, SPINACH, AND CHEESE PIE

The Epirotes are masters of phyllo and cornmeal pies.

One Epirote cook inflated her chest and began to take deep breaths, when I asked her to explain the secrets of a great pie. "Yes," she told me, "our mothers are all wonderful cooks, but I can't believe an American would want to eat such things. Our pies are so poor, so humble, so rough, with nettles, orach, leaf amaranth, bitter chicory, and other kinds of weeds and greens. Well, of course, our wild-green pies are more complex-tasting than the spinach pies made in the cities. And, yes, they really are awfully good. . . ."

In Epirus, making phyllo dough is not only a culinary art but also an important part of one's social life. In the village of Metsovo, I met Maria, a young, blue-eyed Vlach woman with a long black braid down her back, who offered to teach me how to make several local *pittas*.

As she began her demonstration, I was stunned when she paused and then began to pray to her ball of dough not to let her down. When I inquired about this, she told me that it was only the second time in her life she had actually "spoken" to a ball of phyllo. The first time, she explained, was just after she was married, when her mother-in-law stopped by to see how well she cooked. She was trembling, she told me with a grin, and so begged her phyllo dough to behave itself. Then her father-in-law entered the kitchen, saw her shaking, and ordered his wife to stop terrorizing her. "We have had peace in the family ever since," she said.

Maria filled a pie with a fifty-fifty mixture of sorrel and spinach, then added a small handful of assorted wild herbs. If you can't find any, parsley will do.

Makes 32 pieces

Follow the steps on pages 75–76.

1 pound sorrel leaves

1 pound spinach leaves

Coarse salt

2 bunches scallions, chopped

4 tablespoons shredded mint

1 teaspoon sugar

1 scant teaspoon freshly ground black pepper or more to taste

1 cup grated Asiago, Parmesan, or pecorino

1½ cups (6 ounces) grated top-quality fresh unsalted mozzarella or *akkawi*

1½ cups ricotta or cottage cheese

3 to 4 eggs, lightly beaten

1 pound commercial phyllo sheets or 1 recipe Macedonian Phyllo Dough (page 69)

½ cup chopped parsley

½ teaspoon grated nutmeg

Olive oil (mixed with melted unsalted butter, if desired), to brush, spray, or sprinkle each commercial phyllo sheet

Batter topping if you are using commercial phyllo; see note on page 74

GATHERING, CLEANING, AND PREPARING GREENS

The easiest place to gather greens is at your local supermarket or greengrocer's. Small amounts of such leafy greens as mustard or young, tender kale will impart a strong pungent flavor. Tender turnip greens, beet greens, Swiss chard, and spinach will provide velvety weightiness. Arugula or watercress will add pepperiness. Dandelion greens, escarole, and chicory will add a touch of bitterness. Sorrel imbues any pie with tanginess.

If you want to gather edible weeds in the fields, you will need a good book, such as Roger Phillip's *Wild Foods*, to help you with identification. There's hardly any place in the countryside where one cannot find delicious edible weeds: purslane, nettles, goosefoot, lamb's-quarters, orach, amaranth, chickweed, and sorrel. Or you can grow your own (see Appendix C for seed and plant sources).

Once you have gathered your greens, they should be salted or wilted, to reduce them to a small, intensely flavored mass. This done, the greens will not "weep" when cooked, and will impart their intense aromas and distinctive flavors to your pie.

Cleaning and preparing: Wash greens well, then stem and shred coarsely. (In Epirus, cooks use sheep-shearing scissors.) Along with nutrients, greens are full of water; this water must be removed before they are added to pastry.

There are three ways to do this: blanching, salting, and steaming. Strong-flavored leaves should be blanched, refreshed, and squeezed dry. This can be done up to two days in advance if the greens are lightly salted. You can freeze blanched spring greens and keep them in freezer bags to use throughout the year. Tender leaves are best lightly rubbed with salt, then left to wilt. A simple steaming without water will wilt most tough leaves.

The theory behind these various treatments of greens is complicated but fascinating. Cold extraction of liquid, by salting, reduces volume and retains taste without removing nutrients. Hot extraction, by blanching or steaming, also reduces volume (and, with gassy greens, some discomfort) but results in the leakage of some nutrients into the cooking medium. If you continue to cook greens, so that they absorb their expressed liquids, they will be overcooked and tasteless by the time they are cooked, once again, inside a pie.

MACEDONIAN NETTLE AND CHEESE PIE

I like this nettle pie so much that I started growing nettles on my own property where the ground is moist. I purchased the plants from Well-Sweep Farm in New Jersey two years ago, and now have quite a nettle patch, to the chagrin of the boy who mows the lawn, who has often been stung by the hairs. Nettles, however, lose their sting when they are steamed, blanched, or rubbed with coarse sea salt.

Makes 12 squares

1. Wash the nettle tops under running water. Rub with the salt or blanch in boiling water until wilted, then drain and squeeze out moisture. Chop coarsely. Makes about 1¼ cups.

2. In a medium skillet, heat the oil, add the scallions, and cook, covered, over medium heat 2 minutes, stirring, or until soft. Add the nettles and cook about 2 minutes, stirring, or until the oil has been absorbed; transfer to a plate to cool. (Can be prepared up to 1 day in advance to this point; cool, cover, and refrigerate or freeze.)

3. Preheat the oven to 375° F.

4. In a mixing bowl, combine the greens, mint, and cheeses; add salt and pepper to taste; mix well with hands. Stir in the eggs. If the filling seems very dry, add the cream. Makes 1 quart filling.

FILLING
¾ to 1 pound young nettle tops
Coarse salt (optional)
1 tablespoon olive oil
6 scallions, chopped
2 tablespoons snipped fresh mint
1 cup ricotta
1 cup (4 ounces) grated top-quality fresh unsalted
    mozzarella
Salt and freshly ground black pepper to taste
2 eggs, lightly beaten
2 to 3 tablespoons heavy cream (optional)
½ pound phyllo sheets and approximately ⅓ cup olive oil
    for brushing the sheets or 1 recipe Homemade Pastry
    Dough with Olive Oil (page 73)
Batter topping if you are using commercial phyllo; see note
    on page 74

5. If you are using the recipe for Homemade Pastry Dough with Olive Oil, follow steps 3 and 4.

If you are using commercial phyllo sheets, oil or butter a 9½-inch round or square baking dish. Place 6 or 7 folded sheets in the pan, brushing each sheet well with oil. Add the nettle and cheese mixture and spread out evenly. Place another 6 or 7 folded sheets over the nettles, brushing each sheet with oil. Trim edges with a pair of scissors. Mix the remaining oil, flour, and water to make a pancake batter topping and pour over the top. Score the pie and bake until golden brown, about 45 minutes.

*MACEDONIAN LEEK AND WALNUT ROLLS

These wonderful "pie" rolls are baked whole, then sliced into rounds when cold. Reheat and serve warm.

Makes 7 rolls (serves 12)

2 bunches leeks, roots and tough outer leaves removed

2 tablespoons olive oil

Salt

2 cups mixed fresh cheeses (firm farmer cheese, drained cottage cheese, ricotta, or sheep's-milk curds)

1 cup mixed, grated hard sheep's-milk cheese (Asiago, pecorino, or Parmesan)

1½ cups (5½ ounces) shelled walnuts, grated

¼ cup shredded mint

Freshly and finely ground black pepper

14 sheets commercial phyllo dough

Olive oil for brushing phyllo

1. Trim all but the pale green and white leaves from the leeks; quarter each leek lengthwise, then cut crosswise into ¼-inch pieces. Dump into a large sieve, wash thoroughly, and let drain. In a 10-inch skillet, heat 2 tablespoons oil; add the leeks and ½ teaspoon salt, and cook, covered, over medium heat 5 minutes, or until wilted. Transfer to a side dish to cool.

2. Working in small batches, wrap the leeks in cheesecloth and squeeze to extract as much liquid as possible.

3. In a large bowl, combine the leeks, cheeses, nuts, and mint, add salt to taste, and mix well with hands. Adjust the seasoning with plenty of the black pepper. Makes about 3½ cups filling.

4. Preheat the oven to 400° F. Oil a shallow 9-inch square baking pan. Unroll 2 phyllo sheets on a work surface, with the short end facing you. Lightly brush or spray the sheet of dough with oil or butter. Cover with a second sheet of dough and brush or spray it with oil. Place a generous ½-cup filling about 1 inch from the bottom of the dough (the edge closest to you) and shape the filling into a 7-inch log. Loosely roll over the filling once, then fold in the sides of the dough; brush sides with oil; continue to roll into a log. Place opened side down on baking pan and brush top with oil. Repeat with remaining pastry sheets and filling. Place the rolls, side by side, in the pan and use a skewer to prick each three or four times. Bake on the upper middle rack 15 minutes. Reduce the heat to 350°F. and continue baking 45 minutes, or until golden brown and crisp.

5. Transfer the pan to a rack and let stand at least 10 minutes before separating and lifting out the rolls. Allow to cool on a cake rack. Use a serrated knife to cut each roll into 9 even slices. Reheat and serve warm.

NOTES TO THE COOK: The rolls can be baked 1 day in advance, then wrapped in wax paper and stored overnight at room temperature or in the refrigerator. Reheat in a preheated 350° F. oven. Allow to cool slightly before cutting into rounds.

The rolls freeze well. Thaw and place uncut rolls on non-stick baking sheets and bake 10 minutes, then cool slightly before slicing.

Kiki's Cheese Pitta

Of all the cheese *pittas* I've eaten over the years, one of the best was served at a little stone restaurant called Kiki's in the Zagoria region of northern Greece. Zagoria is a beautiful area of gorges, forests, rivers, and mountains of layered rocks, with a stunning monastery perched on a peak 3,200 feet above sea level.

Kiki's restaurant, in the tiny hamlet of Monodendri, is nationally famous for its open-faced fried pies—thin, crisp, fragrant, and warm slices of phyllo covered with a layer of shredded Gruyère-type cheese and crumbled feta. The top has an unusual glossy sheen, impossible if the pie is only fried.

No one besides Kiki's knows the recipe for this *pitta*, and she won't let anyone watch her prepare it. So, when I arrived with my Greek colleague Aglaia Kremezi, we did some heavy-duty detective work. As we waited for our *pitta* (made from scratch, it took forty minutes), we studied the simple restaurant menu: *pitta*, veal or pork chops, salad, feta, beer or wine. There was nothing else. But then we noticed a man entering the establishment carrying a large crate of eggs. Aglaia asked Kiki if there were eggs on the menu. Kiki solemnly shook her head.

Aha! Perhaps she used a very thin egg batter. Back in my Connecticut kitchen, I experimented, making the *pitta* various ways. After a few trials, I came up with an approximation of Kiki's version. I also figured out a way to make the *pitta* in the oven, thus decreasing the amount of butter.

Serve hot in small pieces with drinks, or as lunch for two with a glass of wine.

Serves 4 to 6

1. About 1 hour before serving, preheat the oven to 350° F. Spray a 14- or 15-inch shallow pie dish or pizza pan, preferably lined copper or black steel, with the oil and butter mixture. Stack the phyllo sheets, lightly brushing each with oil mixed with butter, and top with an even layer of the Gruyère and feta. Trim pastry edges to be even with the rim of the dish.

2. In a bowl, combine the egg, milk, flour, and butter, mixing well. Brush or spoon over the entire pie. Bake 15 minutes.

3. With a knife, score through the phyllo sheets, making 2-inch squares. Continue baking until golden brown all over, about 30 minutes longer. Sprinkle lightly with pepper. Let pie rest 5 minutes before serving.

4 phyllo sheets

3 tablespoons olive oil mixed with equal amount melted butter

¾ cup (3 ounces) shredded mild hard cheese, such as Gruyère

5 ounces feta, soaked 10 minutes in cold water, then drained and crumbled

BATTER

Well-beaten ½ small egg

1½ tablespoons milk

2 teaspoons flour

1 tablespoon melted butter

Freshly ground black pepper

*YOGURT AND FRESH HERBS WRAPPED IN GRAPE LEAVES

In the hills surrounding the village of Drama, in eastern Macedonia, Aglaia Kremezi and I came across seven women grape pickers resting in the shade of a large tree. Two were named Georgia, two were named Gramatina, two were named Maria, and the last was named Stavroula.

These women vied with one another to share their kitchen secrets. They told us how they bake kid, simply seasoned with black pepper and oregano, in the oven on a bed of stones, and how they use grated onion as the base for nearly all their stews. We were particularly interested when they described a savory herb and sheep's-milk yogurt bound with cornmeal, wrapped in grape leaves, and fried. It was a village specialty, called *asmapitta* (*asma* means climbing vine leaves in Turkish). Here is an adapted version of the recipe that Aglaia recorded from the grape pickers that day.

These "pies" are best made with wild vine leaves, which are tastier and more tender than the preserved or cultivated variety.

Make the pies as part of a buffet or as a little pass-around with drinks. The contrast of the pungent, crackling vine leaves and lush, creamy yogurt is a delicious and unexpected pleasure.

Makes 12, serving 6

2 cups (16 ounces) plain whole-milk yogurt, drained to
    1¼ cups (see page 410 on draining yogurt)
1 cup finely chopped scallions
¼ cup snipped dill
¼ cup shredded mint leaves
¼ teaspoon freshly ground white pepper
Salt to taste
¼ cup fine cornmeal
24 large vine leaves, fresh or defrosted
2 tablespoons olive oil
Lemon wedges

1. In a mixing bowl, combine the yogurt, scallions, dill, mint, pepper, salt, and cornmeal, mixing well. Makes about 1½ cups very thick filling.

2. Preheat the oven to 275° F.

3. Spread out half the leaves, shiny side down, on a work surface. Trim away the stems. Place about 2 tablespoons filling in the center of each leaf. Fold in on all sides as if making a parcel. Wrap with a second leaf, shiny side out, if desired. (The recipe can be prepared many hours in advance up to this point. Cover the packets with plastic wrap, and keep refrigerated. Return to room temperature before proceeding.)

4. Heat the oil in a medium frying pan, preferably nonstick, and gently fry a few packets at a time until crisp and crinkly on both sides, 2 to 3 minutes. Transfer to a baking sheet and set in the oven to bake 10 minutes longer. Remove and cool to room temperature. Serve with lemon wedges.

With thanks to Aglaia Kremezi, the author of The Foods of Greece, *for sharing her notes and advice*

*Leek, Spinach, and Cheese Pie in a Cornmeal Crust

◦◦

In the Epirote town of Metsovo, the "Switzerland" of Greece, I was a guest of the Averoff family, who have turned their picturesque mountain village into a center of cheese, wine, and handicraft production. With its cobblestone streets, stunning Balkan architecture, glorious flowers, and citizens in traditional dress, Metsovo is a world-class example of how to preserve old customs while preparing to thrive economically in the twenty-first century.

Elena Averoff, a handsome, aristocratic woman in her late thirties, is very proud of the produce of Metsovo, particularly its extraordinary cheeses.

"People live a long time here," she said, offering me delicious thick yogurt from a wooden tub she keeps in her refrigerator. "We eat little meat and practically no sweets, and our old people understand the pharmaceutical use of herbs. We drink cornmeal water and often substitute cornmeal for phyllo in *pittas*. In spring and summer we collect greens to dry, which we use in our *pittas* during winter."

Elena took me to a woman who prepared a homey and delicious cornmeal *pitta*, nicknamed "sprinkle pie" by some northern Greek cooks. She used eight different greens, but mainly leeks and spinach along with a little Swiss chard and some wild mountain greens that she had salted, squeezed dry, and stewed in oil to develop their flavors. The greens were wrapped in a paper-thin gritty crust made of stone-ground cornmeal containing bits of bran. The cornmeal was simply sprinkled onto a greased baking pan; then a little hot water or heated vegetable water was sprinkled on top to soften it. The flavor and texture were utterly delectable.

Serve this rustic pie in squares, with an accompanying glass of buttermilk or a light red wine.

Serves 6 as an appetizer

continued

5 leeks (about 2 pounds), roots and tough outer leaves removed

Coarse sea salt

1¾ pounds spinach

A small handful of at least 2 greens (arugula, Swiss chard, dandelion greens, lamb's-quarters lettuce, sorrel, or some wild greens)

3 tablespoons olive oil

2 tablespoons snipped dill (optional)

¾ pound mixed white cheeses; see Notes to the Cook

Salt to taste

Freshly ground black pepper to taste

1 teaspoon olive oil or melted butter

⅓ cup fine stone-ground yellow cornmeal (available in specialty food markets and health-food stores)

1. Trim all but 3 to 4 inches of green leaves of the leeks, quarter each leek lengthwise, then cut crosswise into ½-inch pieces. Dump into a large sieve, wash thoroughly, and let drain. Soften the leeks by sprinkling with 1½ teaspoons of the salt, tossing, and rubbing well through your fingertips. Leave for at least 1 hour. Meanwhile, wash the spinach and other greens thoroughly; drain well and cut away any thick spinach stems. Shred leaves and fine stems, toss with 1 teaspoon salt, and leave for at least 45 minutes.

2. Rinse the leeks and greens under running water and, working in small batches, wrap separately in cheesecloth and squeeze to extract as much moisture as possible, reserving about ½ cup of the liquid. In a 10-inch skillet, heat 1½ tablespoons of the oil; add the leeks and cook, partially covered, over medium heat 2 minutes, or until the oil has been absorbed, and transfer to a large plate. Add the remaining oil to the skillet; add the greens and cook about 2 minutes, stirring, or until the oil has been absorbed, and transfer to the plate to cool. (Can be prepared up to 1 day in advance to this point, covered, and refrigerated.)

3. Preheat the oven to 400° F. and set oven rack in the center.

4. In a large bowl, combine the leeks, greens, optional dill, and cheeses; add salt and pepper to taste and mix well with your hands. Grease with oil or butter the inside surfaces of a 9-by-1-inch round, non-stick metal or lined copper pie pan; add ¼ cup of the cornmeal, and rotate pan to coat surfaces evenly. Using fingertips, sprinkle 3 or 4 times with the reheated, reserved vegetable liquid until the cornmeal is barely damp. Gently add all the leek-cheese mixture, smooth the surface with moist palms, and sprinkle remaining cornmeal over the top. Lightly press the cornmeal into the mixture, sprinkle 2 or 3 times with hot water, and bake 1 hour, or until a reddish-brown crust forms on the surface. Remove the pie from the oven, sprinkle with a few drops of tap water, and cool on a wire rack at least 20 minutes before cutting and serving with a small spatula.

NOTES TO THE COOK: In Metsovo, only fresh sheep's-milk feta is used. A good mixture to use in the United States could include unsalted grated fresh mozzarella; Bulgarian feta-style sheep's-milk cheese, rinsed in water; Greek *manouri*; well-drained farmer cheese; ricotta *salata*; Monterey Jack; grated Asiago; cottage cheese; ricotta or a small amount of grated Asiago, pecorino, or Parmesan.

To increase the quantity to serve 12 people, triple the leeks; double the cheese; and use only a little additional dill, salt, and pepper. Bake in a 12- or 14-inch deep-dish pie pan 1 hour.

Although you need only a handful of cornmeal, it is important that it be fresh, flavorful, and stone ground (obtainable at health-food stores or by mail order; see Appendix C for mail-order addresses).

Store cornmeal in the refrigerator or freezer.

VARIATION:

A "SPRINKLE PIE" WITH LEEKS

Omit the greens and double the amount of leeks.

PICKLED CABBAGE PIE

This recipe is for one of the great dishes of the Slavic Macedonian country-side—*armiopitta*, or brine *pitta*. Home-pickled cabbage is combined with the finest butter, the best eggs, and the best Hungarian paprika, then baked inside Macedonian Phyllo Dough. Here you will have a chance to practice the Macedonian method of "wrinkling" a sheet of dough over a pie as described on page 70. The steam smoothes the wrinkles, and the dough forms a dome. When the pastry is removed from the oven, it collapses into a crisp, smooth top crust.

Pickling your own cabbage is a lot of work, but the unique flavor rewards the effort. Mildly astringent, home-pickled cabbage does *not* taste like store-bought sauerkraut.

continued

1 small head (2 pounds) green cabbage

3 tablespoons coarse sea salt

2 cups chopped onions

4 tablespoons (¼ cup) corn or olive oil

2 teaspoons Hungarian paprika

1 teaspoon sugar

Salt and freshly ground black pepper to taste

1 cup drained ricotta or crumbled feta

2 teaspoons vinegar (optional)

2 eggs, lightly beaten

1 recipe Macedonian Phyllo Dough (page 69)

2-cup bowl of yogurt

1. Eight to 10 days before serving, put the cabbage into brine. To do this, remove and discard the tough outer leaves of the cabbage. Wash and quarter the cabbage and cut out the core. Place in a deep plastic, enameled, or stainless steel container and top with water and the sea salt. Weigh down the cabbage with a nonreactive object (for example, a Pyrex plate) and let stand 8 to 10 days, stirring up and aerating the brine every day with a long, clean wooden or plastic spatula.

2. Drain the cabbage and squeeze out the excess moisture. It should smell sweet but briny. Shred the cabbage. In a large skillet, sauté the onions over moderate heat in oil until soft and golden. Add the cabbage and stir to coat all the shreds with oil. Raise the heat to medium high and sauté until the cabbage and onions are golden brown around the edges and slightly crisp to the touch, about 5 to 7 minutes. Add the paprika, sugar, and salt and pepper. Remove from the heat and leave to cool.

3. Crumble the cheese. If using feta, soak in water to remove excess salt. Omit the vinegar if the feta tastes tangy. In a bowl combine the cabbage, cheese, and eggs. Fill and bake as directed on page 72. Serve with yogurt.

❧ ARAB AND TURKISH PIES ❧

DAMASCUS-STYLE *BÖREK* IN A TRAY

In this version of the popular cheese *börek* of the eastern Mediterranean, prepared for me in Damascus, the cook, Maja Abrash, used only fresh sheep's-milk cheese, similar to handmade, unsalted mozzarella. "It is good for only one day," she told me. "After that it must be soaked in brine, and it is never as good as it was." Her husband, listening, shook his head as if to say it would be absurd for anyone to think otherwise. Now that fresh, moist, unsalted mozzarella is made daily and is readily available in fine cheese stores and in many supermarkets, you may understand how right he was.

This is an adaptation of Mrs. Abrash's recipe, with a combination of fresh cheeses that, I think, works quite well. Unlike many phyllo pie recipes, this one includes an unusual step—soaking the phyllo sheets with a thin batter. The pie is baked until the top is crisp, golden, and light, and the interior melting, fragrant, and flavorful.

continued

4 tablespoons butter, melted

12 thick phyllo sheets, preferably Apollo #7 (in the East and Midwest) or the Long Beach brand (in the West), or substitute 10 ounces thin phyllo sheets

1 cup milk

1 large egg, lightly beaten

9 to 10 ounces cheese: *akkawi*; grated, moist fresh unsalted mozzarella; or crumbled farmer cheese

¼ cup scissor-snipped parsley

Freshly ground black pepper

Pinch of salt

1 egg yolk

2 to 3 teaspoons all-purpose flour

1. About 1 hour and 20 minutes before serving, begin to assemble and bake the *börek.* Lightly brush a 9-by-13-inch baking dish with 2 teaspoons of the melted butter. Trim the phyllo sheets to fit evenly with rim of the dish.

2. In the oven, set one rack on the uppermost rung and another on the lowest rung. Preheat the oven to 425° F.

3. In a bowl, combine the remaining melted butter, the milk, and the beaten egg. On a work surface or plate, use a fork to crush the cheese with the parsley, pepper, and salt.

4. Line the baking dish with half the phyllo sheets and lavishly and evenly brush each sheet with the milk mixture. (If substituting thinner sheets, brush every other sheet.) Spread the cheese mixture over the surface of the stacked phyllo sheets. Top with the remaining sheets, brushing each one with the milk mixture except the top layer. With a sharp knife, deep-cut the pie into 2-inch squares.

5. Add the egg yolk and enough flour (and water) to the remaining milk mixture to make a light batter and spread on top. Let settle 15 minutes.

6. Set the pie to bake on the lowest rack. Lower the heat to 350°F. and bake the pie 15 minutes. Transfer the pie to the upper shelf and continue baking until the *börek* is golden brown on top and all the liquid has been absorbed, about 30 minutes. Remove from the oven and allow to cool 5 minutes on a cake rack. Loosen the squares and serve while still hot.

NOTES TO THE COOK: Although the *börek* is at its best served straight from the oven, leftovers can be covered with foil and reheated in a 350°F. oven.

If only salted fresh mozzarella is available, cut into slices and soak in several changes of cold water. Chill the cheese until firm, then grate it.

COMMENTS ON OTHER REGIONAL *BÖREKS*
BAKED IN A TRAY

THRACIAN *BÖREKS:* The Turkish region of Thrace is famous for its pies, or *böreks*, because the cheese is of very high quality. The *böreks* are extremely rich, made of lots of eggs, butter, and sheep's-milk yogurt. Thracian *böreks* also have intricate toppings, in which the phyllo is twisted to resemble ribbons, bow ties, and even flattened carnations.

WATER *BÖREKS:* Ayla Algar, in her book *Classical Turkish Cooking*, praises water *böreks* baked in a tray: "This superb creation, a jewel in the crown of the *börek* family, is the final and perfected outcome of the process that began when Turks first rolled dough in their Central Asian homeland almost a millennium ago."

She is describing a kind of glorified noodle pudding. Lumps of an egg based dough, rolled very thin and then dried, are dropped one by one into boiling water. Then immediately pulled out and drained, they are layered in a flat tray with a filling of feta, eggs, chopped parsley, and plenty of butter, then baked until the top turns "gloriously brown."

Other types of Turkish *böreks* include *puf börek* (puff-pastry dough stuffed and fried); *bohça* (yogurt-based pastry stuffed and baked); *sigara* (cigarette-shaped stuffed and fried pastry); *muska* (triangular-shaped stuffed pastry); and *tepsi* (*yufka*-phyllo pie baked in a tray).

ABKHAZIAN TRAY *BÖREKS:* I tasted this *börek* in Tbilisi, but the dish is actually a regional specialty from Abkhazia, along the Black Sea. Noodle dough is layered with cheese and encased in phyllo, then baked until crisp and golden on the outside, while remaining moist and tender within.

PANDELI'S EGGPLANT *BÖREK*

In this rich and delightful *börek*, smoky eggplant flesh is blended with a thick béchamel sauce and two kinds of grated cheese. A specialty at Pandeli's Restaurant in Istanbul, it is served at room temperature with shavings of roasted lamb shank, reminiscent of the great classic Ottoman dish *Hungar Begendi.**

Makes about 20 pieces

3 large eggplants, about 1 pound each

2 tablespoons olive oil

4 tablespoons all-purpose flour

1 cup hot milk

3½ ounces unsalted fresh mozzarella, grated (1 cup)

3 ounces pecorino, Asiago, or Parmesan, grated (1 cup)

Salt and freshly ground white pepper to taste

½ cup milk

2 eggs, beaten

3½ ounces fresh cheese: pot cheese, cottage cheese, farmer cheese, or ricotta

1 pound thick phyllo sheets, preferably Apollo #7 (in the East and Midwest) or the Long Beach brand (in the West)

6 tablespoons butter, melted, mixed with 6 tablespoons olive oil for brushing phyllo

2 tablespoons grated cheese for topping

1 tablespoon grated fresh bread crumbs for topping

1. Grill the eggplants as described on page 26. Peel the eggplants and drain them in a colander 20 minutes; squeeze out excess moisture and roughly chop. Set aside.

2. In a small saucepan over medium heat, warm the oil. Blend in the flour and gradually add the hot milk by tablespoons. Cook, stirring, until thick and smooth, about 10 minutes. Off the heat, add the mozzarella and pecorino cheese, stirring. Return to the stove and cook, stirring, until melted and smooth. Remove from the heat and allow to cool and thicken further. Fold in half the eggplant and season with salt and pepper. (Up to this point the recipe can be prepared 1 day in advance.)

3. Preheat the oven to 425° F. Lightly spray or brush a 9-by-13-by-2-inch baking pan with butter and oil.

4. Loosen the thick cheese sauce with ½ cup milk and beat in the eggs and the fresh cheese. Adjust the seasoning with salt and pepper. Makes about 1 quart filling.

5. Unroll the phyllo sheets and arrange half the sheets in the baking pan, one on top of

*See my *Mediterranean Cooking* for a recipe for this dish.

the other so that they barely overlap the edges, quickly and lightly sprinkle melted butter and oil between all layers. Spread half the filling in one even, thin layer over the pastry base, then scatter the eggplant on top and cover with the remaining filling. Lay the remaining phyllo sheets on top, brushing with more butter and oil between layers. Trim all edges. Brush the top with butter and oil and sprinkle with the grated cheese and bread crumbs. Score the top with a sharp knife for 20 serving pieces. Bake 1 hour, or until golden brown. Cool on a rack, then cut all the way through the scored pieces. Serve warm or at room temperature. Can be reheated 10 minutes in a 350°F. oven.

With thanks to Chef Ismail Demir

TWO DUMPLING
⌁ RECIPES ⌁

GEORGIAN DUMPLINGS WITH CRACKED BLACK PEPPER (*KHINKALI*)

One day, my host family in Tbilisi, Timori Huaberidze and Tsino Natuvlishvili, suggested we visit Timori's parents. Before we departed, Timori telephoned ahead to be sure a lesson in making Georgian dumplings could be arranged. Called *khinkali,* these delicious meat-stuffed dumplings are similar to Russian *pelmeni,* but juicier and a bit larger, shaped like hobo bags with topknots.

Timori's parents live by the Georgian Military Highway, a spectacular mountain road that crosses the Caucasus to Russia. We traveled a steep, twisting route through valleys thick with pine, past deep gorges, stony black riverbeds, and fascinating tree formations. The topography was spellbinding. "The mountains here," Timori said, "can easily possess you."

When we arrived at the village, Timori's mother was busy frying *tabaka* chicken (page 315), weighed down with smooth black stones, in a skillet. She had already prepared rounds of corn bread, which she was keeping warm under her bed pillows until it was time to eat.

A local woman, Izo, had been found to teach me how to prepare *khinkali*. As she kneaded, rolled, flattened, and folded, she told me the story of her life. At the age of eighteen, she had been kidnapped by a shepherd from a mountain village far from her home. His family, disappointed with her culinary skills, berated her terribly. "What good is she?" they asked one another. "She doesn't even know how to make *khinkali!*" They made her life miserable, Izo told me, until she learned to make dumplings better than they did.

After the lesson, Izo took us to a religious festival, the Feast of the Icon, commemorating the resistance of Caucasians against invaders through the centuries. The tribes of the Caucasus claim to be descendants of the Crusaders, and it was at the site of the festival, a remote area in the valley of the Black Aragvi, that they hid their icons whenever they felt threatened.

When we finally arrived at the site, the steep grassy knolls were covered with circles of smoking ashes and littered with the carcasses of more than a hundred lambs, sacrificed to thank God that the hiding place of the icons had never been revealed. The few men remaining at the site told us that, even though the feast was over, it was not too late to join them in a prayer.

These Georgian dumplings require a bit of work, so cooks often get together to make them, to prepare enough to satisfy a crowd. Because *khinkali* are so moist, a Georgian will often hold one up by its dough handle, then lower it into his mouth. The handle, which is thick, is not eaten.

Served with scallions, pickles, sprigs of parsley and coriander, and a sprinkling of freshly ground black pepper, *khinkali* are especially delicious with lemon-flavored vodka. Unlike Russian *pelmeni*, they require neither sour cream nor butter.

Makes 24 dumplings

1. In a wide bowl, combine the beef, pork, onion, garlic, caraway, peppercorns, paprika, and ½ teaspoon salt. Using the palm of your hand, beat in ½ to ⅔ cup cold water, 2 tablespoons at a time; the water should be thoroughly incorporated after each addition. The mixture should be loose and wet. Cover and refrigerate.

2. In a food processor, combine the flour with the remaining ¼ teaspoon salt. With the machine running, add ½ cup plus 1 tablespoon warm water in a steady stream. When all the water has been incorporated, process until well blended, about 45 seconds. Do not overprocess. If necessary, knead by hand to form a soft, warm, and pliable dough. Cover tightly and let rest at least 30 minutes.

3. Divide the dough into 4 equal portions. On a well-floured board, using your hands, roll each piece of dough into a 4-inch log. Flour lightly and cut each log into 6 even pieces. Roll each piece of dough into a 4-inch circle; dust with flour and cover with a clean cloth until ready to stuff.

4. Place a scant tablespoon of meat filling in the center of each circle of dough. Draw up the dough over the meat to enclose it, pleating and pinching the edge to form a knot at the top.

5 ounces ground beef

3 ounces ground pork

1½ tablespoons grated onion

1 small clove garlic, peeled and crushed with salt

¾ teaspoon ground caraway

⅛ teaspoon whole black peppercorns, crushed

Pinch of hot Hungarian paprika

¾ teaspoon salt

1⅔ cups unbleached all-purpose flour

Freshly ground black pepper to taste

continued

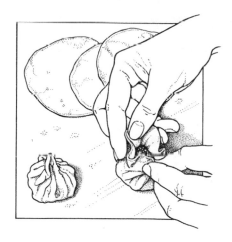

5. Press to seal. Holding a dumpling by its knot, shake gently so that the dough falls into the shape of a purse. Using scissors, cut off the top half of the knot.

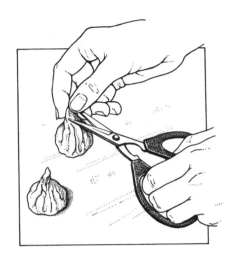

6. Repeat with the remaining dumplings. Place the dumplings on a well-floured tray without crowding—they shouldn't touch—and dust lightly with flour.

7. Fill a large stockpot halfway with water and bring to a boil over high heat. Salt generously and slip in all the dumplings. Stir gently to avoid clumping. Reduce the heat to medium high, cover, and bring the water back to a boil, about 30 seconds. Immediately pour in 2 cups cold water to stop the boiling. Cover and cook 5½ minutes. Then pour in another 2 cups cold water. Cover and return to a boil. The dumplings should cook a total of 8 minutes. Using a slotted spoon, transfer the dumplings to a large, warmed serving platter. Serve immediately, sprinkled with black pepper.

NOTES TO THE COOK: *Khinkali* do not freeze well, and are best eaten immediately after assembling and cooking. They can be boiled and then fried later in butter, just like Chinese fried dumplings.

TURKISH DUMPLINGS WITH YOGURT SAUCE (*MANTI*)

One of the legacies of the Ottoman Empire is the tradition of the food specialist, the expert maker of difficult dishes—lavish, intricate pastries such as baklava, special meat dishes, and *manti*.

I first tasted *manti* at a restaurant in Istanbul. The dish had been described as a cross between Italian tortellini and Chinese pot stickers, but such a description does not begin to describe its delicious, subtle essence. *Manti* consists of small dumplings made of paper-thin dough, stuffed with small quantities of lamb and grated onion. Once formed, the dumplings are baked golden brown to imbue a special toasted flavor, then simmered in a flavorful stock until swollen and tender. After cooking, the dumplings are smothered under a cloak of thick, creamy yogurt. Finally, a teaspoon of sizzling butter, scented with dried mint and finely ground black pepper, is swirled on top.

Since *manti* is one of the finest dishes in the Anatolian repertory, I was eager to find a specialist to teach me to make it. I found such a person in Leman Sezar, whose smile reminded me of Lily Tomlin.

Leman lives high in the mountains above the town of Iskenderun, on the Mediterranean coast. Here, after a divorce, she opened a small café where she serves only *manti*, salads, soft drinks, and the yogurt drink *ayran*. Her energy and talent have made her a great success; frequent appearances on national television have spread her fame throughout Turkey. Now people travel to eat her version of this marvelous dish.

To reach Leman's café, I climbed crumbling steps to the peak of a hilltop. Tables were set on terraces. I lounged, Turkish style, amidst fluffy pillows, to rest a while and enjoy the view.

Later I joined her in her large, cool kitchen, where the sunlight, entering through small windowpanes, danced about, creating a fascinating play of light and shadow on the walls. Here she showed me how to shape the dough into tiny satchels and how to prepare the yogurt garnish.

continued

I immediately liked this woman, the direct way she spoke, the dignified way she held her head. When I asked her "What makes a great *manti?*" her reply was warmly delivered. She had no doubt about who she was and the level of cooking that she stood for. "I use only the finest ingredients," she said, sounding like a serious contemporary California chef. "I personally know the lambs I use and that they've eaten only the wild oregano that grows on these mountains. I grow my own onions and dry them myself. I raise the chickens that lay the eggs that go into my dough. I buy only the best-quality flour. The milk for my yogurt comes from the best farm in the area. To flavor my butter garnish, I use black pepper from India. I grow my own mint, then dry it myself. I make all the dough by hand, beating it until it is almost too lively to handle. I do this so it will stretch to the thinness of paper yet still have strength. Strength is very important, because the dough must be strong enough to withstand baking, porous enough to absorb a tasty stock, and tender enough, when cooked, to melt in a customer's mouth." Leman paused and smiled. "Other than that," she said, "my recipe is just like everyone else's."

Well, please do not be discouraged! You may not have such magnificent ingredients at your disposal, but I promise that if you follow my version of Leman's recipe, you will come up with a delicious rendition of *manti.*

Makes about 120 *manti*

FILLING

8 ounces trimmed and ground leg of lamb

1 large onion, peeled and grated

Salt and freshly ground black pepper

Small pinch of crumbled dried Mediterranean oregano

DOUGH

2 cups (8 ounces) unbleached all-purpose flour

¾ teaspoon salt

1 large egg, lightly beaten

⅓ cup cold water

1½ tablespoons cold milk

2 teaspoons olive oil

1. To make the filling: Place the meat, onion, salt, pepper, and oregano in a mixing bowl and mix well. Refrigerate, covered, up to 1 day.

2. To make the dough: Blend the flour and salt in a bowl or food processor. Add the egg, water, and milk to the flour, mixing to make a dough. (The dough for *manti* is similar to an egg pasta dough, but made with fewer eggs.) Knead 10 minutes by hand or use a food processor, not only to speed up the ordinary kneading time but also to simulate a heavy beating, which is intended to build that

"lively" quality Leman talked about. (I must emphasize that a processor should never be relied upon to knead the dough completely, because of the risk of overprocessing, which turns the gluten in the flour into ropy strands.) Finish the kneading by hand 1 to 2 minutes to give a final silky finish to the dough. Work 2 teaspoons oil into the dough and continue to knead until the dough is smooth, soft, and pliable, about 1 minute longer. Slip the dough into a plastic bag and let rest at least 30 minutes or as long as overnight, refrigerated. Return to room temperature before continuing.

3. To roll out the dough: Ideally, the dough is rolled out with a 3-foot extra-thin rolling pin—an untreated plain wooden broomstick or curtain rod will do. The length and thinness of the pin enable you to roll a round of dough into a gossamer-thin sheet 20 inches in diameter. Once you get used to the thinner pin, you will find it easier to use than rolling out dough with an ordinary pin. And faster, too. (If you are using a thicker pin, roll out a quarter of the dough at a time.) Divide the dough into 2 equal parts. Rewrap one portion. Dust your hands and the work surface, preferably wooden, with flour and lightly knead the dough into a flattened round. Begin to roll out the dough gently in all directions, to keep it even and circular. Lift the dough often, turning it a quarter turn, and dust each time underneath to keep it from sticking.

4. To stretch the dough: Starting at the edge nearest you, dust the dough with flour and roll it up onto the pin, almost halfway to the edge farthest from you. The dough is stretched by the action of the palms and fingers of both hands gliding outward over a sheet of dough that has been curled up around the pin that is rolling at the same time. As if miraculously, you will see a strong, resilient, thin, and translucent sheet of dough appear. It is a thrilling experience and a skill not difficult to learn, though it takes a little practice. Unroll the dough, turn it 90 degrees, dust with flour under and above, and repeat until the round is of even thinness, about 20 inches in diameter. It should be clear enough to read medium-fine print through it. It is very important not to bear down on the dough, or it will stick. Patch any cracks and holes by pinching together.

INGREDIENTS FOR BAKING THE *MANTI*

1 to 2 teaspoons olive oil for greasing the baking dish

2 teaspoons melted butter or olive oil for drizzling over the *manti* before baking

YOGURT SAUCE

4 cups plain low-fat yogurt, drained to 2 cups (see page 410 on draining yogurt)

5 cloves garlic, peeled and crushed with ½ teaspoon salt

2½ cups well-flavored unsalted chicken stock, degreased

½ cup cold water

Salt to taste

4 teaspoons unsalted butter

2 teaspoons dried mint (see Notes to the Cook)

1 teaspoon freshly and finely ground black pepper, preferably Tellicherry

5. To cut and fill the dough: Cut into 2-inch squares. Quickly place a heaping ½ teaspoonful of meat in the center of each square. Pinch all points together; flatten gently, and place, open side up, in a prepared baking dish, 9 by 13 by 2 inches, previously brushed with oil. Place the *manti*, open side up, in one very tight layer, so that it will fill only half the dish. Extra *manti* should be placed on their sides along the inside of the baking dish. Cover with plastic wrap and repeat with the second piece of dough, filling the dish completely. Drizzle with the melted butter or oil. (The *manti* can be prepared in advance up to this point and refrigerated overnight or frozen 2 weeks.)

6. To bake the *manti*: Position a rack in the upper third of the oven; preheat the oven to 400° F. and bake the *manti* until the tops are lightly browned, about 30 minutes. Meanwhile, in a food processor blend the yogurt and garlic and process until smooth and creamy. Leave in the work bowl.

7. In a saucepan, bring the stock to a rolling boil. Pour the stock over the *manti* and return to the oven to finish cooking—that is, until the *manti* have absorbed almost all the liquid and are swollen and tender, about 10 minutes. Set the saucepan aside.

8. Carefully tilt the baking dish and pour the stock into a bowl, add ½ cup cold water, and then add to the yogurt sauce in the processor bowl. Add salt to taste. Process to combine. Now pour the yogurt sauce over the *manti*. In a small skillet, heat the butter to sizzling, and stir in the mint and pepper; allow the flavored butter to come just to a boil and drizzle it over the yogurt-covered *manti* in decorative swirls. Serve at once.

NOTES TO THE COOK: To hold shaped but uncooked *manti* for a few hours, cover with a dry cloth and a sheet of plastic wrap. To hold them longer, store in the refrigerator. Cook directly from the refrigerator, adding an additional 5 minutes' cooking time.

Manti can be flash-frozen on open trays, then stored in an airtight bag up to 3 weeks. Partially defrost before baking.

The first time you make this dough, you may have to cheat a little and lift the dough with your hands to stretch and even it out, but by the second round of dough you will find the knack.

Dried mint is a desirable aromatic and should not be replaced with chopped fresh mint. You can easily dry fresh spearmint leaves in the sun, in the oven, or in a microwave. Crumble, press through a sieve and use as needed. Middle Eastern groceries sell dried mint of excellent quality.

Do not reheat *manti*.

IV

Soups

*W*herever I traveled in the eastern Mediterranean, I encountered the tradition of soup as a main-dish meal, invariably served with plenty of dense, flat bread. And it didn't seem to matter when the soup was served. Sometimes it appeared at breakfast!

Light, creamy, or chunky, lavish, simple, or varied, the healthful, fresh-tasting soups of the eastern Mediterranean offer a vast range of gastronomic experiences. There are yogurt soups, grain and bean soups, soups made with roasted wheat, fish soups, vegetable soups.

All varieties of fresh vegetables are used, as well as lamb or beef, chicken or turkey, shrimp or small fish. Some eastern Mediterranean soups are plain broths, others are hearty; still others are soup-stews thickened with lentils, grains, chickpeas, ground nuts, rice, noodles, or bread. Spices such as cinnamon, safflower, allspice, hot paprika, dried or fresh mint, basil, dill, fenugreek, and coriander are used to add complexity, while lemon, pomegranates, vinegar, rhubarb, sumac, unripened plums or grapes, and yogurt are employed to impart a particular tangy finish. "There are as many soups as there are towns," a Turkish home cook told me.

Most of these soups are created with scarcely more equipment than a heavy pot, sieves, and a good, sharp knife. The techniques are uniformly rapid and straightforward. The key to success is in the choice of ingredients. A potato, a carrot, a quality spice sound easy enough, but making a soup is like building with blocks—each ingredient must hold up its part. Salt, for me, is the keystone in the arch. To paraphrase Brillat-Savarin, a soup without salt is a soup without a soul.

I once invited some friends to a salt tasting. We discovered the fact that some salts are saltier (that is, more intense) than others, and that several commercial brands were decidedly metallic. Among the best, we agreed, were the Mediterranean salts available today at many supermarkets and most fine food stores. Their pure, briny savor adds an edge of dignity to food, especially food that is water based. Since quite a few eastern Mediterranean soups are based on water (as opposed to stock or wine), a good salt has special importance.

Throughout the Islamic Mediterranean world, during the holy fasting month of Ramadan, a nutritious, hearty soup is served at sunset to break the fast. These Ramadan soups, prepared with vegetables, grains, an assortment of chickpeas and favas, and frequently lemon for tartness, are so healthy that their list of ingredients could have been written by a nutritionist inspired by the Mediterranean Diet Pyramid.

ANATOLIAN SOUR SOUP:
MOTHERS AND DAUGHTERS

The Turkish food writer Tuğrul Şavkay explained to me that a Turkish wedding soup, thickened with flour, egg yolks, and vinegar or lemon juice—not unlike the Greek avgolemono—was known a century ago as a "sour soup." "It is still," Tuğrul told me, "one of the finest Turkish soups."*

Today, the term "sour" is a reference to *any* extravagant addition of lemon juice or vinegar by Turkish cooks. I think the following wonderful, refined version, prepared for me in Gaziantep by an elegant blond Turkish woman, Nüket Ersoy, could more rightfully be described as deliciously "tart."

Mrs. Ersoy is a serious cook who knows how to obtain deep flavors without resorting to ersatz combinations. Here she used a turkey stock rather than a stock made from chicken or lamb, to create a flavorful base upon which to build the result: a rich, tangy tomato broth embracing two types of *köfte* balls (some stuffed with pistachios, lamb, spices, and onion; others plain), the whole garnished at the end with a flourish of sizzling oil and mint. Because of the two types of *köfte*, Mrs. Ersoy nicknames her soup "mothers and daughters."

Serves 6

*See my *Mediterranean Cooking* for a delicious recipe for *yoğurt çorbasi.*

1. To make the filling for the *köfte:* In a medium skillet, melt I teaspoon butter over moderate heat. Sauté the meat with the onion, breaking the meat up with a fork, until lightly browned, about 5 minutes. Add 3 tablespoons water (to keep the meat from becoming hard) and salt and black pepper. Cover and cook over low heat until the moisture has evaporated and the meat is very tender, about I0 minutes. Season with more salt and black pepper, and the allspice and red pepper. Fold in the walnuts, pistachios, and remaining butter, mixing well. Cover with plastic wrap and refrigerate.

2. To make the soup base: Warm the butter or oil in a 5-quart casserole and brown the lamb. Add the onion, cover, and steam 5 minutes. Add the poultry stock, the pepper paste, sugar, tomato paste, and salt. Bring to a boil, reduce the heat, cover, and cook until the meat is tender, about 45 minutes. Cool, cover, and refrigerate the soup base until all fat has risen to the top and can be removed. (The recipe can be made to this point up to one day in advance.)

3. To make the *köfte* dough: In a mixing bowl, soak the bulgur with 3 tablespoons water about 5 minutes. Add the meat, onion, flour, salt, pepper, and enough water to make a malleable dough. Moisten your palms with water and knead the mixture, adding teaspoons of water whenever needed to maintain a soft and smooth texture. Divide the mixture

FILLING FOR THE *KÖFTE*

½ tablespoon unsalted butter

¼ cup (I ounce) ground lamb, beef, or turkey

⅓ cup minced onion

Sea salt and freshly ground black pepper to taste

Pinch of ground allspice

Pinch of ground hot red or Near East or Aleppo pepper (page 395)

I tablespoon chopped walnuts

I tablespoon chopped, peeled, unsalted pistachios

SOUP BASE

I tablespoon butter or oil

½ pound lean lamb shoulder, cut into ½-inch cubes

I cup chopped onion

2 quarts well-flavored chicken or turkey stock, degreased

I teaspoon homemade pepper paste (page 389)

Pinch of sugar

2 tablespoons tomato paste

2 teaspoons salt

2 to 3 tablespoons fresh lemon juice

I cup cooked chickpeas, peeled

KÖFTE DOUGH

¾ cup (¼ pound) fine-grain bulgur

I cup (¼ pound) very lean ground lamb or turkey

I tablespoon minced onion

2 teaspoons flour

Sea salt and Near East or Aleppo pepper

FLOURISH

2 teaspoons crumbled mint, preferably spearmint

I teaspoon freshly ground black pepper

2 tablespoons butter

in half. Roll one half into smooth, chickpea-size balls; steam 5 minutes and set aside to cool. Roll the remaining mixture into smooth, marble-size balls and fill each with a little of the filling. See page 268 for details on how to fill *köfte* balls. Carefully seal the openings and roll each between your wet palms until the *köfte* is smooth and round. Steam 5 minutes and set aside to cool.

5. Fifteen minutes before serving, place all the *köfte* balls in a 5-quart casserole. Pour over the chilled soup and slowly reheat to a boil. Add 2 tablespoons lemon juice and the chickpeas, reduce the heat, and slowly cook 5 minutes more. Correct the seasoning with salt and sharpen the taste with more lemon juice if desired. Press the mint and black pepper through a fine sieve. Heat 2 tablespoons butter in a small skillet, add the mint and black pepper, and, when sizzling, pour over the soup. Serve at once.

THE FLOURISH

A sizzling garnish, or finale, is the secret to the explosion of tastes and aromas found in many Turkish dishes, as well as a few from Syria and Lebanon. Sizzling oil or butter, scented with pepper or dried mint (or other herbs or spices and, sometimes, garlic), is swirled into a dish just before serving. In Turkey this technique is called *yüzüne,* in Syria and Lebanon *taklia;* I call it "the flourish." It is reminiscent of an embellishment used by Indian cooks, in which such spices as mustard seeds, cumin, and garlic are swished around in heated butter, or *ghee,* then poured over a cooked dish. In Morocco, too, while an ordinary cook might simply add paprika to a dish, a cook with a more refined technique will achieve significantly greater aroma with a final flourish of paprika-scented hot oil.

THREE MEATLESS
~ LENTIL SOUPS ~

KURDISH HOT AND SPICY
RED LENTIL SOUP

~🐟~

Selim Nazilcam is a Kurdish restaurateur who owns restaurants in Diyarkabir in southeastern Turkey, and a very popular place in Ankara that offers authentic Kurdish home cooking. A strong, burly man with the face of a prize-fighter, he is so religious he won't serve mezze lest their presence encourage people to ask for alcohol—which, of course, he will *not* serve.

Kurdish home-cooked meals, he told me, typically begin with soup. One of the most popular is this red lentil soup, with a wild, earthy, herbal, peppery flavor from its spicing—a popular Kurdish mixture of dried purple basil, ground red pepper, safflower threads, and black pepper.

continued

Serves 6

I cup red lentils

⅓ cup skinned wheat berries or white rice

¼ cup chickpeas, soaked overnight and drained

I cup chopped onion

I cup chopped celery

I cup chopped carrots

2 Italian green frying peppers, cored, seeded, and cut into small pieces

1½ tablespoons tomato paste

I or 2 whole dried red peppers

Sea salt to taste

¼ teaspoon Near East or Aleppo pepper (page 395)

I teaspoon crushed dried mint

Pinch of dried basil (optional)

½ teaspoon freshly ground black pepper

Pinch of safflower threads (*baspir*); see Appendix C (optional)

2 tablespoons butter

I. Place the lentils, wheat berries, chickpeas, and 2 quarts water in a 5-quart saucepan. Cover, bring to a boil, and skim carefully. Add the vegetables, tomato paste, and hot peppers. Cook, covered, I hour. Add the salt and cook 30 minutes longer, or until the chickpeas are fully cooked. Transfer to a soup tureen.

2. Press the red pepper, mint, basil if using, black pepper, and optional safflower through a fine sieve. In a small saucepan, heat the butter; add the powdered aromatics; heat until just sizzling. Pour over the soup in swirls. Cover, wait 5 minutes, and bring to the table. Fold in the aromatic swirls just before ladling the soup into individual serving bowls.

Red Lentil Soup with Caramelized Onions from Aleppo

Here red lentils are cooked with fine-grain bulgur and short-grain rice to make a coarse puree in less than a hour. A skilletful of hot caramelized onions is stirred in at the last minute to create a simple and satisfying main-course soup.

Serves 3 to 4

1. Rinse the lentils, bulgur, and rice and let drain. Place in a deep saucepan with 1½ quarts water, the salt, and the cumin. Bring to a boil; skim, reduce the heat, cover, and simmer 45 minutes, stirring often. If necessary, add cold water to keep the pulses covered.

2. Meanwhile, place the onions and oil in a 10-inch skillet and set over medium-high heat. Cook, stirring, until the onions begin to turn golden brown. Reduce the heat and cook, stirring, until they turn a deep brown, but are not burned, about 35 minutes. Stir the coriander and cayenne into the soup. Pour the entire contents of the skillet over the soup, stir, and serve at once. Makes about 6 cups.

1 cup red lentils
¼ cup fine-grain bulgur
¼ cup short-grain white rice
1 teaspoon sea salt
1 tablespoon ground cumin
2 to 3 large onions (1½ pounds), halved and thinly sliced
½ cup olive oil
1 tablespoon ground coriander seeds
Pinch of cayenne

With thanks to Mrs. Emelie Abdy for sharing her recipe for makloota

BLACK LENTIL SOUP SPECKLED WITH WHEAT BERRIES AND TARRAGON

Here is another soup from Gaziantep that combines skinned wheat berries with dark lentils and tarragon leaves.

Alice Antreassian and Marian Jebejian, in their excellent book *Classic Armenian Recipes*, refer in a footnote to a similar recipe: "In the city of Aintab [Gaziantep] where this soup originates, the feathery, sweeping leaves of the tarragon so resembled a mustache that the soup was known as *bekhov aboor* or literally translated, 'Soup with a mustache.' For this [soup] they dried tarragon in the fall, with great care to keep the leaves intact."

Though I love the mustache imagery the Armenians give this soup, I prefer the more descriptive recipe title of the Turks—*alaca çorba*, meaning speckled soup. Since the skinned wheat berries and black lentils visually predominate, to me this dish looks less like a mustache and more like a speckled chin!

Dried tarragon permeates the soup with an unusual earthy fragrance. To prepare your own: Spread fresh, fragrant tarragon leaves on parchment paper and allow to dry in a low oven or on paper towels in the microwave. Store in a tightly closed jar. Press dried leaves through a fine sieve just before using.

Serves 4 to 6

1. Soak the chickpeas overnight in water to cover.

2. Drain the chickpeas and rinse well. Place the chickpeas, wheat berries, and quartered onion in a large saucepan, add I quart water, and bring to a boil. Skim carefully and cook, covered, I hour. Discard the onion. Pick clean the lentils and wash in several changes of water. Add the lentils, diced peppers, chili, diced onion, salt, and black pepper and another quart water. Bring to a boil, then cook at a simmer, covered, 45 minutes. Remove from the heat. Press the tarragon and red pepper through a fine sieve. In a small skillet, heat oil; add the tarragon and red pepper; heat until sizzling. Pour over the soup in swirls. Cover, wait 5 minutes, and bring to the table. Correct the seasoning with salt.

¼ cup chickpeas

½ cup skinned wheat berries, rinsed

I small onion, quartered

¾ cup black lentils (whole *masoor* dal), Egyptian lentils, French *lentilles de Puy*, or ordinary brown lentils

I small red bell pepper, stemmed, seeded, and cut into ¼-inch dice

½ small, whole, dried red chili

I cup diced onion

Sea salt to taste

Freshly ground black pepper to taste

I tablespoon dried tarragon leaves

¼ teaspoon ground Near East pepper or cayenne

2 tablespoons olive oil

NOTES TO THE COOK: Some Turkish cooks advise that when cooking beans, wheat berries, or chickpeas, one should add a quartered onion to the water and discard after I hour's cooking. They believe that the onion absorbs many of the components that produce gastric upset.

With thanks to Ms. Ayfer Ünsal for sharing this recipe

GEORGIAN WHITE SOUP WITH FRESH HERBS

This light, refreshing, white summer chicken soup, from Kakheti in eastern Georgia, may remind you of the Macedonian version of avgolemono soup, in which vinegar replaces lemon juice. Personally, I think this version, with its finishing embellishment of herbs, is superior.

It's tricky to use both egg whites and yolks to thicken a hot soup; one can easily end up with overcooked egg strands. The Georgian cook stabilizes the liquid with flour and is careful when adding the thickening agent.

Serve with a warm homemade flat bread (page 46).

Serves 4 to 6

7 cups full-flavored homemade chicken stock plus
    2 tablespoons of the solidified fat
½ cup chopped scallions or shallots
2 tablespoons flour
2 large eggs
¼ teaspoon sugar
1 tablespoon mild vinegar, preferably rice wine vinegar
2 tablespoons chopped tarragon
3 tablespoons chopped coriander
Sea salt and freshly ground black pepper to taste

1. Remove the solidified fat from the stock and reserve 2 tablespoons. In a heavy saucepan, melt the chicken fat over moderately low heat. Add the scallions or shallots and cook until softened, about 4 minutes. Increase the heat to moderate, add 5½ cups of the stock, and bring to a boil.

2. Meanwhile, put the flour in a small bowl and gradually whisk in 1 cup of the *cold* stock until smooth. Strain the mixture into the boiling stock and return to a boil. Reduce the heat to low and cook, stirring occasionally, 10 minutes. Remove from the heat and set aside to cool.

3. Beat the eggs with the remaining ½ cup cold stock. Add the sugar and vinegar and whisk vigorously 1 minute. Gradually add a few tablespoons of the hot soup to the egg mixture, then slowly pour the egg mixture into the soup, whisking constantly. Return the soup to the heat and cook, whisking constantly, until thickened and just at the boiling point, about 45 seconds. Off the heat, add the fresh herbs and season with the salt and pepper. Serve at once.

GEORGIAN SPICY AND SOUR BEEF SOUP

Here is a creamy, spicy, slightly sour west Georgian meal-in-a-bowl beef soup-stew traditionally served with unleavened sturdy corn bread (*mchadi*, page 53) or a plate of warm grits enriched with cheese (page 258). The soup goes just as well with a good chewy white flat bread, such as Georgian crackling bread (page 46).

There are numerous versions of this soup. Some call for a little rice, to add body, and a piece of dried fruit leather made from sour plums (*tklapi*) to balance the rich, spicy flavors. Others call for ground walnuts as a thickener, and lemon juice to impart tartness.

In the market town of Zuditi, in the region of Mingrelia, I learned about the spice mixture required for this dish. Inside the covered market there are over twenty stalls set aside for women selling special spice mixtures. The red, gritty, burnished mixture labeled "Specially for Kharcho" smelled richly of garlic and ground coriander seeds. "What else is in this?" I asked the spice woman. "Every dish has its own taste, and *kharcho* must have two special ingredients," she replied. A good *kharcho*, she went on, includes "a mysterious taste from far away." Well, after some research, this epithet turned out to be a reference to the leaves of a variety of fenugreek (*Trigonella coerulea*) called, in Georgian, *utskho suneli*, as well as the husk of the seed, called *ulumbo*. A very similar type of fenugreek can be purchased at Indian spice stores, where the entire seed is called *methi* and the crumbled dried leaves are called *kasoor methi*.

If you decide to leave these ingredients out, you will make a perfectly decent soup, but it will not be a true *kharcho*, with its unique taste and fragrance. Though the spice seller would not reveal the quantities, she did list the other ingredients, which included coriander seeds, savory, dried marigold petals, black pepper, and hot paprika. In the recipe you will find my attempt to duplicate the flavor of the spice packet I bought from her that day.

I use short ribs for their rich flavor, but Georgians will sometimes use chicken wings, lamb riblets, or boneless lean beef. The meat is boiled until fully tender; the bones, gristle, and fat are removed; then onions, garlic, tomatoes, and seasonings are added. Thus the meat ends up butter tender, the vegetables retain their texture, and the spices retain their pungency.

Serve with a plate of fresh herbs: sprigs of coriander, opal basil, tarragon, and mint; bunches of thin scallions; small sweet cucumbers peeled back to resemble an iris. Put warmed-up bread and some brined cheese on another plate.

Serves 6 to 8

3½ pounds beef chuck short ribs, trimmed

2½ tablespoons Spices and Aromatics for *Kharcho* (recipe follows)

2 tablespoons vegetable or olive oil

I large onion, chopped (1½ cups)

2 bay leaves

½ pound plum tomatoes—peeled, seeded, and chopped (I cup)

I cup (4 ounces) crumbled walnuts

3 tablespoons fresh lemon juice or more to taste

Sea salt and freshly ground black pepper to taste

Fresh herbs for garnish: ¼ cup mixed chopped coriander, celery leaves, and parsley

I. In a heavy saucepan, cover the beef with 2 quarts water. Bring to a boil over high heat and skim carefully. Reduce heat, cover, and simmer until the meat is tender, 2 hours. Meanwhile, prepare the *kharcho* spice mixture.

2. In a medium skillet, heat the oil over low heat. Add the onion and bay leaves; cover and cook, stirring frequently, until the onion is very soft, about 10 minutes. Stir in the tomatoes and *kharcho* spice mixture and cook, stirring, 10 minutes. Remove from the heat.

3. Remove the meat from the saucepan and strain the soup through a colander into a deep bowl. Skim the fat from the liquid. Remove and discard bones, gristle, and hard pieces of meat. Cut the meat into I-inch pieces. Return the meat and strained liquid to the saucepan.

4. In a food processor, puree the walnuts to a smooth paste. Add ½ cup of the beef cooking liquid and process until creamy and smooth. Add to the saucepan, along with the onion-tomato mixture, and bring to a boil over moderately high heat. Cook until thick, about 5 minutes. Add the lemon juice and season with the salt and pepper. Bring the soup to a rolling boil, and add a pinch more of the spice mixture and the herbs. Remove from the heat, cover, and let stand 5 minutes before serving. (This heightens the bouquet of the finished dish.)

SPICES AND AROMATICS FOR *KHARCHO*

Makes 2¹/₂ tablespoons

Place the garlic and red pepper in a mortar with some salt; pound to a paste. Stir in the ground fenugreek, fenugreek leaves, paprika, coriander, black pepper, savory, *shaffron*, and sugar; press through a sieve and set aside.

NOTES TO THE COOK: Shaffron is the Georgian word for the dried petals of marigold flowers. The petals impart an earthy tone to many Georgian dishes. But not all marigold petals are the same, and some can be excessively bitter. A few years ago, when researching Georgian food, I grew different marigold strains. I found that Lemon Drops produced the nearest approximation to the earthy but not acrid dried flowers I had brought home from Georgia. If you do not want to harvest and dry your own marigold petals, you can purchase dried marigold petals by mail order (see Appendix C).

With thanks to Tamara Kurdashivili for sharing this recipe for kharcho

2 teaspoons peeled and finely minced garlic

¾ teaspoon red pepper flakes or more to taste

½ teaspoon ground fenugreek seeds and husks

½ teaspoon dried fenugreek leaves, crumbled

½ teaspoon sweet paprika

2 teaspoons ground coriander seeds

¼ teaspoon freshly ground black pepper

½ teaspoon dried savory

½ teaspoon *shaffron* (see Notes to the Cook)

⅛ teaspoon sugar

RED BEAN AND HOT PEPPER SOUP
FROM DAGESTAN

I had never heard of Dagestan, an autonomous republic in the Caucasus on the Caspian Sea, until I found myself invited—along with the Peace Table activist Jerrilyn Brusseau—to visit some villages there and taste the food. For me it was an important trip. I discovered there were more than twenty native nationalities, each with its own traditions and cuisines.

I found the countryside beautiful, but the concrete block towns depressing. Also, I found some excellent recipes. One that particularly stood out was for this hot, rustic bean soup. Served with a sprinkling of fresh herbs and a dollop of yogurt stirred into each serving, it was a recipe worth traveling 5,000 miles to obtain.

Makes 3 quarts, serving 8 to 10

1 pound small red beans
1 small onion, quartered
1 teaspoon olive oil
2 pounds lean lamb breast, trimmed and cut into 8 pieces
2 cups roughly chopped onions
6 cloves garlic
2 bay leaves
2 dried chilis, or 1 teaspoon crushed red pepper flakes or more to taste
2 teaspoons coarse sea salt
4 potatoes, peeled and cut into cubes
1 tablespoon Dagestani Spice Mixture (recipe follows)
6 thin carrots, pared and cut into 1-inch lengths
½ cup chopped celery
3 Italian green frying peppers, cored, seeded, and cut into small pieces

1. Wash the beans under cold running water until the water runs clear. Place in a bowl, add plenty of water to cover, and let stand overnight.

2. Drain the beans. Place the beans and quartered onion in a 5-quart pan and cover with 2 quarts water; slowly bring to a boil. Cook over medium heat until tender. Discard the onion; set aside beans and cooking liquid.

3. Meanwhile, rub a 12-inch skillet with the olive oil. Cook the lamb in one layer in the skillet, covered, over medium-high heat, turning occasionally until well browned on all sides, about 10 minutes. Reduce the heat to medium. Add the chopped onions to the skillet, cover, and cook until well browned, stir-

ring occasionally, 20 minutes. Pour off all the fat in the skillet. Transfer the lamb and onions to a large saucepan. Add 6 cups water and bring to a boil. Reduce the heat and simmer, uncovered, 5 minutes, skimming the surface. Add the garlic, bay leaves, salt, and chilis. Simmer, covered, until the meat is tender, about 1¼ hours. Prepare the Dagestani Spice Mixture.

4. Cool the soup, skim off the fat, and remove the lamb with a slotted spoon to a work surface. Remove all the bones, hard fat, and gristle. Cut the lamb into bite-size pieces. Transfer the beans and 6 cups of the bean cooking liquid to the saucepan. Return the lamb to the saucepan; add the prepared spice mixture, potatoes, carrots, celery, and green frying peppers and cook 30 minutes longer.

5. Remove from the heat; let stand, covered, 10 minutes before serving. Stir in the vinegar and add salt to taste. Serve with a sprinkling of the fresh herbs and a bowl of the yogurt.

With thanks to Mr. Roman Saifullin of Makhachkala, Dagestan

2 tablespoons red wine vinegar

⅓ cup mixed snipped fresh herbs: dill, coriander, and parsley

4 cups of plain yogurt, drained to 3 cups (for directions on draining yogurt, see page 410)

DAGESTANI SPICE MIXTURE

Makes 1 tablespoon

½ teaspoon ground coriander seeds

½ teaspoon ground cumin

½ teaspoon freshly ground black pepper

¼ teaspoon ground caraway or *ajoiwan*

½ teaspoon crumbled dried oregano

Pinch of ground cloves

Pinch of ground cardamom

Pinch of ground cinnamon

Pinch of crumbled dried marigold petals, or small pinch of safflower threads or saffron

MACEDONIAN GREEN CREAM

Here is an easy-to-make, lovely soup made with wild or market greens—young watercress or nettles. Either green makes a wonderful base; I make a point of blanching the leaves, when available, then storing them in the freezer for year-round use.

Nettles are one of the most delicious wild greens and, like purslane, very good for you, chock full of vitamins and minerals.

I first learned about the benefits of nettles in Morocco, where an old Spanish woman who sold wild mushrooms at the market taught me how to forage for wild greens. One day she showed me how to collect nettles. Without gloves, she'd reach into the centers of the young plants, then clip off the tender tops with a knife.

Although I would never dream of gathering fresh nettles without gloves, she contended that when the plants are young and hairless, they don't sting. Back in my kitchen, she worked a little salt into the leaves, rubbing them so that, in her words, "they lose their wildness and yet keep their forest green color when cooked."

Makes about I quart, serving 3

5 cups watercress or nettle tops, washed and stemmed, or
    I¼ cups blanched, squeezed dry, and chopped

I cup water

Coarse salt

2 cups chicken stock

I tablespoon oil

2 scallions with 4 inches of green tops, chopped

I large garlic clove, peeled and crushed with a pinch of salt

I½ cups plain, nonfat yogurt, drained to half the original
    amount (for directions on draining yogurt, see page 410)

I egg yolk

I. Place the greens, water, and salt in a saucepan, cover, and cook 10 minutes. Strain, reserving the liquid. Puree the greens in a food processor with I cup stock by processing 15 to 20 seconds.

2. In a 3-quart saucepan, heat the oil, add the scallions, and cook, covered, for 2 minutes. Add the garlic, remaining stock, and the reserved blanching liquid from step I. Simmer the soup base 5 minutes. (Up to this point, the soup can be prepared in advance.)

3. Return the soup base to medium heat. In a mixing bowl, beat the yogurt, egg yolk, milk, and flour together until smooth. Ladle a little of the simmering liquid into the yogurt mixture, stir back into the pan, then heat, stirring constantly, 10 minutes until slightly thickened and just beginning to boil. Remove from heat, correct seasoning with salt and black pepper, or fresh mint. Serve warm with croutons.

¼ cup milk

1 tablespoon all-purpose flour

Salt to taste

½ teaspoon freshly ground black pepper (optional if using watercress)

1½ tablespoons chopped peppermint (optional if using nettles)

Croutons for garnish

NOTES TO THE COOK: Three quarts of loose leaves yield, after blanching, approximately 1¼ cups (1 scant pound of collected nettles yields 1¼ packed cup of leaves, salted or blanched and squeezed dry).

If you have room in your garden, consider growing nettles in a moist area far from your cultivated garden. If you do grow nettles, remember that once they are established, it is not easy to get rid of them.

You may want to grow sorrel as well, since crushed fresh sorrel leaves are an antidote to the sting of the nettles. Only the tenderest leaves don't sting, so never forage without wearing protective clothing and rubber gloves. And don't eat nettles raw.

Live nettle plants may be ordered by mail from Well-Sweep Herb Farms; in the spring, fresh young leaves can be purchased by the pound from Fox Hill Farms (see Appendix C).

FOUR YOGURT
❧ SOUPS ❧

Yogurt-based soups, hot or cold, give comfort to the mind and body. They can be deliciously subtle. In many parts of the Eastern Mediterranean, they are the backbone of year-round home cooking.

On home tables in Istanbul you will often find a simple hot chicken soup enriched with eggs and yogurt, then garnished with fresh or dried mint and a pinch of cayenne. In the vineyards of Naoussa, in northern Greece, grape pickers eat a chilled, light, and invigorating walnut-mint-garlic-cucumber-olive oil-yogurt soup from large wooden bowls. For recipes for these two dishes, see my *Mediterranean Cooking*.

Yogurt is fragile and can break apart, so great care must be taken when cooking it. Low-fat yogurt is especially vulnerable to break-up if heated too quickly. When you cook yogurt, you must use a stabilizer (i.e., an egg) to protect it from curdling.

Gaziantep cooks are the masters of silky, creamy yogurt soups, which are usually constructed from a base of a poultry or meat broth, and a starch such as wheat berries, chickpeas, or rice. Most often a vegetable is added to the base, then the mixture is thickened with yogurt. Just before serving, a flourish is added in swirls (see page 110).

The themes of these soups are related to the seasons. In early spring, sprouting bulbs (*crocus cancellatus*, Herbert) are used and the soups' flourish is colored with powdered safflower; in mid-spring, a combination of green garlic-scented leaves from unformed garlic cloves and chopped green onions are made into a soup called *şiveydiz*, perfumed with dried mint leaves. Later, fresh peas and chopped scallions are used with mint as the final seasoning (page 127). In late spring, pole beans or whole green almonds (the tender kernels of young almonds) are finished with safflower threads. In summer, slivered fresh onions are used with a flourish of black pepper and dried mint. In winter, simple soups thickened with rice or *tarhana* (a mixture of lightly fermented, cooked wheat berries and yogurt) and enriched with *kibbeh*-type balls are finished with a flourish of mint and black pepper, and large portions of meat or cubes of potatoes are decorated with swirls of safflower (page 126). Other vegetable additions include local truffles, dried favas, and leeks.

To achieve an extraordinary creamy texture, use only all-natural yogurt that has been completely drained. Then add a whole egg and a spoonful of flour as stabilizers. Often a spoonful of olive oil or softened butter is also added to enrich the yogurt. (This works very well when you are using nonfat yogurt since it covers up the chalky taste that people often complain about.) If your yogurt is particularly tart, you can add a small amount of milk to sweeten it.

While the thick yogurt mixture is being gently heated, gradually add the soup base to raise its temperature. Then pour the yogurt back into the remaining base and cook, stirring, until the whole comes just to the boil. At this point, the soup should be removed from the heat and the final flourish added.

For added refinement, the oil or butter for the flourish must be just at the point of sizzling. If it is too hot, the color and taste of the herbs and spices will turn harsh. One way to protect against this is to keep a spoonful of broth nearby to add to the sizzling mixture if you see that the fat is overheating. Another way is to simply add the spice or the herb to the soup, pour the sizzling fat on top, then swirl it in.

The herbs and spices themselves must be specially prepared for this explosive event. Dried crumbled mint or tarragon, as well as safflower threads, ground red pepper, and freshly ground black pepper are pressed through a fine sieve just before using in order to break out their final aromas and ready them for impact with the heat. This sieving produces a powder that when combined with sizzling fat creates deep and beautiful colorings against the white creamy background of the yogurt.

POTATOES AND YOGURT SOUP WITH SAFFLOWER SWIRLS

"Poor man's saffron" is the name given to safflower threads, which give off barely a whiff of aroma and little taste, yet impart a sense of visual excitement to food.

Serves 6

5 ounces boneless shoulder of lamb, trimmed of all fat

⅔ cup dried chickpeas, soaked overnight and drained

4 large boiling potatoes (1½ pounds)

Sea salt to taste

6 cups plain low-fat yogurt, drained to make 3 cups (for directions on draining yogurt, see page 410)

1 whole egg

1 tablespoon all-purpose flour

2 tablespoons olive oil or unsalted butter at room temperature

1 teaspoon freshly ground black pepper

1 rounded tablespoon *haspir* or safflower threads (page 398)

1. Cut the meat into ½-inch cubes. In a 4-quart saucepan, combine the meat and 8 cups water. Bring to a boil and skim carefully. Add the drained chickpeas, reduce heat, cover, and simmer for 1 hour. Up to this point, the soup can be prepared one day in advance.

2. About 1 hour before serving, peel potatoes and cut into ½-inch cubes. Add potatoes and salt to the soup and cook until tender.

3. In a second saucepan, whisk the yogurt with the egg, flour, and 1 tablespoon of the oil or butter, until completely smooth. Set yogurt over low heat, and turn off heat under the soup. Gradually stir 2 cups of the hot soup base into the yogurt mixture in order to raise its temperature. When the temperature of the yogurt is hotter than the temperature of the soup, pour the yogurt back into the soup and set it on medium heat, stirring, until it just comes to a boil, about 15 minutes. Immediately remove soup from heat and transfer to a tureen. Correct the seasoning with salt. Press the black pepper and safflower threads through a fine sieve. Place the powdered spices in the center of the soup. Heat the remaining oil or butter in a small pan or skillet, bring to a sizzle, and pour over the spices, stirring gently to create swirls. Cover and wait 5 minutes before serving.

With thanks to Ayfer Ünsal for sharing this recipe called yoğurtlu patates

SPRING PEAS AND YOGURT SOUP

Serves 6

1. In a medium-sized saucepan, combine the meat and 8 cups water. Bring to a boil and skim carefully. Add the drained chickpeas, reduce heat, cover, and simmer for 1 hour. Up to this point, the recipe can be prepared one day in advance.

2. About 45 minutes before serving, peel the potatoes and cut into ½-inch cubes. Add potatoes and scallions to the soup base and cook until almost tender. Add the peas and salt and cook until almost tender.

3. In a second saucepan, whisk the yogurt with the egg, flour, and 1 tablespoon of the oil or butter, until completely smooth. Set yogurt over low heat, and turn off heat under the soup. Gradually stir 2 cups of the hot soup base into the yogurt mixture in order to raise its temperature.

8 ounces boneless lamb shoulder, cut into small cubes
½ cup dried chickpeas, soaked overnight and drained
2 boiling potatoes
8 chopped scallions (including 4 to 5 inches tops)
1½ cups shelled green peas (about 1½ pounds unshelled or 10 ounces frozen peas)
Salt to taste
6 cups plain low-fat yogurt, drained to make 3 cups (for directions on draining yogurt, see page 410)
1 egg
1 tablespoon flour
2 tablespoons olive oil or unsalted butter at room temperature
Salt
Pinch of Near East or Aleppo pepper (page 395)
¾ teaspoon freshly ground black pepper
1 rounded tablespoon dried mint

When the temperature of the yogurt is hotter than the temperature of the soup, pour the yogurt back into the soup and set it on medium heat, stirring, until it just comes to a boil, about 15 minutes. Immediately remove soup from the heat and correct the seasoning with salt and a pinch of Near East pepper. Transfer to a soup tureen. Press the black pepper and dried mint through a fine sieve and place directly in the center of the soup. Heat the remaining oil or butter in a small skillet, bring to a sizzle, and pour over the mint and pepper. Stir gently to create swirls. Cover the soup and wait 5 minutes before serving.

Yogurt and Wheat Berry Soup with Pistachios

In this yogurt soup, skinned or hulled wheat berries are used to contribute a nutty flavor and a gelatinous texture.

Serves 5 to 6

I cup (½ pound) skinned wheat berries (see Appendix C for mail-order source)

Salt

I onion, quartered

6 cups homemade poultry stock, preferably made from turkey wings

2 cups plain low-fat yogurt, drained to I cup (for directions on draining yogurt, see page 410)

I egg

I teaspoon flour

½ cup cold milk

2 teaspoons olive oil

Pinch of sugar

Salt

2½ tablespoons unsalted butter

2 tablespoons blanched, sliced almonds

2 tablespoons skinned pistachios

½ teaspoon tomato paste

Pinch of Near East or Aleppo pepper (page 395)

1½ teaspoons safflower threads, pressed through a fine sieve to make about I teaspoon powder (page 398)

I tablespoon poultry stock

1. Wash the wheat berries; cover with lightly salted water and leave to soak 4 hours.

2. Drain wheat berries; place in a deep saucepan, add the onion and plenty of water to cover, and cook, partially covered, until tender, about 2 hours. Remove from heat and allow to cool completely. Discard the onion quarters.

3. In a food processor, working in batches, combine the cooked wheat berries with 2 to 3 cups of the poultry stock and blend until smooth. Push the mixture through the fine blade of a food mill into a deep saucepan and add enough of the remaining stock to make a smooth, creamy soup. Up to this point, the soup can be prepared one day in advance.

4. About 30 minutes before serving, reheat the soup. Combine drained yogurt, egg, flour, milk, olive oil, and sugar in a second saucepan; whisk until smooth. Set the yogurt over low heat, and turn off heat under the soup. Gradually stir 2 cups of the hot soup base into the yogurt in order to raise its tem-

perature. When the temperature of the yogurt is hotter than the temperature of the soup, pour the yogurt back into the soup, stirring constantly, over low heat, until it just comes to a boil, about 15 minutes. Correct the seasoning with salt. Transfer to a covered soup tureen.

4. In a small skillet, sauté the nuts in the butter until golden. Drain the nuts and sprinkle over the soup. Stir the tomato paste into the remaining butter and bring to a sizzle, continuing to stir. Add the Near East pepper and sieved safflower threads and swirl once. Then add 1 tablespoon of stock to keep the butter from overheating. Swirl the mixture over the soup, stir once, and serve.

YOGURT AND LEEK SOUP WITH MINT

Serves 6

1. Put the rice and stock in a deep saucepan. Bring to a boil and cook, covered, at the simmer for 30 minutes.

2. Meanwhile, trim the leek root ends, then remove all but 1 inch of the green leaves. Slice each leek thinly crosswise to make 1 quart. Wash and drain. When the soup has cooked 30 minutes, add the leeks and salt; cook 30 minutes longer, or until the rice grains are on the verge of dissolving and the leeks are meltingly tender. Up to this point the soup can be made early in the day.

3. In a second saucepan, whisk the yogurt with the milk, egg, flour, and 1 tablespoon of the butter, until completely smooth.

¼ cup raw short-grain rice, rinsed

2 quarts full-flavored chicken stock, degreased

6 medium leeks

Salt

6 cups plain low-fat yogurt, drained to 3 cups (for directions on draining yogurt, see page 410)

½ cup milk

1 egg

1 teaspoon flour

3 tablespoons unsalted butter, softened to room temperature

Pinch of Near East or Aleppo pepper (page 395)

¾ teaspoon freshly ground black pepper

2 scant tablespoons dried mint

Set the yogurt over low heat and turn off the heat under the soup. Gradually stir 2 cups of the hot soup base into the yogurt in order to raise its temperature. When the temperature of

continued

the yogurt is hotter than the temperature of the soup, pour the yogurt back into the soup, and set it on medium heat, stirring, until it just comes to a boil, about 15 minutes. Immediately remove from the heat. Correct the seasoning with salt and a pinch of Near East pepper. Transfer to a soup tureen. Press the black pepper and dried mint through a fine sieve and place directly on the soup. Heat the remaining butter in a small skillet, bring to a sizzle, and pour over the pepper and mint. Stir gently to create swirls. Cover the soup and wait 5 minutes before serving.

TRAHANA, TARHANA, AND KISHK

In late summer, all through the Balkans, Anatolia, and the Middle East, the village women still make a granular substance called *trahana* (in the Balkans), *tarhana* (in Turkey), or *kishk* (in the Middle East). The taste varies from sweet to tart to extremely pungent; all make a really superb winter staple that can be substituted for rice in soups.

Balkan "sweet" *trahana* is made with fresh milk, preferably ewes' milk, and fine semolina flour. "Sour" *trahana* is made with buttermilk or yogurt.

Here's how Balkan women make sour *trahana:* Semolina flour, salt, and yogurt are kneaded into a stiff dough. Often a little yeast is added, then the dough is left to rise. A special metal sieve is used to form the dough into small pellets. These pellets are left to dry in the sun over a period of days. (Some cooks dry them in a slow oven.) The dried pellets, stored in jars, will keep through two seasons.

Sweet or sour *trahana* can be eaten plain, almost like a kind of porridge. When I visited the Macedonian town of Katerini, a family prepared plain *trahana* for me for lunch. It was so thick it could be eaten with a fork, but the taste, tart with a hint of fermentation, was primitive and wonderful.

You can purchase *trahana* at Greek groceries under the Vlaha or Sico labels. To prepare: For each person, use ¼ cup for each cup of boiling water or stock, adding the *trahana* gradually along with a little butter. Stir constantly until creamy and cooked, about 20 minutes. Add grated or crumbled feta cheese if desired and cook another 5 minutes, stirring. You may find it similar to a cooked breakfast cereal. In fact, in some parts of western Turkey, it *is* eaten for breakfast, accompanied by hot pickled peppers and followed by a sweet dessert.

The most delicious *trahana* I ate was in the town of Kahramanmaraş in southeastern Turkey. Here in the home of a local grower of the renowned Maraş red pepper, I tasted a version like no other. The satin-creamy soup contained little balls made of fine-grain bulgur, chunks of boiled lamb, and lightly bruised garlic cloves, with a final flourish of mint and black pepper.

Meziyet Telbisoğlu, the woman who cooked the soup, sat with hands clasped in her lap, watching me eat. Then with as kind an expression as I have ever seen, she told me how she made it. Hulled wheat berries were cooked, cooled, then blended with completely drained yogurt and spread out in thin layers on cloths to dry. Later lifted off in wafers, they were set in suspended nets on the roof of the house to dry further under the hot sun. These wafer-thin sheets were simply boiled in meat broth, then sieved to make her wonderful soup.

Meziyet also gave me a children's autumn snack: She brought out some of the wafers for me to taste uncooked, then had me dip one in hot water to "heighten its taste" and told me to nibble it along with some fresh walnuts and pistachios. It was superb.

The Middle Eastern variation of *trahana/tarhana* is a cereal/soup base called *kishk*, more finely ground and therefore more quickly cooked. In the rural communities of Syria, Lebanon, and Jordan, it too is eaten for breakfast. And it goes well with sautéed cabbage, kibbeh, and plenty of garlic. It is made by soaking coarse bulgur in yogurt and milk, leaving it to ferment for a fortnight, then salting and drying it in the sun until firm enough to be crumbled into fine powder. *Kishk* is strong stuff, definitely an acquired taste!

V

Small Uncooked Salads

Fresh Summer Salads

*Thracian Summer Salad with Purslane, Tomatoes, and Cucumbers

In late summer, when all the wild mustards, nasturtiums, sorrels, amaranths, dandelions, and lamb's quarters have withered, turned tough and bitter, and gone to seed, there is still one wild green left to enjoy—purslane. Its soft, thick leaves stay fresh even under the hottest sun.

If you don't have a garden or can't find purslane at your local greengrocer's, you can order it fresh or grow it from seeds (page 405). (In Mexican markets, ask for *verdolaga*.)

A healthy, delicious, succulent purslane will stay firm even when dressed with oil and vinegar hours in advance. The whole herb—tender stems, unopened buds, and plump leaves—is good raw, cooked, or pickled.

When Thracians make this salad, they pickle the purslane, but I prefer it raw. Most mixed salads in northern Greece include some form of pickled vegetables: slices of baby eggplant, rippled carrots, purslane sprigs, or pickled hot pepper.

continued

Serves 4 to 6

3 packed cups purslane sprigs

½ packed cup stemmed spearmint leaves

I packed cup arugula leaves

2 red radishes

I small cucumber, peeled, seeded, and diced

I small mild onion, thinly sliced

Fine sea salt

I small clove garlic, peeled

2 tablespoons fresh lemon juice

3 tablespoons extra-virgin olive oil

¼ teaspoon freshly ground black pepper

2 ripe tomatoes, peeled, seeded, and cubed

12 Kalamata olives, pitted

2 or 3 pickled hot peppers or pickled eggplants, sliced

I. Wash the purslane, spearmint, and arugula; discard the stems and any yellow or damaged leaves. Coarsely chop the greens.

2. Sprinkle the radishes, cucumber, and onion with salt and let stand 5 minutes, then rinse and drain.

3. Place the greens, radishes, cucumber, and onion in a salad bowl.

4. In a mortar, crush the garlic with ¼ teaspoon salt. Stir in the lemon juice, olive oil, and pepper, and pour over the greens, radishes, cucumber, and onion. Toss the ingredients in the salad bowl, cover with plastic wrap, and refrigerate up to 2 hours. Just before serving, stir in the tomatoes and correct the seasoning. Garnish with the olives and pickled vegetables.

VARIATIONS:

*DAMASCUS SUMMER SALAD WITH PURSLANE AND SUMMER SAVORY

For a simpler version of the preceding salad, omit the arugula, radishes, pickled peppers, and olives. A few sprigs of fresh summer savory will add the appropriate pungency.

*GAZIANTEP SUMMER SALAD WITH PURSLANE

This tangy salad, called *pirpirim piyazi* is rich and dense, almost like a relish. Serve well chilled with meat kabobs or hot flat bread.

Makes 3 cups

Peel and thinly sliver the onion; sprinkle with salt and leave for 10 minutes. Meanwhile, wash, stem, and chop the purslane to make about 1½ packed cups. Rinse the onion; drain well. Mix onion with the purslane, parsley, tomatoes, pepper, sumac, pepper flakes, lemon juice, and olive oil; blend well. Adjust the seasoning. Serve cold.

1 medium (6 ounces) fresh onion

Coarse sea salt to taste

½ pound purslane

¼ cup chopped parsley

1 cup peeled, seeded, and cubed ripe tomatoes

1 small green bell pepper, stemmed, seeded, and fine-diced to make ½ cup

2 teaspoons sumac

¼ teaspoon Near East pepper or more to taste (page 395)

¼ cup fresh lemon juice or more to taste

2 tablespoons olive oil

*BALKAN FRESH TOMATO SALAD

Here is a simple tomato salad that works well with cherry tomatoes when other ripe tomatoes are out of season.

Serves 4

Arrange the tomatoes, overlapping, on a serving dish. In a bowl, mix the remaining ingredients and spoon over the tomatoes.

3 thinly sliced ripe tomatoes or 16 cherry tomatoes

1 small finely minced long green chili, about 1 tablespoon

2 tablespoons finely minced scallions

1 green bell pepper, roasted until barely soft, stemmed, seeded, deribbed, and julienned

2 tablespoons extra-virgin olive oil

1 tablespoon red wine vinegar

Salt and freshly ground black pepper to taste

*MIDDLE EASTERN CHOPPED SALAD

Whether you call it *salata khodra* in Arabic, *çorban salatasi* in Turkish, or *salata* in Macedonia, this basic, homey chopped salad is served almost everywhere, every day in the summer. It is healthy and straightforward, and can be enhanced as desired with scallions, radishes, crumbled cheese, and shredded Romaine lettuce.

Serves 4

I small cucumber, peeled, seeded, and diced

12 cherry tomatoes, stemmed, roughly chopped, and seeded, or 2 ripe tomatoes, peeled, seeded, and roughly chopped

⅓ cup chopped parsley

⅓ cup shredded spearmint

I clove garlic, peeled

Salt to taste

I teaspoon or more finely chopped fresh green chili

I to 2 tablespoons fresh lemon juice

2 tablespoons extra-virgin olive oil

1. In a salad bowl, combine the cucumber, tomatoes, and herbs.

2. In a mortar, crush the garlic with ¼ teaspoon salt, add the chili, and pound to a smooth paste. Stir in the lemon juice (if the tomatoes are very acidic, use less). Then add the olive oil as if making a mayonnaise. Taste for salt. Pour over the vegetables and mix thoroughly. Chill 1 to 2 hours before serving.

*LEBANESE TOMATO, ONION, AND SPICED CHEESE SALAD

In Lebanon this salad is made with a homemade, fermented sheep's-milk cheese called *shankleesh*, coated with dried thyme and sometimes an assortment of spices. In the United States, I use good-quality ricotta *salata* or a creamy Bulgarian feta, firm enough to cube, which I then coat with a mixture of dried Mediterranean herbs, pepper, and sumac. My rendition of this local cheese is not authentic, but, piled high on a bed of ripe tomatoes, and sprinkled with fresh parsley and olive oil, it makes an utterly delicious summer dish.

Serves 6

1. If the cheese is very salty, soak it in cold water 30 minutes; drain well. Cut the cheese into ½-inch cubes.

2. In a medium bowl, combine the cheese with the oregano, thyme, sumac, and pepper. Let stand 2 to 3 hours, so that it will be imbued with herbal and peppery flavors. Just before serving, add the onion. Spoon the tomatoes onto a serving plate, and top with the cheese and onion. Sprinkle with the parsley and drizzle the oil over the top. Serve at room temperature.

½ pound firm imported feta or ricotta *salata*

½ teaspoon crumbled dried Mediterranean oregano

½ teaspoon dried Mediterranean thyme

½ teaspoon sumac

¼ teaspoon freshly ground black pepper

½ cup finely diced red onion

3 ripe medium tomatoes, peeled, seeded, and cut into ½-inch dice

⅓ cup chopped flat-leaf parsley

3 tablespoons fruity extra-virgin olive oil

*Gaziantep-Style Chopped Salad

This clean, tart variation is a perfect example of how a number of different ingredients, all cut to a small size, can blend harmoniously. The mixture is ideal for dunking a densely textured, lightly toasted piece of bread. Note that the salad doesn't contain any oil.

Makes 4 cups

2 cups fine-diced tomatoes

1 cup fine-diced green bell pepper

1 cup fine-diced red bell pepper

1 teaspoon dried mint, crumbled and sieved

¼ teaspoon Near East pepper or more to taste (page 395)

1 tablespoon ground sumac

2 tablespoons fresh lemon juice or more to taste

Salt to taste

Place all the ingredients in a mixing bowl and toss thoroughly. Chill 30 minutes and serve. If the tomatoes do not express enough liquid, add about 2 tablespoons cold water.

TWO BREAD SALADS

*BREAD SALAD SNACK: THE CAT'S PAWS

Here is the rule: Bread salads will be only as good as the bread that's put into them.

Most readers will know the Italian coarse country bread salad *panzanella*, a standard by which other bread salads can be judged. But I have tasted bread salads just as delicious around the Mediterranean where other breads were used: cubes of toasted semolina bread in Sicily*; crackling pieces of grilled pita bread in Syria (see the next recipe); stale chunks of barley bread tossed with green chilis, onion, and tomatoes in southern Tunisia; and this simple bread salad from southeastern Turkey, in which stale slices of wafer-thin Middle Eastern *lavash, tannour,* or Mükerrem's Unleavened Flat Griddle Bread (page 39) are moistened with grated ripe tomatoes, blended with a creamy fresh mozzarella cheese and two kinds of hot peppers (red and green), then molded into sausage-shaped snack-size ovals. Children have affectionally nicknamed this dish "the cat's paws" because the ovals do slightly resemble them when they are decorated with the onion slivers, representing the fur.

White or whole wheat tandoori bread from Middle Eastern stores is best; stale pita won't do, nor will bread made with eggs or milk.

This salad takes only minutes to prepare, but then must be consumed immediately.

continued

*See "Island of Lipari Spicy Bread Salad," in my *World of Food*.

I small white onion, peeled and slivered

Coarse salt

2 sheets stale *tannour* or *lavash*, crumbled to make 2 cups (3½ ounces), or Mükerrem's Unleavened Flat Griddle Bread (page 39)

I large ripe tomato, halved, seeded, and grated on a coarse grater, then drained in a sieve to make ½ cup pulp

⅓ cup unsalted fresh mozzarella, chilled and grated

Pinch of dried hot red pepper flakes without seeds

I teaspoon extra-virgin olive oil

I teaspoon minced fresh long green chili without seeds

With thanks to Ayfer Ünsal for sharing her charming recipe

I. Sliver the onion, sprinkle with ¼ teaspoon salt, and let stand a few minutes. Rub well, using fingertips to soften and express some of the moisture. Rinse and squeeze out moisture. Let stand while preparing the "paws."

2. Moisten the bread with the tomato pulp, gently kneading it until blended. Add the mozzarella, pepper flakes, oil, and chili, mixing well. Taste for salt. Divide the mixture into 8 equal parts. Use a moistened palm to gently press each portion into a 2-inch sausage or cat's-paw shape. Roll with the onion and serve at once.

*MIDDLE EASTERN BREAD SALAD (*FATTOUSH*)

Here is a wonderful-tasting salad, based on a selection of glossy monochromatic green herbs, chopped and seasoned, then blended with crumbled toasted pita and fresh tomatoes. The addition of two special ingredients makes this salad a *fattoush* rather than merely a Middle Eastern version of Italian *panzanella:* fleshy, textured purslane and lemony sumac.

Purslane grows in almost every cultivated garden in the United States, and shows up in farmers' markets during the summer. Rich in Omega-3 fatty acids, it is incredibly nutritious. In fact, I know a scientist who would like to see it grown in vacant lots all over the country to feed the poor!

Red ground sumac, available at Middle Eastern groceries or by mail order (see Appendix C), infuses the salad with a delightful, slightly sour pungency and aroma.

Make the salad base in advance so that the tastes will have time to mingle; add the crumbled pita and tomatoes just before serving so they will remain partially intact.

Serves 6 to 8

1. In a large salad bowl, combine the pepper, cucumber, scallions, parsley, mint, arugula, and purslane. In a small bowl, combine the garlic, lemon juice, oil, sumac, salt, and pepper. Toss with the ingredients in the salad bowl, cover with plastic wrap, and refrigerate for up to 3 hours.

2. Ten minutes before serving, add the tomatoes and pitas; toss well. Season with additional salt and pepper.

I small green bell pepper, cut into 1/4-inch dice

1/2 cucumber, peeled, halved, seeded, and cut into 1/4-inch dice

I cup chopped scallions

3/4 cup chopped flat-leaf parsley

1/4 cup coarsely chopped mint leaves, preferably spearmint

I cup torn arugula leaves

I cup coarsely chopped purslane

2 cloves garlic, peeled, crushed in a mortar with 1/2 teaspoon salt

1/4 cup fresh lemon juice

1/3 cup extra-virgin olive oil

1 1/2 teaspoons ground sumac

Fine sea salt and freshly ground black pepper to taste

2 to 3 medium ripe tomatoes, peeled, seeded, and cut into 1/2-inch dice

2 large, brick-oven baked pitas, split, toasted, and broken into 1/2-inch pieces

Two
Middle Eastern
Grain Salads

*Bulgur Salad with Red Pepper and Walnuts

Arto der Haroutunian, in his *Middle Eastern Cookery,* describes this unusual dish, known as *bazerghen,* as being Assyrian in origin, and quotes an Assyrian friend, who was angry that the author had earlier described it as Syrian: " 'It's ours,' he protested, indignantly. 'It's been enough to lose one's lands, but it is the ultimate in "massacres" to steal and monopolize even our food. *Bazerghen* is ours!' "

In fact, when an eastern Mediterranean dish is really good, it will spread to other communities in the region. Sephardic Jewish families from Aleppo, including members who have emigrated to the United States, make this dish, which they store in tightly closed jars in the refrigerator for up to a week, where, they say, "it just gets better and better."

In the original Assyrian version, sautéed onions, spices, and dried herbs flavor the bulgur. In the Sephardic version, onions are not usually included, and the dish is flavored with *temerhendy,* a sourish thick syrup made from tamarind.

Grace Sasson, the author of *Kosher Syrian Cooking,* upon whose recipe the following adaptation is based, substitutes a concentrated paste made from cooking down prunes, apples, apricots, barbecue sauce, grape jam, and lemon juice. I've slightly altered Mrs. Sasson's recipe, substituting pomegranate molasses for the syrup and adding fried onions for richness.

Allow the salad to mellow overnight. Serve garnished with a few sprigs of parsley, chopped walnuts, and sautéed pine nuts. It is excellent with grilled meat or just warm pita bread.

Makes about 4 cups, serving 6 to 8

1. Place bulgur in a fine sieve and shake to remove dust. Dampen with cold water and let stand 15 to 30 minutes. Squeeze out excess moisture.

2. In a skillet, sauté the onions in the oil until they become translucent. Remove from the heat to cool. In a mixing bowl, combine the bulgur, onions, and all the remaining ingredients; blend well. Cover and refrigerate overnight before serving at room temperature or chilled. Correct the seasoning with salt and pepper, and garnish with parsley sprigs, walnuts, and sautéed pine nuts.

1½ cups fine-grain bulgur
1 cup finely chopped onions
⅓ cup olive oil
4 tablespoons ketchup
½ cup finely chopped parsley
⅓ cup finely chopped walnuts
1 tablespoon pomegranate molasses or more to taste (page 404)
2 tablespoons fresh lemon juice
1½ teaspoons ground cumin
1½ teaspoons ground coriander
1 teaspoon Near East, Aleppo, or hot Hungarian pepper (page 395)
½ teaspoon ground allspice
1 teaspoon salt
½ teaspoon freshly ground black pepper

GARNISH
6 or 7 short sprigs flat-leaf parsley
2 tablespoons coarsely chopped walnuts
2 tablespoons pine nuts, browned in oil

*Turkish Kisir with Red Peppers and Tomatoes

Here is a red-hued, peppery version of the famous Middle Eastern tabbouleh salad, as it is prepared in Gaziantep, Turkey. The rich red-pepper-paste base provides it with its magnificent color, while pomegranate molasses and lemon juice contribute a fruity tartness. This *kisir* needs less oil than most versions for bulgur salads and is thus less caloric.

Makes about 6 cups

RED PEPPER PASTE
2 fleshy red bell peppers, stemmed, cored, and cut up
  (1¼ pounds)
I red or green chili, cored, stemmed, and seeded

1½ cups fine-grain bulgur
2 vine-ripened medium tomatoes
8 scallions, trimmed and thinly sliced
½ cucumber, peeled, seeded, and chopped
¾ cup chopped parsley
6 tablespoons fresh lemon juice
I tablespoon pomegranate molasses (page 404)
⅓ cup olive oil
I teaspoon salt or to taste
Near East, Aleppo, or hot Hungarian pepper to taste
  (page 395)
Tender Romaine lettuce leaves or boiled vine leaves
Pitas

1. Make the red pepper paste. Grind the peppers and chili with 2 tablespoons water in the workbowl of a food processor until pureed. Transfer to a saucepan and cook over medium heat, stirring often, until reduced to a jamlike consistency yielding ⅔ cup. (Can be reduced, uncovered, in a 2-quart Pyrex bowl in the microwave.)

2. Place the bulgur in a fine sieve and shake to remove dust. Dampen with cold water and let stand 30 minutes. Squeeze out excess moisture. Cut the tomatoes in half, gently squeeze to remove the seeds, and grate the halves with the cut side facing the coarsest side of a four-sided grater or flat shredder. (You should be left with just the tomato skin in your hand; discard it.)

In a mixing bowl, combine the bulgur, red pepper paste, tomato pulp, and remaining ingredients, blending the mixture with your hands or with two forks. Cover tightly with plastic film and chill a few hours before serving. Correct the seasoning and serve surrounded by lettuce or vine leaves and pitas.

Two Pungent
Herb Salads

*Fresh Summer Savory Salad
with Pomegranate

This salad from the Mediterranean coast of Turkey includes the spicy leaves of summer savory as a substitute for the Turkish herb called *kara kekik (Thymbra spicata)*.

When savory is tossed with a handful of tender bitter greens, then dressed with sweet and sour pomegranate molasses, it makes a lively, astringent accompaniment to any rich meat or oily dish. The Turks who eat the herb straight, without the addition of other greens, claim it helps digestion.

Serves 2 to 4

Use your fingertips to rub the savory leaves with a good pinch of sea salt; rinse and drain. (This removes the bitterness and releases the fragrance.) In a small salad bowl, combine the leaves with the shredded greens and the scallions. Separately, combine the pomegranate molasses, garlic, salt to taste, oil, and lemon juice. Drizzle over the greens, scatter with cubes of tomato (if desired), and serve at once.

NOTES TO THE COOK: Fresh sprigs of summer savory can be purchased by the quarter pound from Fox Hill Farm (see Appendix C).

continued

24 10-inch sprigs of summer savory, washed, drained, and stemmed

Coarse sea salt

1 packed cup mildly bitter greens, washed, stemmed, and shredded, or coarsely chopped parsley for a milder salad

¼ cup chopped scallions

½ teaspoon pomegranate molasses (page 404)

¼ teaspoon peeled and crushed garlic

Salt to taste

1 tablespoon extra-virgin olive oil

1 teaspoon fresh lemon juice or more to taste

2 tablespoons cubed tomato (optional)

Seeds for summer savory are available from many nurseries and seed specialists.

Young and tender wild salad greens are no longer an oddity in the United States. Fine groceries, specialty produce markets, and farmers' markets often carry a selection. You can easily grow greens yourself, even in a window box. The Italian *misticanza* mix (see Appendix C) includes an even more tantalizing assortment than the ubiquitous *mesclun*, including wild mustard, Catalonian dandelions, and *puntarella.* The latter two have become personal favorites.

In Turkey in the spring, the fresh leaves are gathered and dried in the sun, then stored upside down from rafters to use throughout the year. To rehydrate, Turkish cooks drop the dried leaves into boiling water, then immediately remove the pot from the flame. The leaves are left for an hour in the covered pot, then drained and chilled. Rehydrated, they are soft as silk.

With thanks to Leman Sezer for sharing her recipe for kekik piyazi

*Oregano Pickle with Fresh Tomatoes and Onion

Many Middle Eastern stores sell oregano pickle in jars, imported from Lebanon, under the Beirut label. In fact, oregano pickle is not oregano at all, according to Mr. Baroodi, the importer, but rather Persian *za'atar* or *za'atar Parsi* (*Thymbra spicata*), the pungent, assertive, flavorful herb that is often confused with the savory substituted in the preceding recipe, and with numerous other herbs in the thyme-oregano-marjoram-savory family. (It should also not be confused with the spice blend called *za'atar*, a mixture of sumac and any one of numerous herbs also called *za'atar*.)

You can obtain plantings of Turkish *kara kekik*/Persian *za'atar* from Well-Sweep Herb Farm (page 407) to grow in a sunny window box. In the meantime, here is how to make the salad using the packaged import.

Serves 2

Drain enough oregano pickle to make 1 cup; rinse, soak in fresh water to remove the brine, and drain again. Mix with the onion, tomato, parsley, oil, and lemon juice, tossing well. Season with salt and pepper to taste.

NOTES TO THE COOK: To preserve the remaining pickle: Store in the refrigerator with a thin layer of olive oil. Always remove the greens with a spoon or a pair of wooden tongs; never use your fingers, lest you introduce bacteria into the brine.

1 cup oregano pickle
1 small onion, minced
1 small ripe tomato, peeled, seeded, and cubed
½ cup chopped parsley
1 tablespoon olive oil
Juice of ½ lemon
Salt and freshly ground black pepper to taste

THREE
OLIVE SALADS

Olives, of course, are delicious with a simple sprinkling of herbs, lemon, and oil, but it is only when one uses them in combination with other foods that one comes to appreciate their incredible versatility and flavor-enhancing quality.

All olives benefit from seasoning: fennel seeds, bay leaves, oregano, chili peppers, cumin, orange, lemon, garlic, or sprigs of thyme or rosemary make fine natural accompaniments, especially with a light sprinkle of olive oil.

*CRACKED GREEN OLIVE AND WALNUT SALAD

This is an exceptionally delicious specialty of Gaziantep, in southeastern Turkey, which includes cracked green olives, walnuts, parsley, and scallions, all chopped by hand and blended with pomegranate seeds into a rich and dense relish—a perfect accompaniment to a simple brochette of grilled meat or a slice of melon.

The combination of pomegranate molasses and lemon juice gives this salad a sweet and sour flavor that balances the richness of the olives and the walnuts.

Makes about 1¾ cups, serving 5 to 6

1. Prepare the salad one or two days in advance for the best flavor. To pit the olives: Place them in a single layer on a double thickness of kitchen toweling. Hit each olive with a mallet or heavy pestle and remove the pit. (The toweling absorbs any expressed oil.) Roughly chop the olives, to make about I cup.

2. Combine the olives with all the other ingredients in a mixing bowl; blend well. Cover with plastic wrap, refrigerate overnight, and return to room temperature before serving.

NOTES TO THE COOK· Choose firm green olives that have not been previously prepared with other seasonings. (The best choices are the French *Picholine* or the Greek *Nafplion*.) Rinse the olives and taste for saltiness and bitterness. If salty, soak them for an hour in water to cover, drain, and rinse well. If bitter, place in a saucepan, cover with water, bring to a boil, and drain. Cover with fresh water and repeat until the olives are no longer bitter.

With thanks to Ayfer Ünsal for sharing this recipe for zetyin piyazi

7½ to 8 ounces cracked green olives, drained

2 tablespoons extra-virgin olive oil

¾ cup shelled walnuts, finely chopped by hand

2 scallions, minced

¼ cup chopped parsley

⅛ teaspoon Near East or Aleppo pepper (page 395) or more to taste

2 teaspoons pomegranate molasses (page 404)

I tablespoon fresh lemon juice

Salt to taste

Freshly and finely ground black pepper to taste

½ cup fresh or defrosted pomegranate seeds

*Black Olive, Orange, and Onion Salad

The salad that follows is a sparkling, fresh combination of orange slices topped with chopped onion, topped in turn by pitted black olives, and garnished with a sprinkling of hot red pepper and olive oil. Nothing could be more straightforward, delicious, and restorative.

Olives and oranges are one of those miracle combinations, like lamb and garlic, before which I sometimes feel I should bow in gratitude. I have known Spanish gourmets who sprinkle olive oil on sliced oranges to make a dessert, and the Moroccan salad of bitter oranges and olives is one of my all-time favorites. What makes this salad unique and places it in the eastern Mediterranean is the addition of onions, which create a textural contrast between the juicy oranges and the soft, chewy olives. The onion you use is important; you don't want a coarse, acrid flavor to destroy the harmony. To moderate the effect of onion in this dish, I always rub them with a little salt before using.

Serves 6 to 8

42 (3½ ounces) black oil-cured olives
I teaspoon grated orange zest
Pinches of crushed red pepper flakes or cayenne to taste
3 tablespoons extra-virgin olive oil
2 to 4 (depending on size) sweet oranges
I medium to large onion, peeled and thinly sliced
I teaspoon coarse sea salt

I. On a wooden work surface lined with a paper towel, tap each olive with a heavy pestle or mallet and slip out the pit, to make about ¾ cup. Toss the olives with the orange zest, a pinch or more of red pepper flakes and the olive oil, cover with plastic wrap, and let stand at room temperature for at least a few hours.

2. Peel the oranges and remove all the outside membranes, using a small knife. Thinly slice the oranges. Arrange the oranges, overlapping, on a flat serving dish.

3. Sprinkle the onion with the salt and leave for a few minutes. Rub the salt into the onion; rinse, drain, and press out all the water.

4. Spread the onion rings over the oranges, then the olives and the marinade; sprinkle with cayenne or crushed red pepper flakes to taste. Serve at once.

*MACEDONIAN BLACK OLIVE AND SCALLION SALAD

Here is a variation on the preceding recipe, without the oranges, adapted from a wonderful cookbook called *Traditional Macedonian Recipes,* one of only two "church" cookbooks that my Macedonian friends in North America consider authentic.

Serves 4 to 6

1. Rinse the olives and taste for saltiness and bitterness. If salty, soak them for an hour in water to cover, drain, and rinse well. Place the olives on kitchen toweling and tap each with a mallet to facilitate removing the pit.

2. Ten to twenty minutes before serving, mix the olives with the scallions, paprika, and oil, tossing well. Mound on a small plate and top with a sprinkling of the crushed red pepper flakes and parsley sprigs.

About 6 dozen (7 ounces) oil-cured black ripe olives, preferably Moroccan or from Thásos, Greece

8 scallions (white part and 2 inches of the green), finely sliced

1 teaspoon sweet paprika

2 teaspoons extra-virgin olive oil

Pinch of crushed red pepper flakes

2 sprigs flat-leaf parsley

VI

Small Cooked Vegetable Dishes

THREE
POMEGRANATE-
FLAVORED
VEGETABLES

*BROILED OKRA WITH POMEGRANATE

In this second Lebanese mountain recipe, okra is grilled over an open fire, then macerated in pomegranate juice. The texture remains quite firm, not slimy or stringy.

This is a good dish to make when you are barbecuing. The okra cooks in less than 10 minutes and is delicious with simply grilled fish, meat, or chicken.

Serves 4

1. A few hours before serving, wash the okra and thoroughly dry with terry toweling. Trim the tops and tips. Skewer the okra and place on a large dish.

2. Combine the oil, pomegranate molasses, water, lemon juice, and garlic; mix well. Brush the okra with the pomegranate mixture and let stand until ready to cook.

3. Grill far from the heat until glazed and browned on all sides, about 10 minutes. Sprinkle with the fresh coriander and serve as soon as possible.

1½ pounds bright green, firm, unblemished fresh okra

2 tablespoons olive oil

1 tablespoon pomegranate molasses (page 404)

1 tablespoon water

1 teaspoon fresh lemon juice

2 medium cloves garlic, peeled and crushed to a paste with ¼ teaspoon salt

5 tablespoons roughly chopped fresh coriander leaves

*GRILLED RED PEPPER STRIPS WITH POMEGRANATE AND CUMIN

At the superb Armenian restaurant Wanes, in the Azizie quarter of Aleppo, every meat dish seems to be glazed with red dye: delicious red-tinted kibbeh; red-tinted skewered meat; steak tinted red, then spread with a thin layer of tomato jam and garnished with a whole pickled red-tinted head of garlic that opens like a flower. The local red wine, Mimas, from Homs, is also very good. When I asked why everything was red, the manager explained that red brings good luck.

The dish that stood out from all this redness, because of its incredibly sparkling freshness, was this red pepper relish flavored with pomegranate molasses and ground cumin. At Wanes it was served with grilled meat, but it goes equally well with poultry or fish.

Makes 1½ cups, serving 6

4 red bell peppers, roasted, peeled, stemmed, seeded, and diced
1 teaspoon red pepper paste (page 389) or more to taste
½ teaspoon ground cumin
1 teaspoon pomegranate molasses (page 404)
1 tablespoon extra-virgin olive oil
½ teaspoon salt or more to taste
½ teaspoon freshly ground black pepper
2 tablespoons fresh lemon juice

1. Place the red peppers in a medium glass serving dish.

2. In a small bowl, combine the pepper paste, cumin, pomegranate molasses, oil, salt, pepper, and lemon juice; mix well. Pour over the diced peppers and mix again. Cover and refrigerate at least 1 hour.

3. Just before serving, taste and adjust the balance of flavors, adding more lemon juice or salt if necessary.

*EGGPLANT WITH POMEGRANATE SAUCE

In this Lebanese mountain recipe, slices of creamy eggplant are macerated with an intensely flavored combination of pomegranate, garlic, and herbs, the whole decorated with glistening crimson pomegranate seeds, which lend a sweet and sour note and a gentle crunch.

When buying eggplants for this dish, choose long narrow ones, taut and smooth, not more than ¾ pound each.

Serves 6

1. Start the preparation the day before serving. Preheat the oven to 425° F. Lightly coat a baking sheet with olive oil.

2. Remove the stem end from each eggplant. Slice the eggplants on the bias into ½-inch-thick ovals. Spread the slices on the baking sheet in a single layer and brush with olive oil. Bake the eggplants 12 minutes on each side, or until golden brown. Using a spatula, transfer the slices, overlapping slightly, to a shallow serving dish.

3. In a small bowl, combine the pomegranate molasses, lemon juice, garlic, sugar, olive oil, and salt; blend well. Drizzle the sauce over the eggplant. Top with the mint, parsley, and pomegranate seeds. Cover with plastic wrap and let stand until ready to serve. Can be refrigerated overnight, but is best served at room temperature.

2 (1½ pounds total weight) long, slender Japanese eggplants
Olive oil

POMEGRANATE SAUCE
2 tablespoons pomegranate molasses (page 404)
1 tablespoon fresh lemon juice
1 small clove garlic, peeled and crushed to a puree with
    ½ teaspoon salt
¼ teaspoon sugar
1¼ tablespoons olive oil
½ teaspoon sea salt
2 to 3 tablespoons shredded fresh mint, preferably spearmint
1 tablespoon chopped flat-leaf parsley
2 tablespoons fresh pomegranate seeds (optional)

NOTES TO THE COOK: To remove the seeds from a pomegranate: Place in a deep sink or basin of water; quarter the fruit; give the skin sides a gentle hit with a wooden mallet and flake the seeds apart with your fingers. Unused seeds will keep up to a year in a sealed plastic container in the freezer.

·❧· FOUR ·❧·
MACEDONIAN
EGGPLANT SALADS

Here are four light, fluffy eggplant salads from the Balkans. Use eggplants that weigh three quarters to one pound. Select for lightness and firmness. (Large eggplants that are heavy in the hand come from older plants; they are very often bitter and contain a plentitude of seeds.)

In the eastern Mediterranean, the color and texture of cooked eggplant flesh is as important as the smokiness of its flavor. The ideal is a shade of cream. To achieve this, cook as instructed over a grill or gas burner; peel while still very hot; immediately soak in a water bath with lemon juice; squeeze well to remove all moisture and bitter juices; then pound with a flat-ended wooden pestle until the flesh is almost translucent. The vegetable is then ready for conversion into a salad.

If you want to serve the first or second salad given here as an individual first course, use the salad to fill 6 roasted, peeled, and cooled red peppers. Serve one to a person, along with plenty of warm pita.

*EGGPLANT AND FRIED VEGETABLE SALAD

A salad for winter.

Makes about 3 cups, serving 6

1. Tightly wrap each eggplant in two layers of aluminum foil. Set over a high gas flame, turning frequently, until each eggplant completely collapses, about 20 minutes. Immediately drop the eggplants and foil covering into a basin of cold water. Remove the foil. Working over the basin, lift one of the eggplants by the stem and begin peeling it from the top down. Immediately place the peeled eggplants into a lemon-water bath (1 cup water, the juice of one lemon, and ½ teaspoon salt). Let stand 20 minutes. (This keeps the eggplant white and allows the bitter juices to seep out.)

2. Meanwhile, warm half the olive oil in a small skillet. Add the peppers, cover, and steam 2 to 3 minutes. Uncover and let sizzle for an instant; add the tomatoes and onion and cook 5 minutes longer, or until the vegetables are soft. Combine the contents of the skillet with the garlic and paprika in the work bowl of a food processor and grind to a smooth mass.

3. Remove each eggplant from the water and gently press out all the moisture (or let it drain in a plastic colander until ready to use). Add the eggplants to the contents in the work bowl and puree everything together until well combined. (You may have to do this in batches.) Add the remaining olive oil, vinegar, and salt and pepper to taste. Allow to mellow in the refrigerator for at least 3 hours before serving. Heap the eggplant mixture onto a flat serving dish, sprinkle with parsley, and surround with crackers.

2 (1¾ to 2 pounds total weight) eggplants
Juice of 1 lemon
Salt
3 tablespoons olive oil
3 Italian green frying peppers, stemmed, seeded, and roughly chopped
1 cup halved and seeded cherry tomatoes
1 cup minced red onion
2 cloves garlic, peeled and crushed with salt
Pinch of hot Hungarian paprika
2 tablespoons mild vinegar
Freshly ground black pepper
Chopped flat-leaf parsley
Crackers

*Eggplant and Raw Tomato Salad

Makes about 3 cups

2 eggplants, 1¾ to 2 pounds total weight

Salt

1 lemon, halved

3 tomatoes, peeled, seeded, and diced

1 medium red onion, minced, rubbed with salt, rinsed in a
   sieve, and drained dry

¼ teaspoon garlic, peeled and crushed with salt (optional)

1 teaspoon minced green chili

⅓ cup extra-virgin olive oil

2 tablespoons aged red wine vinegar

Salt and freshly ground black pepper

3 tablespoons chopped flat-leaf parsley

Grill the eggplants over charcoal or follow step 1 in the previous recipe. Crush the eggplant pulp with a wooden masher or spatula to avoid darkening the flesh. Add the tomatoes, onion, garlic if desired, chili, oil, and vinegar, and salt and pepper to taste. Blend well with a wooden fork or spoon and let stand a few hours before serving. Top with the parsley and serve with warm flat bread.

*MACEDONIAN RELISH WITH GREEN TOMATOES

This tangy relish from Slavic Macedonia includes green, unripe tomatoes—not the kind you find in the supermarket but the really hard, unripe variety sold in midsummer for pickling. When grilled to a state of utter creaminess, these green tomatoes will transform a conventional eggplant-pepper-tomato medley into an unexpectedly delicious relish. The combination of vinegar and hot pepper adds a tart, pungent edge. Serve with grilled meat or fish or with a bowl of lentils and rice (page 237).

Serves 5 to 6

I. Pierce the eggplant with a fork in two or three places. Cook the eggplant, peppers, and tomatoes over glowing coals until soft. The peppers will cook in about 10 minutes; the eggplant and green tomatoes will take about 30 and 40 minutes, respectively. (Cooking times vary considerably, depending on the size and shape of the vegetables and the heat of the coals.)

2. Wrap the garlic in foil and set in the coals to cook until soft, 10 to 20 minutes. Remove the garlic and let cool. Peel it and crush it with ½ teaspoon salt. Place the garlic in a wide mixing bowl, preferably wooden. Add the walnuts and crush to a smooth puree.

continued

1 pound eggplant

1 pound green bell peppers

1 pound green, unripe tomatoes

3 to 4 large cloves garlic, unpeeled

Coarse salt

4 tablespoons peeled, crushed walnuts

½ cup chopped flat-leaf parsley

1½ teaspoons red wine vinegar

Freshly ground black pepper to taste

Hot Hungarian paprika to taste

2 tablespoons fruity extra-virgin olive oil

2 tablespoons flat-leaf parsley and 2 cloves garlic chopped together just before serving for garnish

3. When the peppers have collapsed, set them on a plate, dip in a bowl of cold water, drain, and cool. Core, seed, and slip off the skins of the peppers. Add to the walnut puree. Chill the eggplant in a cold water bath, quickly peel from the stem downward, and soak in lemony water until cool. When the eggplant is cool enough to handle, squeeze out all the moisture and add the eggplant to the bowl. The green tomatoes take the longest to cook; when they are completely soft, remove from the heat and allow to cool. Add the green tomatoes (with skin and seeds) to the bowl. Use a wooden bean masher to crush everything into a smooth, juicy puree. Stir in the parsley and vinegar. Season with salt, pepper, and paprika to taste. Cover with a double thickness of paper towels. Allow to mellow in the refrigerator at least 3 hours.

4. About 20 minutes before serving, remove the relish from the refrigerator. In a small saucepan, heat the olive oil just to boiling and pour over the relish, stirring well to combine. Quickly chop the raw garlic and fresh parsley together and sprinkle on top. Serve directly from the wooden bowl.

*MACEDONIAN SALAD WITH GRILLED VEGETABLES

This salad makes a great dip for floppy warm flat bread or warm cheese corn bread (page 54); it is also a good relish for grilled chicken, fish, or meat. It will keep for a week. If, after a few days, you find some liquid seeping out of the mixture, discard the liquid or reserve to marinate fish or meat in it for a tangy flavor.

Serves 12

1. Prepare coals for grilling.
2. Wrap all but 3 cloves of the garlic in a sheet of aluminum foil. Prick the eggplant in two or three places. Grill the wrapped garlic until soft, 10 to 20 minutes. Grill all the other vegetables until soft. (The vegetables can be roasted in the oven; remove as each collapses.)
3. Peel the roasted garlic and place in a seasoned wooden bowl. As each vegetable collapses, stem, seed, and peel it, and add to the bowl.

1 head garlic, separated into cloves
3 large eggplants
6 green bell peppers
6 tomatoes, halved lengthwise
¼ cup extra-virgin olive oil
1 tablespoon red or white wine vinegar
2 teaspoons salt to taste
1 teaspoon freshly ground black pepper to taste
1 small dried chili, crumbled, or more to taste

4. Immediately after the eggplant collapses, dip into a cold water bath and peel while still hot. Soak in a lemon water bath 10 minutes, then squeeze out all moisture. Use a wooden bean masher to crush all the vegetables into a smooth, loose, and juicy mass. Whisk in the oil, then the vinegar. Adjust the seasoning and add the chili.
5. Peel and chop the remaining garlic and add to the mixture. Use your hands to shape the mixture into a ball and flatten it slightly. Cover with plastic film, wrap, and refrigerate overnight. Bring to room temperature before serving.

TWO STUFFED
❧ VEGETABLES ❧

*BROILED FRYING PEPPERS STUFFED WITH CHEESE AND GREEN CHILIS

❧

One of my favorite stuffed pepper preparations, found on many Salonika restaurant menus, originates from such traditional Macedonian dishes as frying peppers stuffed with fresh cheese, peppers fried with eggs, feta pureed with chilis, and peppers fried with herbs and crumbled feta.

Here the peppers are stuffed with a mixture of cheeses, then slowly grilled on all sides. They are delicious hot, warm, at room temperature, or cold with a glass of ouzo.

Serves 6 to 8

1. Wash the peppers and drain. Use a small knife to make a 1-inch incision halfway around each stem. Cook the peppers until tender in boiling salted water, about 5 minutes, or cook them in a microwave on medium high until they are limp and a dull green color. Set aside to cool.

2. In a small skillet, heat 2 tablespoons of the olive oil to medium hot, add the onion and chili, and cook, stirring, until soft, about 2 minutes. Remove from the heat and set aside.

3. When the peppers are cool enough to handle, carefully remove the seeds. If necessary, rinse the peppers one by one in a bowl of water in order to flush out any large amounts of loose seeds; drain well. (Don't worry if there are just a few pepper seeds left; they are cooked and tender.)

6 to 8 large Italian green frying peppers
Salt
3 tablespoons olive oil
3 tablespoons grated onion
1 tablespoon minced green chili, seeds removed
6 ounces imported feta, soaked in cold water 15 minutes, drained, and crumbled
7 ounces soft sheep's-milk cheese, Greek *manouri*, or ricotta *salata*, or a firm farmer cheese, crumbled
1 egg, well beaten
1½ tablespoons fresh lemon juice
Pinch of crumbled dried summer savory or Greek oregano
Pinch of freshly ground black pepper
2 tablespoons coarsely grated pecorino (optional, if serving hot)

4. In a shallow bowl, crush the two fresh cheeses with a fork, add the contents of the skillet (including the pan juices), the egg, lemon juice, summer savory, and black pepper. Crush until well blended and light. (Do not be tempted to do this in a food processor.) Makes about 1½ cups.

5. Carefully stuff each pepper with equal amounts of the cheese filling. Use a damp cloth to wipe away any overspill. Place the peppers side by side on a foil-lined baking sheet. Brush with half the remaining oil, cover with plastic wrap, and refrigerate. Can be prepared many hours in advance.

6. Thirty minutes before serving, remove the peppers from the refrigerator and preheat the broiler. Set the baking sheet on the rack farthest from the heat source. Broil the peppers until tender and spotted black on the first side, about 6 minutes. Then gently turn them over, brush with remaining oil, and broil on the second side. To serve hot, sprinkle with the grated pecorino. To serve cold, cut in diagonal slices, place a toothpick in the center of each portion, and serve with chilled ouzo.

*EGGPLANTS STUFFED WITH WALNUTS

Not many vegetables taste better than eggplant fried in olive oil. The Georgians have a special frying method that eliminates greasiness without sacrificing taste. They split baby eggplants down the middle, then slip them, flesh side down, into a well-seasoned skillet (I use a non-stick skillet) with a small amount of oil. The skillet is covered so that the eggplants fry and steam at the same time.

Serves 6

12 baby eggplants or 6 Japanese eggplants (about 2 pounds total weight), halved lengthwise

1¾ teaspoons fine sea salt

FILLING

2 cups (7 ounces) walnuts

1 clove garlic, peeled and finely chopped

½ teaspoon hot Hungarian paprika or more to taste

¼ teaspoon ground marigold petals (page 398) or ground turmeric

⅓ cup chopped celery leaves

¼ cup shredded basil leaves

⅓ cup chopped coriander leaves

¼ minced red onion

2 tablespoons mild vinegar, preferably rice wine vinegar

¼ cup pomegranate seeds, plus more for garnish

2 tablespoons olive oil

Flat-leaf parsley for garnish

1. Sprinkle the cut sides of the eggplants with 1 teaspoon of the salt and place, cut side down, on paper toweling. Weight down with plates 20 minutes. Rinse the eggplants under running water and then gently squeeze out the moisture; pat dry with paper towels.

2. Meanwhile, in a food processor, combine the walnuts with the garlic, paprika, marigold petals, and the remaining ¾ teaspoon of the salt. Puree until an oily paste forms. Add ⅓ cup water and process to blend. Transfer the paste to a medium bowl and stir in the celery, basil, coriander, onion, and vinegar. Fold in the pomegranate seeds. Cover and set aside.

3. In a large non-stick skillet, heat the olive oil over moderately low heat. Add all the eggplants, cut side down. Cover tightly and cook until the flesh is golden brown and the eggplants are very tender, about 15 minutes. Transfer to paper towels to drain. (If the skillet is not large enough, you will have to cook the eggplants in batches. Add ½ tablespoon more oil to the skillet before frying the second batch.)

4. With your fingers, press open the middle of the cut side of each eggplant. Mound the walnut filling into each eggplant half and serve warm or at room temperature; garnish with parsley sprigs and pomegranate seeds.

TWO STUFFED LEAF DISHES

*MACEDONIAN GRAPE OR VINE LEAVES STUFFED WITH BULGUR, FAVAS, FIGS, AND HERBS

In this unique version of stuffed grape or vine leaves, the stuffing is made with bulgur (instead of rice) and peeled and cracked favas (instead of pine nuts), and it is seasoned with the popular northern Greek combination of mint, parsley, and dill.

Serves 5 to 6

continued

About 48 young, tender vine leaves, freshly picked or
  defrosted, or grape leaves packed in brine (½ pound)

FILLING
½ cup coarse bulgur
⅓ cup dried, soaked, peeled, and cracked small favas (or
  substitute small black lentils or soaked, peeled, and dried
  cracked chickpeas); see Notes to the Cook
1 cup finely chopped onion
5 tablespoons olive oil
1½ tablespoons chopped parsley
1½ tablespoons chopped dill
1½ tablespoons chopped fresh mint
4 tablespoons chopped dried black figs or dried currants
3 tablespoons fresh lemon juice
Salt and freshly ground black pepper to taste

FOR COOKING THE STUFFED LEAVES
3 tablespoons olive oil
1 cup (approximately) light chicken stock or 1 cup water
  with half a chicken bouillon cube

3 tablespoons fresh lemon juice, plus more for serving
Lemon wedges for garnish

1. If you are using fresh or defrosted vine leaves, blanch small bunches in lightly salted water for ½ minute for defrosted leaves to 3 minutes for fresh leaves. If you are using brined leaves, carefully separate each leaf, then rinse in several changes of cool water to remove the taste of the brine. Blanch in unsalted water 3 to 5 minutes, then refresh under cool running water.

2. Drain the leaves and place them shiny side down on a kitchen towel. Snip off the stems with scissors. If any of the leaves are more than 4 inches across, trim off the excess or cut the leaves in half along the spine of the leaf. Save the stems and spines for step 7.

3. Cover the bulgur with hot water; let stand 15 minutes. (It is essential to use coarse bulgur and hot water so that the wheat expands; otherwise, you will end up with a compact soggy mass.)

4. Wash the soaked, peeled, and cracked favas; place in a saucepan and cover with cold water. Bring to a boil and cook, covered, 15 minutes. Drain in a sieve and set aside to cool. Meanwhile, stir-cook the onion in 2½ tablespoons of the oil until golden, about 5 minutes. Remove from the heat.

5. Drain the bulgur, pressing out as much water as possible. Place the bulgur, onion, favas, herbs, and figs in a mixing bowl. Toss to mix well. Fold in the lemon juice and 2½ tablespoons oil, and add the salt and pepper.

6. To fill the leaves: Put 1 heaping teaspoon of filling on each leaf near the base. Starting at the base, fold the bottom of the leaf over the filling. Fold the sides over the filling to the center. Roll toward the tip of the leaf and squeeze gently so it will be compact and thin. These are best made as small as possible. (At this point they can be wrapped and frozen.)

7. To cook the stuffed leaves: Line the bottom of a 3-quart casserole with a handful of

torn remaining leaves plus the reserved stems and spines, and set the stuffed leaves close together, seam side down, in alternating layers. Sprinkle with a little salt. Add 3 tablespoons oil and cover the rolls with an inverted plate, pressing down slightly. (This is to keep them in place during the cooking.) Add just enough heated stock to come level with the rim of the plate. Bring to a boil, cover, and cook over low heat about 45 minutes for wild and tender leaves. Brined leaves cook in about 1 hour; thick and less tender leaves may take up to 2 hours to cook.

8. Remove from the heat, tilt the pan, add 3 tablespoons lemon juice, and shake gently to combine. Cover the casserole and let the leaves cool in the cooking liquid; they will continue to absorb some of the cooking liquid. Remove the plate. Pour off any liquid. Invert the rolls onto a flat plate, cover tightly with plastic wrap, and refrigerate. (Keeps up to a week in the refrigerator.) Wipe away excess oil, arrange on a flat serving plate, squeeze more lemon juice on top, and serve at room temperature with lemon wedges.

NOTES TO THE COOK: Coarse bulgur and peeled split favas are easily found at Middle Eastern groceries. If unavailable, use whole dried favas; after soaking, peel and crack them in thirds. Or you can use soaked, peeled, and halved chickpeas.

Small black lentils, called *masoor dal* or Egyptian lentils, are also delicious in the stuffing (see Appendix C).

Brined grape leaves are widely available, and fresh leaves can be found on wild grape plants along roads and streams all over the northern United States. In May and June, wild or cultivated grape leaves are tender and ready to be picked, sorted, and frozen in stacks until needed. After defrosting, wash and use right away. Blanch large and tough leaves in salted water to soften. Or you can fill, roll, and freeze them before cooking.

*SWISS CHARD LEAVES STUFFED WITH RICE, CHICKPEAS, AND TOMATO

This Syrian stuffing has a particular freshness and gets better as it mellows. You can substitute tender grape leaves for the Swiss chard, in which case you will need to cook the rolls an extra 20 to 30 minutes.

Serves 6 to 8 as a mezze

FILLING

5 tablespoons extra-virgin olive oil

2 cups chopped red onion

½ cup short-grain white rice, soaked in very hot water for 10 minutes, rinsed, and drained

½ cup chickpeas, soaked overnight, peeled, and halved

¾ cup (about 12) seeded and chopped cherry tomatoes

1½ teaspoons salt

⅛ teaspoon Near East or Aleppo pepper or hot paprika (page 395)

⅛ teaspoon ground cumin

⅛ teaspoon sweet paprika

⅛ teaspoon freshly ground black pepper

1½ cups chopped flat-leaf parsley

3 tablespoons slivered mint leaves, preferably spearmint

1 teaspoon sugar

2 pounds Swiss chard leaves

1½ cups water

3 tablespoons fresh lemon juice

Lemon wedges for garnish

I. In a 10-inch skillet, warm the oil, add the onion, cover, and cook 5 minutes, or until the onion is soft and golden. Remove from the heat. Tilt into a mixing bowl. Add the rice, chickpeas, tomatoes, salt, Aleppo pepper, spices, parsley, mint, and sugar; mix well. Makes about 3½ cups filling.

2. Rinse and drain the Swiss chard leaves. Remove the stalks from the greens and reserve a few for step 4. Dip the leaves into simmering water until pliable, about 10 seconds, and refresh in a basin of cold water. Drain, then gently press out excess moisture. Place the leaves, shiny side down and a few at a time, on a work surface. If the leaves are very large, halve them lengthwise, removing the center rib. Trim each leaf to make an approximate 5-inch square (the ribs should be horizontal, not vertical, for easier rolling).

3. Place a heaping teaspoon of filling below the rib of each leaf. Fold over the filling and roll up to make a firm, thin cigarette shape.

If necessary, squeeze gently in the palm of your hand to firm the roll up. Repeat with the remaining leaves and filling.

4. Line a I-quart heavy saucepan with a few diced stalks. Place the stuffed leaves, open ends down, in tightly packed rows and crisscrossing layers. Weight them down with a plate just large enough to fit inside the saucepan.

5. Pour the water down the inside of the saucepan. Bring to a boil; boil hard for half a minute, cover with a tight-fitting lid, reduce the heat to low, and cook 40 minutes. Remove from the heat and let stand 20 minutes before uncovering. Add the lemon juice to the pan juices and swirl to combine. Serve warm or cold, garnished with lemon wedges.

NOTES TO THE COOK: When eastern Mediterranean cooks have lots of time, they will often skin chickpeas for certain dishes, not only to get rid of the starchy skin, which is somewhat indigestible, but also to achieve a glistening appearance. In nearly all the recipes in this book, I have opted to leave the skins on. This recipe is one of the exceptions. Here the chickpeas must be peeled and halved so that they will cook as quickly as the other ingredients. The extra effort is worthwhile, because peeled chickpeas provide a unique taste and texture, and only a handful is needed for the dish. To peel chickpeas easily: Place soaked and uncooked chickpeas on a kitchen towel, cover with another towel, then gently hit each pea with a rolling pin; rub the peas; the peels will come right off and the pea will split in two.

A GEORGIAN VEGETABLE AND BEAN SAMPLER

THE GEORGIAN KITCHEN

When people first try Georgian food, especially the soups and stews, they often say that the dishes taste "almost Indian." Indian food has certainly been an influence. In the eastern part of Georgia, one will find clarified butter (ghee) used as a cooking medium and a bread that resembles the Indian *naan* that is made in a tandoor oven. In fact, Georgians have long been fascinated with Indian culture; their great twelfth-century epic, a hymn to friendship called *The Knight in the Panther's Skin*, has an Indian hero.

Georgians like to cook with garlic, walnuts, vinegar, dried marigold petals, hot paprika, and onions. And they are masters of cooking with herbs. Fresh coriander, dill, mint, basil, lovage, tarragon, and summer savory are used in great quantities and in multiple combinations to flavor stews, soups, and vegetables, and sometimes even as thickening agents.

I learned that the secret of the best Georgian food lies in the harmony of its flavorings. A Georgian cook told me that if a dish is right, the diner should not be able to single out any herb or spice. "Nothing," she said, "should dominate."

On the other hand, you may notice that most of the Georgian appetizers here contain walnuts, which are ubiquitous in Georgian cooking. A Georgian meal is meant to be voluptuous, and an abundance of walnut-based appetizers fits right in with that concept.

*CREAMY EGGPLANT AND CELERY RELISH

In the town of Pasanauri—along the spectacular Georgia Military Highway, which crosses the Caucasus Mountains into Russia—this excellent relish is brought out as soon as a guest enters a home.

Makes 1½ cups

1. In a 9-inch skillet, slowly cook the onions in the oil until soft and golden, about 20 minutes. Remove from the skillet and set aside. Makes about ¼ cup.

2. Prick the eggplants with a skewer in two or three places. Bake, steam, or boil the eggplants whole until they are completely tender. Separately, boil, steam, or microwave the garlic until soft, 2 minutes. Transfer the eggplants to a slanted wooden board or a large colander; split open lengthwise, place opened side down, cover with a heavy weight, and leave to drain and cool, about 10 minutes. Skin; stem; and discard any hard seeds. Shred the eggplant pulp with your fingers, place in a mixing bowl, and set aside. Peel the garlic.

3. In a mortar or mini-chopper, combine the walnuts with ¼ teaspoon salt, the garlic, ground coriander seeds, and chili. Pound or grind until the walnuts exude their oil and the mixture is smooth. Work in the water to make a light, smooth cream. Combine with the eggplant and, using your fingers, mix in the parsley, celery, tarragon, and fried onions. Sharpen the mixture with the vinegar and season with salt and pepper. Scoop into a shallow serving dish, cover tightly with plastic wrap, and chill for a few hours, but serve at room temperature. Decorate with small torn celery leaves.

2 medium onions, finely chopped (1½ cups)

2 tablespoons vegetable or olive oil

2 medium eggplants (about 13 ounces each), light in hand, smooth-skinned, with bright green stems

2 large cloves garlic, unpeeled

⅓ cup coarsely chopped walnuts

Salt

½ teaspoon ground coriander seeds

2 teaspoons minced green chili

2 tablespoons water

⅛ cup chopped flat-leaf parsley

¼ cup chopped celery leaves

2 teaspoons chopped tarragon, dill, or coriander

2 teaspoons mild vinegar

Freshly ground black pepper to taste

A few torn celery leaves for garnish

RED BEANS, SPICES, AND CHEESE

Georgians know more about blending spices and herbs than any other eastern Mediterranean people, and nowhere do they show off their knowledge to more glorious proof than with a pot of small red beans. Georgians serve small red beans flavored with walnuts, leeks, celery, and spices, accompanied by cornmeal cheese cakes; beans cooked and blended with coriander, savory, and parsley; beans with walnuts, leeks, and coriander; beans with walnuts, leeks, celery, and pomegranates; beans with raisins, honey, and almonds; beans with hot peppers and mint; beans with ham and greens; beans with eggs and butter; beans with walnuts, vinegar, and *tkemali* (page 32); beans simply cooked with spices and a touch of fresh coriander.

The following bean recipe may recall an Indian dal. The special feature of this dish is the combination of sweet spices and sour pomegranate.

Makes about 3½ cups, serving 6 to 8

1 cup small red beans
2 tablespoons vegetable oil
2 medium onions, chopped (1½ cups)
½ teaspoon ground ginger
¼ teaspoon ground cinnamon
¼ teaspoon ground cloves
¾ teaspoon fine salt or more to taste
Freshly ground black pepper to taste
Cayenne to taste
1 to 2 tablespoons fresh pomegranate juice or 2 to
    3 teaspoons mild vinegar
4 tablespoons chopped coriander leaves and ¼ pound
    imported feta for garnish

1. Soak the beans in water, to cover, overnight. Drain, cover with 3 cups cold water, and bring to a boil over medium-high heat. Reduce the heat to medium low and cook, covered, 1 hour, or until beans are very soft.

2. Strain the beans in a colander set over a bowl to collect the cooking liquid. Do not discard the cooking liquid.

3. In a large skillet, heat the oil. Add the onions, cover, and cook over medium-low heat until soft and golden, about 5 minutes. Stir in the cooked beans and cook 5 minutes longer. Increase the heat to moderate and add the reserved cooking liquid, ginger, cinna-

mon, cloves, and salt. Cook, stirring occasionally with a wooden spoon or spatula, until almost all the liquid has evaporated and about half the beans have broken down to a puree. Remove from the heat and adjust the seasoning with salt, black pepper, and cayenne. Scrape into a serving bowl, stir in pomegranate juice or vinegar, half the coriander, cover, and refrigerate at least 8 hours before serving.

4. To serve, bring the beans back to room temperature. Garnish with the remaining coriander and serve with slices of feta.

RED BEANS WITH HONEY AND ALMONDS

One day my Georgian "adopted family" hostess, Tsino Natsulishvili, a generous woman with lovely gray-blue eyes, invited me to join her on a visit to her mother in Kakheti, in eastern Georgia.

It took us about an hour to drive through the flat vineyards of this main wine-making region of the country. When we reached Tsino's mother's house, we found a spread waiting for us on the table. There was a pile of fresh dill, scallions, flat-leaf parsley, coriander, and small tomatoes to be inserted between pieces of delicious, chewy, flat bread, along with opened bottles of the two most famous wines of the region: a fresh white *tsinandali* and a smooth red *mukuzani*, which tasted a little bit like Merlot. After munching, I was invited into the kitchen to watch Tsino's mother prepare our lunch: cabbage leaves stuffed with meat and a platter of red beans flavored with honey.

That evening, passing through a village on the way back to Tbilisi, we ran out of gas—a not unique experience, as there had been severe gasoline shortages for over a month. We walked to the village police station, where my hostess explained our predicament: She was with an American guest, and it would be a "stain on the good name of Georgian hospitality" if she couldn't find gas to get me back to the capital that night. The policemen conferred. Then, to my amazement, they proceeded to open up the gas tanks of all the cars parked in front of the station and siphon off a little gasoline from each. My only thought was "From each according to his abilities, to each according to his needs."

Serves 6 to 8 as part of a Georgian buffet

1½ cups small red beans
2 tablespoons vegetable oil
2 medium onions, chopped (1½ cups)
¼ cup slivered almonds
Freshly ground black pepper to taste
½ cup black raisins
¾ teaspoon fine salt or more to taste
1 tablespoon honey

1. Soak the beans in water, to cover, overnight. Drain, cover with 3 cups cold water, and bring to a boil over medium-high heat. Reduce the heat to medium low and cook, covered, 1 hour, or until beans are cooked.

2. Strain the beans in a colander set over a bowl to collect the cooking liquid. Do not discard the cooking liquid.

3. In a large skillet, heat the oil. Add the chopped onions and cook, covered, over medium-low heat until soft and golden, about 5 minutes. Add the almonds and cook, stirring, until golden. Stir in the pepper, raisins, and cooked beans and cook 5 minutes longer. Increase the heat to moderate and add the reserved cooking liquid and salt. Continue cooking, stirring with a wooden spoon or spatula, until almost all the liquid has evaporated and about a quarter of the beans have broken down to a puree. Remove from the heat and add the honey. Serve warm.

GEORGIAN VEGETABLE PÂTÉS

I think the most characteristic Georgian dish is *pkhali*, a term that refers to a group of vegetable pâtés, each made from a single boiled or roasted vegetable. Most taste better the second day. *Pkhali* can be made with radish tops, cabbage, onion, thistles, beet greens, beets, green beans, nettles, or almost any other vegetable.

Georgians usually serve more than one kind of *pkhali* at a time. Since every vegetable is seasoned with its own set of herbs and/or spices, the recipes are not interchangeable.

Although the flavoring varies, the basic method is fairly constant. After the selected vegetable is cooked, excess moisture is squeezed out. Then the vegetable is mixed with its particular set of chopped herbs, onions, walnuts, and pounded garlic, and its flavor is gently heightened with either pomegranate juice or a mild vinegar.

No matter which vegetable is used, *pkhali* is served molded, usually into an oval loaf. The loaf is marked in crisscross fashion with the blade of a knife, then often garnished with pomegranate seeds, slivered red onions, tiny dabs of sour cream, or a few drops of spiced walnut oil. Diners cut out wedges and eat them with a fork.

*SPINACH PÂTÉ

Makes about 1⅓ cups, serving 4 to 6

I pound young spinach, trimmed, washed, and drained
I large clove garlic, unpeeled
⅓ cup (I ounce) coarsely chopped walnuts
½ teaspoon coarse sea salt
½ teaspoon ground coriander seeds
Pinch of cayenne
¼ cup chopped coriander
2 tablespoons chopped parsley
4 tablespoons grated onion, rinsed and drained
I to 2 teaspoons mild vinegar, preferably rice wine vinegar
¼ teaspoon freshly ground black pepper

OPTIONAL GARNISH
Sour cream or walnut oil
Pomegranate seeds and slivered red onions

I. For the best flavor, begin preparation one day in advance of serving. Steam, boil, or microwave the spinach until almost tender. Add the garlic and cook 2 minutes longer. Remove the garlic, peel, and set aside. Drain the spinach and let cool. Squeeze the spinach by handfuls over a bowl to extract as much liquid as possible; reserve 2 tablespoons of the spinach liquid. Coarsely chop the spinach and transfer to a medium bowl.

2. In a mortar, mini-chopper, or spice mill, grind the walnuts with ¼ teaspoon salt, the garlic, ground coriander seeds, and cayenne. Pound until the walnuts exude their oil and the mixture is pasty. Blend in the reserved 2 tablespoons spinach water.

3. Add the walnut mixture to the spinach and, using your fingers, mix in the fresh coriander, parsley, and onion. Moisten the mixture with the vinegar and season with the remaining ¼ teaspoon salt and the black pepper. Pack firmly into a lightly oiled 1½-cup ramekin or bowl, cover tightly, and refrigerate at least a few hours or overnight.

4. To serve, bring the spinach pâté to room temperature and invert it onto a serving plate. If desired, decorate with tiny dabs of sour cream or drizzle with walnut oil, or garnish with pomegranate seeds and slivered red onions.

NOTES TO THE COOK: If you are using a strong-tasting onion for the garnish, sliver the onion, rub it with salt, and let stand about 4 minutes. Rinse under running water, squeeze dry, and then use as a garnish. This takes out a lot of the bite.

VARIATION:

Here is a hotter version, with red *adzhika* paste (page 390). To make about 1 cup pâté: Combine 1 pound cooked, drained, and finely chopped spinach with 2 to 3 tablespoons *adzhika* paste, the garlic, the herbs, onion, salt, mild vinegar, and an extra tablespoon of ground walnuts. Omit the black pepper, ground coriander seeds, and cayenne. Adjust the salt to taste.

*LEEK PÂTÉ

Makes about 1 ⅓ cups, serving 4 to 6

Follow steps 1, 2, and 3 of the preceding recipe, using the ingredients listed here. To serve, bring to room temperature and invert onto a serving plate. Decorate with pomegranate seeds.

3 large or 6 medium leeks (both the white and tender green parts), washed, trimmed, and sliced ⅛-inch thick

½ teaspoon plus a pinch of salt

3 large cloves garlic, unpeeled

½ cup chopped walnuts

Pinch of hot Hungarian paprika

½ teaspoon ground coriander seeds

⅓ cup mixed chopped herbs: basil, celery tops, and mint

2 teaspoons mild vinegar, preferably rice wine vinegar

2 tablespoons pomegranate seeds

*FRYING PEPPER PÂTÉ

Serves 4

1 pound Italian green frying peppers

Pinch of coarse sea salt

½ cup (2 ounces) coarsely chopped walnuts

2 tablespoons grated onion, rinsed and drained

1 tablespoon chopped coriander

2 to 3 tablespoons fresh pomegranate juice or 1 teaspoon
   very mild vinegar

4 tablespoons pomegranate seeds (optional)

2 pinches of hot Hungarian paprika

1. Place the peppers and 1 inch of water in a small heavy saucepan. Add the salt, cover, and cook over medium heat until the peppers collapse, about 5 minutes. Cool, press out as much moisture as possible, then scrape away the cores, seeds, and peel. Coarsely chop the peppers and follow steps 1, 2, and 3 for the Spinach Pâté (page 176).

2. To serve, bring to room temperature and invert onto a serving plate. Decorate with pomegranate seeds, if available, and hot paprika.

THREE
SOUTHEASTERN
TURKISH SALADS

In southeastern Turkey I found a slew of salads that vaguely resembled the Georgian pâtés called *pkhali*. The similarities were striking: a single leafy green or vegetable combined with scallions or onions and spices, decorated with pomegranates, and containing little or no oil. But instead of the main ingredient being chopped fine and blended almost to a puree as in Georgia, in Gaziantep the main ingredient is chopped, shredded, or slightly squashed so it will absorb the flavorings of the garnishes.

These salads are called collectively *piyazlar*. (Elsewhere in the country the word is used to describe a salad of sliced onion and potatoes or dried legumes—black-eyed peas, chickpeas, or white beans—served with a lemon juice and olive oil dressing and decorated with hard-boiled eggs, sliced tomatoes, and black olives.)

In Gaziantep, such salads are assigned "partners"—dishes that go well with them. For example, the cracked green olive and walnut salad (page 148) goes with ground meat kabobs; the parsley, lemon, and onion salad smothers liver; the tarragon-onion salad is delicious with lentil-bulgur kibbeh (page 274); the purslane and sumac salad (page 134) with cubed kabobs; and the *kekik piyazi* (page 145) is wonderful with *manti* (page 101).

The following cooked salads are also in the *piyazlar* family (but not in the Georgian) and feature mung beans, white beans, and black-eyed peas. They are all wonderful as an accompaniment to flat bread, or may be served very nicely on their own.

*Mung Bean, Scallion, and Pomegranate Salad

This delicious, unique Gaziantep salad is made with the same beans that when soaked turn into bean sprouts. The mung beans are boiled, dressed, and gently crushed with the most traditional *piyaz* ingredients, to be served at room temperature. Serve this, if you like, with ground lamb kabobs.

Makes about 3 cups

1 cup dried mung beans (available at health food stores)
½ cup thinly sliced scallions
½ teaspoon crushed garlic
⅓ cup chopped parsley
¾ teaspoon Near East or Aleppo pepper (see page 395)
1 scant teaspoon salt
¼ cup fresh lemon juice
¼ cup fresh pomegranate seeds or substitute ¾ teaspoon
   pomegranate molasses (page 404)

1. Wash the mung beans under running water until the water runs clear. Soak in cold water for 1 hour; drain.

2. In a heavy saucepan, cook the mung beans in 3½ cups water until tender, about 30 minutes. Drain; reserve ½ cup cooking liquor. Allow the mung beans to cool slightly before adding the remaining ingredients. Set aside to mellow a few hours, then correct the seasoning and serve at room temperature.

With thanks to Mrs. Filiz Hösukolğlu for sharing her recipe for mas piyazi

*White Bean, Parsley, and Onion Salad

In this delightful recipe, popular in northern Syria as well as southeastern Turkey, small white beans are simmered slowly, then tossed while still hot in a mixture of lemon juice and salt. This salad will still be good the following day. Turks eat it as an appetizer and even for breakfast, rolled in flat bread.

Makes about 3 cups

1. Pick over the beans and discard any foreign matter. Soak in water, to cover, overnight. Drain; place in a deep pan, cover with plenty of fresh cold water, and bring to a boil. Lower the heat and cook at a simmer, partially covered, until the beans are tender, about 1½ hours. (You can tell when they are almost done by removing one or two beans with a spoon and blowing gently on them—the skins will burst.) Simmer another 10 minutes, then remove from the heat and drain well in a colander. Reserve a few tablespoons of the cooking liquid for the salad and the remaining liquid for another purpose.

2. Place the beans in a bowl, add the lemon juice, salt, and pepper; toss well and let stand 10 minutes. Add the remaining ingredients and toss again. Lightly crush the beans with the reserved liquid. Serve cold or at room temperature.

I cup dry white beans, preferably navy or Great Northern

3 tablespoons fresh lemon juice or more to taste

I teaspoon salt

½ teaspoon freshly ground black pepper

½ teaspoon Near East or Aleppo pepper (page 395)

¼ cup chopped flat-leaf parsley

¼ cup thinly sliced scallions

¼ cup finely chopped walnuts

¼ cup pomegranate seeds

I ½ tablespoons extra-virgin olive oil

*BLACK-EYED PEAS WITH SCALLIONS, WALNUTS, AND PARSLEY

Makes about 3 cups

1 cup black-eyed peas

4 tablespoons fresh lemon juice

Salt to taste

½ teaspoon Near East or Aleppo pepper (page 395)

¼ cup thinly sliced scallions

¼ cup finely chopped parsley

Freshly ground pepper

½ cup chopped walnuts

¼ cup pomegranate seeds

1½ tablespoons olive oil

Follow the directions for White Bean, Parsley, and Onion Salad (page 181), but do not soak the black-eyed peas. Do not reserve any cooking liquid. Lightly crush the peas with 2 tablespoons water.

VII

Vegetables

Vegetables Simmered in Olive Oil

In the eastern Mediterranean region, there is a special style of cooking vegetables that capitalizes on the unique flavor of olive oil. The vegetables and the oil work beautifully together, each bringing out the taste of the other. These dishes are refreshing, soft-textured, and not at all greasy. To ensure lightness, I have reduced the amount of oil used by eastern Mediterranean cooks by more than half.

The method is simple. The vegetables are stewed in a mixture of olive oil, water, and a small amount of sugar until most of the water evaporates, leaving a syrupy sauce behind. The sugar is added to enrich the syrup, bring out the flavor, and help preserve the shape of the vegetable. The stewing is always slow, with a crumbled wet piece of parchment placed over the vegetables and the pot closed with a tight-fitting lid. This allows slow evaporation of moisture, ensuring the proper butter-soft consistency of the vegetables. It is a truly fine way of cooking, which I urge readers to try. In fact, if you are prejudiced against overcooked vegetables, this method will quickly change your mind, and you will find yourself greatly rewarded.

These vegetable dishes are good served warm, lukewarm, or cold, and they keep well in the refrigerator for several days. They can be eaten by themselves, as part of a vegetarian meal, or as an accompaniment to a main course. Always serve them with bread.

ARTICHOKES, ISTANBUL STYLE

In springtime you will find this dish on counters in restaurants all over Istanbul: cooked artichoke bottoms and assorted vegetables scented with fresh dill, sitting upside down in liquid, their long stalks protruding into the air.

The dish, which can be made in advance, and improves upon sitting at least 5 or 6 hours, is almost a mini-ragout, containing not only artichokes but also carrots, celery root, potatoes, and shallots. The vegetables, all butter tender, are enrobed in a glistening syrupy sauce. Even though sugar is used in the cooking, the final taste, after the vegetables have mellowed, is not at all sweet, but fresh and delightful.

Serves 6

1. Preheat the oven to 300° F.

2. In a deep bowl, combine 1 quart water, the flour, coarse salt, and the juice of 1 lemon. Clean the artichokes (see Notes to the Cook), rub with a lemon half, and immediately place in the bowl.

3. Put the artichokes, stems up, the other vegetables, and 1 cup of the flour-water mixture in a wide casserole. Add ½ cup water, the sugar, remaining lemon juice, the oil, and ½ teaspoon salt. Bring to a boil and allow the liquid to boil vigorously 1 minute. Cover with a sheet of moistened and crumbled parchment paper and a tight-fitting lid, and place the casserole in the oven; cook 1½ hours.

4. Remove the casserole from the oven and let cool before uncovering. Serve the artichokes with the syrupy juices and a sprinkling of the dill. Garnish with lemon wedges. *continued*

2 tablespoons flour

1 teaspoon coarse salt

Juice of 2 lemons plus ½ lemon

6 globe artichokes

2 thin carrots, pared and cut into 1-inch lengths

¼ medium celery root, pared and cut into wedges, or

    1 celery rib, stringed and cut into 1-inch pieces

1 medium potato, pared and cut into wedges

10 shallots, peeled

2½ teaspoons sugar

⅓ cup extra-virgin olive oil

½ teaspoon salt

1 sheet of parchment paper

¼ cup snipped dill or more to taste

Lemon wedges for garnish

NOTES TO THE COOK: One day, while preparing the artichokes for this dish, I discovered that if I used a melon scoop to remove the choke first, and then scraped along the inside walls of the vegetable, I could obtain a larger artichoke bottom than if I worked in the ordinary way, from the outside of the vegetable.

After cleaning the inside, I then worked on the outer side, removing the hard leaves by snapping them back, trimming the leaves straight across, then smoothing out the whole bottom.

With thanks to Chef Ismail Demir of Pandeli's Restaurant, Istanbul, for sharing this recipe

STUFFED BABY ARTICHOKES, IZMIR STYLE

Here is a vegetable and olive oil dish from the city of Izmir, Turkey, where some of the finest Aegean cooking is to be found. Plum-size artichokes are hollowed out, stuffed with dill-flavored rice, then simmered in oil together with fresh favas. The two vegetables together are delicious. If you use baby artichokes, you can eat them whole. Serve cool.

Like many good recipes, this and the okra recipe on page 189 feature a special method. The layering of parchment and a weight inside the pan help regulate the moisture level and keep the artichokes in place, allowing them literally to bathe in the sauce.

Serves 2 to 6, depending upon the menu

1. Wash the rice and rinse in several changes of water; drain. Place it in a small bowl and cover with very hot water. Let stand until ready to use. (This softens and swells the grains.)

2. Gently smack each artichoke on the edge of a hard surface to open up the leaves, then cut away the spiky tips. Remove the hard outer leaves and trim the stem at the base so that it will sit flat during the cooking. Use a vegetable peeler to remove any hard surfaces around the base. Spread the inner leaves and use a melon scoop to remove the choke from the center.

3. Place the artichokes in a mixture of 6 cups water, 3 tablespoons of lemon juice, 1 teaspoon salt, and flour. (The artichokes can sit up to 2 hours without a marring of color, texture, or flavor.)

continued

⅓ cup short-grain white rice
12 baby artichokes (about 1⅓ pounds)
5 tablespoons fresh lemon juice
Coarse sea salt
2 tablespoons flour
4 thinly sliced scallions (⅓ cup)
⅓ cup extra-virgin olive oil
¼ cup snipped fresh dill
3 teaspoons sugar
Salt and freshly ground black pepper
1 large onion, peeled
1 pound fresh favas, shelled
1 large carrot, pared and cut into thick rounds
1 12-by-12-inch sheet of parchment paper
Snipped dill and lemon wedges for garnish

4. Combine scallions, drained rice, 2 tablespoons of the oil, dill, 2 teaspoons of the sugar, and salt and pepper to taste in a bowl; mix well. Drain the artichokes, reserving ½ cup water for step 5. Divide the rice mixture among the artichokes and fill them.

5. Place the onion in the center of a casserole 9 inches in diameter. Surround with the filled artichokes, favas, and carrot. In a small cup, combine the remaining olive oil and sugar, the reserved ½ cup water, and 2 tablespoons fresh lemon juice; beat well. Pour over the artichokes, lay a crumbled piece of wet parchment directly on the artichokes, and set on top of the paper an inverted heat-proof plate just large enough to fit inside the casserole to keep everything in place.

6. Bring 1 cup of water to a boil. Meanwhile, bring the contents of the casserole to a strong boil, then add the 1 cup of boiling water down the inside of the casserole. Boil vigorously 1 minute, lower the heat, cover, and cook slowly about 40 minutes—the artichokes should be very tender and almost all of the liquid absorbed. Remove from the heat and leave to cool without disturbing, 2 to 3 hours.

7. When ready to turn the artichokes out, discard the onion. Transfer the artichokes, favas, and carrot to a shallow serving dish. Spoon the cooking juices over all and decorate with the dill and lemon wedges.

NOTES TO THE COOK: Freeze favas in their skins but out of their pods. Peel when ready to use.

When buying favas, choose beans that have bright green pods and are firm to the touch. Avoid limp pods.

The favas can be omitted from the recipe. Substitute 1 rib of celery, pared and cut into 1-inch lengths.

Short-grain rice is always best for stuffed vegetables, making the filling more compact.

With thanks to Mrs. Sevim Postaeioglü for sharing this recipe

OKRA BRAISED WITH TOMATOES AND ONIONS

If okra is going to be cooked for a fairly long time, it should first be allowed to soak in a vinegar bath to keep it from becoming slimy and stringy. Sautéing before braising enhances its flavor.

The final flourish of heated olive oil, fresh garlic, and coriander adds great aroma. Serve this delicious dish hot or cold.

Serves 4

1. Rinse the okra and carefully pare the cone-shaped tops, taking care not to cut into the pod. Toss with the vinegar and coarse salt and let stand 1 hour. Rinse again and dry on kitchen toweling.

2. In a nonstick skillet, heat 2 table-spoons of the oil, add half the okra, and quickly brown on all sides. Tilt the skillet to keep the oil while removing the okra to a side dish. Repeat with the remaining okra.

3. Add another tablespoon of the oil to the skillet, add the onions and sliced garlic, cover, and cook over medium heat until the onions are wilted and golden, about 2 minutes. Add the tomatoes, sugar, water, and salt and pepper, and simmer, covered, 10 minutes. Add the lemon juice.

4. Meanwhile, lightly oil an 8-inch skillet. Arrange the okra tightly in a spoke pattern, with the tips pointing toward the center. Spoon the tomato and onion mixture over the okra and scatter any remaining okra on top, pressing down gently. Place a sheet of crumbled, wet

I pound firm, crisp okra, each vegetable about 3 inches long
¼ cup white vinegar
I tablespoon coarse salt
5⅓ tablespoons olive oil
2 medium onions, halved and thinly sliced
5 cloves garlic, peeled and thinly sliced
2 large ripe tomatoes, grated (I cup)
I teaspoon sugar
½ cup water
Salt and freshly ground black pepper to taste
Juice of ½ lemon
I 12-by-12-inch sheet of parchment paper
1½ tablespoons roughly chopped coriander
I clove garlic, peeled and crushed with salt

continued

parchment and an inverted plate on top to keep the vegetables in place. Cover with a tight-fitting lid and cook over medium-low heat about 20 minutes.

5. Remove the skillet from the heat, allow to cool about 10 minutes, and then tilt to remove any cooking juices and reserve. Invert the contents of the skillet onto a wide, shallow serving dish. Heat the remaining 2 tablespoons olive oil in the skillet, add the coriander and crushed garlic, and stir once until sizzling; add the reserved juices and bring to a boil, swirling the pan. Spoon over the okra and let stand until ready to serve. The dish is best warm or at room temperature.

*MOTTLED RED BEANS IN OLIVE OIL

"Try to bring back a recipe for those delicious beans!" my stockbroker instructed just before my last trip to Turkey. She was referring to the creamy beans that are simmered in olive oil and served at room temperature. Called *pilaki,* they are a standard item in Istanbul restaurants, and a typical home-cooked Turkish dish.

The trick is to change the water twice: first, just after soaking, and second, after the beans are half-cooked. This reduces the possibility of gas after eating, and gives the beans a fresher taste than if served in their original cooking liquid.

Serve no sooner than 6 hours after the beans have finished cooking. They are delicious with fresh, warm flat bread; as an accompaniment to grilled fish; or as part of a small buffet in summer.

Serves 6

1. Pick over the beans and remove all foreign matter, as well as any broken beans. Cover the beans with cold water and let soak overnight at room temperature. Discard any beans that float to the top of the water.

2. The following day, drain the beans and place in a deep saucepan; cover with cold water and bring to a boil. Skim carefully, then cook the beans, partially covered, over medium heat 20 minutes.

3. Meanwhile, peel and slice the onion into thin strips; peel the potato and carrot and cut into small cubes. Chop the celery to make ⅓ cup.

4. Heat the olive oil in a 10-inch-straight-sided skillet and add the onion. Cover and cook 2 to 3 minutes. Add the potato, carrot, and celery and toss over medium heat another minute. Add the garlic, sugar, red pepper flakes, tomato paste, mustard, if desired, and 1 cup cold water. Bring to a boil and then cook, covered, at a simmer 10 minutes.

½ pound dried mottled beans, preferably cranberry, borlotti, pinto, or Roman (see Notes to the Cook)
1 small onion
1 medium waxy potato
1 medium carrot
1 small rib celery
⅓ cup olive oil
5 very small garlic cloves, unpeeled
2 teaspoons sugar
Good pinch of dried red pepper flakes
1 teaspoon tomato paste
¼ teaspoon Dijon mustard (optional)
1½ cups boiling water
Salt and freshly ground black pepper to taste
2 tablespoons chopped parsley
Fresh lemon juice to taste
Lemon wedges for garnish

5. Drain the beans and add to the skillet. Add 1½ cups boiling water and continue to cook, covered, until most of the liquid has been absorbed and the beans are tender. Add salt and pepper. Pour into a deep serving dish, sprinkle with the parsley, and let stand at room temperature at least 6 hours before serving. (Can be refrigerated up to 2 days. Bring back to room temperature to serve.) Add lemon juice and garnish with lemon wedges.

NOTES TO THE COOK: The Turkish beans for this dish are called *barbunya*, a word used both in Turkey and Greece for baby red Aegean mullets. The pinkish color of these beans is almost the same as that of cooked borlotti beans.

GREEN BEANS AND TOMATOES
IN OLIVE OIL

"These beans have their own dignity, don't you think?" a woman from Salonika remarked as we sat down to a simple lunch of a bowl of putty-colored beans enrobed in oily sauce and napped with tomatoes, onions, and scallions, accompanied by a slab of cheese and crusty bread.

Don't worry about a loss of nutrients. The nutrient content of green beans is fairly low; the high fiber content is not affected by "overcooking."

Like most Greek vegetables cooked in olive oil, these beans are best served at room temperature.

Serves 4

1½ pounds tender green beans, trimmed

¼ cup olive oil

1 cup minced onion

Salt to taste

1 teaspoon sugar

⅓ cup tomato sauce

1 cup boiling water

1 12-by-12-inch sheet of parchment paper

Place all the ingredients in a heavy saucepan. Bring to a boil and boil vigorously 1 minute. Cover with crumbled wet parchment and a tight-fitting lid. Cook over low heat or in a 300° F. oven 2 to 3 hours, or until most of the liquid has been absorbed. Serve lukewarm.

ASSORTED VEGETABLES AND GREENS

*DANDELION GREENS WITH CRISPY ONIONS

This can be a delicious mezze, a vegetable accompaniment, or a simple main dish for lunch. All sorts of other winter greens (escarole, curly endive, kale, mustard greens, Swiss chard, or spinach) can be prepared in the same way, but I personally think dandelion greens work best.

The greens and the onions are simmered in olive oil until the onions turn sweet, and the dish turns thick and rich. It is then garnished with crisp fried onions and served warm or at room temperature. Garnish with lemon wedges and sliced radishes.

Serves 2 to 3 or up to 6 as a mezze

I. Heat the oil in a 9- or 10-inch skillet. Pat the onions dry between paper towels. Add the onions to the skillet; cook over medium-low heat, stirring often, until golden, about 10 minutes. Remove half the onions with a slotted spoon and set aside to cool. Increase the heat and continue cooking the remaining onions, until crisp and golden brown, about 5 minutes. Transfer the fried onions with a slotted spoon to paper toweling to drain.

continued

3 tablespoons olive oil
2 medium onions, peeled and thinly sliced
1½ pounds dandelion greens, washed and stemmed
Pinch of coarse sea salt
1 garlic clove, peeled and crushed with salt
2 tablespoons fresh lemon juice
Salt and pepper to taste
4 lemon wedges for garnish
2 sliced radishes

2. Meanwhile, blanch or microwave the greens with the sea salt until just tender. Drain, refresh, and squeeze out excess water. Shred the greens and chop the reserved golden-stage onions. Place the greens and these onions in the skillet, add the garlic, and cook until thick and soft to the bite, about 5 minutes, stirring often. Stir in the lemon juice and adjust the seasoning with salt and pepper. Serve warm, sprinkled with the crisp onions and surrounded with the lemon wedges and radishes.

NOTES TO THE COOK: The fried onions can be prepared separately and kept, uncovered, 1 to 2 days in a cool place.

ADZHARIAN-STYLE GREEN BEANS WITH CINNAMON-FLAVORED YOGURT SAUCE

This light, flavorful, creamy, putty-hued dish of beans is a famous accompaniment to Chicken *Tabaka* (page 315). The beans are cooked until really soft—first in boiling water to break down their woodiness, then gently in buttery juices. After this procedure, even the toughest beans finally fall into silken "strings." The beans are served coated with a cinnamon-flecked yogurt sauce, with the usual extravagant Georgian assortment of herbs.

Serves 2 to 4

1. In a large bowl, combine the yogurt, cinnamon, sugar, and saffron, if desired; blend well. Set aside.

2. Bring a large saucepan of water with sea salt to a boil and cook the beans 10 minutes, or until just tender; drain. When cool enough to handle, press out excess moisture. Cut into 1-inch pieces.

3. In a large skillet, melt 1 tablespoon of the butter over moderate heat. Add the scallions and the garlic, cover, and cook 2 minutes. Add the beans and the remaining butter, cover tightly, and reduce the heat to low. Cook until the beans are soft, about 10 to 15 minutes, depending upon their thickness. Remove from the heat and mix in the dill and mixed herbs. Season with salt and pepper. Add the yogurt mixture and toss with the beans over low heat for an instant to blend the flavors. Serve warm or at room temperature.

¾ cup plain low-fat yogurt
¼ teaspoon ground cinnamon
⅛ teaspoon sugar
Pinch of powdered saffron (optional)
Sea salt
½ pound string beans, washed, with ends snapped off
4 tablespoons unsalted butter
3 scallions, chopped (½ cup)
1 small garlic clove, peeled and chopped
2 tablespoons chopped dill
2 tablespoons chopped mixed herbs, such as summer savory, coriander, mint, and tarragon
Salt and freshly ground black pepper to taste

NEVIN HALICI'S MIXED VEGETABLES WITH TWO SAUCES

⁌⁓⁍

Nevin Halici, a scholar and cookbook author, has the face of a monastic saint. Calm, self-contained, spiritual, and imbued with an almost mystical approach to cooking, she always wears a white dervish turban when out of doors.

To visit Nevin, in the central Anatolian city of Konya, I drove three hours south from Ankara. Konya, set in a vast plateau, is perhaps the most traditional and religious city in Turkey. Its skyline is dominated by a single, perfect green-tiled fluted tower—the tomb of one of the world's greatest mystics, the thirteenth-century ecumenical saint named Mevlana, founder of the Order of the Whirling Dervishes.

Mevlana, in his writings, often related life to the kitchen, referring to it as the "sacred heart, a temple." These writings got Nevin interested in researching and recording Turkish regional cuisine. So far she has published five books on the subject, with more to come. She and her family also sponsor a biannual food festival, cooking competition, and international food symposium.

In Konya, when I was Nevin's guest, she and I spent mornings at the market, and long, lazy afternoons talking about food and cooking. As it turned out, we had the same shopping strategy, always preferring to see what is available and fresh rather than planning our meals in advance.

At Konya's central open-air market, I was impressed with the impeccable quality of the locally grown fruits and vegetables: juicy cherries, plums, and loquats, and magnificent eggplants, peppers, zucchinis, onions, and tomatoes. But I was struck, too, by the lack of such common vegetables as carrots. Nevin explained that a Turkish cook, forced to use the same ingredients again and again, must know numerous ways of combining and preparing them, and, through the use of spices, herbs, aromatics, and techniques, ways of infusing ingredients with bold and extraordinary flavors.

A good example was an impromptu dish she made for me one day with a sampling of what we had bought. "This is similar to an old-time dish people prepared from vegetables in their gardens," she said, while she sliced some eggplants and zucchinis and fried them in oil, then stewed several tomatoes.

"If a guest showed up, the cook would simply run out to her garden, gather some vegetables, then put together something personal and tasty to eat."

She layered the fried vegetables to look like the petals of a flower, then topped them with two sauces—the first, a fresh tomato sauce with a mild tart edge of vinegar, and the second, on top of the tomato sauce, a superb silken-textured yogurt sauce made by diluting concentrated yogurt with fresh water. The result— sweet, creamy, healthy, and wonderfully embellished vegetables. I found the simple dish absolutely superb. In this adaptation, the vegetables are baked in the oven.

Serves 2 to 4

1. Remove the stem and blossom ends from the eggplants and zucchinis. Slice on the diagonal into ½-inch-thick rounds. Spread the slices on paper towels, sprinkle with the coarse salt, and let stand 20 minutes. Rinse and pat dry.

2. Meanwhile, preheat the oven to 425° F.

3. Gradually whisk the cold water into the yogurt until creamy and smooth. Beat in the pureed garlic and set aside to mellow.

4. Lightly coat a baking sheet with olive oil; arrange the eggplants, zucchinis, and chilis on the sheet in a single layer and lightly coat with oil. Bake the vegetables 10 to 12 minutes. Remove the chilis and reserve. Turn the eggplants and zucchinis over and bake until golden brown and fully cooked, about 15 minutes. Using a spatula, transfer the slices, overlapping slightly, to a flat serving dish.

¾ pound garden-fresh zucchinis
¾ pound garden-fresh eggplants
Coarse salt

YOGURT-GARLIC SAUCE
2 to 3 tablespoons cold water
⅔ cup all-natural (no gum stabilizers) nonfat plain yogurt, drained to one half its volume; for directions on draining yogurt, see page 410
¼ teaspoon garlic, peeled and crushed with ⅛ teaspoon salt
Olive oil
2 mildly hot New Mexican (Anaheim) green chilis

TOMATO SAUCE
3 medium ripe tomatoes
1 teaspoon olive oil
½ teaspoon sugar
Salt to taste
¾ teaspoon red wine vinegar
⅛ teaspoon garlic, peeled and crushed with salt

5. Halve the tomatoes, squeeze out the seeds, and roughly chop the flesh. In a small skillet, gently heat 1 teaspoon olive oil and add the tomatoes. Cook about 10 minutes, uncovered, until the tomatoes absorb their juices and reduce to about 1 cup. Push through a strainer and return to the skillet. Add the sugar, salt, vinegar, and ⅛ teaspoon crushed garlic and bring to a boil, stirring, and reduce to about half. Cover the skillet, reduce the heat to very low, and cook 2 to 3 minutes. (To preserve the fragrance of the vinegar and garlic, do not uncover the skillet until ready to assemble.) Spoon the tomato sauce over the arranged vegetables. Top with the yogurt sauce, surround with the chilis, and serve at once.

ALL-MIXED-UP VEGETABLE STEW

If a country has a popular national dish that combines all the bright and earthy vegetables of the sun—eggplants, tomatoes, peppers, and garlic—that country most likely borders on the Mediterranean. Georgia, of course, is not on the Mediterranean but, as mentioned earlier, is definitely Mediterranean in spirit, as this all-mixed-up vegetable stew surely attests. The Georgians call it *adzapsandali* (which means, literally, "making a mess").

It is similar to a ratatouille, but heady with herbs, spices, and hot pepper.

The dish is better if made 1 to 2 days before serving; the flavors have time to mingle, and the stew will look less like a mess and more like a well-formed whole.

Serves 6 to 8

1. Layer the eggplant cubes in a colander, sprinkling them with the coarse salt. Weight and leave to drain at least 30 minutes. Rinse the eggplant and squeeze gently to extract the bitter juices.

2. In a large nonstick skillet, heat the oil over high heat. Working in batches, add a single layer of eggplant to the skillet and sauté, turning to brown on all sides, about 2 minutes. With a slotted spoon, transfer the cubes to a strainer set over a bowl; reserve any oil that drains out.

3. Reduce the heat to low and return any drained oil to the skillet. Add the onions, cover, and cook 1 minute. With a slotted spoon, transfer the onions to a large Dutch oven; set aside. Add the potatoes to the skillet and cook, stirring, 1 minute, then add them to the Dutch oven. Add the red and green peppers to the skillet and cook, stirring, until glossy, about 2 minutes; set aside.

4. Layer the eggplant cubes over the onions and potatoes in the Dutch oven, followed by the tomato slices and pepper rings. Add the crushed garlic, minced chili, cinnamon, sugar, and salt and pepper. Cover and cook over low heat until the potatoes are tender, about 15 minutes. Stir in the chopped herbs, cover, and cook 1 minute longer. Let cool to room temperature; cover and refrigerate 1 to 2 days.

5. Let the vegetables return to room temperature before serving. If desired, add a little mild vinegar and more salt and pepper. Sprinkle with more herbs before serving.

2 medium eggplants (about 1¾ pounds total weight), peeled and cut into 1-inch cubes

1 teaspoon coarse salt

⅓ cup olive oil

3 medium yellow onions, coarsely chopped (about 3 cups)

1 pound waxy potatoes, peeled and cut into 1-inch cubes

1 medium red bell pepper, cored, seeded, and sliced into ¼-inch rings

1 medium green bell pepper, cored, seeded, and sliced into ¼-inch rings

3 medium ripe tomatoes, thinly sliced

3 cloves garlic, peeled and crushed with salt

½ long, thin green chili, seeded and minced (about 1½ teaspoons)

¼ teaspoon ground cinnamon

¼ teaspoon sugar

Salt and freshly ground black pepper to taste

1 cup chopped herbs—a combination of basil, mint, coriander, and parsley—plus 1 to 2 tablespoons for garnish

Mild vinegar to taste (optional)

SPINACH ROOTS AND STEMS WITH LEMON AND OLIVE OIL

When you clean fresh spinach, don't throw away those roots and stems. Turks smother a lamb stew with them (page 351), and they can be used in this delightful and different-tasting salad, earthy and pungent.

The salad is small and can be quickly made to be served as a separate dish, even if you are also serving spinach leaves. It is also good with an almond or pine nut *tarator* dressing (page 20).

Serves 2 to 4

1½ to 2 dozen bunches of fresh spinach roots and stems
   (collected from approximately 2 pounds fresh spinach)
3 tablespoons extra-virgin olive oil
Juice of ½ lemon
Salt to taste
Freshly ground black pepper to taste

Wash spinach in several changes of water. Cut off the leaves and save for some other purpose. Halve each "clump" of stems and roots and soak in water to loosen any grit. Steam the stems and roots until just tender. Refresh under cool running water; drain and gently press out excess moisture. Place in a salad bowl. Combine the remaining ingredients, pour over the stems and roots, toss once, and serve.

STEWED POTATOES WITH TOMATOES AND FETA

Here is a simple peasant dish from northern Greece. The potatoes are cut into thick wedges, like apples cut for a pie. The dish is equally good served hot or warm, with feta.

Serves 2

In a 10-inch deep-sided skillet, heat the oil and sauté the onion over moderate heat until soft and golden. Add the garlic, tomato sauce, water, parsley, and salt and pepper. Bring to a boil, add the potatoes, cover tightly, lower the heat, and cook 30 minutes, or until the potatoes are tender and the sauce is thickened. Serve warm or hot, with slices of feta on the side and good crusty bread.

1½ tablespoons olive oil
1 cup chopped onion
2 cloves garlic, peeled and minced
1 cup tomato sauce
1 cup water
2 tablespoons chopped parsley
Salt and freshly ground black pepper to taste
4 waxy medium potatoes (1 pound), peeled and cut into 6 wedges
4 slices imported feta

FOUR
EGGPLANT
~ DISHES ~

EGGPLANT TROTTERS STEAMED
IN TOMATO SAUCE

Here is an extremely easy, low-fat eggplant dish so good that I recommend you use a piece of bread to wipe up the sauce. The strange name is a reference to the bouncy feature and garlic-vinegar pungency of a plate of well cooked lamb's trotters.

Serves 4 to 6

6 eggplants (1½ pounds total weight)

3 cups water mixed with the juice of 1 lemon

1 teaspoon olive oil

1½ pounds ripe tomatoes, peeled, seeded, and cubed, with juices reserved

Juice of ½ lemon

Salt

1 12-by-12-inch sheet of parchment paper

6 to 7 cloves garlic, peeled

4 to 5 tablespoons mild white wine vinegar

2 tablespoons chopped parsley for garnish

1. Peel the eggplants and cut into 1-by-2-inch pieces. As you peel the eggplants, drop them into a bowl of the water mixed with lemon juice.

2. Drain the eggplants and place in a 10-inch skillet. Add the olive oil, tomatoes, lemon juice, and ½ teaspoon salt. Wet and crumble a sheet of parchment; place it directly over the contents in the skillet, cover with a tight-fitting lid, and set to cook over medium heat 10 minutes, shaking the pan from time to time.

3. Meanwhile, chop enough garlic to make I tablespoon. Sprinkle with salt and crush to a puree. Dilute the garlic with the vinegar and stir into the tomato sauce. If the pan juices are a little dry, add some of the reserved tomato juice. Recover the dish with crumbled wet parchment and the lid and cook another 10 minutes. Remove the skillet from the heat without removing the cover. Allow to cool to room temperature. Serve with a garnish of the chopped parsley.

TWO VARIATIONS

In Izmir, fried minced green chilis are added to make a hotter version.

To create a rural Aegean variation, add fried chunks of Italian green frying peppers.

DEEP-FRIED EGGPLANT FANS WITH RED CABBAGE SALAD

In this recipe, thin Italian or Japanese eggplants are fan sliced (left attached at the stem), poached in salted water, drained dry, dusted in flour and beaten egg, then fried until crisp and golden. They look beautiful and taste great, covered with a salad of shredded red cabbage, chopped cherry tomatoes, and small black olives dressed with a lemon vinaigrette. You can also serve these fried fans the way it is done in the town of Trabzon, Turkey, by the Black Sea, with a yogurt-garlic sauce (page 27).

Serves 4

continued

4 Japanese or elongated Italian eggplants, garden fresh with
    bright green stems
Coarse sea salt to taste
I cup olive oil
2 eggs, well beaten
¼ cup water
Flour for dredging

RED CABBAGE SALAD
I cup shredded red cabbage
10 cherry tomatoes
½ cup chopped parsley
½ teaspoon garlic, peeled and crushed with salt
I tablespoon olive oil
I teaspoon cider vinegar

1. Wash the eggplants and make an inch-wide continuous strip from one side of the stem to the other side. Using a long, thin knife, make three slits, lengthwise, through each eggplant. Gently press down on each to create fans.

2. Place the eggplants in a nonreactive saucepan; cover with salted water and an inverted plate to keep them submerged. Bring to a boil and cook over medium-high heat 7 to 10 minutes. Use a slotted spatula to transfer the eggplants to kitchen toweling and leave to drain. When cool, gently flatten each eggplant to express moisture. (Up to this point the recipe can be made up to 2 hours in advance.)

3. Combine all the ingredients for the salad and set aside.

4. Slowly heat the olive oil in a 9-inch skillet to hot but not smoking. Beat the eggs with the water. Dredge the eggplants in flour, dust off the excess, and dip into the egg mixture. Fry, turning once, until golden on both sides. Drain on paper towels. Serve hot or at room temperature with the prepared salad.

Inspired by a recipe in Turkish Cooking *by Gülseren Ramazanoğlu*

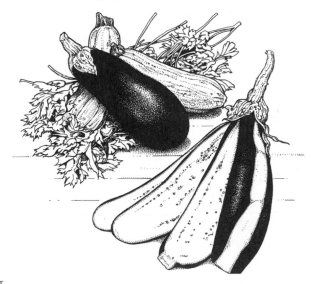

SLOW-GRILLED EGGPLANTS

This wonderful, exceedingly simple preparation is a specialty of Sotiri's Place in Salonika, a modern, very "in" *ouzeria*, known to the cognoscenti for the wry humor of its owner and its delicious food.

Use only garden-fresh medium-large glistening eggplants, thick around the middle. Cook slowly over hot coals coated with ash, so that the interiors will be moist and buttery and the skin will turn completely black. The longer and slower you cook the eggplants, the creamier they will be. I have left eggplants over hardwood coals for as long as an hour.

Serve whole, to be eaten like a baked potato as a first course.

Serves 4

1. Begin the charcoal fire and allow the coals to turn to ash before cooking. You will need a supply of coals to keep a steady heat for about half an hour.

2. Wash and dry the eggplants and prick each one once with a toothpick. Place the eggplants far enough from the hot white coals so that they will cook slowly and evenly. Turn the eggplants only as each side becomes black and soft. They are done when they have turned completely black and soft on all sides. Transfer to a serving dish and peel off the skin on the top side. Let cool 5 minutes.

4 thick, plump purple-black eggplants (each 10 to 11 ounces)
1½ tablespoons extra-virgin olive oil
1 tablespoon fresh lemon juice
Pinch of crumbled dried Mediterranean oregano
¼ teaspoon fine salt
Pinch of sugar
Pinch of freshly ground black pepper
2 tablespoons chopped parsley

3. Meanwhile, combine the oil, lemon juice, oregano, salt, sugar, and pepper in a small bowl.

4. Slip each eggplant onto an individual dish so that the peeled side is up. Use a small knife to make 3 or 4 crisscrossing slashes into the buttery pulp, whisk the olive oil dressing until well combined, and spoon a little over each serving. Gently press the dressing into the pulp with a fork. Top with the parsley and serve.

GRILLED BABY EGGPLANTS WITH EGG AND LEMON SAUCE

Here is a quick version of the preceding recipe that you can prepare on a stove-top burner.

Serves 2

2 6-ounce eggplants
I large egg
Juice of ½ lemon
½ cup heated poultry stock

I. Wrap eggplants individually in foil; place over stove-top burners set to high heat; cook until eggplants collapse on all sides, about 20 minutes. Split open on one side.

2. Meanwhile, in a small heavy saucepan, beat the egg until pale and foamy. Slowly beat in the lemon juice, a few drops at a time. Then gradually drizzle in the stock and cook, stirring, over low heat until thickened. Do not allow the sauce to boil, but cook it about 3 minutes, then pour immediately over the eggplants and serve.

THREE VEGETABLE ·❧· DISHES WITH A MEATY FLAVOR

SMOKY EGGPLANT-YOGURT FOAM WITH LAMB CRISPS

The Turkish name of this Gaziantep specialty is *Ali Nazik*, which means "the gentle pasha." It is a dish of thick yogurt blended with the palest, creamiest eggplant flesh, and topped with crumbly, crispy bits of lamb. At the end a flourish of sizzling butter and red and black pepper is poured on top.

In the original recipe, coarse-ground lamb shoulder cooks slowly in a deep pan in its own fat, with gradual additions of boiling water to keep it tender. In the end, it is allowed to fry crisp before it is drained and highly seasoned with spices.

In my adaptation, I use meat from the leg (or a slice of tender beef), cut into tiny dice and cooked quickly in a nonstick skillet so it turns crispy but stays juicy within.

The finesse of the dish lies in its subtleties, one of which is keeping the eggplant flesh as pale as possible. The trick is to place the peeled eggplant in water mixed with lemon juice in order to "bleach" it and sharpen its taste.

For superior flavor, grill the eggplants over hardwood coals (see page 401 for mail order sources).

This recipe is served as a main course for 4 in Gaziantep, but also works well as a vegetable dish for 6. Plan to use a shallow 8-inch serving dish, and accompany it with sliced green chilis, flat bread, and salad.

Serves 6 as a vegetable dish

continued

2 large very fresh eggplants (I pound each)

8 to 10 ounces cubed lean beef steak or I thin slice leg of
lamb, trimmed of fat and center bone removed

I cup water

5 tablespoons lemon juice (juice of 2 lemons)

1/4 teaspoon salt

2 cloves garlic, peeled and crushed with 1/4 teaspoon salt

4 cups low-fat plain yogurt, drained to 2 cups (for directions
on draining yogurt, see page 410)

2 teaspoons unsalted butter or I 1/2 teaspoons olive oil

Salt and freshly ground black pepper to taste

Near East or Aleppo pepper to taste (page 395)

FLOURISH

2 teaspoons butter or olive oil

3/4 teaspoon freshly ground black pepper, pressed through a
sieve

Pinch of Near East or Aleppo pepper

I. To grill the eggplants over hardwood coals: Begin a hardwood fire and allow the coals to turn to ash. Prick each eggplant three or four times with a toothpick. Bury them in ashes or set on a grid far enough from the hot coals so that they cook slowly and evenly. Turn as each side becomes black and the flesh very soft, about 30 minutes total cooking time. Transfer immediately to a bowl of cold water.

2. Meanwhile, with a mallet, pound the beef or lamb until it is 1/8-inch thick. Cut into 1/8-inch cubes.

3. As soon as an eggplant is cool enough to handle, lift and hold it by the calyx and quickly peel away the skin from the top down. Place the peeled eggplants in a bowl with the water, 4 tablespoons of the lemon juice, and the salt. Allow the flesh to "bleach" for at least 20 minutes. Remove the eggplants; gently press out all the moisture and place on a wooden work surface. Chop with a stainless steel knife. Add the garlic and the remaining lemon juice. Loosen the yogurt with 2 to 3 tablespoons water, then gradually fold into the mashed eggplant.

4. Spread an even layer of the eggplant mixture into the bottom of a shallow heat-proof 8-inch serving dish. Cover the dish and set over simmering water or in a low oven in order to warm it gently.

5. Heat the butter or olive oil in a medium-size nonstick skillet, add the meat, and cook over high heat, stirring I minute. Reduce the heat to medium, cover, and cook 5 more minutes, shaking the skillet occasionally. Season liberally with salt, black pepper and Near East pepper, and remove from the heat.

6. To make the flourish: Spread the crispy lamb bits over the eggplant in one even layer. Wipe out the skillet; add fresh butter or olive oil and heat to just a sizzle. Add the sieved black pepper and the pinch of Near East pepper, and let sizzle for an instant. Spoon over the meat and serve at once.

STEWED GREENS WITH A MEAT FLAVOR

Boiled vegetables will always taste better after a quick sauté in olive oil or with a little olive oil poured on top. A delicious Armenian way to flavor them is to stew them in meat juices.

Serves 4

1. Heat the butter in a large skillet and add the meat bones. Cover the skillet and cook the bones over medium heat, turning them occasionally, until well browned on all sides. Add 1 cup water, ½ teaspoon pepper, and a pinch of salt, and cook at a simmer, uncovered, 10 minutes. There should be only about 1 to 2 tablespoons thick, intensely flavored meat juices left in the skillet. Discard the bones or use them to make a light stock.

1½ teaspoons unsalted butter
½ pound lamb or beef bones
Freshly ground black pepper
Salt
12 ounces beet greens, spinach, nettles, or any other leafy spring greens
½ cup yogurt-garlic sauce (page 27)

2. Meanwhile, wash, stem, and drain the greens. Cook, covered, in a saucepan until wilted, about 5 minutes. Immediately drain and refresh under cold running water. Squeeze dry and roughly chop.

3. Reheat the reduced juices in the skillet. Add the greens and cook gently, stirring, 5 minutes. Season with salt and pepper to taste. Pile the greens onto a shallow serving dish, mound the yogurt-garlic sauce in the center, and serve warm or at room temperature.

NOTES TO THE COOK: Hard and acrid leafy greens should be blanched awhile in plenty of boiling water to preserve nutritional value, flavor, and color, while removing some of their pungency, gassiness, and sharpness.

If you have 1 cup degreased meat stock on hand, boil it down to 2 tablespoons and begin with step 2.

OKRA WAIKI

"We take food very seriously here, and we are great carnivores," said my hostess, Souhelia Talos, a fine home cook in Aleppo. Souhelia, dressed in a gray track suit, was about to prepare a meal of five dishes, each of which was to include some form of lamb or beef. The dishes ranged from kibbeh and meat-stuffed vegetables to delicious preparations in which ground meat was used as a condiment or sauce thickener. The large proportion of vegetables to meat is typical of Mediterranean stews. In fact, I calculated that each person at that meal consumed less than 3 ounces of meat.

Serves 4 to 6

1 pound small, tender okra

2 sweet red peppers, seeded, deribbed, and cut into small pieces (1 pound total weight)

½ long red or green chili, seeded, deribbed, and minced

Pinch of salt

2 tablespoons olive oil

¾ pound ground beef

1½ tablespoons garlic, peeled and crushed with salt

2 teaspoons ground coriander seeds

2 tablespoons tomato paste

Salt and freshly ground black pepper to taste

1 cup water

1 tablespoon fresh lemon juice or more to taste

Pinch of sugar

Fresh coriander sprigs, lemon slices, and pita triangles (for garnish)

1. To simulate the tiny okra, the size of thumbnails, required for this dish, prepare the okra the night before. Wash it under cool running water and drain. Cut off the entire top stem, then cut the pod into ¾-inch lengths. Spread out on kitchen towels and leave to dry overnight at room temperature.

2. To make a red pepper paste, grind the peppers and chili with ½ cup water and a pinch of salt in the work bowl of a food processor. Transfer to a saucepan and cook over high heat, stirring often, until reduced to a jamlike consistency and yielding about ½ cup.

3. Heat the oil in a heavy 3-quart casserole. Add the beef. Cook over medium-high heat until browned and glistening, about 5 minutes. Stir in the okra, garlic, ground coriander seeds, ½ cup red pepper paste, tomato

paste, and salt and pepper. Cover tightly and cook over low heat 20 minutes. Shake the pan from time to time to avoid scorching. (Up to this point, the recipe can be prepared many hours in advance.)

4. Twenty minutes before serving, stir in 1 cup water, lemon juice, and sugar. Reheat, gently, 10 minutes before serving. Garnish with 2 or 3 sprigs of fresh coriander, lemon slices, and pita triangles.

VIII

Stuffed Fruits & Vegetables

STUFFING FRUITS AND VEGETABLES

In the culinary world of the eastern Mediterranean region, home cooks vie for acclaim for the ingenuity of their stuffed fruits and vegetables. The best of their recipes play intricate balancing acts, combining sweet and savory tastes—with rice, pine nuts, dried currants, and spices, then pitting these combinations against pungent, concentrated flavors, such as those of pomegranates, lemons, sumac, or tamarind.

Nuances of texture are important too. For example, the subtle crunch of almonds matched with chicken and spices, all stuffed inside an apple, or the firm but buttery addition of cracked chickpeas to rice, lemon, and chopped herbs stuffed inside Swiss chard leaves.

Exploring the dishes, I found fascinating combinations, most of which appear in this chapter: tomatoes and chickpeas with allspice; cabbage and rice with mint and garlic; quinces and almonds with cloves; eggplants and pomegranates with pine nuts; green tomatoes and walnuts with cilantro, basil, and dill.

In the recipes that follow, the fruits and vegetables are not used merely to contain a second food. In a properly stuffed fruit or vegetable dish, the shell and filling always work together, the former giving body and the latter multidimensional flavor. Many of these recipes require vegetables cooked to a point of melting tenderness, antithetical to crisp young vegetables cooked al dente, so much in vogue today.

As the seasons turn, regional cooks construct stuffed vegetable dishes out of the produce available in the markets. In winter, Macedonians stuff whole cabbages or their separate leaves with meats, bread, or rice and all sorts of spices and aromatics, then braise them to a succulent texture.

Turks use small baby eggplants that have been hollowed out and carefully dried the previous summer. The taste of a rehydrated eggplant is stronger than that of a young fresh eggplant and calls for a lusty filling, such as bulgur, peppers, and a little meat, all simmered in a sumac-flavored broth.

In spring and early summer, tender vine leaves, sorrel, spinach, beet greens, and Swiss chard are stuffed, each having its own special flavor and texture.

continued

The great season for stuffing is the end of summer, when the bulk of the harvest floods in. Then there are eggplants to be hollowed out or halved, and juicy, ripe tomatoes to be scooped and stuffed. Large, leafy collard greens are stuffed with meat and rice and flavored with tomatoes and mint. Dewy squash blossoms, picked in the early morning, are an ideal stuffing medium, as are zucchinis and peppers of all colors and flavors.

Finally, in autumn, apples, quinces, pumpkins, and artichokes are all ready for stuffing.

Once stuffed, these fruits and vegetables can be baked, poached, fried, steamed, or grilled. Most can be prepared in advance. Little skill is required, but such dishes do take time and are not suitable for the hurried cook. Rather, they are for the cook who loves to work with produce and who knows that good food cooked lovingly always repays its maker a hundred times.

After years of fascination with the whys and hows of successfully stuffing vegetables, here are my collected guidelines, the combined wisdom of numerous eastern Mediterranean home cooks.

Short- or medium-grain white rice is best for stuffing, because it naturally becomes compact instead of turning fluffy. In theory, you should use a raw rice filling for eggplants, peppers, cabbages, and artichokes, for which the cooking time is fairly long, and partially cooked rice for Swiss chard leaves, tender vine leaves, tomatoes, and young zucchini. (This isn't possible if you're preparing a dish of mixed stuffed vegetables that includes eggplants, zucchinis, peppers, and tomatoes. In that case, use raw rice.)

If you use large-grain bulgur for stuffing, use it moistened but raw. Bulgur cooks more quickly than rice.

When filling the cooking vessel, pack the rolls or vegetables as close together as possible, then cover with an inverted plate, to hold the vegetables in place and to reinforce the tight fit. Add only enough boiling liquid to reach the outer rim of the plate. (With some bulky vegetables, the liquid level should be lower, about I inch below the top.)

The major point in the difference between properly and improperly cooked stuffed vegetables is this: Adding too much liquid at the beginning produces a lot of liquid left in the pan after the cooking. If you have to reduce a large quantity of liquid by boiling, the taste of the stuffing will not be as good.

The liquid should be brought quickly to a boil and left to boil 1 minute; then the pot should be covered with a tight-fitting lid, the heat turned down, and the cooking time followed as given in the recipe.

After the cooking is completed, turn off the heat and leave the vegetables covered, so that they can settle and absorb more liquid. The vegetables can then be left to cool and to be served or reheated later on.

When serving, drain any juices from the saucepan into a dish. In some cases you might want to invert the entire pot onto a shallow serving dish and then pour the reserved juices over the top.

*STUFFED EGGPLANTS WITH TOMATO-
POMEGRANATE SAUCE

Here is one of the great stuffed vegetable dishes of the Middle East; it is called according to Anne-Marie Weiss-Armush, the author of *Arabian Cuisine* (whose recipe I have adapted here), "the sheikh" of stuffed vegetable dishes, because it contains only meat—no rice or breadcrumbs. It is usually served as part of a buffet, but it can also be served warm or hot as a main course. Accompany it with rice pilaf and a small selection of vegetable dishes.

It is easy to scoop out the pulp from zucchinis or eggplants if you have a special vegetable reamer for that purpose. Otherwise, you can use an apple corer and a demitasse spoon.

Makes 4 to 5 servings as a side dish

8 to 10 small Japanese or Italian eggplants (each 3½ ounces and 4 inches long)

Coarse sea salt

2 tablespoons unsalted butter

I large onion, finely chopped

¾ pound lean lamb shoulder, coarsely ground

½ teaspoon Syrian Mixed Spices, Number I (page 397)

¼ teaspoon freshly ground black pepper

½ cup (2 ounces) pine nuts, toasted

I tablespoon olive oil

¼ green frying pepper or bell pepper, thinly sliced

1½ tablespoons tomato paste

1½ teaspoons pomegranate molasses (page 404)

I 12"-x-12" sheet of parchment paper

½ teaspoon fresh lemon juice

Sugar

4 to 5 flat-leaf parsley sprigs for garnish

I. Gently roll each eggplant back and forth 4 or 5 times on a work surface to soften it and facilitate the removal of the insides. Remove the stems and discard. Use a vegetable reamer or an apple corer and a demitasse spoon to tunnel through the eggplant to within ¼ inch of the end. Rotate the reamer or corer to scoop out the pulp, leaving a ⅛-inch shell and taking care not to break through the skin; discard the pulp. Fill a large bowl with water, stir in 2 teaspoons coarse sea salt until dissolved, add the eggplants, and set aside to soak.

2. In a heavy medium skillet, melt I tablespoon of the butter over moderately low heat. Add the onion, cover, and cook 5 minutes. Uncover and cook, stirring occasionally, until soft but not brown, about 10 minutes. Increase the heat to moderate and add the lamb, breaking up the meat with a fork. Cook until no longer pink, about 3 minutes. Stir in ½ teaspoon coarse sea salt, the mixed spices, black pepper, and 3 tablespoons water. Cook until all the water has evaporated, about 2 minutes. Remove from the heat and fold in the pine nuts. Season to taste with salt and black pepper. Set aside to cool. Wash out the skillet.

3. Drain the eggplants and pat dry with paper towels. Using a small spoon or melon baller, pack each eggplant with the meat stuffing. Reserve any extra stuffing.

4. In the same skillet, heat the oil and the remaining butter, add the stuffed eggplants, and fry in batches, turning, until lightly browned on all sides. In a 5-quart casserole, arrange the eggplants in one layer. Add any leftover filling, then tuck the pepper slices between the eggplants.

5. Drain any excess fat from the skillet and add 1½ cups water, the tomato paste, pomegranate molasses, lemon juice, and pinches of salt and black pepper to taste; bring to a boil over high heat. Pour the sauce over the eggplants, top with a round of wet, crumbled parchment, then a lid; cook, covered, over low heat until very tender, about 30 minutes. Allow the eggplants to rest 10 minutes in the casserole.

6. Carefully transfer the eggplants to a serving dish. Strain the pan juices. If the sauce is too thin, rapidly reduce it to a creamy consistency. Adjust the seasoning with salt, black pepper, and sugar to taste. Spoon over the eggplants, scatter the parsley on top, and serve warm.

NOTES TO THE COOK: You can substitute small zucchinis for the Japanese eggplants. If you do, reduce the cooking time to 15 minutes.

STUFFED EGGPLANTS WITH YOGURT

‑‑‑

My husband, who collects Middle Eastern daggers, struck up an acquaintance with the director of the Military Museum in Damascus. When the subject changed to food, the face of the courtly curator lit up like a lantern. "My favorite dish of all," he said, "is *fatta al batignan*, because of the melting quality of the eggplant—the way it holds its shape but still melts in your mouth like butter."

The curator left us for a few minutes, then returned to tell us that he had just spoken to his wife and we were invited to his home the following evening to taste the dish, or even earlier if I wanted to learned how to make it—which, of course, I did.

His wife, Maja, which means "zebra's eyes," was beautiful and serene, with porcelain-white skin. She, her two daughters, and two sons proceeded to prepare a feast, serving some of the finest Damascene specialties, including this glorious stuffed eggplant dish, her husband's favorite.

Serves 5 to 6 as a main course

10 to 12 small Italian eggplants (each about 3½ ounces and 4 inches long)

2 teaspoons coarse sea salt

FILLING

1 tablespoon unsalted butter or olive oil

1 pound lean boneless lamb shoulder, coarsely ground

½ teaspoon salt

¼ teaspoon freshly ground black pepper

¾ teaspoon Syrian Mixed Spices, Number 1 (page 417)

3 tablespoons water

½ cup pine nuts (2 ounces), toasted

1. Gently roll each eggplant back and forth 4 or 5 times on a work surface to soften it and facilitate the removal of the insides. Remove the stems and discard. Use a vegetable reamer or an apple corer and demitasse spoon to tunnel through the eggplant to within ¼-inch of the end. Rotate the reamer or corer to scoop out the pulp, leaving a ⅛-inch shell and taking care not to break through the skin; discard the pulp. Fill a large bowl with water, stir in sea salt until dissolved, add the eggplants, and set aside to soak.

2. Make the filling: In a 10-inch straight-sided skillet, melt the butter or olive oil over

moderately low heat. Add the meat, cover, and steam 3 minutes. Uncover and cook, stirring occasionally, until the meat is broken up and no longer pink, about 2 minutes. Pour off the fat, add the salt, pepper, mixed spices, and 3 tablespoons water; cook, uncovered, until all the water has evaporated, about 2 minutes. Remove from the heat and fold in the toasted pine nuts. Season again to taste with salt, pepper, and mixed spices. Set aside to cool. Wash out the skillet.

3. Begin making the tomato-onion sauce: Heat 1 tablespoon of the butter or oil in a 5-quart casserole, add the onions, and cook, covered, over low heat for 10 minutes, stirring often, until the onions are very soft. Stir in the tomato paste and allow it to sizzle, about 1 minute. Add the salt, mixed spices, green pepper, and 6 cups water; bring to a boil and continue simmering while preparing the eggplants.

4. Drain the eggplants and stuff each with the cooled filling. If necessary, use a demitasse spoon or a small melon baller to gently push in the stuffing. Heat remaining 2 tablespoons butter or oil in the washed skillet over medium heat. Place the eggplants, side by side, in the skillet, and sauté each until the eggplant is golden brown on one side, about 5 minutes. Turn and continue browning on the second side, 5 minutes.

5. Add pomegranate molasses to the casserole with the tomato-onion sauce, stirring to combine. Use a slotted spoon to transfer the eggplants to the simmering sauce. Place a weight such as a heat-proof plate or a glass lid just large enough to fit inside the casserole directly on the eggplants. Add additional water if necessary to just barely surround the rim of the plate. Bring to a boil, boil vigorously 1 minute, lower the heat, cover the casserole, and simmer 30 minutes. Remove from the heat and do not uncover for 10 minutes. (Up to this point, the recipe can be prepared many hours in advance.)

THE TOMATO-ONION SAUCE

3 tablespoons unsalted butter or olive oil

4 large red onions (2 pounds), thinly sliced

3 tablespoons tomato paste

1 teaspoon salt

½ teaspoon Syrian Mixed Spices, Number 1

¼ cup chopped green bell pepper

6 cups water

1 tablespoon pomegranate molasses (page 429)

Salt, freshly ground black pepper, sugar, and fresh lemon juice

THE YOGURT SAUCE

4 cups plain low-fat yogurt

2 tablespoons sesame seed paste (tahini)

2 cloves garlic, peeled and crushed with ½ teaspoon salt

Pinch of Syrian Mixed Spices, Number 1

6 stale whole wheat pitas (12 ounces), toasted and diced

GARNISH

⅓ cup blanched almonds, toasted or browned in unsalted butter

¼ cup pomegranate seeds

½ teaspoon Syrian Mixed Spices, Number 1

¼ cup chopped flat-leaf parsley

6. Make the yogurt sauce: In a bowl, combine the yogurt with the sesame seed paste, garlic, and mixed spices. Set aside.

7. Ten minutes before serving, reheat the eggplants in the tomato-onion sauce until hot. Remove the eggplants to a side dish. You should have about 4½ cups tomato-onion sauce; if not, reduce by rapidly boiling to a creamy consistency. Adjust the seasoning with salt, pepper, sugar, and sharpen the sauce with a few drops of lemon juice.

8. Spread a layer of pitas on individual plates. Spoon equal amounts of tomato-onion sauce over each portion of bread and cover with a thin layer of yogurt sauce. Arrange the eggplants on top and coat with the remaining yogurt sauce. Garnish with almonds, pomegranate seeds, mixed spices, and parsley.

ZUCCHINIS STUFFED WITH BULGUR, TOMATOES, AND HOT PEPPER

This is a simplified version of one of the most extraordinary *dolmas* (stuffed vegetable) I have seen.

Mrs. Aysel Budak, a champion cook in Gaziantep, prepared seven different kinds of stuffed vegetables, all cooked in the same pot, to create, she said, "a total *dolma* experience."

When she opened the pot, I was astonished by the array of vivid colors: both rehydrated and fresh eggplants, rehydrated and fresh hot and sweet green and red peppers, and pale green zucchinis—all stuffed with a meaty, spicy mixture of cracked wheat, tomatoes, and chopped green chili.

My favorite was the stuffed zucchini, with its striking silken texture. Mrs. Budak later gave me her recipe, then whispered its "secret": Add the lemon juice when the zucchinis are fully cooked.

Serve hot or warm, with a bowl of cool yogurt blended with crushed garlic.

Serves 4 to 6

1. One day before preparing the stuffed zucchinis, prepare the yogurt-garlic sauce. Keep refrigerated until ready to serve.

2. Gently scrub each zucchini; cut off about ½ inch from the flower end, and pare the end to use as a plug. Hollow out the zucchini with a vegetable reamer or an apple corer. Put a pinch of salt in each zucchini and let stand 1 hour.

3. Meanwhile, warm the oil in a wide skillet, add the onion and meat, cover, and cook over medium heat, stirring occasionally, until the meat is browned and separated, about 5 minutes. Add the tomato and cook, stirring, for an instant. Remover from the heat, add the bulgur, *baharat*, tomato paste, chili, and ¼ cup water; mix well to blend. Season well with salt and pepper. When the filling is cool enough to handle, gather it into a ball and knead until well blended.

4. Drain the zucchinis of any accumulated liquid. Loosely stuff each zucchini with the prepared mixture and plug with the pared ends. (Up to this point, the recipe can be prepared 4 to 5 hours ahead. Keep covered in the refrigerator. Add an extra 5 minutes to the cooking time in step 5.)

5. Pack the zucchinis in a 4- or 5-quart casserole. Add 1 cup water mixed with ¾ teaspoon salt and pinches of sugar and black pepper. Place a heavy, inverted plate on top of the zucchinis and gently press down so that they remain intact during cooking. Cover with a tight-fitting lid and bring to a boil. Reduce the heat to low and simmer gently ¾ hour.

6. Remove the casserole from the heat; allow to rest 15 minutes before removing the cover and plate.

7. Tilt the casserole and add the lemon juice to the remaining juices (about ½ cup) and swirl to blend the liquids. Serve warm, with the pan juices poured on top, lemon wedges, and the chilled garlic-flavored yogurt sauce on the side.

YOGURT-GARLIC SAUCE

2 cups all-natural lowfat yogurt drained to one half its volume (see page 410 for directions), blended with ½ cup water, salt to taste, and ½ teaspoon garlic, peeled and crushed with salt

12 to 16 tender zucchinis, each no larger than 6 inches, with firm, gleaming skin

Salt

1 teaspoon olive oil

1 medium onion, finely chopped

5 to 6 ounces lean ground lamb or beef

1 ripe tomato, halved, seeded, and grated (about ½ cup)

1 cup coarse-grain bulgur

½ teaspoon Turkish *baharat* (page 392)

1 teaspoon tomato paste

1 tablespoon minced fresh green chili, seeds removed

Freshly ground black pepper to taste

Sugar to taste

Juice of ½ lemon

Lemon wedges for garnish

STUFFED CABBAGE, ALEPPO STYLE

These highly seasoned stuffed cabbage leaves are formed like thin cigars. The ends are left open to allow the filling to take on more flavor from the liquid.

Mrs. Emilie Abdy, of St. Ann's Melkite Catholic Church in West Paterson, New Jersey, gave me this Aleppine recipe. She suggests blanching the cabbage leaves with an onion in the water to reduce the possibility of gastric irritation.

Serves 6

I tablespoon coarse salt
2 to 2½ pounds fresh cabbage
I medium onion, peeled

MEAT AND RICE FILLING
½ pound lean ground lamb or beef
¾ cup medium- or short-grain white rice, rinsed and drained
I grated onion
I½ teaspoons salt
¾ teaspoon freshly ground black pepper
½ teaspoon Near East or Aleppo pepper (page 395)
I cup cold water
I½ teaspoons ground allspice
4 tablespoons toasted pine nuts (optional)

COOKING LIQUID
6 cloves garlic, peeled and crushed with salt
I tablespoon dried mint
I cup tomato sauce
I tablespoon pomegranate molasses (page 404)
½ cup water
Salt and freshly ground black pepper to taste
2 lamb bones

I. Bring a large kettle of salted water, over medium-high heat, to a boil. Remove wilted or bruised outer leaves from the cabbage; cut out and discard the core, loosen the leaves at the base. Put the cabbage and the onion into the boiling water; when the water returns to a boil, cook, uncovered, 10 minutes. Drain the cabbage leaves, then rinse under cool running water; remove to a colander and drain again.

2. Meanwhile, mix the ingredients for the filling; knead well to make a loose mixture. Keep refrigerated until ready to fill the cabbage leaves.

3. Loosen the cabbage leaves. Trim thick ribbing with a thin-bladed knife. Spread the cabbage leaves out on a large work surface, outer side of the leaves down. Cut large leaves in half along the ribbing.

4. Place 2-tablespoon lumps of stuffing along one edge and roll up without tucking in the sides. Repeat the procedure with the remaining filling. Chop the remaining leaves and reserve.

5. Line a 4- or 5-quart saucepan with the reserved cabbage and lamb bones. Arrange the cabbage rolls, seam side down, on top of the trimmings. When all the rolls are in the saucepan, weight them down using a heat-proof upside-down plate just large enough to fit inside, on top of the rolls.

6. In a bowl, combine the remaining ingredients and pour around the inside of the casserole. Bring the liquid to a vigorous boil; boil 1 to 2 minutes, cover tightly, reduce the heat, and cook 30 minutes. Remove the pan from the heat and allow to rest 30 minutes. (The rolls will continue to absorb juices during this time.) The leaves can be served at once but are better if left to stand about 6 hours. Reheat gently and serve hot.

BALKAN STUFFED CABBAGE

H ere is a fine Balkan stuffed cabbage recipe. The touch of vinegar at the end provides an intriguing sharpness, which substitutes for the brined cabbage called for in the original recipe. This dish, also known as *sarma*, goes beautifully with the Balkan cheese bread on page 54.

For best flavor, make the cabbage rolls through step five early in the day or the day before. The cheese bread is best when freshly baked.

Serves 6 to 8

½ cup short-grain white rice

¼ cup chopped smoked ham or prosciutto (about 2 ounces)

I teaspoon peeled, minced garlic

4 tablespoons chopped parsley

½ teaspoon sweet paprika

Salt and freshly ground black pepper

I 3-pound head white cabbage

3 tablespoons corn oil

2 medium onions, I minced and I slivered

¾ pound ground pork

½ pound ground veal

2 eggs, lightly beaten

4 ounces smoked or slab bacon, smoked ribs, or smoked sausages, sliced (see Notes to the Cook)

I carrot, sliced

I 14-ounce can sliced tomatoes, undrained

I small lemon, thinly sliced

I tablespoon tomato paste

2 to 3 tablespoons sour cream

I teaspoon white wine vinegar

I. Soak the rice in hot water 10 minutes; drain well and place in a large mixing bowl. Add the ham, garlic, 2 tablespoons parsley, paprika, ¾ teaspoon salt and a pinch of pepper, and mix well. Set aside.

2. Bring a large kettle of salted water, over medium-high heat, to a boil. Remove wilted or bruised outer leaves from the cabbage; cut out and discard the core. Loosen the leaves at the base. Put the cabbage into the boiling water; when the water returns to a boil, cook, uncovered, 10 minutes. Drain the cabbage leaves and rinse under cool running water; remove to a colander to drain again.

3. Choose 24 of the largest leaves; trim thick ribbing with a thin-bladed knife, sprinkle the leaves with black pepper, and set aside. Chop the remaining cabbage. Press out all the moisture and set aside I cup for the stuffing in the next step and the remainder for step 6.

4. In a large skillet, heat 2 tablespoons

of the oil over medium-high heat. Add the minced onion; sauté, stirring, until lightly browned, 3 to 4 minutes. Add 1 cup of the chopped cabbage; sauté, stirring, until all the moisture has evaporated and the cabbage is lightly browned, about 5 minutes. Reduce the heat to low; add the ground meats and sauté, breaking up the meat with a fork and stirring, about 1 minute. Add to the rice mixture, stirring until well mixed. Set aside to cool, then stir in the eggs.

5. Spread the cabbage leaves out on a large work surface, the outer side of the leaf down. Place 4 tablespoons of the stuffing along one edge of a cabbage leaf; turn the cabbage over the filling and roll up. Tuck in sides. Repeat with the remaining leaves and filling.

6. Heat the remaining 1 tablespoon oil in a 5-quart casserole over medium heat. Add the bacon, ribs, or sausage slices and cook, covered, until the fat is rendered, 2 to 3 minutes. Tilt the casserole and skim off all but 1 or 2 tablespoons fat. Add the carrot, slivered onion, and remaining chopped cabbage. Sauté, stirring, until lightly browned, about 5 minutes. Arrange the cabbage rolls, seam side down, on top of the trimmings, scattering the tomatoes, their juices, and lemon slices between layers. When all the rolls are in the casserole, weight them down with a heat-proof, upside-down plate just large enough to fit inside the casserole.

7. Dilute the tomato paste in 1 cup water and pour around the inside of the casserole. Bring to a vigorous boil, boil 1 minute, cover tightly, and cook over reduced heat 2 hours. (Can be set in a 350° F. oven to bake 2 hours.) Remove from the heat and let stand 30 minutes. (The rolls will continue to absorb juices during this time.)

8. Arrange the cabbage rolls in a shallow ovenproof serving dish. Mix any pan juices with the remaining parsley, sour cream, and vinegar and season with salt and pepper to taste. Reheat the rolls until hot, spoon the mixture over the rolls, and serve at once.

NOTES TO THE COOK: The strongly flavored smoked bacon available in German and Hungarian butcher shops is preferred for this recipe. If it is unavailable, regular slab bacon may be substituted.

BAKED GREEN TOMATOES STUFFED WITH MIXED HERBS AND WALNUTS

This Georgian summer dish includes green tomatoes, baked, cooled, then stuffed with chopped walnuts. About an hour before serving, a thick, aromatic mixture of chopped herbs is gently heated and poured over each tomato.

Serves 4

4 mature green tomatoes, about 1½ pounds

Salt and freshly ground black pepper to taste

1 teaspoon sugar

1 tablespoon each chopped parsley, dill, and basil

½ teaspoon coarse salt

Pinch of cayenne

Vinegar, preferably one that is aromatic, such as sherry wine vinegar, Greek *glykadi*, or balsamic vinegar to taste

1 cup chopped walnuts

1 clove garlic, peeled

2 sprigs coriander

Strips of roasted red pepper dusted with chopped dill for garnish

1. Slowly grill the tomatoes over warm glowing coals until fork tender and blistery (or bake them in a 400° F. oven). Immediately dip them into a bowl of cold water and leave to cool on a plate.

2. Carefully core the tomatoes, and scoop out the seeds and pulp, leaving only the outer walls; sprinkle the insides with salt, pepper, and the sugar. Reserve 2 tablespoons of strained juices.

3. In a small glass or ceramic bowl, combine the parsley, dill, and basil with the coarse salt, cayenne, and enough of the reserved juices to make a thick sauce, about 1½ teaspoons. Add a few drops of the vinegar.

4. In a food processor, combine the walnuts, garlic, coriander, 2 teaspoons reserved tomato juices, and a few drops of vinegar to taste. Process until just combined. Makes ½ cup filling. Stuff the tomatoes with the walnut mixture and stand them in a shallow serving dish. Heat the herb sauce in a microwave or in a small saucepan until lukewarm. Use a spoon to drizzle about 1 tablespoon over each tomato. Cover loosely and set in a cool place for at least 1 hour. Garnish just before serving with strips of roasted red pepper.

QUINCES STUFFED WITH CHICKEN, GOLDEN RAISINS, AND ALMONDS

This recipe was inspired by a description in a book by Lesley Blanch, *From Wilder Shores: The Tables of My Travels.* The author describes a chicken dish she tasted in Syria: "At Homs, a small, smiling town, the rushing waters of the Orontes River have turned the huge creaking water wheels for centuries, and there are balconied houses and little cafés hanging over streams. There I ate apples stuffed with small pieces of chicken, rice, sultanas, chopped blanched almonds, honey and cloves, which is a good way to make the remains of a chicken go a long way without seeming apologetic."

When I was in Syria, I decided to track down this dish, only to discover that Ms. Blanch, who now lives "in France in a bamboo thicket with two adored cats," had mixed her towns and her memories. It is Hama, the rival town across the river from Homs, that has the water wheels and the famous restaurants, but I went from one to the other without finding anyone who knew the dish. In the meantime, Syrian-Armenians have confirmed that it has indeed been made in Syria, probably prepared by an Armenian chef a long time ago.

Here is the recipe as I developed it with quinces. For those readers who don't want to wait until they have some leftover chicken on hand, I suggest using 5 or 6 chicken thighs. After cooking, remove all the skin, gristle, and hard parts and roughly chop the juicy meat.

Serve these stuffed quinces on a buffet table with grilled vegetables, pickles, and rice.

Serves 6

continued

2 teaspoons unsalted butter

FILLING

2 teaspoons olive oil

1 small onion, coarsely chopped

¼ cup basmati rice, washed until water is clear, and drained

2 tablespoons blanched almonds, toasted and chopped

⅓ cup golden raisins, soaked in warm water 10 minutes and
    drained

3 tablespoons cider vinegar

¼ teaspoon ground cloves

¼ teaspoon freshly ground white pepper

Sea salt to taste

Pinch of cinnamon and cayenne

1 cup cooked chicken in ¼-inch dice

6 quinces (8 to 10 ounces each)

1½ tablespoons fresh lemon juice

2 tablespoons unsalted butter, at room temperature

1 tablespoon honey

4 teaspoons cider vinegar

1. Preheat the oven to 350° F. Butter a 12-inch oval baking dish and set aside.

2. In a medium skillet, heat the oil. Add the onion, cover, and cook over low heat 5 minutes. Add the rice and cook 2 minutes, stirring constantly. Add the almonds, raisins, 3 tablespoons cider vinegar, the cloves, white pepper, salt, cinnamon, cayenne, and ¾ cup of water. Increase the heat to high and cook, stirring frequently, until most of the moisture has evaporated, about 5 minutes. Remove from the heat; stir in the chicken, season with salt and white pepper, and set aside.

3. Wash the quinces; cut off about 1 inch of the tops and reserve them. Remove and discard the cores. Scrape out enough of each quince to make a ⅓-inch-thick shell; reserve and chop the scrapings. Dab the inside of each quince with lemon juice to prevent discoloration. Using a skewer, lightly prick the quince skins at 1-inch intervals. Mix the scrapings with a pinch of sea salt and ¾ cup water. Spread the scrapings evenly in the prepared baking dish. Arrange the quinces right side up in the dish and fill with the chicken and rice mixture. Set the reserved tops alongside the quinces and cover the dish with foil. Bake 1¼ hours.

4. In a small bowl, mix 2 tablespoons butter, the honey, and 3 teaspoons of the vinegar. Dot each quince with 1 teaspoon of the honey butter, cover with the reserved tops, and bake, uncovered, 10 to 15 minutes longer, until the quinces are tender.

5. Transfer the quinces to a shallow serving dish. Strain the contents of the baking dish into a small skillet, pressing down on the solids; discard the solids. Boil the liquid until reduced to ¼ cup. If desired, season with the remaining 1 teaspoon vinegar. Spoon the sauce around the quinces and serve warm.

NOTES TO THE COOK: My choice for the honey is a German pine forest variety, dark colored with a strong, pungent flavor, sold under the Langanese label. Other bitter honeys, such as chestnut, also work well.

Mediterranean apples are usually tart, and can be used interchangeably with quinces. If you make this dish with apples, cook 30 minutes less.

From late fall, American markets offer a wonderful variety of apples, each with its own special taste, texture, and degree of juiciness. However, not all apples hold their shape when baked, and not all hold up their end of the flavor balance in this highly seasoned chicken dish. The best apple choice here is the bittersweet Northern Spy, with its creamy texture and tart flavor. If you use a sweeter apple, adjust with a final fillip of cider vinegar just before serving.

IX

Pilafs, Pulses, & Corn

·❧ PILAFS ❧·

A pilaf can be made with any of a number of primary ingredients—rice, lentils, bulgur, green wheat, even skinned wheat berries. The concept is of a grain (or in one case below, lentils) combined with almost anything else, traditionally served as a main course, but often served today as a starch supplement.

Pilaf is honest food and elegant in its simplicity—light, fragrant, and easily digestible. For me, any cuisine that makes plain starches so beguiling is a cuisine of great sophistication.

Here is a brief rundown of the primary ingredients in the pilafs presented in this book.

·❧ RICE ❧·

There are many ways to cook rice, depending upon which variety you choose. American rice doesn't need washing or soaking, unlike imported rice, which always needs a good washing. My first choice is aromatic basmati rice, but long-grain rice is also good. Middle Easterners traditionally use butter in their hot pilafs, but I have found that healthy, savory pilafs can be made well with olive oil. A good rice pilaf should be like a good strand of spaghetti—firm but tender and tasting of the grain.

·❧ BULGUR ❧·

For pilafs that call for bulgur, use coarse or medium-grain. You will not have to rinse or soak bulgur when making pilaf. Darker-grain bulgur available from Middle Eastern groceries is particularly tasty.

In the Turkish countryside most pilafs were traditionally made with nutty-tasting, mildly toasty bulgur. Rice, not grown in Turkey, was treated as a luxury import. Called *pligouri* in Greece, *bourghoul* in Lebanon, *bulgur* in Turkey, sturdy, honest, and nutritious bulgur has rarely been "romanced" the way pasta, rice, or couscous have been. But bulgur's hearty, nutty flavor is as deserving of respect as the more popular staples.

↘ LENTILS ↙

Two kinds of lentils are used in eastern Mediterranean pilafs: small, slate-colored black lentils, which are unhulled red lentils and cook to a creamy state without collapsing; and ordinary greenish brown supermarket lentils (see Appendix C for mail-order sources). The black ones can be found at Indian shops; Kalustyan; and Dean and DeLuca, New York, where they are called "Indian whole *masoor* dal." Lentils don't require soaking, and all types can be cooked in less than 40 minutes.

↘ GREEN WHEAT ↙

Green wheat (*freekeh* in Syria, *frik* in North Africa, *fireek* in Egypt, *firik* in Turkey) is one of those original "poor people's foods," like pig's feet and wild greens, that have become chic in recent years.

In early spring, when the stores of winter wheat have been used up and the new wheat is not yet ready for harvest, farmers will gather piles of immature wheat from the fields, carefully set them afire, then thresh the charred sheaves. The idea is to let the chaff and straw burn, but to preserve the moist kernels of immature wheat. As a result of this burning, the kernels become imbued with a wood-smoke flavor that is delicious, earthy, and unique. It takes time to clean green wheat, but it is well worth the effort. Green wheat is nutritious, too, with a high vitamin, mineral, and protein content (see Appendix C for mail-order sources).

RICE PILAF WITH NOODLES

Here is a simple all-purpose eastern Mediterranean rice pilaf to accompany any and all stews, grilled meats, and stuffed vegetable dishes.

Serves 5 to 6

1. In a 2-quart casserole, sauté the vermicelli in butter and oil until golden, stirring constantly. Stir in the rice and fry until glazed, about 1 minute. Add the boiling liquid and the salt and allow it to boil 1 minute. Reduce the heat to low and simmer, covered, until liquid has been absorbed, about 18 minutes. Place a folded paper towel or terry towel over the rice, cover the pot, and let rest, with the heat turned off, 10 minutes before serving.

2. Sprinkle with one of the spices and fluff the rice with a fork.

¾ cup vermicelli, broken into one-inch lengths
1½ tablespoons melted butter
1½ tablespoons olive oil
1½ cups long-grain rice
3 cups boiling water or chicken broth
1¼ teaspoons salt
Freshly ground black pepper, ground cinnamon, or ground cloves for garnish

VARIATION.

SYRIAN-STYLE WHITE RICE WITH NOODLES

Soaking rice may not be popular with nutritionists, but it produces an extremely tender grain of rice. Soak it in hot water 1 hour; drain and follow the directions in the preceding recipe, but reduce the boiling liquid to 2½ cups and the simmering time to approximately 13 minutes.

RICE PILAF WITH ANCHOVIES, CURRANTS, AND PINE NUTS

A few miles from Istanbul, along the Bosporus, there is a charming little restaurant called Pafuli, which caters to the Laz people from the extreme eastern portion of the Turkish Black Sea coast, nostalgic for the humble home cooking of their native region. The repertory of anchovy dishes here is staggering: anchovy pancakes; anchovies baked in bread; anchovies wrapped and baked in fig leaves; anchovy sauce poured over cornmeal cakes. But the pièce de résistance of the restaurant is this anchovy pilaf *(Hamisi Pilavi)*, served with side dishes of pickled anchovies, smoked anchovies, and anchovy pâté!

Tuğrul Savkay, Istanbul's leading restaurant critic, took me to Pafuli to acquaint me with this dish, which he called a variation on a "rite of passage into the world of pilafs." I was astounded. The pilaf was not only unusual, it was great—an extraordinary mingling of aromatic rice, tasty anchovies, toasted pine nuts, tart and sweet currants, and chopped herbs.

The nostalgia that this dish evokes among Pafuli's small but loyal clientele causes them to hang around after dinner to sing regional folk songs to the accompaniment of a lute.

Serves 6

1. Wash the rice in three changes of water, rubbing the rice with your hands to remove excess starch. Soak the rice in a quart of boiling water mixed with 1 tablespoon coarse salt until the water cools. Drain and rinse until the water runs clear. (If substituting ordinary long-grain rice, do not wash or soak; simply rinse and set aside.)

2. Open up each fish and pull out and discard the central bone. Discard the head and rinse the fish under cool running water. Mix 1½ teaspoons salt, ½ teaspoon of the sugar, and ½ teaspoon pepper and season the fish evenly. Wrap the fish in plastic and refrigerate.

3. In a wide nonstick skillet, heat the oil and sauté the pine nuts and onions until golden. Add the rice to the skillet and cook, stirring occasionally, 3 to 4 minutes. Add the spices, currants, remaining sugar, salt, plenty of pepper, and up to 3 cups boiling water, or enough to come about an inch above the surface. Bring to a boil and stir once. Cook, covered, over high heat 2 to 3 minutes, then reduce the heat to very low and cook 10 minutes. Remove from the heat.

4. Preheat the oven to 375° F. Oil a 9-inch square or round ovenproof baking dish, preferably lined copper.

5. Spread one third of the fish, skin side down, on the bottom of the prepared pan. Cover with a layer of rice, then a layer of opened fish, and then another layer of rice. Place the remaining fish attractively in a spokelike pattern on top. Brush lightly with olive oil and bake 45 minutes. Just before serving, gently fork in the herbs and some pepper. Serve hot, warm, or cold.

With thanks to Mr. Bekir of the Pafuli Restaurant

1½ cups basmati or long-grain rice
Coarse salt
1 pound fresh anchovies or small smelts
2½ teaspoons sugar
Salt and freshly ground black pepper
2 tablespoons extra-virgin olive oil
3 tablespoons pine nuts
3 medium onions, chopped
1 teaspoon ground allspice
1 teaspoon ground cinnamon
3 tablespoons dried currants, soaked in warm water until plump, then drained
3 cups boiling water (or as needed)
2 tablespoons olive oil
2 tablespoons chopped parsley
2 tablespoons snipped dill

STEAMED CRUSTY RICE PILAF
WITH POTATOES

This unusual pilaf, from Tripoli, Lebanon, requires tasty, perfumed basmati rice and also an ample amount of butter for the right flavor. Potatoes, cut into thin slices, are arranged on the bottom of the pan, then browned until crusty, imbuing the rice with an earthy, buttery fragrance. The dish is served turned out, the potatoes on top.

Serves 4 to 6

2 cups basmati rice
Salt
1 medium onion, thinly sliced
6 tablespoons unsalted butter
2 medium waxy potatoes, peeled and thinly sliced
Pinch of freshly ground black pepper

1. Wash the rice in three changes of water, rubbing the rice with your hands to remove excess starch. Soak the rice in a quart of water mixed with 1 tablespoon salt at least 2 hours before cooking.

2. About 1 hour before serving, bring 1 quart water and 1 tablespoon salt to a boil in a deep saucepan. Drain the rice, add to the boiling water, and cook over high heat 5 minutes, stirring often. Drain the rice and rinse it in several changes of water.

3. In a 10-inch nonstick skillet, sauté the onion in 1½ tablespoons of the butter over medium heat until soft and golden, about 5 minutes. Transfer the onion to a side dish and add 2 tablespoons butter to the skillet. Make an overlapping layer of potato slices, then top with the sautéed onions. Season with salt and a pinch of pepper. Tightly cover the skillet and place over medium-low heat 3 to 4 minutes to steam.

4. Spread the drained rice on top of the potatoes and onions. Place a paper towel over the rice and cover tightly with a lid to keep steam from escaping. Cook 10 minutes over medium-low heat, then reduce the heat to low and cook another 30 minutes. Melt the remaining butter and drizzle over the rice. Cover again, remove from the heat, and allow to rest 5 minutes. Invert onto a wide, flat plate. If the potatoes stick to the bottom of the skillet, loosen them with a thin-bladed spatula, and replace them on the rice bed. Serve hot.

RICE AND LENTIL PILAF MEGADARRA

I discovered this simple brown lentil and rice pilaf topped with strands of crisp browned onions in 1968 in Claudia Roden's wonderful *A Book of Middle Eastern Food*. Since my work involves field-researching recipes, I rarely cook from other people's books, but Claudia's introduction was so intriguing I knew I had to try it. She described the dish, a modern version of a medieval recipe, called *megadarra*, then went on to relate how her aunt always served it with this apology: "Excuse the food of the poor!" In response, her guests would invariably reply, "Keep your food of kings and give us *megadarra* every day!"

I have cooked this pilaf many times, always smiling at this little story. Over the years I have changed the recipe slightly to suit my own taste, but Claudia's proportions are perfect; when I tried to cut down on the oil, the dish was not the same.

A good accompaniment would be a bowl of yogurt-garlic sauce and a bread salad such as *fattoush* (page 140).

Serves 4

1. Clean and sort the lentils; wash, drain, and cook them in 1½ quarts water for 20 minutes.

2. Meanwhile, cook the onions in the oil over medium-high heat, stirring, until the onions begin to turn golden brown. Reduce the heat and continue to cook, stirring often, until the onions are medium brown. Use a slotted spoon to remove half the onions to paper towels to drain and turn crisp. Continue to cook the remaining onions until they turn a deep brown.

1½ cups brown lentils
2½ cups slivered onions
½ cup olive oil
1 cup long-grain rice
Salt to taste
2 teaspoons freshly ground black pepper
2 cups yogurt-garlic sauce (page 27)

continued

3. When the lentils have cooked 20 minutes, add the rice, salt, pepper, and enough water to cover, and bring back to a boil. Reduce the heat and cook, covered, at a simmer another 20 minutes.

4. When the onions have turned a deep brown, add them along with the cooking oil to the lentils. Remove from the heat and let stand, uncovered, about 10 minutes before serving. Serve piled in a mound in a small, deep bowl, with the crisp onions on top. Serve warm, at room temperature, or cold with a bowl of yogurt-garlic sauce and *fattoush*.

NOTES TO THE COOK: If you want to use less oil, remember that the onions will not crisp properly in the skillet. You can crisp them in the microwave by spreading them out on a microwave-proof towel; then dry them 30 seconds. The dish will lack a certain richness.

AYFER ÜNSAL'S BLACK LENTIL PILAF
WITH GREENS

A yfer Ünsal, who taught me this delicious dish, is a live-wire practical cook, a modern Turkish woman who rises early, prepares dinner for her family, then goes off to work as a crusading journalist, exposing bribery and corruption.

She lives in Gaziantep, in southeastern Turkey, located on an ancient caravan route near the Syrian border. Gaziantep is not beautiful, but it has two great charms: its people, who are exceptionally friendly, and its food, deliciously spicy and robust, influenced by Arab, Armenian, and Kurdish cooking.

Ayfer's robust, spicy cooking style is grounded in her region. "All the women here know the same dishes," she told me, "we all cook them and our repertory is large because we cook with the seasons." Fascinated with her region's food, Ayfer has sponsored local cooking competitions.

This homey, homely combination of mildly acidic purslane and earthy lentils is typical Gaziantep home cooking. The sour flavor is invigorating, the assorted peas and grains are nourishing, and yet the dish is surprisingly light. Sometimes there is a fine line between a pilaf and a soup. This dish can best be described as a soupy pilaf—so soupy, in fact, that it is eaten with a spoon.

It can be served hot or warm. Traditionally it is eaten with scallions or a smashed onion. To smash an onion, wrap it in a kitchen towel and hit it with a mallet. The cloth will absorb the acrid juices and the onion will be sweet. Peel the onion, separate the leaves, and sprinkle lightly with salt.

Purslane—a thick, fleshy green that grows weedlike in almost everyone's garden in late summer—is delectable raw or cooked. There are no inedible lookalikes; the major danger is from gardening chemicals and pesticides. If you practice safe gardening, you will be thrilled to discover that you can eat the weed instead of thinking of ways to eradicate it. Purslane also happens to be exceptionally healthy, the richest source of Omega-3 fatty acids of any vegetable so far examined.[*]

continued

* "Purslane: A Terrestrial Source of Omega-3 Fatty Acids" by Artemis Simopoulos, M.D. in the *New England Journal of Medicine*, vol. 315 (1986), p. 833.

⅔ cup black lentils (Indian whole *masoor* dal), or Egyptian lentils, or substitute French *lentilles de Puy* or ordinary brown lentils

6 ounces trimmed boneless leg of lamb

2 tablespoons olive oil

I medium onion, chopped

I½ teaspoons tomato paste

I½ teaspoons homemade pepper paste (page 389)

6 to 7 cups purslane leaves and stems, or 5 cups stemmed sorrel leaves

¼ cup cooked black-eyed peas

¼ cup cooked chickpeas and ¼ cup cooking liquor

2 tablespoons coarse-grain bulgur

3 garlic cloves, peeled and crushed with ½ teaspoon salt

3 tablespoons fresh lemon juice or more to taste (reduce to one half if using fresh sorrel leaves)

Salt and freshly ground black pepper to taste

¼ teaspoon Near East or Aleppo pepper (page 395)

I teaspoon dried mint, pressed through a fine sieve

Lemon wedges

4 small onions or 8 scallions as garnish

I. Pick the lentils clean and wash in several changes of water. Put in a saucepan, add 3 cups water, and bring to a boil. Simmer 30 minutes.

2. Meanwhile, cut the meat into small pieces and pound each portion with a flat mallet to make it as thin as scaloppine. Cut into tiny cubes. Place the meat and half the olive oil in a 4- or 5-quart casserole. Cover and cook over medium-high heat 5 minutes, stirring occasionally. Reduce the heat to medium, add the onion, and continue cooking, covered, 2 minutes longer. Stir in the tomato and pepper pastes and ½ cup water. Bring to a boil, cover, and cook at a simmer 20 minutes.

3. Wash the purslane in several changes of water; trim the roots (the leaves and stems are edible). Chop coarsely. (If using sorrel, place in colander in a deep bowl, pour on boiling water, and let stand 3 minutes; drain, discard the water, refresh the leaves, and squeeze dry. Shred the leaves coarsely.)

4. To the casserole, add the greens, the lentils, and 2 cups of the lentil cooking liquor, the black-eyed peas, the chickpeas with ¼ cup of their cooking liquor, bulgur, garlic, and just enough water to barely cover. Simmer, covered, 15 minutes. Remove from the heat and stir in the lemon juice and salt and pepper to taste. Let stand, covered, until ready to serve. (The pilaf is best served warm.)

5. Transfer the pilaf to a serving bowl. Heat the remaining oil, add the Near East pepper and mint, and allow to sizzle. Immediately drizzle over the pilaf, making swirls. Fold in the swirls at the table to distribute the red pepper and mint. Pass a plate with lemon wedges and onions or scallions.

NOTES TO THE COOK: The correct lentil for this dish is the black Indian or Egyptian lentil—dark-skinned with an orange center. When skinned, it cooks to a state of creaminess; with the skin on, it holds its shape and turns creamy within. These lentils are available at many Middle Eastern and Indian markets, as well as by mail order from Dean and DeLuca (see Appendix C).

If you substitute small French *lentilles de Puy,* the pilaf will be different, with a firmer texture but still delicious.

For those without access to purslane, sorrel is a good substitute (Fox Hill Farm can furnish either of these greens in huge amounts; see Appendix C).

You can buy seed, to grow a succulent yellowish purslane, from The Cook's Garden, P.O. Box 535, Londonderry, Vermont 05148.

Blanched purslane freezes perfectly, and can be used to make this pilaf year-round.

BULGUR PILAF WITH COLLAPSED EGGPLANT AND LAMB

Here is a very old Gaziantep dish, originally made in autumn with the interiors of eggplants which have been scooped out of shells that were to be dried and saved for winter stuffing. Without the skin the eggplant flesh did not hold firm, thus the adjective "collapsed."

This extremely rustic but tasty dish appears in different versions: In parts of the southeast, and at other times of the year, it is made with bulgur and the leftovers of a homey stew of meat, eggplant, and vegetables. In the town of Kilis, an hour's drive from Gaziantep, cooks add carrots to this mixture to make a pilaf they call "the traveler." In Gaziantep, without the carrots, the pilaf is called "the visitor."

Serves 4

continued

1 medium eggplant (or the scooped-out interiors of 10 small
    Italian eggplants)

Coarse salt

1 medium onion, chopped

2 tablespoons olive oil

8 ounces lean lamb, trimmed of all fat and bone, diced fine
    or coarsely ground

½ long green chili, stemmed, seeded, and chopped

1½ teaspoons tomato paste

1 tablespoon homemade red pepper paste (page 389)

1 cup coarse-grain bulgur

GARNISH

1 teaspoon freshly ground black pepper

2 teaspoons unsalted butter

1. Peel the eggplant and cut the flesh into 1-inch chunks. Salt the eggplant and leave to drain in a colander for at least 1 hour. Rinse, squeeze gently, and keep rolled in a damp kitchen towel until ready to use.

2. In a straight-sided 10-inch nonstick covered skillet, sweat the onion in the oil 2 minutes. Stir in the lamb, cover, and cook until the meat throws off its moisture, reabsorbs it, and begins to brown, about 3 minutes. Add the eggplant, stirring it to lightly sear on all sides, 2 minutes. Add the chili, tomato and pepper pastes, and 1 cup water. Bring to a boil, cover, and cook over medium heat 20 minutes.

3. Place the bulgur in a fine sieve; shake to remove dust, but do not wash the grains. Stir in the bulgur. Add 1¼ cups boiling water and ¾ teaspoon coarse salt, bring back to a boil, and stir once. Cover the pan, lower the heat, and cook 20 minutes, or until all the liquid has been absorbed.

4. Remove the skillet from the heat and place a folded kitchen towel over the contents in the skillet, cover tightly, and set in a warm place 15 to 20 minutes, or until the bulgur is completely swollen.

5. When ready to serve, prepare the garnish: Press the black pepper through a fine sieve. In a small saucepan, heat the butter to sizzling, add the black pepper and, swirling the pan once, spoon the bubbling mixture all over the pilaf. Serve at once with a well-chilled cucumber-garlic-yogurt sauce.

NOTES TO THE COOK: The Kurds not only dry eggplant shells for winter, but also the stems by scoring them in two or three places, then hanging them up. They don't actually eat the dried stems, using them instead to flavor bulgur pilaf. The diner doesn't swallow them, just chews on them to extract their mushroomlike taste.

With thanks to Mrs. Filiz Hösukoğlu for sharing her recipe for ezik dolma as

BULGUR AND GREEN WHEAT PILAF WITH EGGPLANT, TOMATOES, AND CHILIS

A delicious variation on the preceding recipe that uses roasted green wheat. This pilaf, too, is good with yogurt sauce.

Serves 6 to 8

1. Heat the oil in a 4-quart Dutch oven. Add the meat, cover, and cook over medium heat about 10 minutes, stirring often, until the meat is browned but not crisp.

2. Meanwhile, wash and clean the green wheat, as described on page 247.

3. Add the onion and cook, stirring, about 2 minutes. Do not brown. Add the tomatoes and chilis and cook, stirring, 2 minutes longer. Add 1½ cups water and the salt and bring to a boil. Reduce the heat, cover, and cook at a simmer until the meat is tender and the liquid is completely reduced to a glaze, about 30 minutes.

4. Add the eggplant and mixed spices and cook, stirring, a few minutes. Then stir in the green wheat and bulgur or cracked wheat and cover with 3½ cups water. Simmer, covered, 30 minutes, or until the grains are tender and the liquid is almost completely absorbed.

5. Prepare the garnish: In a small saucepan, heat the butter, add the black pepper, and drizzle over the cooked eggplant and grains. Cover Dutch oven with a folded kitchen towel and the lid and cook 5 minutes longer. Remove from the heat and let stand 5 to 10 minutes more. Carefully stir once and spoon the pilaf onto a serving dish. Serve hot or warm with the garlic-yogurt sauce.

With thanks to Mrs. Fikriye Gulenler for sharing this recipe

1 teaspoon olive oil
⅓ pound lean lamb or beef, cubed
1 cup green wheat (page 232)
1 medium-large onion, chopped
2 ripe tomatoes, halved, seeded, and grated
2 long green chilis, stemmed, seeded, and minced (about 1 tablespoon)
1 teaspoon salt
½ pound eggplant, peeled and cut into ¾-inch cubes
½ teaspoon mixed spices or Turkish *baharat* (pages 392–93)
1 cup coarse-grain bulgur or cracked wheat

GARNISH
2 tablespoons unsalted butter
½ teaspoon freshly ground black pepper, or more to taste
1½ cups yogurt-garlic sauce (page 27)

BULGUR PILAF WITH SPINACH AND FRIED ONIONS

A rural Arab dish that goes well with simmered meats and chickpeas and a bowl of thick yogurt.

Makes 3½ cups, serving 4 to 5

3 large onions

3 tablespoons olive oil

I pound fresh spinach, washed, stemmed, and shredded

I cup coarse-grain bulgur

I cup unsalted meat, poultry, or vegetable stock, heated to boiling

½ teaspoon ground allspice

I teaspoon salt

½ teaspoon freshly ground black pepper

I. Halve the onions and cut each lengthwise into thin strips (Arabs call these "wings"). Heat the oil in a heavy 10-inch skillet and cook the onions, covered, 30 minutes, stirring often, until they are golden brown.

2. Meanwhile, wilt the spinach in a 3-quart saucepan 5 minutes. Stir in the bulgur, stock, allspice, salt, and pepper. Cover and cook over low heat until the bulgur is tender, about 20 to 25 minutes. Remove from the heat and let stand 5 minutes.

3. Gently stir in the fried onions and adjust the seasoning, adding more pepper to taste.

BULGUR AND LENTIL PILAF WITH CARAMELIZED ONIONS

This recipe is a kind of variation on the rice and lentil pilaf called Megadarra (page 237). Here bulgur replaces the rice, becoming the base of the dish. Serve with glasses of icy yogurt drink or bowls of thick yogurt.

Serves 6 to 8

1. Place the lentils in a saucepan with 3 cups water, bring to a boil, and simmer until the lentils are tender. Reserve the lentils and any remaining cooking liquor. Measure the cooking liquor and add enough stock to make 3½ cups. Set aside.

2. Heat the butter and oil in a large skillet and cook the onions until they turn golden brown, about 30 minutes.

3. Meanwhile, place the bulgur, lentils, salt, tomato paste, pepper paste, and liquid in a heavy 4-quart saucepan and bring to a boil, stirring. Reduce the heat to low and cook, covered, 15 minutes. Place a paper towel over the bulgur, cover the pan, and place it over a flame tamer to continue cooking another 10 minutes.

4. When the onions are golden brown, add the black pepper and Near East pepper and bring to a sizzle. Pour over the bulgur and stir gently.

With thanks to Mrs. Filiz Hösukoğlu for sharing this recipe

I cup black lentils (whole *masoor* dal), picked over and washed
About 3½ cups chicken or meat stock
3 tablespoons clarified butter
3 tablespoons olive oil
5 medium onions, peeled, halved, and thinly sliced
2 cups coarse-grain bulgur
Sea salt to taste
I tablespoon tomato paste
I tablespoon red pepper paste (page 389)
¼ teaspoon freshly ground black pepper
½ teaspoon Near East or Aleppo pepper (page 395) or ¼ teaspoon crushed red pepper flakes

Bulgur Pilaf with Toasted Noodles

Please remember that bulgur easily overcooks and turns mushy if too much liquid is used. Don't soak it, cook in about 1¾ cups hot meat or chicken broth for every cup of large grains.

Serves 3

4 tablespoons butter
½ cup broken spaghetti or vermicelli
I teaspoon salt
I cup coarse-grain bulgur
1½ cups chicken or meat broth
¼ teaspoon freshly ground black pepper

I. In a saucepan, melt 3 tablespoons of the butter over medium heat. Add the spaghetti or vermicelli and fry, stirring often, until golden brown. Add I teaspoon salt and the bulgur, stirring.

2. Bring broth to a boil. Pour in broth and allow the mixture to boil about 3 minutes. Cover, reduce the heat, and cook at a simmer 10 more minutes, or until all the liquid has been absorbed. Place a kitchen towel or double layer of paper toweling on the grains, replace the cover, remove from the heat, and let stand 10 to 15 minutes before serving.

3. Heat the remaining I tablespoon butter; add the pepper and let sizzle. Pour over the bulgur and serve.

GREEN WHEAT PILAF WITH GROUND LAMB SAUCE, PEAS, AND PINE NUTS

Use this pilaf as a bed for slices of roasted lamb or as a starch to accompany vegetables. Green wheat, as mentioned, has a crunchy texture and smoky flavor that go beautifully with the traditional spice combination of cinnamon, allspice, and cloves—a popular seasoning for lamb in Syria.

Though you can eat this dish right away, it is more delicious if it sits a day; reheat just before serving.

Serves 4 to 6

1. Heat 2 tablespoons of the butter in a 9-inch skillet. Add the onion and cook, covered, over medium heat until softened. Add the lamb and sauté until it is browned and crumbly. Add the pine nuts, allspice, pepper, cinnamon, cloves, and salt to taste (start with ½ teaspoon). Cook 2 minutes. Add 1¾ cups water. Bring to a boil, reduce the heat, cover, and cook at a simmer 5 minutes.

2. Meanwhile, place the green wheat in a sieve in a deep bowl and cover with cool water. Rub the wheat kernels between your palms vigorously to feel for stones or other foreign matter. Wash in several changes of water until the water runs clear and the kernels feel free of grit. Let soak 2 to 3 minutes. Skim off and discard any husks that float to the top.

5½ tablespoons butter
½ cup chopped onion
½ pound lean ground lamb
⅓ cup pine nuts
1 teaspoon ground allspice
½ teaspoon freshly ground black pepper
¼ teaspoon ground cinnamon
Pinch of cloves
Salt
1 cup green wheat (page 232)
½ cup fresh or frozen tiny peas, thawed
3 tablespoons coarsely chopped pistachios

3. Melt the remaining butter in a second large skillet, preferably nonstick. Add the green wheat. Sauté over medium heat until the wheat is very hot. Add the simmering lamb sauce. Reduce the heat, cover, and cook 25 to 30 minutes, or until the wheat is tender and the liquid is almost absorbed. Add the peas, cover, and cook 5 minutes longer. (Can be prepared 1 day in advance and reheated just before serving.)

4. Pour onto a flat plate, sprinkle with the pistachios, and serve.

∾ PULSE AND ∾
CORN DISHES

Of all the pulses of the eastern Mediterranean area, none matches the chickpea in versatility and usefulness. Delectable, nourishing, economical, and easy to cook, chickpeas are used almost with abandon: They are added to salads; rolled in olive oil and dressed with vinegar and onion rings; slipped into sauces; thrown into pilafs, couscous dishes, soups, and stuffings. Chickpeas are eaten as snacks and even show up in one of the most unusual and delicious Turkish desserts, where they are mixed with husked wheat berries, apricots, figs, almonds, pine nuts, sugar, and rose water (see Noah's Pudding, page 367).

Dried chickpeas must be soaked overnight in plenty of soft water; a quick one-hour soak isn't enough. If your water is hard, I suggest you use a bottled variety; otherwise, add a teaspoonful of baking soda to the soaking water, remembering to rinse the chickpeas in several changes of water in the morning. This technique will yield the desirable soft texture of the chickpea.

Cook chickpeas either in lots of unsalted water in a covered pot or in much less water in a pressure cooker.

An Arabian Stew of Chickpeas, Eggplant, and Tomatoes

Moussaka is a layered dish of vegetables and meat, with a luxurious mixture of eggs and yogurt in the Balkans (see page 362 for Moussaka with Fried Kale), or a cheese-rich béchamel topping in Greece. But in Syria the term *mussaka'a* is applied to a melange of fried vegetables, frequently arranged in layers, baked, or cooked together in a shallow dish, often without meat. In this recipe, peeled chickpeas substitute for the meat; added richness comes from the spices and the contrast of sweet and sour.

This *mussaka'a* is very good served warm or at room temperature as a supper dish, along with a bulgur pilaf with noodles (page 246) and a bowl of cucumber, garlic, and yogurt sauce (page 29).

Serves 6

1. Peel and halve the chickpeas; set aside.

2. Remove and discard 3 vertical strips of skin from each eggplant, leaving it striped, then cut the whole eggplant into 2½-inch chunks. Salt the pieces and leave to drain in a colander for at least 1 hour.

3. Rinse the eggplant, squeeze gently, and pat dry with paper towels. Working in batches, lightly fry the chunks in 5 tablespoons hot oil until golden brown; drain. Sprinkle the eggplant with pepper and set aside.

4. In a 2- or 3-quart casserole with a tight-fitting lid, warm the remaining olive oil and add the onions. Sweat them over low heat 10 minutes, stirring occasionally, until limp and golden. Add the chickpeas and fry 2 min-

continued

1 cup chickpeas, soaked overnight

1½ to 2 pounds large eggplants (about 2)

Coarse salt

8 tablespoons olive oil

Freshly ground black pepper to taste

2 large onions, halved and cut lengthwise into thin strips

10 small cloves garlic, unpeeled

1 cup fresh or canned tomatoes, seeded and chopped, juices reserved

1 tablespoon tomato paste

½ teaspoon Near East or Aleppo pepper (page 395)

3 cloves garlic, peeled and crushed with 1 teaspoon salt

3 tablespoons chopped parsley

1 tablespoon red wine vinegar

2 teaspoons sugar

¼ teaspoon ground allspice or cinnamon

Fresh lemon juice

Sprigs of fresh mint

utes. Stir in the drained eggplant, unpeeled garlic, tomatoes and their juice, tomato paste, and Near East pepper. Cover tightly and cook over reduced heat without stirring 40 minutes. Carefully fold in the crushed garlic, parsley, vinegar, sugar, and allspice. Cook 10 minutes longer, or until thickened. (Up to this point, the dish can be made one day in advance. Cool, cover, and refrigerate so that the flavors will meld.)

5. To serve, return to room temperature, adjust the seasoning with salt, pepper, and allspice, and sharpen the taste with a few drops of lemon juice. Garnish with the mint.

WARM CHICKPEAS WITH WHITE OIL

In Syria, there are special restaurants where chickpeas are prepared in numerous ways by a specialist, called a *hamsani*. The chickpeas, cooked very slowly in a fired oven, have a meltingly soft texture and delicious flavor.

This dish of cooked chickpeas and oil, crumbled pita, and onions is a favorite among men when they get together to play cards. It is called *fattet be zeit*, which means "shredded bread with oil." It is literally a dish that can be eaten while someone shuffles the deck.

The white oil used is an unusual mixture of cold water, baking soda, garlic, and cold old olive oil, which is highly acidic. Such an oil is second quality; I mention it only as a curiosity. In my adaptation I use good fresh olive oil. The dish makes a delightful simple snack.

While Syrian men eat this snack in the evening as they play cards, in neighboring southeastern Turkey a similar dish is eaten for breakfast. Again, it is a dish prepared for men by other men. Though I think it is interesting to relate, it is not nearly as good to eat.

In the central market of Gaziantep, I came upon a covered shelter along one wall—shaded, cool, dimly lit, nearly as large as a railroad station waiting room. Here a couple of hundred men were sitting around sipping tea and eating *nohutlu dürrüm*, a rolled-up round of thick pita filled with chickpeas, slivered onions, parsley, Near East pepper, and sumac. The chickpeas had simmered all night in a broth flavored with lamb bones.

Serves 4

1. Preheat the oven to 350° F.

2. Toast the pita in the oven until golden brown. Remove and break into small pieces. Place in a wide shallow serving bowl.

3. In a saucepan, reheat the chickpeas in their cooking liquor. Add the garlic. Quickly tilt the saucepan and moisten the pita with the chickpea liquor, then toss the pita well. Spread the garlicky chickpeas on top.

4. Beat the olive oil with the cold water and drizzle over the chickpeas. Sprinkle with the cumin and Near East pepper; garnish with the scallions and serve at once.

With thanks to Mr. Anaz Al Zarzour of Damascus

½ pound pita, split

1⅓ cups freshly cooked chickpeas, with I cup chickpea liquor

2 cloves garlic, peeled and crushed with a pinch of salt

3 tablespoons olive oil

2 tablespoons cold water

¼ teaspoon ground cumin

2 pinches of Near East or Aleppo pepper (page 395)

6 to 8 scallions, thinly sliced

MACEDONIAN CHICKPEAS, EGGPLANTS, AND TOMATOES

At a conference on the traditional ways of Greek cooking, organized by the Oldways Preservation & Exchange Trust, in Porto Carras, I was in the blissful state that the Greeks call *kefi*. Against the background of Mount Olympus, the sparkling Aegean Sea, and the clear Greek light, I learned and shared while enjoying the fruits of the Grecian table—good food, good wine, superb oil. But the final banquet was the best. We walked into a dining room lit only by tall candles, with ancient Christian music echoing from the walls. We listened to clerical prayers, then sat down to a Lenten meal, served at long tables. This was a Greece I didn't know—a Greece of tribute, reflected in marvelous food made to feed the mind and soul as well as the body.

Among the dishes served that night was this Macedonian version of chickpeas, eggplants, and tomatoes. I liked it so much I asked my Greek food-writer friend Aglaia Kremezi to find the recipe. The secret, it turned out, is preparing the dish in an earthenware pot so that the correct amount of moisture is released during cooking. A dish as good as this need be accompanied only by dense, chewy bread.

Serves 6

1. Drain the chickpeas; place in a saucepan, add fresh water to cover, bring to a boil, and simmer, covered, over low heat until half-cooked, about 45 minutes. Set aside.

2. Meanwhile, peel the eggplant and cut into 1-inch cubes. Sprinkle lightly with salt and let stand in a colander to draw off excess moisture, about 45 minutes. Set aside.

3. Preheat the oven to 300° F.

4. Heat the oil in a 12-inch skillet. Add the onions, frying pepper, and chili; stir 3 minutes. Add the eggplant and sauté without browning it, 2 more minutes. Add the garlic, tomatoes with juice, parsley, oregano, and 1 teaspoon coarse salt; cook at a simmer 10 minutes, stirring often.

½ pound dried chickpeas, soaked overnight

1 1-pound eggplant

Coarse salt

¼ cup olive oil

2 chopped onions

1 Italian green frying pepper, cored, seeded, and cut into small pieces

2½ teaspoons chopped long green chili

1½ teaspoons garlic, peeled and crushed with a pinch of salt

2 cups canned tomatoes with juice

½ cup chopped parsley

1 teaspoon *rigani*, or Mediterranean oregano

1 bay leaf

1 12"-x-12" sheet of parchment paper *(optional)*

5. In a 4-quart bean pot, clay casserole, or earthenware lined electric cooker, mix the chickpeas, 1¾ cups of the cooking liquid, the bay leaf, and the contents of the skillet. Cover the pot with a clay plate or a round of parchment and fasten with a string. Bake in the oven about 2½ hours or all day in the electric cooker. The aroma will be extremely fragrant and the chickpeas very tender. Remove the paper, increase the oven heat, and bake 10 minutes more to allow excessive moisture in the dish to evaporate. The finished sauce should thickly coat the chickpeas.

SMALL BROWN BEANS (FUL)

"The rich eat *ful* for breakfast, the poor eat *ful* for lunch, but only animals eat *ful* for dinner." So goes the Egyptian proverb. *Ful*, pronounced "fool," is made from dried favas and is the national dish of Egypt. In Syria and Lebanon it is eaten as a soupy mass for breakfast, along with slabs of feta-style cheese, glossy black olives, cucumbers, and plenty of pita.

In the following recipe the *ful* is tossed with parsley, garlic, and scallions and is served as a room-temperature brunch dish.

Every type of dried favas, small and round, large and flat, skinned and cracked, can be used to make a bowl of *ful*, but the best version is made, in North America, with small, smooth beige-brown favas from Canada. *Ful mdammes* is available in cans at Middle Eastern groceries. If you decide to make this dish on the spur of the moment and don't have any home-cooked beans on hand, you can easily substitute a can of *ful mdammes*. In that case, omit steps 1 and 2.

Makes 3½ cups, serving 8 as part of an Arab-style breakfast

1. The day before you plan to serve the dish, pick over the beans, wash them until the water runs clear, and soak them in water to cover 12 to 18 hours. (In summer, soak them in the refrigerator.) Discard any beans that float.

2. Drain the beans and rinse again. In a heavy, deep 4-quart saucepan with a tight-fitting lid, bring about 3½ cups soft water to the boil, add the beans, and cook, covered, over high heat 10 minutes.

3. Add the lentils and onion to the pot. Cover, return to a boil, and cook, without stirring, over reduced heat until the beans are tender, about 2 hours. (Cooking the beans in a deep saucepan reduces excessive evaporation. If necessary, add cold water to keep the beans covered.) Stir in ¾ teaspoon salt. Remove from the heat and allow to cool. Discard the onion. (*Ful*, without other seasonings, will keep 2 to 3 days in a tightly covered container in the refrigerator.)

4. About ½ hour before serving, place the beans and the cooking liquor (or the total contents of two cans of *ful mdammes*) in a heavy saucepan. Simmer 10 minutes, or until the beans absorb almost all the cooking liquor. Remove from the heat and beat in the garlic, lemon juice, and 4 tablespoons of the oil. Partially crush the beans. Fold in the parsley. Correct the seasoning with salt and pepper to taste. Pour into a wide, shallow serving dish. Drizzle the remaining oil on top. Garnish with the tomato, lemon wedges, and scallions. Serve warm.

NOTES TO THE COOK: To achieve the soft, soothing quality of a well-cooked *ful*, you should soak and cook the favas in soft water. The Canadian favas I use take about 2½ hours to cook. But keep in mind that the age and quality of dried beans will affect their cooking time, sometimes by as much as 200 percent.

MOTTLED BEANS WITH COLLARD GREENS, BLACK SEA STYLE

This is a popular home-style dish from the Black Sea coast of Turkey. The local people, called Laz, serve it with hot corn bread. A similar dish is made in neighboring Georgia, with the addition of slivers of country ham.

Serves 6

½ pound mottled red beans, such as cranberry, bolita, or Roman, soaked overnight

2 tablespoons olive oil

I cup chopped onion

2½ teaspoons chopped long green chili

I Italian green frying pepper, cored, seeded, and cut into small pieces

I teaspoon garlic, peeled and crushed with salt

2 cups tomato sauce

½ cup chopped parsley

I teaspoon sea salt

I pound fresh collard greens

Freshly ground black pepper to taste

2 teaspoons butter

Good pinch of cayenne

1. Drain the beans; place in a saucepan, add fresh water to cover, bring to a boil, and simmer, covered, over low heat until half-cooked, about 45 minutes. Set aside.

2. Meanwhile, heat the oil in a wide, deep skillet. Add the onion, chili, and frying pepper and cook 3 minutes, stirring occasionally. Add the garlic, tomato sauce, parsley, and salt and simmer 10 minutes, stirring often.

3. Drain the beans and reserve the cooking liquid. Add the beans and about I cup liquid to the skillet, cover, and continue cooking until the beans are tender.

4. Soak and clean the collard greens. Shred the leaves finely to make about 4 cups. In a medium saucepan, bring 3 cups water to a boil. Add the collards and cook 20 minutes. Drain the collards; add them to the skillet along with more reserved bean liquid if necessary and continue cooking 10 minutes. Adjust the seasoning with salt and pepper.

5. In a small saucepan heat the butter to sizzling, add the cayenne, swirl once, and pour over the contents in the skillet. Serve hot or warm.

VARIATION

Omit the greens and serve the beans at room temperature.

CREAMY GIANT WHITE BEANS AND GREENS CASSEROLE

The beauty of this plain, pure-tasting, simple-to-make dish resides in the honesty of the well-mellowed beans. Try this dish with an accompaniment of thick yogurt and a plate of mildly piquant pickled peppers or a thick, garlicky *tsioula* dip (page 18).

Serves 4

1. Soak the beans overnight. Discard all beans that float. Drain and rinse well.

2. In a deep saucepan, cook the beans in plenty of vigorously boiling water 10 minutes; drain. Return the beans to the pot, add fresh water to cover, and cook gently 1 hour.

3. Meanwhile, preheat the oven to 300° F. Put 3 tablespoons of the olive oil, the onions, garlic, and chili in a 6-cup, 7-cup, or 8-cup baking dish. Mix the ingredients well, cover, and place the baking dish in the oven to cook 1 hour.

4. Drain the beans, reserving about 2 cups of the cooking liquid. Add the beans, bay leaf, and reserved cooking liquid to the dish in the oven. Bake another hour. Meanwhile, wilt the greens in a skillet in the remaining olive oil.

½ pound dried white beans, such as *gigantes* or sweet runners
4 tablespoons olive oil
2 large onions, peeled and thinly sliced
5 to 8 cloves garlic, peeled and thinly sliced
1 small dried red chili, crumbled, or ¼ teaspoon red chili flakes
1 bay leaf
1½ cups blanched Swiss chard, sorrel, and/or escarole leaves
Salt
Freshly ground black pepper
1 bowl drained yogurt (for directions on draining yogurt, see page 410)

5. To the dish in the oven, add the greens, salt, and pepper and stir to combine. Return the dish to the oven and bake, uncovered, 15 minutes. Remove from the oven and allow to settle 3 hours before serving with the yogurt. (Do not refrigerate—the beans will lose their fresh taste.)

NOTES TO THE COOK: The large, creamy white *gigantes* from Kastoria, in Greek Macedonia, are plump and hold their shape well in long-simmered dishes. They are sold in Greek groceries, or substitute sweet runners from Dean and DeLuca, New York (see Appendix C).

GEORGIAN GRITS WITH CHEESE

"Paula, honey, these are just plain ole grits!" said Martha Villas from North Carolina, when she tasted this dish from the Republic of Georgia. I had brought back carefully tagged envelopes of the rough-textured pale particles in order to make what my Georgian friends had insisted on translating as "polenta," but which I knew had to be something else. Well, to quote from Joni Miller's wonderful book *True Grits*, "Few people meet a pearly, farina-like mess of grits late in life and fall in love with its flavor."

Southern Americans who call grits "ambrosial comfort food" serve them with redeye gravy. In the Republic of Georgia, people eat them warm or cold with spicy food such as *kharcho* (page 117). If you're an American southerner, I'm sure you already have a good grits recipe, but if you're new to the dish, you might want to try the following recipe and enjoy its warming, soothing qualities. Then again ... its qualities may escape you.

While American southerners will use a sharp cheese to enrich a bowl of grits, Georgians will add shavings of smoked or fresh mozzarella-type cheese, allowing it to soften as the grits cool down. They also blend and cook fresh cheese with their grits until it becomes thick and well blended. This is called *elargi* and is, to my northern taste, even better.

Makes about 1 quart, serving 8 to 10

5 cups water
1 cup whole heart, stone-ground grits
8 ounces moist salted fresh mozzarella, grated

1. In a 2-quart heavy saucepan, bring the water to a rolling boil. Gradually stir in the grits, return to a boil, and reduce the heat. Cover; cook slowly 15 minutes, stirring occasionally.

2. Meanwhile, grate the cheese (to avoid stringiness). Stir the cheese into the thick grits and cook, stirring, another 5 minutes.

X

Kibbeh

FIFTY VARIETIES
~ OF KIBBEH ~

Kibbeh has been called the masterpiece of the Middle Eastern table. In its most classical form (and there are innumerable variations), it is a 3-inch long football-shaped brown food, with a crisp or tender outer shell made of ground lamb kneaded with moistened bulgur, and a juicy interior or stuffing of cooked meat, spices, and nuts.

Good kibbeh is not bland or dry, but moist, well-seasoned, and light—a juicy combination of meat, nuts, and spices that can be baked, poached, steamed, or fried. Armenians call it *kufta*; Assyrians, *kittel*; Cypriots, *koupas*; Israelis *kibbe*; Palestinians, *kubba*; Turks, *Içli köfte*; and Syrians and Lebanese, kibbeh.

Kibbeh, believe me, is *not* an overrated meatball! When well made, kibbeh is one of the most interesting forms of ground meat cookery. The Middle East, in fact, is the only part of the world where the meatball is truly exalted. Elsewhere, meatballs are considered a poor person's way of stretching meat. Kibbeh, it should be noted, is not made with odds and ends, but with only the finest, leanest lamb, ground to a paste, which enhances its elastic ability to blend with moistened bulgur. Then, by dexterous hand movements, this lamb-bulgur combination is worked into a thin shell. And this, remember, is just one kind of kibbeh, for the dish can also be made with cooked cold rice, semolina, or matzo meal instead of bulgur; with fish; spinach; red lentils, pumpkins; potatoes; veal; beef; rabbit; and turkey.

The fifty varieties listed below all include bulgur, the most popular kibbeh component in the regions covered by this book. I have personally cooked all fifty, but, for lack of space, I include recipes in this chapter for only eleven (noted here with a circled number). Several other kibbeh recipes can be found in other chapters, as noted in the list. So, why do I list all? First, because I think the list is fascinating, conveying the possibilities of the dish. Second, if any reader is interested in cooking any of the kibbeh dishes not fully described, please write to me, care of the publisher, and I will provide details by mail.

Finally, please don't be afraid of kibbeh. Most of these variations can be made by the average North American cook. Of course, some are easy and others require a deft hand, but with effort all can be mastered. See the detailed illustrations after the list.

FRIED KIBBEH

1. Kibbeh Ovals Stuffed with Nuts. *Qras Maqliyyeh*, Syria
2. Extra-Crisp Ovals Stuffed with Pistachios. *Içli Köfte*, Gaziantep, Turkey
3. Baby-Size Kibbehs Stuffed with Braised Lamb Shank, Tomatoes, and Onions. Kibbeh *Hamis*, Damascus, Syria
4. Tennis-Ball-Size Kibbeh. Kibbeh *Halaby*, Aleppo, Syria. Huge ovals, crisp on the outside and juicy within. "The pride of Aleppo."

VEGETARIAN KIBBEH

5. Pumpkin Kibbeh Stuffed with Spinach, Chickpeas, and Walnuts. Lebanon
6. Fish Kibbeh Flavored with Fresh Coriander and Grated Orange, and Stuffed with Onions and Pine Nuts. Kibbe *Samak*, Lebanon
7. Vegetarian Red Lentil Ovals with Tarragon-Onion Salad. *Malhitali Köfte*, Gaziantep, Turkey
8. Potato Kibbeh Stuffed with Fried Onions, Chickpeas, and Cinnamon, and Baked in a Tray. Kibbeh *Batata bi-Siniyyeh*, Lebanon

continued

GRILLED KIBBEH

9. Flat Pancakes Stuffed with Walnuts, Butter, and Spices. Kibbeh *Sajiya*, Syria

10. Dome Kibbeh Stuffed with Lamb Kidney Fat, Hot Pepper, Walnuts, Pomegranate Molasses, and Pomegranate Seeds. Kibbeh *Michwiya*, Syria

11. Small or Large Skewered Balls or Sausages (see Kibbeh Kabobs, page 343). These kibbeh are either stuffed or unstuffed, but always highly seasoned with herbs and spices.

12. Kibbeh Grilled and Served in a Meat and Quince Stew, Garnished with Onions, Carrots, Pomegranate Juice, and Tomatoes. *Safarjaliah*, Aleppo, Syria

POACHED AND STEAMED KIBBEH

13. Ground Beef or Veal Shells Stuffed with Meat, Celery, Walnuts, and Spices. Kibbeh *Hamud*, Syria. This kibbeh is poached in a tart vegetable broth flavored with mint. A popular dish in the Jewish community of Aleppo.

14. Steamed Marble-Size Unstuffed Bulgur Balls Served in Tangy Tomato Soup (see Anatolian Sour Soup: Mothers and Daughters, page 108). *Eksili Akitmali Ufak Köfte*, Gaziantep, Turkey

15. Kibbeh with Eggplant and Sumac. *Soumaqieh*, Aleppo, Syria. The "Cadillac" of kibbehs.

16. Lamb and Sour Cherries with Kibbeh. Kibbeh *bi Karaziah*, Aleppo, Syria

17. Kibbeh with Glazed Carrots and Pomegranate. Kibbeh *bi Jazareeyeh*, Aleppo, Syria

18. Kibbeh Steamed in Pomegranate Juice Thickened with Cornstarch. Kibbeh *bi Romaneya*, Lebanon

19. Kibbeh Poached in Yogurt Sauce with Garlic and Mint or Coriander or Tarragon. *Labaniyeh*, Lebanon and Syria

20. Lamb Dumplings and Kibbeh in Yogurt Sauce (see my *Mediterranean Cooking*). *Shish Barak bi Laban*, Lebanon

21. Apricot-Shaped Kibbeh Poached in Yogurt Sauce with Sautéed Fresh Favas and Tarragon. *Michemchiya*, Damascus, Syria

22. Kibbeh and Chicken Poached in Yogurt-Enriched Broth. *Madzoon Kufte*, Armenia

23. Kibbeh with Cauliflower and Chickpeas in Yogurt-Tahini Sauce. *Fakheteya-Arnabeya*, Syria. This dish, tart with pomegranate juice, is topped with fried coriander and garlic.

24. Kibbeh Cooked with Favas and Swiss Chard in Yogurt Sauce. Syria

25. Kibbeh Poached in Fermented Yogurt-Bulgur Sauce. Kibbeh *Kishk*, Syria

26. Kibbeh Poached in a Fermented Yogurt-Bulgur Sauce with Fried Cabbage. Lebanon

27. Steamed Kibbeh with Hot Pepper Sauce. Kibbeh *Flefla Hamra*, Syria

28. Green Kibbeh with Swiss Chard and Walnut Sauce. Armenia and Syria

29. White Kibbeh with Yogurt-Tahini Sauce. Kibbeh *Baida*, Syria

30. Poached Stuffed Kibbeh with Tahini Sauce Garnished with Walnuts and Parsley. Syria

31. Poached Kibbeh with Tahini-Walnut Sauce, Fried Onions, and Chickpeas. Kibbeh *Ladanea*, Latakia, Syria

32. Poached Kibbeh Stuffed with Almonds, Fried Onions, and Meat, Garnished with Chickpeas and Lamb Shanks, and Served with Tahini Sauce and Hot Pepper. Kibbeh *Arnabeya*, Syria and Lebanon

33. Large Kibbeh Stuffed with Hard-Boiled Eggs, Poached in a Fava, Coriander, and Swiss Chard Stew. Kibbeh *Faleya*, Syria

34. Kibbeh Poached in Eggplant & Meat Stew. Syria and Lebanon

35. Kibbeh Poached in Artichoke and Meat Stew. Syria

36. Kibbeh Poached in Pumpkin and Meat Stew. Syria

BAKED KIBBEH

37. Tray *Köfte*, Gaziantep Style. Turkey
38. Kibbeh Patties Stuffed with Mixed Nuts and Sumac. Lebanon
39. Two-Layer Kibbeh Stuffed with Meat, Onions, and Nuts, Baked in a Tray. Kibbeh *bi Siniyyeh*, Lebanon and Syria

40. Tray Kibbeh Baked in a Tray with Tahini Topping. Israel
41. Potato Kibbeh Stuffed with Onions and Pine Nuts. Known as Kibbeh *Hileh,* or "trick kibbeh," because there is no meat. Syria
42. Coil-Shaped Kibbeh Stuffed with Pine Nuts, Walnuts, and Meat. Kibbeh *Mabrumih,* Damascus, Syria

LEFTOVER KIBBEH

43. Leftover Kibbeh Simmered in an Onion and Tomato Stew. Syria
44. Leftover Kibbeh Simmered in Onion Sauce with Chickpeas and Tahini. Syria
45. Fried Kibbeh Topped with Scrambled Eggs, then Baked. Syria
46. Red Lentil and Bulgur Blended with Leftover Filling of Ground Meat, Fried with Minced Onions and Pine Nuts. Damascus, Syria. This kibbeh is spread out on a plate, and topped with a sauce made with the remaining ground meat.

RAW KIBBEH

47. Flat, Cold Raw Kibbeh Topped with Warm Meat, Onions, and Walnut Sauce, Garnished with Mint and Parsley. Syria
48. Flat, Cold Raw Kibbeh Topped with Mint, Scallions, Parsley, and Olive Oil, and Served with a Warm Meat, Onion, and Tomato Sauce. Syria
49. Flat, Cold Raw Kibbeh Garnished with Olive Oil, Parsley, and Tomato, Lebanon
50. The Tank. Kibbeh *Debbaboh,* Damascus, Syria. Made with a raw shell stuffed with cooked meat, this kibbeh is shaped like a rocket and heavy like a tank.

MAKING KIBBEH: DETAILED INSTRUCTIONS

In stages, kibbeh is easily prepared. The filling can be made in advance, then frozen. You can shape and stuff kibbeh and store it in the refrigerator overnight, or freeze it up to one month. (Freezing actually produces extremely tender kibbeh.) Always prepare the stuffing first so it will be cold when you insert it into the shell.

THE STUFFING

The inside of a well-made kibbeh should be as juicy as possible. The classic stuffing consists of a little cooked meat, some stewed onions, a few toasted pine or other nuts, and spices. Some cooks enrich their kibbeh stuffing with butter or chopped lamb fat to obtain a juicy effect; I substitute more onions and very well drained yogurt.

Some kibbehs are so small there is no room for nuts in the stuffing. In some there is no stuffing at all, except maybe a chickpea-size ball of spiced butter. Others contain only stewed onions and sumac for a fruity, sour taste. A vegetarian kibbeh of pumpkin might have spinach and chickpea stuffing (page 276).

MAKING THE TRADITIONAL MEAT-AND-BULGUR SHELL

In the Middle East, there are women famous for having "kibbeh fingers." It is a pleasure to watch these specialists at work. Their dexterity is amazing, and the speed of their production nearly incredible.

Over the years I have watched Middle Eastern women shape kibbeh shell ovals on their forefingers, but I was almost thoroughly astonished by Aleppo's famous kibbeh maker Amal al-Jabri—a cheerful, middle-aged woman who invited me to her apartment for a lesson. Assisted by her old wet nurse, Amal dazzled me with her faultless dexterity, spinning out huge baseball-size shells on her thumb.

It helps to have a long forefinger around which to fashion the thin kibbeh shell. Once fashioned, the shell is carefully slipped off the finger, stuffed, and sealed with moistened fingertips.

Do not lose hope! If your forefinger is too soft or you don't have time to practice, you can still make patties and meatballs with the same kibbeh recipes.

To make a shell properly, you must understand the following different components of its assembly.

The Meat

To avoid tough kibbeh, use extremely lean lamb, from the loin or the leg, cleaned of all sinews, fat, and gristle so that it can be turned into a smooth paste.

Lean veal scallops, beef, turkey, and rabbit can be substituted for lamb, but because these meats do not have the same elastic powers, you will need to add a little flour or beaten egg to the mixture.

The Bulgur

The bulgur should be of the smallest grain variety. Place the bulgur in a fine sieve and shake it to release and remove any dust or dirt. It should then be moistened with just enough water to make it swell, but not so much that it turns mushy.

The Flavorings

Grated onion in small amounts can radically change the flavor of the shell. During handling, its mildly acrid flavor vaporizes, while its exuded liquid helps the mixture to bind. The correct proportion for salting is 1 to 1½ teaspoons salt per cup of meat paste, plus any or all of the following spices to taste: freshly ground black pepper, hot paprika, ground cumin, ground coriander seeds, ground cinnamon, ground allspice, or mixed spices.

The Water

It is important to understand that cold water is added gradually, not all at once. As the bulgur begins to swell, it turns hard, and more water is added to maintain a workable dough. If you add too much water, simply allow the mixture to stand until the water is absorbed, then add a small additional amount of bulgur to absorb the rest.

There comes a point, however, when the bulgur has absorbed all the water it possibly can and the addition of any more will push the mixture out of balance. At this point, you may want to add a little flour or beaten egg or a little mashed potato.

The Bulgur-Meat Ratio

Bulgur-meat ratios vary from recipe to recipe. Poached, baked, and fried kibbeh patties usually call for twice as much meat as bulgur. "Blind," or raw kibbeh (kibbeh without a filling), usually requires three times as much meat as bulgur. To cut down on the meat and still attain a high-quality kibbeh, I use mashed potato or an egg to help bind the shell.

Dietary Note

The average serving of three small kibbeh or one large kibbeh, including the filling, is about 2½ to 3 ounces meat. According to the American Heart Association's recommended guideline of 300 milligrams of dietary cholesterol per day, the cholesterol contained in a 3-ounce serving of lamb kibbeh amounts to less than 25 percent of the recommended maximum.

MIXING THE KIBBEH SHELL

Wash the bulgur in a sieve under running water, then allow it to drain. Puree the onion in the work bowl of a food processor. Add the meat and seasonings and process until smooth and pasty. Add a few tablespoons ice-cold water to the meat and process about 5 seconds, until well mixed. Add the bulgur and process for an instant. (You can do this in batches.)

Turn the mixture out onto a work surface, then knead the dough until it is smooth and pliable. Separate it into batches. Return one part to the food processor and knead in short bursts. Repeat with the second batch. (You don't want the mixture to heat up, lest it turn mushy.) Kibbeh dough should be cold, smooth, and a little sticky. Chill the dough in the refrigerator or freezer if it is soft.

continued

SHAPING THE SHELL

To facilitate shaping your kibbeh ovals, fill a wide, shallow bowl with cold water mixed with a tablespoon of cornstarch and a good pinch of salt. The salt inhibits the bulgur from turning mushy.

For easiest handling, wet both palms before shaping each oval and keep hands, fingers, and shell moist at all times.

Pinch off a piece of the ground lamb and bulgur mixture and roll into a smooth oval (below, left).

If you are right-handed, hold the ball in your wet left hand and make a hole in it with the forefinger of your right hand. Use the palm and cupped fingers of your left hand to mold a thin, egg-shaped, smooth oval around your forefinger (below, center).

Make quick open-and-closing motions with your left hand and fingers. Meanwhile twist your entire right hand from the wrist to the forefinger, making short half turns always in a clockwise direction. Left-handed cooks carry out this operation with opposite hands. Seal any breaks by briefly dipping the shell in the prepared water, then smoothing the dough.

STUFFING THE SHELL

Quickly slip the prepared filling into the shell. Pinch ends to seal, using a few drops of cold water to bind. Use fingertips to smooth out dough (below, right).

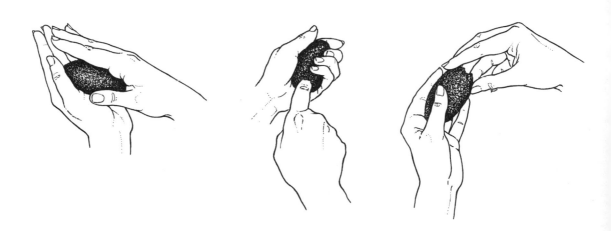

Gently squeeze the oval with wet palms to form a smooth football shape.

Spray the ovals with butter-flavored oil or olive oil, cover with plastic wrap, and refrigerate until ready to cook.

∽ COOKING THE KIBBEH ∾

The traditional way to cook kibbeh ovals is to fry them in oil until brown. (Some cooks insist kibbeh should be crackling crisp, whereas others prefer a soft, tender shell.) The same kibbeh can also be shaped into patties and broiled or pan fried in a nonstick skillet or baked until tender and brown. There are also many recipes for poaching or steaming kibbeh, to be served either warm or cold.

Whichever method you choose, to achieve a tender and moist result, do not overcook the kibbeh.

FRIED KIBBEH

KIBBEH OVALS STUFFED WITH NUTS

When you bite into this fried kibbeh, you should hear a little crackle, like the crunch of good baklava. The small amount of cornstarch in the water, used for molding the kibbeh into ovals, will help produce a crisper shell, by creating a thin cloak and thus keeping out the oil.

Serve this kibbeh hot or warm, with any of the dips on pages 22 to 24.

Makes 12 medium-size kibbeh ovals, serving 4 to 6

FILLING
½ cup chopped onion
I tablespoon olive oil
5 ounces ground lamb shoulder
¼ cup pine or other nuts, toasted
Pinch of Syrian Mixed Spices Number I (page 392)
Salt
Freshly ground black pepper
⅓ cup chopped parsley
6 tablespoons plain, low-fat yogurt, drained to 3 tablespoons
  (see page 410 for directions on draining yogurt)

I. To prepare the filling: Place the chopped onion and oil in a medium skillet and cook until golden and soft. Add the lamb and brown lightly, breaking up the meat with a fork, 5 minutes. Add ½ cup water and cook, uncovered, over low heat 15 minutes, or until all the water has evaporated and the meat begins to brown in its own fat. Add the pine nuts, mixed spices, salt, pepper, and parsley, and cook I to 2 minutes longer, stirring. Remove to cool. Fold in the yogurt.

2. Prepare the kibbeh dough as directed on page 267. Pinch off pieces of dough the size of apricots. Follow the instructions on page 268 for shaping and filling the ovals. Set the prepared ovals, ½ inch apart, on a flat tray, spray with oil, and freeze or refrigerate until ready to cook.

3. Fry a half dozen kibbeh at a time in hot oil until brown and lightly crisp. (Can be broiled on all sides.) Serve warm or at room temperature.

SHELL

¾ cup fine-grain bulgur

8 ounces fresh extra-lean ground leg of lamb

2 tablespoons grated onion

I teaspoon fine salt

¼ teaspoon freshly ground black pepper

¼ teaspoon Syrian Mixed Spices Number I

Pinches of cayenne and grated nutmeg

2 to 3 tablespoons cold water

Olive oil or butter-flavored oil spray

Oil for frying (optional)

EXTRA-CRISP OVALS STUFFED WITH PISTACHIOS

Here is a delicious, crunchy Turkish version of kibbeh called *Içli köfte*. I learned this recipe from Mrs. Fikriye Gulenler, a prize-winning cook in Gaziantep. The shell is extraordinarily crisp, because of the addition of a little mashed potatoes.

When I went to Mrs. Gulenler's home to take a lesson, I saw her prize, a 2-foot-high embossed Ottoman-style room heater called a *pasa mangali*, made of copper. It was on prominent display in her living room.

Mrs. Gulenler recalled how she had won the contest organized by the local newspaper: "I prepared *Içli köfte* for two hundred people. That was eleven years ago, and I'm still recovering." She paused. "You don't win first prize unless you take that extra step." Then she added, with humility, *"Inshallah"* (God willing).

Here is my adapted version. Serve it with one of the yogurt soups on pages 126–130, or as part of an eastern Mediterranean buffet.

continued

FILLING

½ cup chopped onion

1 tablespoon olive oil

5 ounces ground lamb shoulder

½ cup water

¼ cup pistachios, peeled and chopped

¼ cup chopped walnuts

½ teaspoon Near East or Aleppo pepper (page 395)

¼ teaspoon freshly ground black pepper

Dashes of ground cinnamon and allspice

Salt to taste

2 tablespoons chopped parsley

2 tablespoons butter or well-drained yogurt (see page 410
    for directions on draining yogurt)

SHELL

1 small boiling potato

6 ounces extra-lean ground leg of lamb

½ cup fine-grain bulgur

¼ cup grated onion

Salt

½ teaspoon freshly ground black pepper

⅛ teaspoon Near East or Aleppo pepper

Olive oil or butter-flavored oil spray

Oil for frying (optional)

1. To prepare the filling: Place the onion and olive oil in a medium skillet and cook until golden and soft. Add the lamb, breaking up the meat with a fork, and brown lightly 5 minutes. Add ½ cup water and cook, uncovered, over low heat 15 minutes, or until all the water has evaporated and the meat begins to brown in its own fat. Allow the meat to become crispy. Add the nuts, spices, salt, and parsley. Cook 1 to 2 minutes longer, stirring. Remove to cool. Fold in the butter or yogurt.

2. To make the shells: Prepare the kibbeh dough as directed on page 267. Boil the potato, then peel and mash it. Blend the dough with the mashed potato until completely homogenous. Pinch off walnut-size pieces of the mixture. Follow the instructions on pages 268 to 269 for shaping and filling the ovals; the ovals should be thin and small. Set ovals on a flat tray spaced ½ inch apart, spray with oil, and freeze or refrigerate until ready to cook.

3. Fry a half dozen shells at a time in hot oil until brown and crisp. (They can be broiled on all sides.) Serve warm or at room temperature.

BABY-SIZE KIBBEHS STUFFED WITH BRAISED LAMB SHANK, TOMATOES, AND ONIONS

These kibbehs, the lightest and tenderest of all, are a must at Damascene weddings. They are fried until brown but are not crisp lest they turn dry.

Serve with an assortment of dips, including *Baba Ghanoush* (page 26).

Makes about 36 kibbeh

1. Strip the meat off the bone and cut into 1-inch chunks. (Save the bone for some other purpose.) In a medium nonstick skillet, sauté the onion in the butter or oil over moderate heat until soft and golden, about 5 minutes. Add the meat and brown lightly. Add the tomato paste, water, salt, pepper, and spices and stir. Bring to a boil, partially cover, and cook over low heat until the meat is very tender and almost all the liquid has evaporated, about 45 minutes.

2. Cool the meat, then chop or pulse it 10 times in a food processor. Adjust the seasoning and chill before continuing. Makes about 1 cup filling.

3. See page 267 for making the kibbeh dough. Pinch off walnut-size pieces of the bulgur-meat dough to make, shape, and fill the kibbehs. See pages 268 to 269. The ovals should be thin and small. Set them out, ½ inch apart, on a flat tray, spray with oil, and freeze or refrigerate until ready to cook.

4. Fry a half dozen kibbehs at a time in hot oil until brown but not crisp. (They can be broiled on all sides.) Serve warm or at room temperature.

FILLING

1 large lamb shank, trimmed of excess fat

1 small onion, minced

2 tablespoons butter or olive oil

1 tablespoon tomato paste

2 cups water

Salt and freshly ground black pepper to taste

Pinch of Mixed Spices, Number 2 (page 393)

SHELL

3 cups fine-grain bulgur

1¼ pounds extra-lean ground leg of lamb

3 tablespoons ice water

3 tablespoons grated red onion

Olive oil or butter-flavored oil spray

Oil for frying

Vegetarian Kibbeh

Vegetarian Red Lentil Ovals with Tarragon-Onion Salad

The split, hulled red lentils found at health food stores and ethnic markets lose their shape when cooked, turning creamy and yellow. Mild-tasting on their own, they require assertive flavoring. In this superb vegetarian recipe, they are shaped into peppery ovals called *malhatali köftes*, after being blended with soaked cracked wheat, tarragon, and hot spices.

This dish is much loved in Gaziantep, where the local women keep it in the refrigerator (where it can be stored 2 to 3 days), to be brought out as a quick snack along with a tarragon and onion salad and a glass of chilled ayran, the popular yogurt drink (page 411).

Makes about 32 *malhatali köftes*, serving 4 to 6

1. Place the lentils in a medium-size heavy saucepan, cover with 3 cups salted water, and bring to a boil. Skim; reduce the heat to medium-low and cook until lentils turn yellow and mushy and the water is absorbed, about 30 minutes. (Add cold water if necessary to keep the lentils from burning. Cold water is said to make these lentils creamier.)

2. Add the red pepper and tomato pastes to the lentils and bring to a boil, stirring. Rinse the bulgur and place in a large bowl. Pour the boiling contents of the saucepan over the bulgur. Stir well and set aside until the bulgur has absorbed all the moisture, about 30 minutes.

3. In a small skillet, sauté the onion in the oil until golden brown. Add the garlic, cumin, and black pepper and cook over low heat 2 minutes longer. Add to the lentil-bulgur mixture and knead well. Mix in the red pepper, parsley, and tarragon and knead well again. Add lemon juice, salt, and more red pepper to taste. Use wet hands to pinch off plum-size pieces of the mixture and shape each into a small oval. Arrange on a large flat serving dish in a circle.

4. Mix together all the ingredients for the salad and place in the center of the dish. Surround with the romaine leaves. Serve warm or cold.

With thanks to Mrs. Filiz Höstulğu for sharing this recipe

I cup hulled red lentils, rinsed and drained

Salt

I ½ teaspoons homemade red pepper paste (page 389 or page 390)

I ½ teaspoons tomato paste

½ cup fine-grain bulgur

I large onion, peeled and finely chopped

2 tablespoons olive oil

2 small cloves garlic, peeled and chopped

I ½ teaspoons ground cumin

¼ teaspoon freshly ground pepper

Pinch of ground red pepper

⅓ cup chopped parsley

I tablespoon chopped tarragon

A few drops of lemon juice, or more to taste

Salt to taste

TARRAGON-ONION SALAD (*TARHIN PIYAZI*)

I cup tarragon leaves

⅓ cup thin-slivered onion

¼ cup chopped green bell pepper

I red ripe tomato, peeled, seeded, and chopped

⅓ cup chopped parsley

I teaspoon ground sumac

3 tablespoons fresh lemon juice

Salt to taste

Separated romaine lettuce leaves

Pumpkin Kibbeh Stuffed with Spinach, Chickpeas, and Walnuts

Serve with quartered lemon, a bowl of *Baba Ghanoush* (page 26), and Spiced Cheese with Red Onion and Tomatoes (page 137).

Makes 24, serving 4 to 6

FILLING

1/3 cup chopped onion

I tablespoon olive oil

1/2 cup cooked chickpeas, peeled and halved

1/4 cup chopped walnuts

1/3 cup cooked and chopped spinach, drained well (8 ounces fresh)

1/4 teaspoon sumac or more to taste

Salt and freshly ground black pepper to taste

Pinch of hot Hungarian paprika

2 to 3 teaspoons fresh lemon juice

PUMPKIN SHELL

I cup canned or fresh cooked pumpkin

2 cups fine-grain bulgur, unwashed

1/3 cup flour

2 tablespoons grated onion

2 teaspoons salt

I teaspoon freshly ground black pepper

Pinch of hot paprika

Oil for frying

I. To prepare the filling: In a small skillet, sauté the onion in the oil over moderately low heat until soft but not brown, about 5 minutes. Mix the onion with the chickpeas, walnuts, spinach, seasonings, and lemon juice.

2. In a mixing bowl, mash the cooked pumpkin to a puree. Place the bulgur in a fine sieve and shake it to loosen and remove any dust or dirt. Mix the dry bulgur, flour, grated onion, and seasonings with the pumpkin puree; blend well. Set aside 10 minutes. If the dough is too hard, add a few drops of water and knead well.

3. To shape the kibbeh: Knead about 2 tablespoons of the pumpkin mixture until it holds together; shape as directed on pages 268 to 269 and use about I teaspoon of the filling. After every two kibbehs have been shaped and filled, knead in a few more drops of cold water. Knead well after each addition so that the mixture remains malleable.

4. Heat oil to 375° F. Fry 4 or 5 kibbehs at a time, until golden on all sides, about 1½ minutes. Drain on paper toweling. Serve hot, warm, or cold.

With thanks to Mrs. Samira Ghorra for sharing this recipe

POACHED
AND STEAMED
❧ KIBBEH ❧

Poached and steamed kibbehs should be firm yet tender, but not soft like stuffed vegetables. Homely on their own, without an appetizing color, they enrich all kinds of stews made with fruits (quinces or cherries) or vegetables (artichokes, eggplants, or carrots). When made small, the size of marbles, they are steamed 5 minutes and added to soups. Small ovals are also smothered in yogurt or tahini sauces.

Poached and steamed kibbehs are lighter and easier to digest than those fried or baked. They are excellent served cold, to be dipped into thick yogurt, tahini, or chunky sauces made with greens, nuts, and spices.

KIBBEH WITH EGGPLANT AND SUMAC

This dish includes meltingly soft eggplant and lemony sumac, while allspice and cinnamon add a warm, spicy flavor. Some might call this dish "good grub" because of its abundant reddish-brown gravy, but Aleppines refer to it as the "Cadillac of kibbeh."

Serves 4

FILLING

1 large onion, chopped

1 tablespoon olive oil

5 ounces ground lamb shoulder or turkey

3 tablespoons pine nuts

½ teaspoons ground allspice

Salt and freshly ground black pepper to taste

⅓ cup chopped parsley

3 tablespoons drained yogurt (see page 410 for directions on draining yogurt)

SHELL

¾ pound extra-lean ground lamb or turkey

½ cup plus 1 tablespoon coarse-grain bulgur

2 tablespoons cold water

½ small onion

Salt

Freshly ground black pepper

½ teaspoon ground cumin

¼ teaspoon ground allspice

1 to 2 tablespoons flour if turkey is used

1. To prepare the filling for the kibbeh: Place the onion and oil in a medium skillet and cook until golden and soft. Add the lamb and brown lightly, breaking up the meat with a fork, 5 minutes. Add ½ cup water and cook, uncovered, over low heat 15 minutes, or until all the water has evaporated and the meat begins to brown in its own fat. Add the nuts and allow them to brown lightly. Then fold in the allspice, salt, pepper, and parsley and cook 1 to 2 minutes longer, stirring. Remove to cool. Fold in the yogurt.

2. Prepare the shell mixture as described on page 267. Pinch off 16 walnut-size pieces of shell mixture. Shape and fill as directed on pages 268 and 269. The ovals should be thin and small. Reserve any extra filling. Place a collapsible steaming rack in a wide saucepan. Add water to the pan, making sure it doesn't reach the rack. Bring to a boil, place half the kibbeh on the rack, cover the pan, and steam

the kibbeh 5 minutes. Repeat with the remaining kibbeh. (The kibbeh can be prepared ahead of time and kept in the refrigerator until 15 to 20 minutes before serving.)

3. To make the eggplant stew: Remove 5 vertical strips of skin from the eggplant, leaving it striped, then cut it into 8 thick wedges. Lightly salt the wedges and leave to drain in a colander 30 minutes.

4. Combine the sumac and 1 cup hot water in a small saucepan and bring to a boil. Remove from the heat and let stand while following step 5.

5. In a 5-quart casserole, heat half the oil

SUMAC-FLAVORED EGGPLANT STEW

1 large eggplant

Coarse salt

4 tablespoons sumac

3 tablespoons olive oil

1 or 2 pieces meaty lamb bones or 1 lamb chop cut into small pieces and trimmed of fat

1 large onion, cut into 8 pieces

1 cup cooked chickpeas

1 tablespoon tomato paste

1 cinnamon stick

Lemon juice (optional)

2 tablespoons chopped parsley

and brown the meaty bones. Transfer to a side dish. Add the onion to the casserole; brown over moderate heat 5 minutes. Return the meaty bones to the casserole. Add the chickpeas, tomato paste, cinnamon stick, and 3 cups water. (If you have extra filling, add it to the casserole.) Bring the liquid to a simmer, cover, and cook over moderately low heat 20 minutes.

6. Line a sieve with cheesecloth and strain the sumac liquid, squeezing the cheesecloth to remove as much liquid as possible. Add to the casserole. Discard the sumac.

7. Rinse the eggplant, squeeze gently, and pat dry with paper toweling. In a small skillet, heat the remaining oil, add the eggplant, and fry lightly, turning to brown on all sides. Drain and add to the casserole. Cover and cook about 1 hour, or until the eggplant is so tender that it is on the verge of collapsing.

8. Fifteen minutes before serving, add the partially cooked kibbeh and a little more water, if necessary, to keep the contents covered and continue simmering 15 minutes, covered. Discard the cinnamon stick.

9. Transfer the kibbeh to a heated large, deep serving platter. Sharpen the sauce with a squeeze of lemon juice, if desired. Ladle the vegetables and sauce over the kibbeh and serve with a sprinkling of chopped parsley. Serve with rice and a chopped vegetable salad (page 136).

With thanks to Adnan Al-Jabri for sharing this recipe

KIBBEH WITH GLAZED CARROTS AND POMEGRANATE

This very light, very good kibbeh is a popular family dish from Aleppo. I think that this dish requires no accompaniments except warm flat bread. For dessert, try semolina cakes stuffed with dates and walnuts (page 382).

Serves 4 to 6

FILLING

⅔ cup plain nonfat yogurt drained to one half (see page 410 for directions on draining yogurt)

Ground allspice to taste

Salt and freshly ground black pepper to taste

SHELL

7 ounces extra-lean ground leg of lamb

½ cup coarse-grain bulgur

1½ tablespoons ice water

3 tablespoons grated onion

¼ teaspoon ground allspice

Salt and freshly ground black pepper to taste

Olive oil or butter-flavored oil spray

POMEGRANATE-FLAVORED CARROT STEW

1 pound meaty lamb neck bones

Sea salt

Freshly ground black pepper

1½ pounds carrots

3 tablespoons butter or oil

1½ teaspoons garlic

2 teaspoons dried mint

1 teaspoon pomegranate molasses (page 404)

1. To make the filling: Blend the drained yogurt with the allspice, salt, and pepper and chill in the refrigerator.

2. To make the shell: Prepare the kibbeh dough as directed on page 267. Divide into 20 equal pieces. Follow instructions on pages 268 to 269 for shaping the kibbeh dough. Insert a teaspoon of the seasoned yogurt in each piece and seal. Set the prepared kibbehs on a flat tray, spaced ½ inch apart; spray with oil and freeze or refrigerate until ready to cook.

3. To make the stew: In a wide, deep saucepan, place the meaty bones and enough water to cover; bring to a boil and remove from the heat. Drain the meat and rinse it briefly under cold water. Rinse the pot. Return the meat to the pot, cover with 1 quart water, add the sea salt, and simmer, covered, until the meat is tender, about 1¾ to 2 hours.

Transfer the meat to a work surface. Use a small knife to work the bones loose, and discard them. Season the meat with salt and pepper. Degrease the cooking liquid. Return the meat to the liquid. (Up to this point, the dish can be made in advance.)

Pare and cut the carrots on the diagonal into thin slices. Heat the butter or oil in a large skillet. Add the carrots, cover, and cook over medium heat 20 minutes, turning the slices occasionally. The carrots should be glazed and aromatic. Add to the meat, along with the garlic, mint, and pomegranate molasses. Turn the heat to medium, cover the pan, and continue to cook 20 minutes.

4. Add the kibbeh to the simmering broth, cover the pot, and poach 5 to 10 minutes. Serve hot with rice or noodles.

With thanks to Mrs. Emilie Abdy, editor of Eating with Sitto, *published by St. Ann's Melkite Catholic Church in West Paterson, New Jersey, for sharing this recipe*

Green Kibbeh with Swiss Chard and Walnut Sauce

Here is a summery presentation of steamed kibbeh. The sauce is so good that you will want to use it for dipping bread.

Makes 12 kibbeh ovals

FILLING

2 tablespoons (1 ounce) pine nuts

2 tablespoons (1 ounce) walnuts, finely chopped

1 tablespoon olive oil or butter

1 cup chopped onion

5 ounces ground lamb shoulder

Salt and freshly ground black pepper to taste

1/8 teaspoon ground cinnamon

1/3 cup chopped parsley

1/2 cup plain low-fat yogurt, drained to 1/4 cup (see page 410 for directions on draining yogurt)

SWISS CHARD AND WALNUT SAUCE

3 tablespoons tahini

1/2 teaspoon crushed garlic

1/2 teaspoon salt

1/3 cup fresh lemon juice

1 1/2 pounds Swiss chard leaves, stemmed, steamed, refreshed, chopped, and squeezed dry

3 ripe tomatoes, halved crosswise, seeded, and the cut side rubbed on a four-hole grater to make 1 1/2 cups foamy pulp

1/2 teaspoon Near East or Aleppo pepper (page 395)

1/4 cup chopped parsley

1/4 cup chopped scallions

1/4 cup chopped walnuts

1. To make the filling: In a medium skillet, sauté the nuts in a teaspoon of the oil or butter until golden; remove to a paper towel to drain. Add the chopped onion and remaining oil and cook until golden and soft; then add the lamb and brown lightly, breaking up the meat with a fork, 5 minutes. Add 1/2 cup water and cook, uncovered, over low heat 15 minutes, or until all the water has evaporated and the meat begins to brown in its own fat. Add the salt, pepper, cinnamon, and parsley and cook 1 to 2 minutes longer, stirring. Remove to cool. Fold in the yogurt. Chill until ready to fill the kibbeh.

2. To make the sauce: Combine the tahini with the garlic and salt. Beat in the lemon juice to make a "tight" sauce. Thin with 2 tablespoons water, stirring. Add the Swiss chard and remaining ingredients for the sauce and thin with just enough cold water to create a napping consistency. Cover and chill at least 2 hours to blend the flavors.

3. To make the shell: Prepare the kibbeh dough as directed on page 267. Divide into 12 parts and shape and fill as di-

rected on pages 268 to 269. Place a collapsible steaming rack in a wide saucepan. Add water to the pan, making sure it doesn't touch the rack. Bring to a boil, place half the kibbeh ovals on the rack, cover the pan, and steam the ovals about 7 minutes. Repeat with the remaining ovals. Set aside to cool about I hour.

4. To serve, arrange the kibbehs on a flat platter, spoon over the sauce, and serve.

SHELL

6 to 8 ounces lean leg of lamb, trimmed of all fat and ground to a paste

¾ cup fine-grain bulgur

Pinch of ground cumin

¼ teaspoon ground allspice

1½ teaspoons salt

¼ teaspoon freshly ground black pepper

I small onion

Cayenne to taste

BAKED
❧ KIBBEH ❧

Kibbeh baked in a round tray is one of the easiest types of kibbeh to prepare successfully, since it requires no shaping. But it must be cooked carefully to maintain moistness. If for some reason it emerges too dry, you can use it to make the delicious recipe for leftover kibbeh at the end of the chapter.

Some cooks baste their baked kibbeh with stock, while others cook it with great quantities of fat. The trick is to use a tray or cake pan deep enough to keep the meat from drying out as the interior cooks and the surface browns to a crisp shell. It is better to undercook and finish browning under the broiler than to bake kibbeh too long and end up with a dry, inedible mass.

TRAY KÖFTE, GAZIANTEP STYLE

This version of tray *köfte* is very thin, no more than ⅔ inch high. Serve warm or hot with yogurt, salads, and dips.

Serves 10

1. Gently cook the meat and salt in the oil in a deep casserole until the meat throws off liquid. Add the onion and continue cooking, breaking the meat with a fork, until the meat begins to turn brown. Add the spices and nuts; cook until the meat is tender and a little crisp. Remove from the heat. Tilt the casserole and spoon off the excess fat. Cool and fold in parsley and yogurt. Chill well.

2. To make the shell: Place the bulgur in a sieve and wash under cool running water to moisten. Let stand 10 minutes.

3. Place the meat, onion, salt, and spices in a food processor and grind to a smooth and glossy paste. Remove half the meat mixture. Add half the bulgur and an ice cube and process 20 seconds. Remove and repeat with the remaining meat, bulgur, and ice cube. Combine and knead with the potato and more salt to taste until the mixture is like bread dough—smooth and elastic. (You may need to add extra spoonfuls of water.)

4. Preheat the oven to 375° F. Butter or oil a 9-by-13-by-2-inch baking dish.

5. Divide the mixture into 10 equal parts. Moisten hands with cold water. Press one portion of the kibbeh dough into an even ¼-inch-thick patty and place on the bottom of the pan. Repeat with 4 other parts and completely line the bottom of the pan, then use cold fingertips to smooth the pieces together. Spread the filling on top and gently press into the surface. Repeat with the remaining kibbeh dough to form a smooth top layer. Use the tip of a knife to score the entire top layer with crisscrossing lines, going three fourths of the way down. Loosen the edge with a spatula. Sprinkle with a little cold water and spread pistachios and melted butter or oil evenly on top. Bake 15 minutes and baste. Continue baking 10 minutes longer. Run under a broiler to brown the top. (Can be frozen cooked or uncooked.)

FILLING

10 ounces ground lamb shoulder
Pinch of salt
1 tablespoon olive oil or clarified butter
1 large onion, chopped
1 teaspoon Near East or Aleppo pepper (page 395)
1 teaspoon freshly ground black pepper
Pinches of ground cinnamon and allspice
⅓ cup chopped walnuts
⅓ cup skinned and chopped pistachios
4 tablespoons chopped parsley
3 tablespoons well-drained plain yogurt (see page 410 for directions on draining yogurt) or 1 tablespoon butter

SHELL

2 cups fine-grain bulgur
1¾ pounds ground lean lamb
½ large onion, grated
1 tablespoon salt
½ teaspoon Near East or Aleppo pepper
1 teaspoon freshly ground black pepper
2 ice cubes
1 large potato, boiled, peeled, and mashed (¾ cup)
12 skinned pistachios for garnish
¼ cup clarified butter or olive oil

KIBBEH PATTIES STUFFED WITH MIXED NUTS AND SUMAC

This delicious kibbeh, with its tart-flavored filling, is from the Chouf Mountains, above Beirut. I suggest you make small, round patties rather than ovals, since they are easier to form and can be baked instead of fried.

Serve with quartered lemons, any dip containing eggplant, or a bowl of plain yogurt mixed with crushed garlic, then sprinkled with fresh mint leaves (page 27).

Makes 30 to 36 kibbeh patties, serving 6

FILLING

4 teaspoons unsalted butter

⅓ cup pine nuts or chopped walnuts

I medium onion, finely chopped

½ pound ground lamb shoulder

Pinch of salt

¼ teaspoon freshly ground black pepper

I tablespoon ground sumac

½ teaspoon ground allspice or 2 teaspoons pomegranate molasses (page 404)

7 tablespoons plain low-fat yogurt, drained to 3½ tablespoons (see page 410 for directions on draining yogurt)

SHELL

¾ cup fine- or medium-grain bulgur

½ pound extra-lean ground leg of lamb

½ small onion, grated

Pinches of ground cumin and hot paprika

½ teaspoon fine salt

I. To make the filling: In a small skillet, melt I teaspoon of the butter, add the pine nuts or walnuts, and sauté until golden brown; remove from the heat. Add 3 teaspoons butter over moderate heat, stir in the onion, and cook, covered, until it is soft and golden, about 3 minutes. Add the meat to the skillet and cook, breaking the meat up with a fork, until lightly browned, about 3 minutes. Add ¾ cup water, a pinch of salt, the black pepper, and the sumac to the meat. Cover and cook over low heat until the moisture has evaporated from the skillet and the meat is very tender and juicy, about 30 minutes. Remove from the heat.

2. Add the allspice or pomegranate molasses and yogurt to the filling, crushing it into the mixture. Adjust the seasoning adding salt to taste. Store covered in the refrigerator until ready to use. (Up to this point, the filling can be prepared I to 2 days in advance.)

3. To make the shell: Prepare the kibbeh dough as directed on page 267, using the ingredients above. To shape the kibbeh into patties, wet both palms in the bowl of water with ice cubes before you shape each patty. Pinch off about 1 tablespoon of the dough. Place in the palm of one hand. Flatten it with moistened fingers into a 2¼-inch round patty. Place about 2 teaspoons of the chilled filling on the patty, then cup your palm to partially enclose the filling. Moisten your hands again and work the dough gently, stretching it into a thin shell to enclose the filling. Pinch to seal. Repeat with the remaining dough and filling. Gently flatten the patties and place in a single layer on a lightly greased baking sheet. Brush with oil or butter, cover with plastic wrap, and refrigerate until ready to cook. (They can be frozen at this point.)

4. To bake the patties, preheat the oven to 450° F. Remove the wrapping from the patties and bake them, turning once, 3 to 5 minutes on each side, until lightly browned outside but still juicy inside. (Add 5 minutes extra cooking time if using frozen patties.) Serve hot, at room temperature, or slightly chilled. Squeeze lemon juice over the patties and decorate with chopped mint shortly before serving.

NOTES TO THE COOK: This kibbeh can be fried in oil, broiled, or pan fried in a nonstick skillet until crisp.

½ teaspoon freshly ground black pepper
2 to 3 ice cubes in a bowl of water
½ to 1 tablespoon oil or clarified butter

Lemon juice
Chopped mint

LEFTOVER KIBBEH SIMMERED IN AN ONION AND TOMATO STEW

Leftover tray kibbeh, or simple poached or fried kibbeh without sauce, can be used to make this dish. In fact, it is worth making kibbeh if only to create leftovers with which to execute this delightful recipe.

Serves 2

About 6 ounces leftover cooked kibbeh

1 large onion, thinly sliced

2½ tablespoons olive oil

1 large ripe tomato, halved and grated to a pulp on a box grater

½ tablespoon tomato paste

Salt to taste

Pinch of Near East or Aleppo pepper (page 395)

Pinch of sugar

Freshly ground black pepper to taste

2 tablespoons chopped parsley

Cut the kibbeh into bite-size pieces and set aside. In a covered skillet, steam the sliced onions with the olive oil and ¼ cup water 15 minutes. Add the tomato, tomato paste, salt, and ½ cup water and cook, covered, 10 minutes. Fold in the kibbeh pieces and the seasonings, cover, and cook 5 minutes longer. Serve hot with a sprinkling of chopped parsley.

XI

Fish

*O*ne of the saddest things about the eastern Mediterranean region is the depletion of its once great fishing grounds. This has driven the price of good fish sky high, especially along the coast of the Levant. The waters still provide a fine selection, and the Greeks manage to find good fish too. But sometimes I suspect that the fish I am served in Greek restaurants is imported from Japan.

When an eastern Mediterranean cook buys a good-tasting fish, she is most likely to fry it or grill it simply over coals, and serve it with any number of sauces based on garlic, tahini, eggplant, coriander, walnuts, tomato, or chilis. If the fish has little taste, the cook is likely to braise it for a stew or boil it for soup. Don't expect the complex fish dishes you find in Western European cuisines. When you eat fish in the eastern Mediterranean, nine times out of ten it will be very simply cooked.

The most delicious fish for grilling is the sweet red mullet (our Caribbean goatfish) known as barbouni *in Greece,* tekir *in Turkey,* and Sultan Ibrahim Sakhri *in Syria and Lebanon. Mullets are not gutted, but grilled whole over hard charcoal.*

In inland parts of the region, fish is not very popular, perhaps because of memories of the years before refrigeration, when fish arrived in less than prime condition. Still, some salted fish and dried fish eggs play a minor role in the cooking of the region: Macedonians batter and fry rehydrated salt cod and serve it with a garlicky dip (page 18) and Syrians and Lebanese serve batrakh, *made with the dried and pressed roe of mullet. The best comes from Egypt, packed in creamy wax; they are cut into thin rounds and served simply with thin slices of garlic and a drizzle of olive oil.*

The region offers an assortment of flavorings that flatter fresh fish: pomegranate and coriander, cumin, cinnamon, and raisins. It is the use of such flavorings that distinguishes eastern Mediterranean fish dishes from those of Italy, France, and Spain.

FRYING FISH

Olive oil is the medium for frying fish. I hope readers won't be turned off by the notion. Fish properly fried can be light, delicious, and not at all fat soaked. Careful frying fits well with the healthy Mediterranean diet.

How is this possible? First, the fish must be very fresh. Second, only olive oil should be used. Third, the frying pan should be deep, wide, and made of heat-conducting steel thin enough to react to the cook's quick decisions. Fourth, the temperature of the oil must be absolutely correct—a frying thermometer is essential. (Oil at the correct temperature quickly seals the fish, locking in juices and flavor and locking out oil absorption.) Fifth, fish should not be crowded in the oil; cook in batches, allowing the oil to return to the correct temperature before continuing. Finally, flouring is important. Expert fryers use cake flour or other flour equally fine, with which they dust the fish quickly just before frying, shaking off the excess.

Most varieties of fish fry best at 375° F., usually in less than 5 minutes. There are two exceptions, small sardines and baby red mullets, which eastern Mediterranean cooks fry at 300° F. These two- to three-inch-long fish weigh about ¾ ounce, cook at the bottom of the pan, then rise when done, emerging crisp, golden, juicy, and oil-free. The olive oil used to fry them may be used many times since it is never allowed to reach its smoke point.

To store olive oil for reuse, cool and strain through cheese cloth that has been wrung out in vinegared water. Store in a cool place.

RAINBOW TROUT FILLETS WITH EGGPLANT AND POMEGRANATE

I recommend that you use red-fleshed rainbow trout when preparing this superb Georgian recipe. The visual contrast of crispy pink-fleshed fish and creamy black-skinned eggplant is stunning, the combination of flavors is intriguing, and the pomegranate juice adds a final tang.

Serves 4

1. Salt the fish and let stand 1 hour.

2. Cut the eggplant lengthwise into ⅓-inch-thick slices. Sprinkle the flesh with 1 teaspoon coarse sea salt; stack in layers in a nonreactive colander and press down with a weight. Let stand 30 minutes.

3. Rinse and dry the eggplant. Brush with olive oil and broil until golden brown on both sides (or you can dust them with flour and fry in hot oil until golden on both sides). Set aside.

4. Preheat the oven to 375° F. Arrange the fish in a 13-by-9-inch baking and serving dish. Sprinkle with pepper. Spread the scallions and herbs on top and cover with overlapping slices of eggplant. Bake, basting twice with the diluted pomegranate juice, until the trout flakes when touched with a fork, about 20 minutes. Serve warm with a sprinkling of coriander and parsley.

Coarse sea salt

4 6-ounce red-meat rainbow trout or baby salmon fillets, each ¾ to 1 inch thick (skin on)

1 8-ounce Japanese eggplant, stemmed and bottom end trimmed

Olive oil

½ teaspoon freshly ground black pepper

1½ tablespoons chopped scallions

2 tablespoons shredded basil leaves

2 tablespoons chopped coriander

2 teaspoons pomegranate molasses (page 404) diluted in ⅓ cup water

Chopped coriander and parsley for garnish

Spicy Fish Fillets with Bulgur and Caramelized Onions, Latakia Style

One of the most popular baked fish dishes of the Levant is called *sayyadiah*. It is a casserole of fish, rice, and onions, sometimes tinted red by saffron or turmeric, with yellow raisins and pine nuts added for sweetness. In this version from the Syrian coast, the dish is tinted red with delicious Aleppo pepper, part of a chunky salsa-style topping of tomatoes, garlic, spices, and lemon juice. The topping is spread over the fish, which is then baked until glazed. Coarse-grain bulgur replaces rice, and the onions are allowed to caramelize. The result is spicy and wonderful.

In Latakia, a whole fish is used. The cook fries the fish in oil to firm up the body, removes it from the skillet, and lifts off the fillets. The skin, frame, and head are then returned to the skillet to flavor the oil, which is used to flavor the bulgur.

In this simplified version, fish fillets are firmed up with a light dusting of flour and a quick searing in a nonstick skillet. Then the skillet is deglazed to make a simple broth.

The first 4 steps may be completed early in the day.

Serves 4

1. Season the fish fillets with a mixture of salt, pepper, ¼ teaspoon of the mixed spices, and cloves. Cover with plastic wrap and refrigerate until ready to cook.

2. Peel, quarter, and slice the Spanish onion lengthwise. (These are locally called "wings.") Heat half the oil in a heavy 9-inch skillet, add the onion wings, stir once, cover, and cook over low heat 20 minutes.

3. Meanwhile, heat I tablespoon oil in a small saucepan and stir in the bulgur, half the cumin, and half the oregano; fry, stirring constantly, 2 minutes. Add ½ teaspoon salt and the boiling water. Allow the bulgur to boil about 5 minutes, then cover, reduce the heat, and cook 15 minutes, or until all the liquid has been absorbed. Set aside, covered, to finish cooking.

4. In a small skillet, heat another tablespoon oil, add the chopped onion, and cook, stirring, I minute. Add the tomato, garlic, ¼ teaspoon salt, Aleppo pepper, remaining oregano, cumin, and ½ teaspoon mixed spices and cook, stirring often, 5 minutes. Add the lemon juice and 2 tablespoons water. Bring to a boil, stirring, and remove from the heat to rest 15 minutes, then stir up with a fork. (Up to this point, the recipe can be prepared up to 2 hours in advance.)

5. Thirty minutes before serving, preheat the oven to 400° F. Spread the onion wings in a 6- or 8-cup shallow baking dish and spread the bulgur on top in one even layer. Pat the fish fillets dry with paper toweling; dredge in flour and dust off the excess.

6. Heat the remaining I tablespoon oil in a nonstick skillet and sear the fish I minute on each side. Place the fish fillets on top of the bulgur and coat with the tomato mixture. Bake 15 minutes. Serve with a topping of chopped coriander.

4 small, delicate fish fillets (farmed catfish, halibut, rainbow trout, or bass)
Sea salt
Freshly ground black pepper
¾ teaspoon Syrian Mixed Spices, Number Two (page 393)
Pinch of ground cloves
I extra-large Spanish onion
6 tablespoons olive oil
I cup coarse-grain bulgur
½ teaspoon ground cumin
I teaspoon Mediterranean oregano
1½ cups boiling water
½ cup chopped onion
I fresh or canned tomato, peeled, seeded, and chopped
2 teaspoons crushed garlic
¾ teaspoon Aleppo or Near East pepper (page 395) or to taste
Juice of ½ lemon
Flour for dredging
2 to 3 tablespoons chopped coriander

BAKED FISH FILLETS WITH WALNUT AND FRESH CORIANDER SAUCE

⬦

This fish dish, with its rich and aromatic sauce, is best made in autumn when walnuts are fresh but the weather still warm enough to serve fish tepid. The sauce is a tasty marinade for cooked fish, so you should make the dish hours in advance. Refrigerate it up to one day, but bring it back to room temperature before serving.

Serves 2 to 4

2 to 4 small fillets of white-fleshed fish, each fillet weighing about 5 ounces

Sea salt

WALNUT AND CORIANDER SAUCE

2 ounces shelled walnuts, finely grated or chopped

Sea salt

½ scant teaspoon hot Hungarian paprika

⅓ cup warm water

2 plump cloves garlic, peeled and halved

3 tablespoons olive oil

1 packed cup chopped coriander

Juice of 1 lemon or more to taste

Lemon wedges or slices for garnish

1. Rinse the fish fillets, dry them, and sprinkle with salt. Cover and refrigerate for at least 1 hour.

2. To make the sauce: In a mortar, mini-chopper, or spice mill, grind the walnuts with ¼ teaspoon salt and the paprika. Pound until the walnuts exude their oil and the mixture is pasty. Gradually blend in just enough warm water to make the walnuts turn creamy and light-colored. Scrape into a small bowl.

3. Crush the garlic, together with a pinch of salt. Heat the oil in a small skillet over medium-low heat. Add the garlic and coriander and cook, stirring, until the oil just begins to sizzle, 2 to 3 minutes. Add to the walnuts, along with the lemon juice and enough of the remaining water to make a sauce of napping consistency. Correct the seasoning. Makes about 1 cup.

4. Preheat the oven to 400° F. Spread the fish fillets on an oiled baking sheet. Lightly brush with oil and bake the fish until just cooked, 5 minutes. Transfer the fish fillets to a shallow serving dish. Leave to cool.

5. Spread an even layer of sauce over each fish fillet, garnish with lemon wedges, and serve at room temperature.

Adapted from a recipe by Sima Osman Yassine and Sadouf Kamal

FISH POACHED IN CUMIN-FLAVORED TOMATO SAUCE

This simple, homespun dish for two requires little time and only one skillet. Good with a rice pilaf and sautéed spinach.

Serves 2

I. Rinse the fish, pat dry with paper towels, and sprinkle with sea salt. Let stand I hour.

2. Meanwhile, peel and thinly slice the onion, celery, and garlic and gently steam with the olive oil in a covered skillet 2 to 3 minutes. Add the cumin and red pepper and cook, stirring, I minute longer. Add the tomato and ½ cup water and bring to a boil. Add a pinch of salt and black pepper to taste and cook, stirring, I minute.

3. Fold each fillet in half and slip into the simmering sauce, cover, and cook over medium-low heat 5 to 8 minutes, or until the fish is done (the time varies with the thickness of the fillet). Transfer the fish to a shallow serving dish. Boil the pan juices to reduce to a napping consistency. Pour over the fish and let stand until ready to serve. Serve warm with parsley sprinkled on top.

2 6-ounce white-fleshed fish fillets

Sea salt

I large onion

I large rib celery

I clove garlic

I teaspoon olive oil

½ teaspoon ground cumin

Pinch of Near East or Aleppo pepper (page 395) or cayenne

I ripe tomato, halved crosswise, seeded, and rubbed on a box grater to make ¼ cup pulp (discard the skin)

Pinch of salt

Freshly ground black pepper to taste

Chopped fresh parsley for garnish

Fish Poached in Morel Sauce

*I*n Turkey I learned how to poach fish fillets in a thick, intensely flavored poaching liquor of chunky vegetables, grated tomatoes, and sliced morels, which was then used as the sauce. Made with black morels picked in the woods near the city of Izmir, the result was divinely aromatic.

Nearly all the recipes in this book were gathered from women working in simple home kitchens. Aybek Surdam, executive chef at the Istanbul Hilton, was one of the very few exceptions. This is his superb version of a traditional dish, *lev-rek bugulama.*

Serves 4

5 fresh morels, stems removed, heads quartered if large

2 teaspoons olive oil

⅓ cup chopped red onion

2 Italian green frying peppers, stemmed, cored, and thinly sliced

1 long green chili, stemmed, cored, and thinly sliced

2 tablespoons chopped parsley

1 large vine-ripened tomato, halved crosswise, seeded, and rubbed on a box grater, to make ½ cup pulp (discard the skin)

½ cup fruity white wine

Salt

Freshly ground black pepper

1 pound turbot fillets or sea bass, fluke, flounder, or sole fillets

A few drops lemon juice

1. Wash the morels in a bowl of water; swish to release dirt, drain, and pat dry inside and out with a cloth. Set aside.

2. In a 12-inch nonstick skillet, heat 2 teaspoons olive oil over low heat. Add the onion, cover, and steam until wilted, about 1 minute. Add the sliced peppers, chili, half the parsley, and the morels and cook over medium heat 1 minute, stirring. Add the tomato, wine, and salt and pepper to taste. Cover and cook over medium heat 5 minutes.

3. Season the fish lightly with salt and pepper. Fold each fillet in half and slip into the simmering sauce, cover, and cook over medium-low heat 5 to 8 minutes, or until done (the time varies with the thickness of the fish fillet).

4. Transfer the fish to a shallow serving dish. Boil the pan juices to reduce to a napping consistency. Correct the seasoning and sharpen the flavor with a few drops of lemon juice. Pour over the fish and let stand until ready to serve, warm or at room temperature (not hot) with the remaining parsley.

FISH SMOTHERED IN A TAHINI SAUCE

A lean white fish baked with tahini makes a rich, sensual combination. Tahini doesn't preserve its smooth look when cooked, but heating brings out its nutty flavor. To enhance the appearance of this splendid recipe, I took an idea from a photograph in *In a Caliph's Kitchen* by David Waines, a book on medieval Arabic cooking, and added toasted hazelnuts on top. Serve at room temperature or chilled. A plate of pickled vegetables is just the thing to serve with the fish.

Serves 6

1. Season the fish with the salt, pepper, and cayenne. Sprinkle with lemon juice and set in the refrigerator for 1 hour.

2. In a medium skillet, heat the oil over moderately low heat. Add the onions and cook, stirring occasionally, until soft and a deep golden brown, about 15 minutes.

3. To make the sauce: Mix the tahini with the garlic and lemon juice in the work bowl of a food processor. With the machine on, slowly add ½ cup cold water until the sauce is creamy and smooth.

4. Preheat the oven to 375° F. Oil a 10-inch ovenproof serving dish. Place the fish in the baking dish, cover with a sheet of foil, and partially cook 10 minutes. Cut the fillets into bite-size chunks, fold in the fried onions, and mix lightly.

5. Spread the tahini sauce over the fish and onions, scatter the hazelnuts on top, and return to the oven to bake 15 minutes longer.

2 pounds thick white-flesh fish fillets, such as halibut
¾ teaspoon sea salt
½ teaspoon freshly ground black pepper
Pinch of cayenne, or more to taste
2 tablespoons fresh lemon juice
3 tablespoons olive oil
2 onions, peeled and cut into eighths

TAHINI SAUCE
¼ cup tahini
2 cloves garlic, peeled and crushed with ½ teaspoon salt
½ cup lemon juice
½ cup cold water

3 tablespoons chopped hazelnuts

PEPPER FISH

❧

In this Lebanese party dish, a whole fish is stuffed with a combination of green pepper and walnuts, then coated with a lemony tahini sauce. Decorated with pomegranate seeds, walnut halves, coriander sprigs, and lemon slices, it makes a beautiful presentation.

A good red snapper is ideal. If you use fillets, arrange them in an attractive baking dish, with the stuffing smeared in between; serve directly from the dish.

Serves 6

1. About 3 hours before serving, season the fish with sea salt, half the black pepper, and the red pepper.

2. To make the stuffing: In a 10-inch skillet, heat the oil, add the onions, and cook, covered, until they are soft and golden, about 5 minutes. Add the green pepper, chili, and walnuts and cook 2 to 3 minutes. Season lightly with salt and black pepper. Remove from the heat and stir in half the parsley and coriander.

3. Preheat the oven to 350° F. Oil an oval baking dish for the whole fish or a 9-inch round or square baking dish for the fillets.

4. Stuff the whole fish, close the opening with string, coat with oil, and bake, basting often, 45 minutes. If you are using fillets, place half in the prepared dish, spread with the onion-pepper-walnut mixture, and top with another layer of fish. Brush with oil and bake 20 minutes, or until the fish flakes when touched with a fork.

5. Combine the tahini, garlic, and lemon juice in a food processor and blend until white and "tight." With the machine on, slowly add water until a mayonnaise consistency is reached.

4 pounds whole red snapper or 2 pounds lean white-flesh fish fillets
1½ teaspoons sea salt (use ¾ teaspoon salt for fish fillets)
1 teaspoon freshly ground black pepper
½ teaspoon Near East or Aleppo pepper (page 395)

STUFFING

2 tablespoons olive oil
2 medium onions, chopped (2 cups)
1 small green bell pepper, chopped (1¼ cups)
1 tablespoon minced green chili or more to taste
¾ cup finely crushed walnuts (3 ounces)
Sea salt
Freshly ground black pepper
⅓ cup chopped parsley
⅓ cup chopped coriander

TAHINI SAUCE

1 cup tahini
3 large cloves garlic, peeled and crushed with 1 teaspoon salt
½ cup fresh lemon juice or more to taste
⅔ cup cold water

Olive oil for the baking dish and for basting the fish
lemon wedges
2 tablespoons fresh pomegranate seeds
6 coarsely chopped walnuts

6. Remove the fish from the oven and pour the tahini sauce over the fish. Just before serving, garnish with lemon wedges, pomegranate seeds, walnuts, and the remaining parsley and coriander. Serve warm.

Adapted from Lebanese Cookbook *by Dawn, Elaine, and Selma Anthony*

Marinated and Fried Small Fish with Rosemary

This old northern Greek recipe has always fascinated me. Numerous small fish are first fried, then soaked in a marinade of salt, garlic, rosemary, sugar, and vinegar. If well covered, the dish will keep for some time. It tastes delicious around day five!

Whenever I have been served this dish, there have been sprigs of rosemary in the sauce. In fact, rosemary is an excellent preservative of fried foods, and its distinctive flavor adds a special quality.

Serve cold with crusty bread and a shredded romaine lettuce salad.

Serves 6

1 pound very small fish, such as smelts (about 20), fresh or defrosted, cleaned, head on, rinsed and wiped dry

Sea salt

Freshly ground black pepper

Juice of ½ lemon

8 tablespoons extra-virgin olive oil

Flour or semolina for dredging

1 tablespoon crushed garlic

4 teaspoons finely chopped fresh rosemary

⅓ cup white wine vinegar

1 cup dry white wine

½ teaspoon sugar

1 tablespoon dried currants

1 ripe tomato, halved crosswise, seeded, and rubbed on a box grater, to make ½ cup pulp (discard the skin)

1 tablespoon chopped flat-leaf parsley

Sprigs of rosemary for garnish

1. Open up each fish, pull out the central bone, and discard. Rinse the fish.

2. Mix 2 teaspoons sea salt with ¼ teaspoon black pepper, and season the fish evenly. Sprinkle with the lemon juice. Cover and refrigerate at least 1 hour.

3. Heat 4 tablespoons of the oil in a 9-inch skillet. Thoroughly dry the fish with paper towels. Dust them lightly with flour, and fry in batches in the hot oil until crisp and golden, about 2 minutes to a side, turning only once. Transfer to a 10-inch round porcelain or glass serving dish. Pour the oil through a strainer. Wipe out the skillet and return the oil to it.

4. Stir 1 tablespoon flour into the oil and brown lightly. Add the garlic, rosemary,

vinegar, wine, sugar, a pinch of salt, and the currants and heat, stirring, until boiling; simmer, uncovered, I to 2 minutes.

5. Add the remaining 4 tablespoons oil, tomato, and parsley and bring just to a boil. Pour the simmering marinade over the fish. Let the mixture cool completely, cover with plastic wrap, and refrigerate at least 3 days and preferably 4 to 5 days. Be sure to turn the fish daily to keep them moist and to allow the marinade to flavor the flesh. Serve the fish chilled with a garnish of rosemary sprigs.

MARINATED AND FRIED CATFISH, ALEPPO STYLE

This well-spiced fish is usually served with a cold salad of boiled cubed potatoes mixed with plenty of chopped parsley and scallions, seasoned with a dash of Aleppo pepper and ground cumin, and dressed with plenty of lemon juice and olive oil.

Serves 3

1 thick fillet farmed catfish (about 1 pound)

MARINADE
1 tablespoon grated onion
½ teaspoon crushed garlic
1 teaspoon sea salt
¼ teaspoon Syrian Mixed Spices, Number 2 (page 393)
1 teaspoon Near East or Aleppo pepper (page 395)
½ teaspoon ground cumin
Grated peel of ½ orange
½ tablespoon strained fresh lemon juice

Flour for dusting
Olive oil for frying

1. Divide the catfish fillet into 3 serving pieces. Combine the ingredients for the marinade and let soak about 1 hour.

2. Heat enough oil to the depth of 1 inch in a frying pan. Drain the fish, wipe dry with paper toweling, and dust lightly with flour. Fry in the hot oil until cooked and dark brown on both sides. Serve hot or cold with a parsley-rich potato salad.

SARDINES WRAPPED IN GRAPE LEAVES

In the eastern Mediterranean region, fish are often wrapped in leaves before they are cooked. In Turkey and northern Greece fresh sardines are wrapped in grape leaves before grilling; in Turkey, turbot are wrapped in wilted Swiss chard leaves before baking; and in Georgia I ate tiny river trout, no longer than my index finger, wrapped in walnut leaves and pan fried. This leaf-wrapping creates wondrous effects, preserving moistness and imbuing fragrance. If you decide to wrap a fish in jarred grape leaves, be sure first to rinse the leaves well of the brine.

If fresh grape leaves are available, use them without blanching.

This wonderfully simple dish of sardines wrapped in grape leaves and grilled over hot coals is from Turkey. Here the leaves are not eaten but simply used to keep the sardines' natural juices from escaping during cooking and to imbue the fish with their mildly pungent flavor.

The sardines must be absolutely fresh. I use frozen sardines, imported from Portugal, and sold in 2-pound bags in Latin American and Portuguese fish markets.

Salt the sardines while still frozen to ensure firmness as they defrost. The salt will also flavor the flesh.

Serves 6

1. Rinse partially defrosted sardines and pat them with paper toweling. Sprinkle them with sea salt and pinches of hot paprika on both sides and keep in the refrigerator until ready to grill.

2. Heat hardwood charcoal until you have hot coals. Wrap each sardine with 1 leaf, shiny side out, and place on the grill. Grill about 2 minutes to a side. Remove the sardines from the grill and serve at once with lemon wedges. Each person removes the leaves and flavors the fish with lemon juice.

12 large sardines

Coarse sea salt

Pinches of hot paprika

12 large grape leaves, fresh or packed in brine

12 lemon wedges

SWORDFISH PILÂKISI

Poaching fish or mussels (and also dried mottled beans) in a light olive oil–based sauce rich with chunks of diced carrots, potatoes, celery, onion, and garlic is a popular method called *pilâki* in Turkey. Whether you are cooking fish, mussels, or beans, the vegetables are first sautéed in olive oil, then the fish or beans are added along with seasoning, including a small amount of sugar, which gives the sauce a thick, syrupy quality and makes it glisten. The dish is served at room temperature.

In restaurants around Istanbul you are likely to find this sauce served with mullet or mussels, but I use it with swordfish—a popular combination in people's homes.

Serves 4

1½ pounds swordfish, cut into 4 portions

Sea salt

Freshly ground black pepper

2 tablespoons olive oil

1 medium onion, halved and finely sliced

1 carrot, pared and diced (⅓ cup)

1 potato, pared and diced (⅓ cup)

1 small rib celery, diced (2 tablespoons)

6 small cloves garlic, peeled but left whole

¼ teaspoon sugar

1 ripe tomato, halved crosswise, seeded, and rubbed on a box grater, to make ½ cup pulp (discard the skin)

½ lemon, peeled, seeded, and thinly-sliced

4 to 5 sprigs dill

Juice of ½ lemon

¼ cup roughly chopped flat-leaf parsley

1. Lightly sprinkle the fish with the salt and pepper and set aside.

2. In a 10-inch skillet, heat the oil. Add the onion, cover, and cook over medium heat until the onion just begins to turn golden, about 5 minutes. Add the carrot, potato, celery, garlic, and sugar and cook, stirring, until the vegetables just begin to brown and turn glossy, about 5 minutes. Add the tomato and 1 cup water and bring to a strong boil and cook, uncovered, over high heat 30 seconds; then lower the heat, cover the pan, and cook 10 minutes.

3. Slip in the portions of fish, baste with the vegetables, arrange a slice of lemon on each piece of fish, and top with the dill. Cover the skillet and cook over low heat 10 more minutes. Sprinkle with the lemon juice and

baste to mix well. Set aside for at least 2 hours before adjusting the seasoning. Serve at room temperature, garnished with the parsley.

With thanks to Tuğrul Şavkay

SKEWERED SWORDFISH

Eastern Mediterranean cooks often treat fish with marinades. In Georgia, when both sturgeon and pomegranates are in season, Georgian cooks combine the two before barbecuing, then serve the finished dish with a thick sauce of reduced pomegranate juice.

One of the best swordfish marinades is used by Turks. They literally soak the fish steaks or cubes in lots of lemon juice flavored with slivers of garlic, crumbled bay leaf or Mediterranean oregano, and a little olive oil for about 1 hour. This marinade has an almost magical effect, moistening and bringing out flavor.

Serves 2

1. In a shallow glass or porcelain dish, mix the lemon juice, garlic, oil, sea salt, pepper, and bay leaves or oregano. Add the swordfish cubes and let soak for at least 1 hour.

2. Skewer the swordfish, alternating with bay leaves if you are using them. Grill over hot coals, 4 inches from the flame, about 2 to 3 minutes to a side. The cubes should be fully cooked but still moist. Serve at once with lemon wedges.

3 tablespoons strained fresh lemon juice

2 cloves garlic, peeled and sliced

2 tablespoons olive oil

½ teaspoon sea salt

Freshly ground black pepper to taste

2 imported bay leaves, halved, or 2 pinches crumbled dried
    Mediterranean oregano

¾ pound swordfish, cut into 1¼-inch cubes

Lemon wedges for garnish

MUSSELS SAGANAKI

In this popular recipe from Salonika, mussels are simmered in a shallow pan with two handles (called a *saganaki*), along with green chili, herbs, tomatoes, and powdered mustard. Cubes of feta are added just before serving. The combination may surprise you, but be assured this is an intensely flavorful first course.

Note that steps 1 through 4 can be completed many hours in advance.

Serves 3 to 4

3 pounds unshelled mussels

Sea salt

Freshly ground black pepper

Fresh lemon juice

1 tablespoon olive oil

1 long green chili, stemmed, seeded, and finely chopped
   (2½ teaspoons)

⅓ cup chopped flat-leaf parsley

5 large spearmint leaves, shredded

¼ teaspoon crumbled dried *rigani* (Greek oregano)

½ teaspoon peeled and crushed garlic

Pinch of hot red pepper flakes

1 teaspoon powdered mustard

½ cup peeled, seeded, and chopped tomatoes, fresh or
   canned (if canned, drain well)

3 ounces imported feta, preferably Bulgarian

2 tablespoons chopped flat-leaf parsley for garnish

1. Scrub the mussels, pull off the beards, and rinse in several changes of water. Place the mussels in a bowl of lightly salted cool water and let stand at least 30 minutes so they purge themselves of sand. (Farmed mussels do not need soaking; if soaked, they lose all their flavor.)

2. Put the mussels and ½ cup water in a wide, deep skillet or saucepan, cover and cook until they open, about 2 minutes. (If the shells are just beginning to open, leave them 1 minute longer, but do not overcook.) Transfer the mussels to a bowl in order to catch their juices. Strain the cooking liquid through several layers of damp cheesecloth and reserve. When the mussels are cool enough to handle, remove them from their shells and cut off any remaining byssus threads. Sprinkle the mussels with the black pepper and a few drops of lemon juice. Strain any collected liquor in the bowl and add to the reserved broth.

3. In a 9-inch skillet, heat the oil over medium-low heat. Add 2 teaspoons of the chili and the parsley and cook 1 minute, stirring. Add the mussel cooking liquid, mint, *rigani*, garlic, hot red pepper flakes, mustard, tomatoes, and ¼ teaspoon black pepper and quickly bring to a boil. Cook over medium heat 5 minutes, stirring often, or until the sauce has thickened to about 1¼ cups. If desired, add the remaining green chili to taste. Bring back to a boil for an instant, then remove from the heat and allow to cool, about 10 minutes.

4. Add the mussels to the sauce, cover, and refrigerate. (Up to this point, the dish can be made 1 day in advance.)

5. Twenty minutes before serving, soak the feta in cold water 15 minutes, then drain and cut into small cubes. Reheat the mussels and the sauce in a wide skillet over medium-low heat to heat through. Do not allow the sauce to boil. Add the cubes of feta and cook, stirring, about 2 minutes longer. Adjust the seasoning and serve at once with a sprinkling of the parsley.

MARINATED AND GRILLED OCTOPUS

Here is a delectable appetizer to serve hot or cold, accompanied by a glass of chilled white wine, raki, or ouzo. One reason you might like octopus: It eats only shellfish, and its flesh is delicate and sweet.

Your fishmonger can get you frozen octopus, or you can buy it "freshly defrosted" during Lent, when fish markets usually double or triple their selection. During the rest of the year try Greek, Italian, or Oriental markets.

Since octopus is sold frozen, you won't need to tenderize it by beating. Freezing does the tenderizing for you.

Serves 6 to 8 as an accompaniment to drinks

I large octopus (about 4 pounds)
Coarse sea salt

MARINADE
½ cup red or white wine vinegar
2 teaspoons dried oregano
3 bay leaves
I½ teaspoons coarse sea salt
¾ teaspoon sugar
I lemon, peeled, seeded, and diced
Olive oil (enough to cover the octopus during marination)

Freshly ground black pepper
Lemon wedges for garnish

1. Up to 2 weeks before serving, defrost the octopus overnight in a bowl of lightly salted water. Detach the tentacles in one piece and press out the beak. Clip the eyes from the head and discard them. Turn the hood inside out and discard the viscera. Wash and rinse thoroughly under cool running water.

2. Place the octopus in a deep, heavy casserole and cover with a lid. (Do not add liquid.) Set the octopus over medium heat and cook until the water produced evaporates and the flesh is tender and rosy red, about I½ hours. If necessary, add a little water and continue cooking. Be sure to turn the octopus often for even cooking.

3. Drain the octopus in a colander and rinse under running water; rub off the skin and discard. Shake the octopus dry, rub the flesh with coarse sea salt, and leave to dry on a towel-lined plate in the refrigerator at least 12 hours.

4. Cut the chilled octopus into a 2-inch pieces and tightly pack in a I-quart wide-mouth Mason jar. In an enamel or stainless steel pan, combine the vinegar, oregano, bay leaves, salt, and sugar and bring to a boil. Ladle the boiling liquid into the jar. Add the lemon pulp and the olive oil, filling to within 1/8 inch of the top. Cover, cool, and refrigerate up to 1 week.

5. Remove from the refrigerator about 1 hour before serving. Arrange the pieces of octopus onto 8 skewers; reserve the marinade. Broil about 3 inches from hot coals until browned along the edges and just heated through, turning once and brushing with the reserved marinade. Serve at once with a grinding of black pepper and wedges of lemon.

VARIATION:

Remove the octopus from the marinade about 1 hour before serving. Drain; cut into bite-size pieces and spear with toothpicks. Do not grill the octopus. Top with a grinding of black pepper and garnish with lemon wedges. Serve at room temperature.

XII

Poultry

CHICKEN BROILED WITH LEMON AND YOGURT MARINADE

This is a dish Macedonians call Golden Chicken, because of its crisp, golden skin. It is very easy to make. Serve with boiled potatoes, onions, and rehydrated hot peppers mashed to a puree and seasoned with oil, vinegar, and garlic.

Serves 4

1. Trim the chicken to remove excess fat.

2. Mix the lemon juice, garlic, paprikas, allspice, salt, and black pepper; coat the chicken pieces with this mixture. Cover and refrigerate overnight.

3. Bring the chicken to room temperature.

4. Start a hardwood charcoal fire in an outdoor grill or heat the broiler. Brush the broiling rack with oil and set about 6 inches from the heat source.

5. Place the chicken skin side down, coat with the yogurt, and grill or broil, basting often, until the chicken is very tender, 25 to 30 minutes.

8 chicken thighs

⅓ cup fresh lemon juice

3 cloves garlic, peeled and crushed with salt

1 teaspoon sweet paprika

½ teaspoon hot Hungarian paprika

Pinch of ground allspice or cinnamon

Salt and freshly ground black pepper to taste

1 cup plain non-fat yogurt, drained to ½ cup (see page 410 for directions on draining yogurt)

Rolled Breast of Chicken Glazed with Pomegranate

Here is a variation on a Georgian dish in which a chicken breast is flattened, stuffed with a fresh mozzarella type of cheese, then basted during broiling with a sweet-and-sour pomegranate glaze. It is as good as it sounds!

Serves 3 to 4

2 large boneless chicken breasts (2½ pounds), halved, skinned, and pounded ¼ inch thick, with skin reserved

Salt and freshly ground black pepper to taste

4 ounces fresh unsalted mozzarella, cut into finger-size pieces

½ teaspoon hot Hungarian paprika

1 tablespoon olive oil

1 medium red onion

2 tablespoons pomegranate molasses (page 404)

¼ cup mayonnaise

¼ cup pomegranate seeds

Sprigs of coriander and flat-leaf parsley

1. Place the breasts flat, boned side up, on a work surface and season with salt and pepper. Place the cheese down the center of each breast, sprinkle with the paprika, then roll each breast tightly into a sausage shape. Cover the opening side with one quarter of the reserved skin. Tie the rolls securely with string at 1-inch intervals. Be sure that the cheese is entirely enclosed. Brush all over with the oil; set on a flat dish, wrap in plastic, and refrigerate until 45 minutes before serving.

2. Meanwhile, peel the onion, cut into thin slices, and separate into rings. Rinse the onion under cool running water and squeeze dry. Set aside until ready to serve. (Up to this point, the dish may be prepared many hours in advance.)

3. Bring the chicken to room temperature. Preheat the broiler or prepare a moderately hot charcoal fire. Brush the rack with oil.

4. Brush the chicken with the pomegranate molasses and then with the mayonnaise. Broil or grill the chicken pieces 6 to 7 inches from the heat, basting often with the pan juices and turning them over often. Cook until the juices run clear when pricked with a skewer, about 12 minutes. Let the rolls rest 5 minutes before slicing. Untie the strings and cut each roll into 6 slightly diagonal slices. Arrange the slices, cut side up, on a serving platter. Sprinkle the chicken with any pan juices and serve at once, garnished with the onion rings, pomegranate seeds, and sprigs of coriander and parsley.

GEORGIAN CHICKEN *TABAKA* WITH TWO SAUCES

This famous Georgian dish, a superb preparation for a small chicken, yields a juicy interior and a nicely crisp skin. The technique is simple and ingenious. The chicken is separated along its breast bone, then flattened and weighted so that all its fat runs out while it fries. In the meantime, the wings and legs protect the breast from overcooking.

In Georgia, *tabaka* chicken is served cut up into small pieces to be eaten with the fingers, with numerous thin dipping sauces served on the side.

Following the main part of the recipe, you will find recipes for two popular dipping sauces: *badza,* an uncooked walnut sauce with Georgian spices; and *isrim makvali,* a fresh, pureed blackberry sauce flavored with coriander, hot paprika, and garlic. An additional sauce appears elsewhere in the book: the classic Georgian sour plum sauce, *tkemali* (page 32). All three are excellent and definitely worth making.

You may also serve *tabaka* chicken as they do in the region of Adzharia on the Black Sea. There the chicken pieces are piled in the center of a platter, surrounded by a garnish of green beans simmered in butter, then smothered in herbs and cinnamon-flavored yogurt (page 195).

Serves 2; more if part of a Georgian feast of many dishes

I. Cut down the center of the breast bone of the chicken, separating the breast into halves. Place the chicken inside up and spread it open. Hit the chicken with the flat side of a meat cleaver to flatten it further. Fold the wing tips under the breast so that each wing covers and protects each upper breast. Make a small hole at the bottom of the breast skin on each side and slip into each the end of a drumstick. Be sure that each leg is protecting a lower

1 2-pound broiler-fryer chicken or 2 squabs, weighing
    1 pound each
Salt
Freshly ground black pepper
2 cloves garlic, peeled and crushed with salt
3 teaspoons butter, softened

portion of the breast. Season the chicken with the salt, pepper, and garlic, then rub the skin with 2 teaspoons of the butter. Let stand at least I hour before cooking.

2. Lightly brush a nonstick 12-inch skillet or griddle with the remaining butter and set it over moderate heat. Add the chicken, skin side up. Top with a heavy cast-iron casserole or large skillet, and fill with heavy pans or bricks. Cook the chicken over medium heat 10 to 15 minutes. Remove the weights, turn the chicken over, and pour off any pan juices and reserve. Return the chicken to the skillet, skin side down; add the weights and cook 10 to 15 minutes longer. (If using 1-pound squabs, cook only 10 minutes to a side.) Serve hot, warm, or at room temperature, cut into small pieces if desired.

NOTES TO THE COOK: If the skillet juices are not burned, still another sauce can be prepared. Combine the juices with some crushed garlic and a little boiling water or stock. Boil down to a slightly thickened consistency and pour over the chicken after it has been cut up. Serve at once, without any of the accompanying sauces suggested above.

BADZA WITH GEORGIAN SPICES

There are literally dozens of walnut sauces in Georgian cooking. One of the most famous for poultry is *satsivi*, flavored with dried coriander, dried marigold petals, cinnamon, cloves, and a huge amount of garlic, all combined with beaten egg yolks. It's good, but too rich for me. I much prefer this flavorful and colorful uncooked walnut sauce, called *badza*, which has the consistency of a smooth velouté, yet is incredibly light.

I offer two ways to make it: a quick way, which is not quite as light and refined; and the more demanding traditional method, which includes a fascinating technique for extracting oil from walnuts.

My hostess, Tsino Natsulishvili, a generous woman with incredible gray-blue eyes, taught me the traditional method. She first ground a pound of walnuts with some red pepper, dried coriander, dried marigold leaves, and garlic, pushing everything through a meat grinder twice before beginning to pound portions of it into a paste. She kneaded the mixture like dough until it "tightened," then began to add tablespoons of cooled stock as she continued to knead until a bright, burnished yellow-colored oil was expressed. Next, she pressed the whole walnut mixture through a fine sieve, then added just enough stock to make a napping sauce. She set aside about half of the expressed oil for another time; she drizzled the rest over the sauce, giving it a suave finesse.

Serve the sauce with boiled, fried, or roasted chicken and grits with cheese (page 258), Georgian corn bread cakes (page 53), or warmed thin crackling bread (page 46).

Makes 1 cup, serving 4

1. *The quick version:* In a food processor, combine the walnuts, salt, garlic, coriander, fenugreek, marigold petals or turmeric, and paprika; process until well blended as a paste. With the machine on, add the vinegar and chicken stock; pulse to obtain a smooth sauce.

2. Press through a medium sieve and discard the solids. Cover the sauce and refrigerate to blend the flavors, at least 2 to 3 hours. Season with more salt just before serving.

3. *The traditional version (also using a food processor):* Grind the walnuts. Crush the garlic with salt until pulpy. Add the garlic and spices to the food processor and blend until the walnuts begin to turn oily. Then, with the machine running, slowly add 2 to 3 tablespoons chicken stock or water until you begin to see beads of oil ooze out of the mass. Stop the machine immediately. Transfer a small clump of the walnut mixture to a piece of damp cheesecloth. Gather up the ends and squeeze the walnut mixture until the oil runs out into a small bowl. Repeat with the remaining clumps of walnut mixture. Reserve the oil.

1 heaping cup shelled walnuts (4 ounces)

¼ teaspoon salt

1 small clove garlic, peeled

¾ teaspoon ground coriander seeds

¼ teaspoon ground fenugreek

½ teaspoon dried marigold petals or ⅛ teaspoon ground turmeric

About ¼ teaspoon hot paprika

2 to 3 teaspoons rice wine vinegar

¾ cup chicken stock or water at room temperature

Double the recipe for Georgian Chicken *Tabaka* (page 315)

continued

Return the walnuts to the food processor; add the vinegar and enough stock or water to loosen the mixture and process until smooth. Then thin with the remaining liquid. Strain, discarding the solids, and use as a dip for chicken *tabaka*. You can also use it as a "soak," or loose sauce, for small pieces of boiled chicken.

4. Drizzle some of the oil over the sauce. Save the remainder to flavor other Georgian dishes, such as the vegetable pâtés on pages 176–78.

⃕

FRESH BLACKBERRY SAUCE

This delicious, quick sauce—*isrim makvali*—goes beautifully with *tabaka* chicken. The blackberry imparts an intense and invigorating flavor, and the chopped coriander adds a fresh spiciness. Make the sauce about 5 hours before serving so that all the elements can meld. But don't make it any earlier—this sauce tends to spoil quickly.

Makes ⅔ cup, serving 2

1 small clove garlic, peeled
¼ teaspoon coarse salt
½ pint blackberries
2 tablespoons chopped coriander
Pinches of hot Hungarian paprika
2 teaspoons fresh lemon juice

One recipe for Georgian Chicken *Tabaka* (page 315)

1. In a mortar, crush the garlic with the salt. (Or use the blade of a large knife to mash the garlic with salt.)

2. Using a wooden spoon, push the blackberries through a fine nonmetallic sieve; discard the seeds.

3. In a small porcelain, glass, or ceramic bowl, combine the sieved blackberries with the garlic, coriander, paprika, and lemon juice, mixing well. Set aside, covered, at room temperature 5 hours to blend the flavors before serving.

MUSAKHAN

This is a Middle Eastern village dish—a succulent combination of chicken, olive oil, lots of stewed onions (some cooks use as much as half the weight of the chicken), homemade flat bread, and aromatic lemony sumac, cooked together in a deep outdoor oven, then garnished with browned pine nuts just before serving.

I have eaten many versions of *musakhan* over the years, but the best rendition was at the home of Mrs. Hayat Taghi in Amman, overlooking the university where her husband is a professor of American literature. There were many guests that day, including a prominent Palestinian filmmaker and visiting relatives, away from the chaos of Beirut. The conversation was serious and literary, but when the *musakhan* appeared, everyone adjourned to a low table and dug in with fingers, the traditional way.

"You must eat with your fingers so you can *feel* the chicken. And be *sure* to smell your hands," my hostess instructed.

"The aroma of the olive oil is a big part of the pleasure. We like to revel in the sensuality of this dish," the filmmaker added.

The quality of the oil is very important, and you must use Middle Eastern bread, such as a good store bought Mountain *Lavash* or Syrian *saj* bread (page 13). The bread is torn into small pieces to make a bed for the chicken and sauce. Garnish with thin rings of red and green bell pepper.

Serves 4

continued

I frying chicken, quartered

I½ tablespoons ground sumac

⅛ teaspoon ground nutmeg

⅛ teaspoon ground cinnamon

¼ teaspoon freshly ground black pepper

Sea salt

Juice of I lemon

I pound red onions, peeled and thinly sliced

2 tablespoons olive oil

½ cup rich chicken stock

½ pound Mountain *Lavash* or Syrian *Saj* bread, torn into
    small pieces

¼ cup pine nuts, toasted

I. Rinse the chicken and pat dry. Trim off excess fat.

2. Combine the sumac, spices, and salt. Set aside 2 teaspoons and mix the rest with the lemon juice. Rub into the chicken flesh and marinate up to I day.

3. Place the onions in a large skillet, toss with I½ tablespoons of the olive oil, half the chicken stock, reserved spices, and a pinch of salt. Cover and cook gently 30 minutes. (Up to this point, the dish can be prepared I day in advance.)

4. Bring the chicken to room temperature and preheat the oven to 400° F.

5. Place the chicken, skin side down, on a nonstick baking sheet. Divide the onions into 4 parts and spread them over the chicken; cover with foil and bake 20 minutes.

6. Lightly brush a large ovenproof serving dish with the remaining oil. Scatter the torn bread in one or two layers on the bottom; sprinkle with the remaining chicken stock and carefully flip the chicken-and-onion quarters onto the bread so that the skin side is up. Return to the oven and bake 20 minutes, until tender and crispy brown. Serve at once with a sprinkling of the pine nuts.

CHICKEN WITH OKRA

This fine yet homey traditional dish of northern Greece demonstrates how pleasantly crunchy, tender, and tasty okra can be.

Choose the smallest okra you can find, preferably the dwarf variety. (American farmers' markets often sell these in midsummer.) Greeks don't like the slimy quality of cooked okra and have a clever way to deal with it. After trimming the tops and tails, they toss the okra in vinegar and salt, then leave it in the sun for an hour to dry. After a simple rinsing and drying, the okra is ready to be sautéed—a step that further enhances their flavor.

I have adapted this recipe from one attributed to a home cook from Thrace in a six-volume encyclopedic work on regional Greek cooking. Thrace, the area closest to Turkey, is home to the least known but most savory cooking in all of Greece, perhaps because it is here that Greek, Turkish, Bulgarian, Pontian, and Macedonian culinary traditions meet. In the original recipe, the pods are threaded onto skewers made from long oregano branches, adding aroma and making it easy for the cook to turn the vegetable while sautéing. Afterward, the okra is cooked along with the chicken, tomatoes, green frying pepper, and herbs.

Serves 4

1. Carefully pare the cone tops of the okra pods and trim the tips if they are black, but do not cut into the pods. Place on a flat tray, sprinkle with the vinegar, dip each cone top in a small mound of sea salt, and leave 1 hour, preferably in the sun—or at least in a warm place.

2. Meanwhile, bring the chicken to room temperature, wash, and pat dry.

3. Rinse the okra; dry carefully, divide evenly among the skewers, and thread the pods closely.

4. Preheat the oven to 400° F.

5. Heat half the oil in a heavy 12-inch skillet over moderately high heat. Add the tomatoes and cook until soft, thick, and lightly caramelized, about 10 minutes. Season with pinches of salt, black pepper, and cinnamon. Use a slotted spoon to transfer the tomatoes to a side dish. *continued*

¾ pound small, firm okra pods, rubbed with a towel to remove any fuzz

3 tablespoons cider vinegar

Coarse sea salt

2½ pounds chicken parts (legs and thighs)

4 tablespoons olive oil

4 vine-ripened tomatoes, cored, halved, seeded, and cut into large chunks, or 1¾ cups chopped canned tomatoes

Salt and freshly ground black pepper

Pinch of ground cinnamon

¾ cup grated onion, squeezed dry

1 Italian green frying pepper, cored, seeded, and minced (¼ cup)

Pinches of crumbled dried Mediterranean oregano

Pinches of hot pepper flakes

2 tablespoons fresh lemon juice

¾ teaspoon sugar

3 tablespoons chopped flat-leaf parsley

6 6-inch bamboo skewers

6. To the juices remaining in the skillet, add the onion and green frying pepper and rapidly cook over medium heat, stirring, until all moisture evaporates and the onions begin to turn golden brown, about 10 minutes. Add ¼ cup water and simmer 5 minutes longer. Sprinkle with 2 pinches each of the oregano, hot pepper flakes, salt, and black pepper. Scrape the onions into a 9-by-12-inch baking dish and add the tomatoes.

7. Wipe out the skillet, add the 2 tablespoons remaining oil, and set over medium-high heat. Sprinkle the chicken parts with salt and black pepper, place them skin side down in the skillet, and brown well, about 5 minutes. (If necessary, brown the chicken in batches to avoid crowding the pan.) Remove the chicken to a side dish. In the same fat, brown the skewers of okra, 1½ minutes to a side.

8. Slip the okra into the tomato-onion sauce and place the chicken on top. Cover the baking dish with foil and bake 1 hour.

9. Raise the oven heat to 500°. Push aside the chicken pieces and remove the skewers of okra to a side dish. Add the lemon juice and sugar to the sauce and adjust the seasoning. Turn the pieces of chicken in the sauce. Place the baking dish on the highest shelf of the oven and allow the chicken and sauce to glaze and brown, about 10 to 15 minutes.

10. Slip the okra off the skewers and surround the chicken with the okra in an attractive pattern. Sprinkle the chicken and okra with the parsley and serve the dish warm.

ROAST CHICKEN STUFFED WITH LAMB, RICE, AND PINE NUTS

This is one of the really good chicken dishes of the Arab world, subtly spiced and beautifully balanced. It requires, first of all, real "hands-on" cooking, which I find pleasurable, and it brings together a variety of diverse ingredients, sour and sweet tastes, and crunchy and soft textures into a finely tuned equilibrium.

The chicken, incredibly moist because of a preliminary steaming in broth, is finished in a hot oven until golden brown and glazed. Serve it with a few Middle Eastern salads and a bowl of yogurt, cucumber, and mint sauce (page 29).

Serves 6

1. About 2 hours before serving, begin to prepare the stuffing. In a wide nonstick skillet, melt 1 teaspoon of the butter. Add the lamb or veal and cook slowly until lightly brown. Add the remaining butter and the pine nuts and fry until golden brown. Add a good pinch of the mixed spices and ½ teaspoon salt and stir 1 minute. Add the rice, pistachios, and walnuts; moisten with 2 cups water, bring to a boil, cover, and simmer over low heat until the liquid is absorbed, about 10 minutes. Allow the rice to cool slightly. Add the lemon zest and correct the seasoning with salt and pepper.

2. Wash the chicken inside and out; dry; then rub with salt, black pepper, and a good pinch of the mixed spices.

3. Stuff the chicken and truss it. Place in a deep pot; add the cinnamon stick and 3 cups

continued

STUFFING

2 teaspoons butter

¾ pound lean lamb or veal, coarsely ground

⅓ cup pine nuts

1 teaspoon Syrian Mixed Spices Number 1 (page 392)

Salt

1 cup long-grain rice, washed and drained

⅓ cup peeled and chopped pistachios

2 tablespoons chopped walnuts

1 teaspoon grated lemon zest

Salt and freshly ground black pepper

1 plump roasting chicken (5 to 6 pounds), neck, gizzard, and
 heart reserved

1 cinnamon stick

12-by-12-inch sheet of parchment paper

Butter-flavored oil spray

Fresh lemon juice

water; bring to a boil. Wet parchment, crumble it, and place it over the chicken. Cover the pot and cook at a simmer 1 hour.

4. When the chicken has simmered 45 minutes, preheat the oven to 450° F.

5. Carefully transfer the chicken to an open roasting pan, spray it with the butter-flavored oil, and surround it with the simmering liquid from the pot. Roast until the chicken is tender and golden brown, basting often, about 20 minutes. Remove the chicken, cover with a foil tent, and allow to rest 10 minutes. Meanwhile, skim the pan drippings of all fat and reduce the juices slightly. Add a few drops of lemon juice. Carve the chicken and arrange, along with the stuffing, on a large, warm serving platter. Pour the pan juices over all and serve at once.

NOTES TO THE COOK: If you have too much stuffing, place the remainder in a shallow baking dish, cover, and bake 20 minutes.

A Circassian's
"Circassian-Style" Chicken

Here is a Circassian's version of the legendary eastern Mediterranean chicken dish known as Circassian Chicken, in which moist chunks of poached chicken are bathed in a rich, smooth, beige-colored walnut sauce garnished with swirls of spicy, red-tinted oil. This final fillip yields an intensely sharp bouquet.

Various forms of this dish are served throughout the region, but—and this was a revelation—the dish is cooked differently within the small, influential Circassian community of Amman, Jordan. (It is called *chet shipsupasta* in Circassian.)

I had been invited to the handsome villa of Mrs. Hayat Mufti, a sprightly woman with the striking blue eyes and blond hair that are characteristic of Circassians—converts to Islam who migrated to the Middle East from the Caucasus and were among the first settlers in Amman.

Mrs. Mufti's version differed from the usual recipes in three important respects: Her sauce was thickened with toasted flour; her walnut sauce was cooked, as opposed to the raw sauce served in Turkey; and she served the dish warm, while Georgians and Turks serve it cool and sometimes even cold. I found her version light and highly digestible. "You cannot overcook the sauce," she advised me, "but you *can* undercook it"—a lesson I urge you to remember when you try your hand at making it.

For the best flavor, begin preparing this dish at least two days in advance of serving; this chicken improves with time. It keeps up to a week in the refrigerator if carefully covered. Serve warm, not hot, with a simple bulgur or rice pilaf.

Serves 16

continued

6 pounds chicken quarters

2 teaspoons olive oil

2 small onions, sliced

1 tablespoon garlic, peeled and chopped with salt

Salt and freshly ground black pepper

Pinch of saffron

⅓ cup all-purpose flour

1 teaspoon Near East or Aleppo pepper, or more to taste
   (page 395)

Pinch of ground allspice

2¼ cups (8 ounces) shelled walnuts

1 tablespoon fresh lemon juice

RED-TINTED OIL

1 tablespoon walnut oil

¼ teaspoon Near East or Aleppo pepper

1. To make the chicken and sauce: Wash the chicken and pat dry. Trim off excess skin and fat.

2. Heat the oil in a 5-quart casserole. Add the onions; cook until soft. Add the chicken and 2 teaspoons of the chopped garlic; sprinkle with salt, black pepper, and saffron. Cover with 1 quart water; simmer until chicken is tender. (Slow, gentle cooking helps to keep the chicken intact.)

3. Meanwhile, toast the flour in a 9- or 10-inch heavy nonstick skillet, turning it constantly until it becomes a lovely light beige. Add the Near East pepper and allspice, and continue stirring over low heat 30 seconds longer. Remove from the heat.

4. Skin, bone, and cut the chicken quarters into smaller serving pieces. Lightly season with additional salt and black pepper if desired. Strain the chicken broth and degrease. You should have 3½ cups. Mix the remaining garlic with 1 cup of the broth and pour over the chicken to keep it moist.

5. In a food processor, grind the walnuts and seasoned flour to a smooth paste. Slowly add 1 cup of the chicken broth and process until smooth. Then slowly add the remaining broth to make a creamy sauce.

6. Scrape the sauce into the skillet, set over medium-low heat, and bring to a boil. Cook, stirring occasionally, 20 minutes.

7. Drain the chicken pieces and place in one layer in a 9-by-13-by-2-inch ovenproof serving dish. Add 1 cup of the walnut sauce and the lemon juice; mix well. Thin the remaining sauce with water to a napping consistency and correct the seasoning with salt. Pour the sauce over the chicken. Let the mixture cool completely, cover with plastic wrap, and refrigerate for at least 2 days before serving.

8. To make the red-tinted oil: Gently reheat the cooked chicken in a 350° F. oven until warm. Heat the walnut oil in a very small saucepan, add the Near East pepper, and swirl to combine; heat just to a sizzle. Remove from the heat and allow the pepper to settle. Dribble the red-tinted oil over the surface of the dish, making decorative swirls.

DUCK WITH QUINCES

‹❦›

If ducks were less fatty and quinces were a year-round fruit, you would most likely want to eat this dish often. The play of tart, fragrant quinces, against spicy, aromatic cinnamon bark and rich duck is unforgettable.

This recipe, which comes from the Georgian Black Sea coast, was given to me by Zurhan Amirashivili. He recalled that his grandmother always prepared this dish for his birthday. She simmered the duck in water until half-cooked, stuffed it with the cores and peelings of quinces, then browned it in a very hot outdoor oven until the skin turned incredibly crisp. She then thickened some of the duck broth with mashed quinces, serving the sauce and quinces as a garnish when the duck was brought from the fire to the table.

Serves 4

I. Empty the duck, if frozen, and set aside the giblets for some other purpose. Remove all fat from the cavity and around the neck and tail, and cut out the fat under the wings. Cut out the wishbone and discard. Prick the duck all over with a fork. With a small paring knife make deep slits in thick, fatty areas.

2. Place the duck, breast side up, in a deep heavy casserole, preferably oval, and add 2 cups water, the peppercorns, cinnamon stick, and onion. Bring to a boil. Cover the duck with a sheet of wrinkled and dripping-wet parchment. Tightly cover the pot and cook over low heat I hour.

3. Meanwhile, wash the quinces and rub

1 duck, about 5 pounds
½ teaspoon black peppercorns
1 cinnamon stick
1 small onion, halved
1 12"-by-12"-sheet of parchment paper
3 large fragrant, lemon-yellow quinces
Sea salt
Freshly ground black pepper
1 lemon, halved
½ teaspoon ground cinnamon
3 tablespoons butter, rendered duck fat, or olive oil
2 cups chopped onions
Fresh coriander sprigs

each with a wet cloth to remove any dirt and fuzz. Cut each quince into eighths; peel and

continued

core the quinces, and reserve all the debris for stuffing the duck. Mix the debris with sea salt and black pepper, the pulp of half a lemon, and the cinnamon and set aside.

4. Heat 2 tablespoons of the fat in a 10-inch skillet; add the quince slices and sauté until golden on all sides. Remove from the skillet. Add the onions and another tablespoon fat to the skillet, cover, and cook over medium heat 10 minutes. Return the quince slices to the skillet; mix with the onions and set aside.

5. Lift the duck out of the pot and drain its juices back into the pot. Let the duck sit 10 minutes on a work surface while you preheat the oven to 350° F. Skim the cooking liquid and add it to the onions and quince slices. Stuff the cavity of the duck with the seasoned debris. Rub the duck skin with the remaining lemon half. Set the duck on a rack to roast in the oven until crisp and golden, about 1 hour, basting often with small amounts of lightly salted water.

6. Raise the oven heat to 475° F. and continue roasting the duck 20 minutes. Meanwhile, cook the onions and quinces, uncovered, stirring often, until the quinces are completely tender. Crush one or two pieces of the quinces into the juices to help thicken the sauce. Adjust the seasoning and check for a good sweet and sour balance with lemon juice or sugar. Quarter the duck and serve nestled in the quince sauce. Snip the coriander and scatter over the duck.

Notes to the Cook: One good, rich duck should be enough to serve four people. If you want to double the recipe, first simmer one duck, then another, then roast both together to complete the cooking.

You might want to use this trick of Julia Child's: Remove the wishbone from the duck breast before cooking; this will make it a lot easier to cut the meat off the carcass in thin slices.

XIII
Meat

GRILLED MEATS

Grilled meat techniques are much the same around the world, but nowhere are they better used than in Turkey, justifiably famous for its shish kebab.

Shish kebab means, simply, cooked skewered meat. The skill lies in the choice of meat, seasonings, marinades, and accompanying salsas, salads, or relishes.

I was thrilled to travel to Gaziantep, in southeast Turkey, the mecca of skewered meat dishes and also the pastry confection baklava. I soon found an excellent source, Burhan Çadğas, the chef and owner of Çadğas Restaurant, the city's most famous meat restaurant for over a hundred years.

Among other things, Burhan explained to me why some shish kebab skewers are four-sided, others very thin, and still others flat. The four-sided variety is for cubed meat, so that it can be turned to cook evenly on all four sides. The thinner swords are used to weave into meat strips, while flat skewers are best for ground meat kabobs, where the meat is molded directly onto the steel. Burhan's expertise on numerous other points is reflected in the following recipes: Marinated Grilled Lamb Loin Strips with Burhan's Onion-Parsley Salad; *Köfte* with Warm Eggplant Salad; Molded Eggplant and *Köfte* Kabobs; *Köfte* with Loquats; *Köfte* with Garlic Heads; and *Köfte* with Shallots. In the eastern Mediterranean all meat is served well done.

MARINATED GRILLED LAMB LOIN STRIPS WITH BURHAN'S ONION-PARSLEY SALAD

The accumulation of several small details make this one of the most delicious of all lamb shish kababs. The cut of the meat; the size of the meat pieces; the intensity of the heat; and speed of cooking together combine to make this one of the best of its type.

In this recipe you need to use meat from the loin; no other cut will do. (This is more economical than it seems, because if you substitute lamb leg, you will need to remove every piece of gristle, sinew, and fat, then use only the leanest pieces.) The meat is first cubed, then butterflied into strips. The heat of the fire must be intense. The meat is grilled very quickly; thus the juices are sealed in. The marinade is not for tenderizing but for a bold and spicy taste.

Serve with onion, parsley, and sumac salad (page 332).

Serves 4

1. Cut the meat into 1-inch cubes and then butterfly each piece, but do not pound the flesh to even it out—this will destroy the texture. Combine the ingredients for the marinade in a nonreactive mixing bowl, blending well. Add the lamb and stir to coat it evenly. Cover and refrigerate 9 to 12 hours, turning the meat occasionally.

2. About 2 to 3 hours before serving time, remove the lamb from the marinade and string onto 8 long, thin skewers. Reserve the marinade.

3. Light the grill or hibachi, preferably filled with hardwood charcoal for the hottest coals.

continued

1 pound lean lamb, from the loin

MARINADE

1 tablespoon tomato paste

1 tablespoon homemade pepper paste (page 389); see also Notes to the Cook

1 to 3 tablespoons olive oil

1 teaspoon garlic, peeled and crushed with salt

1 teaspoon Turkish *baharat* (page 392)

½ teaspoon freshly ground black pepper

8 long, thin skewers

4 mildly hot poblano or long green peppers (optional)

4 Middle Eastern thin flat breads, such as *saj, tannour,* Afghan, or mountain, flour tortillas; or soft *lavash* (optional)

4. Grill the peppers and set them aside. When the coals are white and hot, brush the meat with the marinade and place the skewers between grid bars directly over the coals so that they brown and cook quickly, turning and brushing them with the marinade, about 2 to 3 minutes total time. Just before serving, heat the bread, if you are using it, over the coals. Push the kabobs off the skewers into the center of the bread, fold over, and serve at once with the onion-parsley salad, below, and the grilled poblanos.

NOTES TO THE COOK: For the marinade, see page 389 for a delicious homemade red pepper paste, to be made each year in late summer. Out of season, make the quick variation on the same page. You can also use *selin aci biber sosu,* an imported red pepper sauce from Turkey, available at many Middle Eastern food markets, or any other red pepper paste, such as the Indonesian *sambal oelek.*

BURHAN'S ONION-PARSLEY SALAD

Serve this excellent salad with Marinated Grilled Lamb Loin Strips, above, or with any simple skewer of *köfte* or cubed meat.

Makes about 1¼ cups

2 white or red onions, peeled and halved
Coarse salt
½ cup chopped parsley
1 teaspoon ground sumac or more to taste

1. Thinly slice the onions and toss with 1 teaspoon coarse salt. Rub the salt into the strands and let stand 5 minutes.

2. Rinse and drain the onions thoroughly. Mix with the parsley and sumac. Serve within 30 minutes.

ERRATA

HarperCollins regrets the following two typographical errors on the endpaper maps: The region designated "Serbian Macedonia" should be designated "Slavic Macedonia"; and the correct spelling for the town in southeastern Turkey is "Gaziantep."

Caucasian Marinated Pork Kabobs

The marinade here can also be used for kabobs of lamb or beef. Again, the purpose of the marinade is not to tenderize but to impart a strong, bold flavor.

Serves 8

1. Trim excess fat from the pork. Cut into 1¼-inch cubes.

2. Combine the diluted 1½ tablespoons pomegranate molasses, 2 tablespoons of the olive oil, onion, dill, salt, pepper, and sugar in a bowl. Pour over the pork, cover, and refrigerate overnight or up to 2 days.

3. One hour before serving, remove the meat from refrigerator, drain, and thread on the skewers. Let stand ½ hour while you heat the coals. Oil the rack with remaining olive oil and place 5 to 6 inches from the hot coals. Grill the kabobs, covered, until the meat is cooked and charred at the edges on all sides, but still very juicy within, approximately 15 minutes. Remove the kabobs from the heat, brush with the diluted 4 tablespoons pomegranate molasses, and serve with onion-parsley salad.

2½ pounds boneless pork shoulder

MARINADE

1½ tablespoons pomegranate molasses (page 404), diluted in ½ cup water

3 tablespoons olive oil

½ cup grated onion

2 tablespoons chopped dill

1 teaspoon salt

1 teaspoon freshly ground black pepper

Pinch of sugar

8 four-sided skewers

4 tablespoons pomegranate molasses, diluted with 3 tablespoons water for brushing and dipping

Burhan's Onion-Parsley Salad (opposite)

SEVEN
GROUND MEAT
KABOBS

A love of ground meat dishes is not unique to the eastern Mediterranean, but the methods by which Macedonians prepare their *kyofteh,* Turks their innumerable varieties of *köfte,* Georgians their *kotelettis,* and Middle Easterners their kibbeh kabobs are interesting to any cook who wants to make light ground meat dishes and, at the same time, cut down on meat consumption by "stretching." The word "stretching" refers to additions to the meat, important in cultures where meat is regarded as an expensive luxury. When I lived in Morocco, lamb was sold at the same price per kilo, whatever the cut. The rich bought the unadulterated lean cuts, while the poor bought the fatty cuts, then stretched them in stews or in meatball recipes.

In Macedonia and southern Turkey, I watched cooks add soda water or baking soda to their meat mixtures, to attain lightness and make it easier to shape the ground meat around a skewer. In Georgia, cooks whip in plain water, then bread the exterior. Some add mashed potatoes to create extremely light meatballs. Middle Easterners use grated onion to enhance the flavor, maintaining that the change in color and taste is admirable. "You must never actually see the onion," a housewife in Aleppo told me as she kneaded onion-enhanced meat with bulgur to make kibbeh kabobs.

The first five recipes that follow are adaptations of dishes served at Çadğas's Restaurant in Gaziantep. Burhan Çadğas chops the breast of young male lambs* with sheep's tail fat and salt to make his delicious *köftes.* For health reasons I have greatly reduced the fat content and heightened the seasoning in an attempt to compensate.

One excellent trick I learned, which reduces the dryness of ground meat without a lot of fat, is to remove certain types of *köfte* from the skewers, along with the accompanying fruit or vegetable, when the meat is only half-done, then finish the cooking in a covered pan with a little water or sauce to maintain juiciness. I recommend this technique when making the following molded eggplant and *köfte* kabobs, as well as the *köfte* with loquat, garlic heads, or shallots.

KÖFTE WITH WARM EGGPLANT SALAD

Here, in one of Burhan Çadğas's most popular *köfte* and eggplant dishes, the traditional *köfte* is grilled, then presented in a creamy eggplant sauce with slivers of crunchy raw onion and hot pepper. The raw and the cooked create a kind of Turkish ying-yang.

In summer this makes a terrific supper dish just as it is, with warm pita.

Serves 2 to 3

continued

---

* Every Eastern Mediterranean cook I have discussed this with has advised me to buy the meat of male lambs, since it is more tender. But there's no way to do this in American supermarkets. The cooks insist that only chopping with a knife into minute bits of meat provides the memorable melt-in-your-mouth sensation. This we can accomplish, but it's time-consuming. Pulsing in a food processor also produces good results.

KÖFTE

¾ pound lean ground lamb or beef

3 tablespoons chopped parsley

I large clove garlic, peeled and crushed with ½ teaspoon salt

¾ teaspoon Turkish *baharat* (page 392)

Salt and freshly ground black pepper

Pinch of Near East or Aleppo pepper (page 395)

2 teaspoons flour

2 tablespoons soda water

WARM EGGPLANT SALAD

I or 2 eggplants (I pound)

Juice of I lemon

3 medium vine-ripened tomatoes

I to 2 teaspoons slivered medium-hot green chili

3 tablespoons slivered Italian green frying or green bell pepper

Salt, freshly ground black pepper, and sugar to taste

3 teaspoons fresh lemon juice, plus more to taste

2 tablespoons chopped parsley

2 to 4 flat-sided skewers

½ cup slivered white onion

FLOURISH

I½ teaspoons unsalted butter

¼ teaspoon Near East or Aleppo pepper

Warm pita bread

I. To make the *kofte:* In a mixing bowl, combine the lamb, parsley, garlic, *baharat,* salt, black pepper, Near East pepper, flour, and soda water. Knead until smooth and well blended. Divide into 4 parts.

2. To make the eggplant salad: Prick the eggplants several times with a skewer. Grill them over coals until they collapse completely, about 30 minutes. Alternatively, wrap each eggplant in two layers of aluminum foil and set over high flames on a stove burner. Dip immediately in cold water, then peel away the skin and discard the stem. After either cooking method, soak the eggplants in I cup water mixed with the lemon juice I5 minutes. (This keeps the flesh white.) Drain the eggplants and squeeze the flesh to express all moisture, as well as any bitter juices. In a wide mixing bowl, crush the flesh with a wooden fork, spoon, or potato masher.

Broil or grill the tomatoes. Peel, seed, and crush them, draining off excess liquid. Combine the tomatoes with the eggplant, slivered chili and green pepper, salt, black pepper, sugar, lemon juice, and parsley. Cover and keep at room temperature up to 2 hours.

One hour before serving time, light a charcoal grill or hibachi. Mold the *kofte* onto the skewers and grill over glowing coals until firm and crusty, turning once. (The *kofte* can also be shaped into patties and pan-broiled.)

Rub the onion slivers with salt and let stand a few minutes, then rinse and drain. Fold into the eggplant mixture and set over low heat until just warm. Adjust the seasoning with salt, black pepper, sugar, and lemon juice to taste.

3. To make the flourish: Remove the *köfte* from the grill. Gently reheat the eggplant salad in a heat-proof serving dish on top of the stove or in a microwave or regular oven. Slip the *köfte* off the skewers into the warm salad. Immediately heat the butter in a small pan, add the Near East pepper, let the butter sizzle, swirl once and drizzle over the dish. Serve at once with warm pita.

MOLDED EGGPLANT AND *KÖFTE* KABOBS

These rich, savory kabobs flavored with tomatoes, chilis, and pomegranate molasses, are very popular. Graduated slices of eggplant, alternated with spicy ground lamb, are grilled over hardwood coals until the meat is crusty and firm. Since the eggplant is barely cooked, the kabobs are finished off in a covered skillet until they have absorbed all the delicious juices from the meat and sauce. The eggplant texture will be creamy, and its black skin (which always hardens when grilled) will remain moist and supple.

When shopping, look for the straightest, smallest, firmest, and most unblemished eggplants you can find.

Serves 4

continued

4 small Italian or Japanese eggplants, each approximately
   4 ounces
4 12-inch bamboo skewers
Salt

KÖFTE
¾ pound lean ground lamb or beef
I to 2 tablespoons unsalted butter (optional)
⅓ cup coarsely chopped parsley
I large clove garlic, peeled and crushed with ¾ teaspoon salt
¾ teaspoon Turkish *baharat* (page 392) or ½ teaspoon
   ground allspice and ¼ teaspoon hot Hungarian paprika
Good pinch of cayenne or red pepper flakes if you are using
   baharat
¼ teaspoon salt
Freshly ground black pepper
2 teaspoons flour
2 tablespoons soda water
Olive oil spray

TOMATO SAUCE
4 large ripe tomatoes
I hot green chili
½ cup water
Salt to taste
Freshly ground black pepper to taste
I teaspoon pomegranate molasses (page 404)

Burhan's Onion-Parsley Salad (page 332)
Warm pita bread

I. Wash and hull the eggplants. Slip a skewer through each eggplant lengthwise. Using a thin-blade knife, make crosswise slices at ¾-inch intervals along the length of the eggplant. Soak the skewered eggplants in a bath of lightly salted water. (This maintains a light color.)

2. To make the *köfte:* Combine the lamb, butter if you are using it, parsley, garlic, *baharat,* cayenne, salt, black pepper, flour, and soda water and knead until smooth and well blended. Divide into 4 parts.

Drain the eggplants and shake off excess moisture. Stuff marble-size lumps of meat between the eggplant slices and reshape the eggplant with moistened palms, smoothing the surface on all sides. (It helps to roll the eggplant on a work surface.) The kabob should be almost double in length. Spray each kabob lightly with oil, wrap individually in plastic wrap, and refrigerate up to 6 hours before continuing.

3. To make the tomato sauce: One hour before serving time, light hardwood charcoal in a grill or hibachi. Roast the tomatoes and chili until the skins begin to blister and the flesh is very soft. Remove to a colander or sieve set over a 12-inch skillet or a 13-by-9-inch baking pan, and use a wooden pestle or a bean or potato masher to crush and press the chili and tomatoes through the sieve into the skillet. Discard the skin and seeds. Add ½ cup water, salt, black pepper, and the pomegranate molasses and blend well. Set aside.

4. Make the onion-parsley salad.

5. Grill the kabobs over glowing coals, turning on all sides until firm and crusty, about

10 minutes. Remove the kabobs from the grill. Place the skillet or baking pan directly over the coals. Cover with a lid or foil and allow the kabobs to finish cooking, basting often, about 20 minutes.

6. To serve, transfer the eggplant kabobs carefully to individual plates, spoon sauce over them, and serve at once with the salad and warm pita.

KÖFTE WITH LOQUATS

Few fruit and meat kabobs work as well as this Turkish combination of *köfte* and loquats, pigeon-egg size, apricot-colored fruit, similar to Japanese medlars. When I first tasted this dish it was late May, the height of the loquat season in southern Turkey. The fruit was everywhere—bruised, tart-sweet, delicious.

Here the fruit scents the meat, while the intricately spiced meat flavors the fruit. The result is exceptional.

You want firm, unblemished loquats for grilling. (For eating, loquats are best when brown and bruised.) Texas and southern California have loquats in season, and my supermarket in New England carries loquats imported from Chile in late fall.

If it's too cold to grill out of doors, you can make the dish with a good broiler. Brown the meat under the broiler, then finish it in a covered skillet with a little water added.

Serve with chopped scallions and parsley. If the loquats are too sweet, add a drop of lemon juice along with salt and pepper.

Serves 4

continued

KÖFTE

¾ pound lean ground lamb or beef

3 tablespoons chopped parsley

I large clove garlic, crushed with ½ teaspoon salt

¾ teaspoon Turkish *baharat* (page 392)

Pinch of cayenne

2 teaspoons flour

2 tablespoons soda water

Salt and freshly ground black pepper to taste

10 loquats

4 thin skewers

Oil for brushing the kabobs

½ teaspoon pomegranate molasses (page 404), diluted in
⅔ cup water

I teaspoon fresh lemon juice

2 tablespoons chopped scallions

I tablespoon chopped parsley

Warm pita bread

I. To make the *köfte:* Combine the lamb or beef, parsley, garlic, *baharat*, cayenne, flour, soda water, and salt and pepper; knead until smooth and well blended. Divide into 16 equal portions.

2. Halve each loquat around the middle, remove the pits, and trim the ends. Use a melon scoop to remove the inner hard membrane. Skewer alternately with portions of meat, pressing meat and fruit firmly. Brush with the oil.

3. Grill over charcoal or under a broiler preheated to its highest setting. Brown well, turning the skewers often. Slip the meat and fruit off the skewers into a wide skillet. Try to keep the meat and fruit intact. Add the pomegranate molasses diluted in water and the lemon juice. Cover the skillet and continue cooking the kabobs over medium-low embers or on top of the stove 20 minutes. When almost all the liquid has been absorbed, carefully transfer the kabobs to individual serving dishes. Scatter the scallions and parsley on top and serve at once with warm pita.

VARIATION:

KÖFTE WITH GARLIC HEADS

Serves 4

8 plump heads garlic, roots trimmed, one layer of paper skin removed, and halved

4 thin skewers

Olive oil

4 small sheets *saj* or *tandir* bread or 2 pitas, halved

Follow the previous recipe, substituting 8 garlic heads for the loquats. Skewer the *köfte* and garlic and brush with oil. Set over low-burning coals and cook slowly, turning often, until the garlic cloves soften and the meat is well browned, about 10 minutes. Use thin bread slices to transfer the *köfte* and garlic to a

10-inch skillet. Add ½ cup water, cover, and place the skillet over the coals. Cook slowly 20 minutes, adding more water if necessary to keep the *köfte* and garlic juicy. Serve in small serving dishes with warm bread sheets.

VARIATION:

KÖFTE WITH SHALLOTS

Follow the recipe for loquats, but substitute 12 whole unpeeled shallots. Add ½ teaspoon pomegranate molasses to the simmering water.

CUMIN-FLAVORED *KÖFTE* WITH TWO SAUCES

For this popular and delicious Turkish summer dish, grilled minced lamb or beef kabobs are served atop a bed of savory, nutty bread croutons, topped first with a flavorful tomato sauce and then with a crown of thick, creamy yogurt. The final flourish of a small quantity of bubbling butter seasoned with cayenne provides a radiant touch. The resulting dish is a study in textures, flavors, and colors.

The original version calls for smothering the dish with butter, but in my recipe the bread layer is bolstered by simmering toasted cubes of stale bread in a savory chicken broth, creating so much extra taste and succulence that the butter can be cut down by three quarters.

Turkish *pide* is a dense bread made of whole-meal flour enriched with milk, usually the size of an individual pizza and about ¾ inch thick. Many markets sell it under the name "Mediterranean pita" or "pocketless pita." If it is unavailable, any dense bread cut into ¾-inch cubes may be substituted. A baked empty pizza shell will work too, in a pinch.

Accompany this dish with a platter of watercress and mint sprigs and a few young scallions, with no seasoning.

Serves 4

continued

KÖFTE

¾ cup cubed stale, firm white bread, crustless

1¼ pounds lean ground lamb or beef

1 small onion, grated

¼ teaspoon ground cumin

Salt

¼ teaspoon freshly ground black pepper

1 egg, well beaten

4 12-inch flat skewers

2 teaspoons olive oil

BREAD BASE

6 ounces day-old *pide* (see above)

½ tablespoon unsalted butter

Pinch of salt

⅓ cup meat or poultry stock

TOMATO SAUCE

2 teaspoons olive oil

2 ripe tomatoes, peeled, seeded, and chopped, about
  1⅔ pounds

1 teaspoon chopped medium-hot green chili

Pinches of salt and sugar

¼ teaspoon crushed garlic

1 teaspoon red wine vinegar

YOGURT SAUCE

1 cup plain low-fat yogurt, drained to ½ cup (see page 410
  for directions on draining yogurt)

Salt to taste

FLOURISH

2 tablespoons unsalted butter

1 teaspoon Near East or Aleppo pepper (page 395)

1. To make the *köfte:* In a bowl, pour warm water over the bread cubes and let them stand for a few minutes. Press out and discard the liquid. Leave the bread in the bowl.

Add the meat, onion, cumin, salt, and black pepper and knead until well blended. Add the egg to the mixture and knead with a fork until light and well combined.

Divide into 12 equal parts and gently mold each into a sausage shape. (It helps to keep hands moistened to avoid sticking.) Mount onto the skewers, oil the surface of the meat, cover with plastic wrap, and keep refrigerated for up to half a day.

2. To make the bread base: Cut the *pide* into ¾-inch cubes—you will have about 3 cups. Melt the butter in an 8- or 9-inch non-stick skillet; add the salt and the bread cubes. Quickly sear/toast on all sides over high heat, stirring constantly, about 1 minute. Add the stock, cover, and cook over medium heat until all the moisture has been absorbed, about 3 minutes. Set aside with the cover in place.

3. To make the tomato sauce: In a second skillet, warm the olive oil; add the tomatoes and chili and cook over high heat, stirring until thick. Add the salt, sugar, garlic, and vinegar and bring to a boil, stirring. Set aside. Makes about 1 cup.

4. To make the yogurt sauce: Place the yogurt in a small bowl; gradually beat in ¼ cup water until smooth and creamy. Add the salt. (Up to this point, the dish can be prepared in advance.)

5. Prepare the hardwood coals.

6. Five to 7 minutes before serving, grill the meat on both sides; cook until desired degree of doneness. Meanwhile, reheat the bread and the tomato sauce. When the tomato sauce is boiling, add the vinegar, cover, and remove from the heat.

7. To make the flourish: Melt the 2 tablespoons butter in a small saucepan. (You can do this right over the coals.) Add the cayenne, but do not allow it to burn. Divide the bread among 4 serving dishes. Top each with the grilled meat, the tomato sauce, and then the yogurt. Drizzle the bubbling butter on top and serve.

NOTES TO THE COOK: Minced meat is traditionally molded onto wide, flat skewers, to which it adheres better than to the four-sided or round variety. You can find these skewers at many Middle Eastern markets, but they are not a necessity. The objective is to preserve juiciness and obtain the taste of meat grilled over coals.

Loin chops marinated in grated onion with salt and pepper can be substituted for the *köfte*.

With thanks to Aybek Surdam for sharing this recipe

BROILED KIBBEH KABOBS WITH PARSLEY, LEMON, AND WALNUT SAUCE

In Aleppo, large apple dumpling–shaped kibbeh stuffed with peppery butter or chopped sheep's tail fat are mounted on skewers and broiled until crusty on the outside and juicy within. In Damascus, a smaller unstuffed version is preferred—more highly seasoned with spices and served under a blanket of parsley, lemon, and walnut sauce.

Makes 18 kibbeh, serving 5 to 6

continued

PARSLEY, LEMON, AND WALNUT SAUCE

2 medium lemons

¼ teaspoon coarse salt

Pinch of freshly ground black pepper

Pinch of Near East or Aleppo pepper (page 395)

⅓ cup coarsely chopped walnuts

¾ cup chopped flat-leaf parsley

½ teaspoon garlic, peeled and crushed with pinch of salt

6 tablespoons shredded mint leaves

2 tablespoons olive oil

2 tablespoons water

KIBBEH KABOBS

1 cup fine-grain bulgur

1 pound lean lamb, beef, or turkey, ground to a paste in a food processor

1 small onion

1¼ teaspoons salt

½ teaspoon *each* freshly ground black pepper, allspice, and cumin

2 tablespoons olive oil

2 pinches of Near East or Aleppo Pepper

1½ tablespoons flour

6 flat-sided skewers

Butter-flavored oil spray or 1 tablespoon olive oil

Warm pita or *saj* (page 43)

1. To make the sauce: Peel the lemons, discard the seeds, and chop the flesh to make ½ cup. Season with the salt, black pepper, and red pepper. In a bowl, mix the lemons with the remaining ingredients and let stand about 1 hour before serving.

2. To make the kabobs: Wash the bulgur in a sieve under running water. Squeeze out excess moisture. Combine bulgur with all the other ingredients in the work bowl of a food processor. Process 40 seconds. Finish the blending by hand, adding water as necessary to form a soft mass.

3. Divide the mixture and mold onto the skewers. Spray or coat with oil. Broil close to the heat source until brown and crusty on both sides. Serve at once, in warm pita, with the parsley, lemon, and walnut sauce spread on top.

VARIATION:

Substitute a thick yogurt and garlic sauce (page 27) for the walnut sauce. Enrich the yogurt sauce with chopped parsley.

THREE MEATBALL
DISHES

GEORGIAN *KOTELETTIS* WITH FRESH HERBS
AND RED ONIONS

Here is an unusual method for infusing moisture into *köfte* balls—or *kotelettis*, as they are called in western Georgia. Tsitsi Ratishivili, a Mingrelian housewife, showed me how to gradually whip spoonfuls of cold water into a ground pork and beef mixture until it is almost soupy, and then, with moistened palms, flip the meat into long, smooth ovals, to be floured, egged, and breadcrumbed before frying.

I offer below a lower-fat version, without eggs and breadcrumbs. The neat patties are brushed lightly with a little butter-flavored oil (for flavor); broiled until seared on both sides; then finished in a medium oven until fully cooked, about 20 minutes. They shrink a little but are still juicy.

Serve with warm sheets of Mükerrem's Unleavened Flat Griddle Bread (page 39), and with roughly chopped fresh coriander and parsley, and sliced red onions.

Serves 6

continued

KOTELETTIS

1 pound lean ground beef

1 pound lean ground pork

⅓ cup chopped coriander

1½ teaspoons freshly ground black pepper

2 teaspoons fine salt

1½ teaspoons hot Hungarian paprika

Oil mixed with some melted butter for brushing the patties (optional)

OPTIONAL COATING

2 cups soft breadcrumbs

2 eggs, beaten

Oil mixed with some melted butter for frying

GARNISH

1 medium red onion, peeled and thinly sliced

½ cup roughly chopped flat-leaf parsley

¼ cup roughly chopped coriander

¼ teaspoon hot Hungarian paprika

Pinch of salt

Freshly ground black pepper to taste

6 large tandoori bread rounds, 12 flour tortillas, 12 Mükerrem's Unleavened Flat Griddle Breads, or 12 *saj* bread rounds (pages 39 and 43)

Lemon wedges

I. In a mixing bowl, combine all the ingredients for the *kotelettis*, blending well. Gradually beat in 1½ cups water. Separate the mixture into 12 equal portions and form each part into a sausage-shaped roll. To do this, roll the meat mixture back and forth between wet palms until it "flips" into a roll. Chill thoroughly under plastic wrap.

2. Optional coating and frying: Dip the prepared *kotelettis* in the breadcrumbs and egg for a complete coating. Let air-dry while heating oil mixed with some butter (for flavor) in a wide skillet. Fry the *kotelettis*, until crisp and golden brown, about 7 minutes to a side. Drain and set in a 200° F. oven until ready to serve.

3. For a less fattening version, broil until crisp and well cooked, about 20 minutes.

4. Meanwhile, mix the ingredients for the garnish and pile onto a serving dish. Heat the bread over a low flame or under the broiler until each side just begins to soften and spot brown. Keep warm in a plastic bag or a linen towel until ready to serve.

5. To serve, place the *kotelettis* side by side on top of the garnish mix; add lemon wedges. Pass the warm bread.

MACEDONIAN MEATBALLS
ROLLED IN PARSLEY

*H*ere is a superb version of meatballs in an egg and lemon sauce, as served in the northern Greek city of Kastoria. The meatballs are extremely light, tangy, and attractive.

The plentiful sauce is based on beaten eggs and lemon juice, and calls for the same technique as the well-known avgolemono sauce. Sprinkle a little freshly ground black pepper on top just before serving. Accompany with steamed rice.

Serves 5 to 6

Complete steps 1 and 2 many hours in advance, so that the flavors blend and mellow.

1. In a food processor, combine the meat with the onion, garlic, 1½ teaspoons fine salt, 1 teaspoon black pepper, mint, rice, vinegar, 1 tablespoon of the oil, and the lightly beaten egg. Process until you have a smooth paste, then transfer to a bowl, cover, and refrigerate until firm enough to handle, about 30 minutes.

2. Spread the parsley on a flat surface. Gently divide the meat mixture into 16 equal parts. Moisten your hands with cold water and gently shape each part into an elongated oval and roll in a bed of chopped parsley. Arrange the rolls on a flat plate, cover with plastic wrap, and refrigerate.

3. About 1 hour before serving, bring 6 cups water to a boil in a 5-quart casserole,

continued

1½ pounds extra lean ground meat (beef, veal, or lamb or a combination of two)
1 large grated onion, rinsed and drained
1 clove garlic, peeled
Salt
Freshly ground black pepper
1 teaspoon crumbled dried mint, preferably spearmint
½ cup raw white rice
3 tablespoons aged red wine vinegar or 2 tablespoons lemon juice and 1 tablespoon wine vinegar
2 tablespoons olive oil
1 egg, lightly beaten
2 cups finely chopped flat-leaf parsley

SAUCE
2 egg yolks
1 teaspoon cornstarch
3 tablespoons fresh lemon juice or more to taste
Salt and freshly ground black pepper to taste

wide enough to hold all the ovals in one layer. When the water boils, add 1 teaspoon salt and the remaining 1 tablespoon of oil. Add the meatballs one by one, without losing the boil. (Constant boiling keeps the parsley coating in place.) Skim off the foam that rises to the surface. Cover and cook at a slow boil until the rolls are soft and tender, about 35 minutes.

4. With a slotted spoon carefully transfer the ovals to a heated serving dish. Cover to keep moist. Turn off the heat. For the sauce, place the egg yolks in a small, heavy saucepan with the cornstarch, and beat until pale and light. Add the lemon juice and beat 30 seconds longer. Set the saucepan over medium-low heat. Gradually add a scant 2 cups of the cooking liquid into the egg mixture and continue beating until thick and creamy. Adjust the seasoning with salt and pepper and sharpen the sauce with a few drops of lemon juice. (Avoid boiling, or the mixture will scramble.) Spoon over the meatballs, sprinkle with black pepper, and serve at once.

With thanks to Maria Papadina for sharing this recipe

PEAR-SHAPED MEATBALLS STUFFED WITH CREAMY EGGPLANT

Just when I thought that I had seen just about everything one can do with an eggplant, a Syrian acquaintance shared yet another recipe. In this Aleppine version, baby eggplants, chosen for their pear shape and long stems, are peeled, fried, steamed, chilled, and coated with a ground meat mixture, then browned and finally baked in a spicy tomato sauce. Serve with a rice and fried noodles pilaf (page 233).

Serves 4

Prepare the eggplant and meat mixture early in the day.

1. Wash, dry, and peel each eggplant, but do not remove the calyx or stem.

2. In a 10-inch skillet, heat 2 tablespoons olive oil over medium heat. Add the eggplants, cover the skillet, and cook until the flesh is golden brown on all sides and very tender, about 15 minutes. Add ½ cup water and cook, covered, turning the eggplants occasionally, over low heat another 20 minutes. Carefully transfer the eggplants to a flat dish, cover, and refrigerate. Pour off the pan juices.

3. To make the meat mixture: Combine the meat, onion, spices, salt, and black pepper in the work bowl of a food processor and process until pasty. Turn out onto a work surface and knead in the flour and egg white; mix to a light, malleable paste. Divide into 8 smooth balls, cover, and refrigerate.

4. About 45 minutes before serving, preheat the oven to 350° F.

5. Working with wet palms, make a deep cavity in each ball and place a whole eggplant in it. Mold the meat mixture evenly around the eggplant, leaving the stem and calyx exposed. With wet hands pat and press the meat firmly so that the rolls resemble pears. In a medium nonstick skillet, fry half the "pears" in 3 tablespoons olive oil until brown on all sides, 3 minutes. Transfer to a 10-inch round, ovenproof serving dish. Repeat with the remaining "pears."

8 Italian eggplants, with long stems attached (1¼ pounds total weight)

2 tablespoons olive oil

GROUND MEAT MIXTURE

1¼ pounds lean ground lamb, beef, or turkey

1 medium onion, grated

1 teaspoon Syrian Mixed Spices, Number 2 (page 393), or 1 teaspoon ground allspice

Good pinch of Near East or Aleppo pepper (page 395)

1 teaspoon salt

½ teaspoon freshly ground black pepper

3 tablespoons flour

1 egg white, beaten frothy

3 tablespoons olive oil

SPICY TOMATO SAUCE

⅓ cup grated onion

½ teaspoon garlic, peeled and crushed with salt

4 medium vine-ripened tomatoes, peeled, seeded, and chopped, or 1½ cups light tomato sauce

½ teaspoon ground allspice

¼ teaspoon ground coriander seeds

⅓ teaspoon Near East or Aleppo pepper or to taste

Salt to taste

1 to 2 teaspoons fresh lemon juice

continued

6. To make the tomato sauce: Discard all but I tablespoon fat from the skillet. Add the onion and cook, stirring, for an instant. Then add the garlic, tomatoes, spices, and salt. Bring to a boil, pour over the meat rolls, and set in the oven to finish cooking, about 30 minutes, basting occasionally. Sprinkle with lemon juice and serve hot or warm.

Thanks to Adnan Al-Jabri for sharing this recipe for ormuk kebabi

A Regional Sampler of Meat Stews

In the six regional stews that follow, the meat is literally smothered in vegetables, fruits, or herbs—the most popular eastern Mediterranean stewing method. This smothering perfumes the food, heightens its taste, and makes boiled, stewed, or fried meat very attractive.

Turkish Meat Stew Smothered in Spinach Stems and Roots

Here is a use for those spinach stems and roots that are usually discarded. The taste is special, earthy, and just the slightest bit bitter, not at all like that of spinach leaves. In fact, I like these stems and roots so much, I often use them in a simple warm salad dressed with lemon and oil (page 200).

In this economical stew, 3 shoulder lamb chops and the stems and roots of 2½ to 3 pounds fresh spinach will make a meal to serve 4 or 5. Serve the leaves as a vegetable on the side, using the bones from the chops for added flavor (page 209).

The egg yolk–lemon liaison used at the end should be very light, more like a veil than a traditional avgolemono sauce. Serve with rice pilaf.

continued

2½ to 3 pounds fresh spinach, with 2½- to 3-inch pinkish
    stems

2 tablespoons unsalted butter or olive oil

Pinch of salt

3 lamb shoulder chops

I cup grated onion

⅓ teaspoon Near East or Aleppo pepper (page 395) or
    ¼ teaspoon cayenne and a pinch of ground allspice

¼ teaspoon sugar

Salt to taste

I egg yolk

I tablespoon flour

2 tablespoons fresh lemon juice

I. Cut away the spinach leaves and save for a pie, soup, or simple vegetable dish. Discard damaged outer stems from each clump and trim the roots. Cut each clump in half (without separating the stems from the root base) and soak in several changes of water.

2. Drain the spinach stems and place them in a 10-inch skillet. Add half the butter or oil and salt; cover and stew over moderate heat 5 minutes. Strain off the expressed liquid and reserve. Set the stems aside. Rinse out the skillet.

3. Bone and trim the meat and cut into ¾-inch cubes.

4. Heat the remaining butter or oil in the skillet over moderately high heat, add the meat, and cook, covered, 5 minutes. Uncover and boil off the liquid in the pan, stirring often. Allow the meat to gently brown in the fat, stirring often. Add the onion and cook, stirring, for another minute. Place the spinach stems on top, add the reserved liquid, ½ cup water, spices, sugar, and salt; cover and cook over medium heat 30 minutes, or until the meat is tender.

5. Ten minutes before serving, in a small saucepan beat the egg yolk and flour, I tablespoon cold water, and lemon juice until well blended. Tilt the skillet and ladle about I cup of the skillet juices into the egg-yolk mixture. Gently cook the egg-yolk mixture over low heat, stirring, until creamy and thick. Set aside for an instant.

6. Using a slotted spoon, place the lamb in a warm serving dish, arrange the stems on top in an attractive manner, and cover to keep warm. Pour the remaining skillet juices into the saucepan and continue to cook, stirring, until creamy and light. (If the sauce is too thick, add a little water.) Correct the seasoning and pour over and around the meat and spinach stems. Serve at once.

Inspired by a recipe in The Delights of Turkish Cooking, *by Neset Eren*

MACEDONIAN LAMB STEW SMOTHERED IN SPINACH LEAVES

H ere is a wonderful Slavic Macedonian dish. Salting the spinach leaves an hour before cooking causes them to exude their moisture but not their vitamins, and they keep their bright green color in the sauce.

The perfect accompaniment to this dish is garlic-flavored yogurt.

Serves 4 to 5

1. Remove any thick spinach stems and cut the larger leaves into smaller pieces. In a wide bowl, toss the leaves with coarse salt and let stand 1 hour.

2. Meanwhile, trim the meat and cut into 5 or 6 pieces.

3. In a nonstick skillet, brown the lamb in 1 tablespoon of oil. Season with coarse salt and black pepper, then add the boiling water. Cover tightly and cook over medium-low heat until the lamb is tender, ¾ to 1½ hours, depending upon the age of the lamb. You should have about 2 cups cooking juices in the skillet.

4. Gently squeeze the spinach in batches to remove as much water as possible and set aside. (This makes about 4 cups.) Roughly chop the spinach.

1½ pounds fresh spinach, washed in several changes of water
2 to 3 teaspoons coarse salt

2 pounds shoulder of lamb
2 tablespoons vegetable or olive oil
½ teaspoon coarse salt
¼ teaspoon freshly ground black pepper
3 cups boiling water
16 scallions (white part plus 4 inches green shoots), cut on the diagonal into 1-inch pieces
1 heaping teaspoon Hungarian paprika
1 tablespoon tomato paste

2 cups yogurt, drained to 1 cup (see page 410 for directions on draining yogurt)
½ teaspoon crushed garlic

5. Drain the lamb; degrease and reserve the cooking juices. Heat the remaining tablespoon of oil in a 12-inch skillet. Add the scallions and gently sauté until wilted. Stir in the paprika, tomato paste, and reserved cooking juices and bring to a boil. Simmer 5 minutes.

continued

6. Meanwhile, cut the lamb into bite-size pieces. Discard bones and gristle. Add the meat and spinach to the skillet. Partially cover and continue cooking over gentle heat until the spinach is cooked, about 10 minutes. Taste for salt. Sprinkle generously with more black pepper and serve with a bowl of thick yogurt mixed with crushed garlic.

AUTUMN LAMB STEW WITH SQUASH, LEMON, AND MINT

This spicy dish from Gaziantep is traditionally served with a bulgur pilaf.

Serves 4 to 5

1 pound lean shoulder of lamb or veal, cut into 1-inch cubes and including all bones
1¼ teaspoons freshly ground black pepper
3 tablespoons olive oil
1 cup chopped onion
1 tablespoon tomato paste
1 tablespoon homemade pepper paste (page 389)
1½ teaspoons minced garlic
1½ cups cooked chickpeas
1 large ripe tomato, peeled, seeded, and chopped
6 cups peeled and cubed hubbard, banana, or butternut squash (about 4 pounds squash or 2 pounds trimmed weight)
½ teaspoon salt
4 tablespoons fresh lemon juice
2 teaspoons dried mint
Pinch of Near East or Aleppo pepper (page 395)

1. Trim the meat of excess fat and sprinkle with half the black pepper. Heat 2 tablespoons of oil in a 4-quart pan over medium heat. Add the meat and cook, stirring, until all moisture evaporates, about 7 minutes. Add the onion and cook, stirring, for 10 minutes.

2. Add the tomato and pepper pastes, and cook, stirring, 5 minutes. Add 1½ cups water and bring to a boil. Cover and cook over medium-low heat until the meat is tender, about 45 minutes.

3. Add the garlic, chickpeas, tomatoes, cubed squash, and salt. Add water to barely cover the contents and cook, covered, until the squash is tender, 25 minutes.

4. Stir in the lemon juice and remove from heat. Transfer the contents of the casserole to a shallow serving dish.

5. Press the mint, red pepper, and remaining black pepper through a fine sieve. Heat the remaining 1 tablespoon of olive oil in a small saucepan until sizzling; add the powdered aromatics and stir for an instant. Swirl the oil over the stew, stir once, and serve hot.

Adapted from a recipe called kabaklama *given to me by Mrs. Ayfer Ünsal*

GEORGIAN MEAT STEW SMOTHERED WITH FRESH HERBS AND SOUR FRUITS

In Georgia, in springtime, you will find families feasting on this dish outdoors in the hills surrounding Tbilisi. Georgian men like to make this stew of spring lamb, lots of herbs, and a few unripe plums, "perhaps because it is easy," explained my friend Tamara when I asked her why it was a male specialty.

Three-month-old lamb cooks very quickly; older lamb may require double the cooking time. (Fresh, young veal breast is often cooked this way too.) Georgians living in the United States suggest substituting fresh cranberries when the traditional sour plums are not available.

This dish will be even better if made early in the day, cooled to room temperature, then chilled. Remove all fat and reheat slowly just before serving. (It is also good at room temperature.) Serve with warm and crisp bread, such as Buba Khotoveli's Crackling Flat Bread (page 46).

Serves 6

continued

3 pounds lean lamb shoulder on the bone, cut into 1½-inch
    chunks

3 cups minced onions

½ cup boiling water

I packed cup tarragon leaves

I packed cup parsley leaves

¾ packed cup coriander

I cup fresh or frozen cranberries, stemmed, washed, and
    drained

¼ teaspoon hot paprika or more to taste

¼ cup dry white wine

Salt

2 sprigs tarragon for garnish

I. Rinse the lamb and place it, dripping wet, in a large casserole. Cover and cook over moderately low heat 15 minutes. Add the onions and boiling water. Cover, reduce the heat to low, and simmer until the meat is tender, about 1½ hours (see note above for young lamb). With a slotted spoon, transfer the lamb to a deep serving dish. Skim as much fat as possible from the cooking liquid.

2. Meanwhile, chop together the tarragon, parsley, and coriander. Add them, with the cranberries and paprika, to the skimmed cooking liquid. Boil over moderate heat until the cranberries burst, about 5 minutes. Add the wine and return to a boil. Season with hot paprika and salt to taste. With a slotted spoon, remove the cranberries and add to the lamb. Boil the liquid, skimming until thick, about 6 minutes. Pour the sauce over the meat. Garnish with sprigs of tarragon and serve warm.

With thanks to Tsino Natsuvlishvili for sharing this recipe for chakapuli

MACEDONIAN PORK SMOTHERED IN LEEKS

When I asked the Greek cookbook author Vefa Alexiadou to name her favorite recipe from her book *Greek Cuisine*, her husband, Kostas, interrupted to say that *his* favorite was this Macedonian stew of pork and leeks. My husband also thinks this dish is great—lusty and succulent.

This dish is rich. Please don't bother trying it with a leaner cut of pork—it won't be the same and you'll be disappointed.

Really good dishes made with very few components require absolutely top-quality ingredients. For example, since this is a winter dish, use home-preserved chopped tomatoes or a can of chopped tomatoes from Italy, not hothouse tomatoes.

The pork should be from the shoulder; loin pork is far too lean. I buy a 2¾-pound pork shoulder butt, then trim off most of the fat.

Leeks are cheap in Macedonia but expensive in the United States. You should choose leeks that are more white than green, and that are about 1 inch in diameter.

Serves 4 to 6

1. Brown the pork lightly in hot oil in a 12-inch covered skillet over moderately high heat. Turn the pieces after 8 minutes and continue to brown. Uncover, boil down the juices, and pour off almost all the fat.

2. Add the onion and brown, stirring, 5 minutes. Add the tomatoes or tomato sauce, 2 cups water, celery, and salt and pepper; cover and cook 30 minutes.

2¾ pounds pork shoulder butt, untrimmed, or 1¾ pounds trimmed, and cut into 1-inch cubes
1 tablespoon olive oil
1 medium onion, grated
1 cup chopped canned tomatoes or homemade tomato sauce
1 small rib celery, chopped
Salt and freshly ground black pepper to taste
9 to 12 leeks, trimmed of roots and tough green tops

3. Peel away the coarse outer leaves of the leeks. Wash the leeks well to remove all sand; cut the white and pale green parts into 2-inch lengths, lay them in a large skillet, add 1½ cups water, cover, and simmer 10 minutes. (The leeks can be blanched in a microwave.)

4. Refresh, drain, and add the leeks to the skillet. Partially cover the skillet and cook until the meat is tender and almost all liquid has been absorbed, about 1 hour. Serve with a good sprinkling of freshly ground black pepper.

LAMB WITH APPLES

This terrific winter dish, from southeastern Turkey, uses red apples, called *nidge*, sour and hard as stones. I substitute the pretty, delicate lady apples grown in California, New York, and Washington State, which are available around Christmas.

The fry-steam technique here is often used in eastern Mediterranean cooking for tougher pieces of meat. The meat throws off its juices, reabsorbs them, then finally fries in the small amount of fat in the pan.

Pomegranate molasses gives this dish a delicious piquant taste, underscored by the well-established Gaziantep combination of red pepper and tomato paste.

Serves 4 to 6

1½ pounds boneless lamb shoulder, trimmed and cut into 1-inch cubes

1 tablespoon olive oil

1 cup grated onion

1 scant tablespoon pomegranate molasses (page 404)

1 teaspoon Near East or Aleppo pepper (page 395) or to taste

½ tablespoon tomato paste

Approximately 20 (1½ pounds) lady apples, unpeeled, cored, and cut to the same size as lamb cubes

Salt to taste

1. Put the meat and oil in a 10-inch non-stick skillet, cover, and cook over medium-high heat 10 minutes, shaking the pan often. Remove the cover; allow the juices in the pan to be reabsorbed by the meat and then let the meat brown on all sides, 5 to 10 minutes.

2. Add the onion and cook, stirring, 5 minutes. Stir in the pomegranate molasses, 1 cup water, and the red pepper and tomato pastes. Cover the skillet again and cook the meat 40 minutes. Add the apples to the stew and continue to cook 20 minutes longer. Correct the seasoning with salt. Serve in a shallow dish.

With thanks to Filiz Hösukoğlu for sharing this recipe for Elma Tavasi

THREE CASSEROLE DINNERS

It is actually easier to prepare either a rustic or a sophisticated one-dish casserole meal ahead of time than to cook a main dish-and-two-vegetables "sixty-minute" dinner just before your guests arrive. For one thing, there will be a lot less stress, and for another, your home will be filled with the welcoming aroma of good food.

The casserole dishes that follow are flavorful, pleasingly aromatic, and also economical. The recipes can be doubled or even tripled to feed larger crowds. None requires a complicated accompaniment—just good chewy bread or a bowl of fluffy bulgur pilaf, a simple salad, and, for those who want a sweet, a fruit compote or store-bought treat.

"HIDDEN MEATS"

The yellow headlights sliced through the mist, revealing the pine trees that lined the road. Every so often I'd catch a glimpse of the lights of Salonika, Greece's "second city," sparkling far below. I was ascending a mountain, in search of a special restaurant in the village of Hortiatis, which I'd heard about even in Athens, 300 miles to the south.

I found it, finally—the Pistaria Klimataria, a small, humble chalet-type place, with thick wooden tables and white stuccoed walls, exuding the aroma of grilled and roasted meats. Most diners were feasting on the house specialty, a unique regional version of the fascinating Greek "hidden meat" dish called *klephtika*.

continued

Chef and owner Panayiotis Kamanikas told me he makes his version out of cubes of fresh ham, feta, onion, garlic, red chili, and leeks packed into a large sausage skin so that all the flavor is retained. But his father, he added, between dashes to the kitchen and stops at the tables of his happy clientele, would wrap the same combination of meat and seasonings in an animal skin, then cook it by burying it in hot ashes until the hair on the skin burned off.

Klephtika is actually a whole class of fascinating "secret" Greek dishes, originally cooked in the hills by guerrilla fighters hiding from the Turks. They are "secret" because, being sealed inside containers and then cooked slowly amidst embers, they do not raise smoke and thus give away the mountain campsites of their preparers. I refer anyone interested in kitchen versions of *klephtika* to Diane Kochilas's *The Food and Wine of Greece*, particularly her Veal Baked in Bread *(Exohiko Thessalias)*.

Kurdish Eggplant Casserole with Lamb, Garlic, and Sumac

Many parts of Turkey and the Balkans offer a similar dish, called *guvech*, for which a large earthenware casserole is filled with a small amount of meat, usually lamb, plus every kind of vegetable imaginable: cauliflower, celery root, green beans, okra, leeks, pumpkins, eggplants, green peas, carrots, peppers, and tomatoes—all cubed, layered, then slowly baked together.

In this version, from the Kurdish city Diyarkabir in southeastern Turkey, the rule of less is more applies. A wide, shallow earthen dish is filled with eggplants, tomatoes, sweet and hot peppers, and a small amount of lamb, then cooked in a thick, rich, sumac-flavored liquid. Just before serving, the dish is sprinkled with a generous handful of chopped garlic and parsley.

Serve *guvech* with a simple bulgur pilaf.

Serves 3 to 4

1. In a 5-quart pot, cook the meat with the onion, salt, pepper, and 2 cups water, covered, over medium heat until almost tender, 1½ hours.

2. Meanwhile, trim the eggplant tops and discard. Cut each eggplant lengthwise into ½-inch slices. Peel the end slices only. Sprinkle the eggplant with coarse salt and let stand 1 to 1½ hours. Rinse the eggplant well and squeeze out the water by pressing between palms. Pat dry. Fry the eggplant slices in hot oil until golden brown or arrange the slices on a lightly oiled baking sheet and bake 10 minutes on each side in a preheated 425° F. oven.

3. Combine the sumac and ¾ cup water in a small saucepan and bring to a boil. Remove from the heat and let stand while following step 4.

4. Remove the meat from the pot, discard the onion, and reserve and degrease the cooking liquid for the accompanying pilaf. Separate the meat from the bones and trim away all hard fat. Arrange the meat on the bottom of a 1½-quart ovenproof dish, preferably made of earthenware. Sprinkle with salt, black pepper, and hot pepper flakes.

5. Arrange the eggplant and frying peppers on top of the meat in one layer. Cover with the tomato sauce, seasoned with salt, pepper, and sugar. Arrange a layer of tomato slices and whole chilis on top of the sauce.

6. Preheat the oven to 375° F.

7. Strain the sumac liquid through a fine sieve into a bowl, stir in the lemon juice, and pour over the contents of the casserole. Loosely cover with foil and bake 45 minutes. Just before serving, sprinkle with the garlic mixed with the parsley.

Adapted from a recipe called Meftuna, *given to me by Mrs. Selim Nurileam*

---

2 pounds lamb neck

1 medium onion, quartered

½ teaspoon salt

¼ teaspoon freshly ground black pepper

3 eggplants (2 pounds total weight)

Coarse salt

Vegetable or olive oil for frying or baking

¼ cup ground red sumac

Pinch of hot pepper flakes, with few seeds

2 Italian green frying peppers, stemmed and cut into 1-inch chunks

1 cup homemade or canned tomato sauce

Pinch of sugar

2 tomatoes, sliced

2 long green chilis

Juice of ½ lemon

3 large cloves garlic, peeled and crushed with salt

2 tablespoons chopped parsley

BALKAN MOUSSAKA WITH FRIED KALE

This unusual Balkan version of moussaka features kale instead of eggplant. The blanched and dried kale leaves are dipped in a very light batter and then fried, producing a delicate, crisp bed for a spicy ground meat filling, topped with a tangy, moist combination of yogurt and milk lightly enriched with egg—far lighter than the traditional, floury béchamel. For this recipe, everything can be prepared in advance, then simply assembled 30 minutes before baking. This moussaka is particularly good served with a salad of marinated red and green peppers.

Serves 8

BATTER

I large egg

1¼ cups low-fat milk

I cup all-purpose flour

I teaspoon baking powder

2 bunches small, crisp kale leaves

1¼ pounds lean ground meat: lamb shoulder, beef chuck, or
    turkey

½ teaspoon salt

¼ teaspoon freshly ground black pepper

Hot Hungarian paprika

½ teaspoon ground cinnamon

I tablespoon olive oil

I cup chopped onions

I cup chopped parsley

I tablespoon peeled, minced garlic

I tablespoon tomato paste, diluted in ¾ cup water

Olive oil for frying

5 tablespoons fine breadcrumbs

I cup freshly grated Parmesan, Kefalotyri, or Asiago

I. To make the batter: Mix the egg with the milk, then stir in the flour and baking powder, mixing until smooth. Cover and let stand at room temperature 30 minutes.

2. Wash the kale and remove thick stems. Steam, blanch, or boil the leaves until just tender, about 10 minutes. Refresh under cool running water and pat dry. Cut large leaves into thirds. Drain dry.

3. In a large skillet over medium heat, place the ground meat, salt, pepper, pinch of paprika, cinnamon, and oil. Brown gently, breaking up any chunks, about 10 minutes. Drain off fat.

4. Add the onions, parsley, and garlic. Cook, covered, until the onions are soft, 10 minutes over medium heat. Stir in the diluted tomato paste and bring to a boil, stirring. Remove from the heat.

5. Pour 1½ inches oil in a large, heavy

skillet or electric skillet set at 375° F. Mix the kale into the batter, stirring to coat all the leaves evenly. When fat reaches 375° F. on deep fat thermometer, fry leaves in small batches 2 to 3 minutes, turning to brown on all sides. Drain on a cake rack set over brown paper or paper toweling.

TOPPING

4 large eggs
I cup plain yogurt
2 cups lukewarm low-fat milk
Dash of hot Hungarian paprika

6. Oil a 3-quart shallow baking dish and dust the bottom with the breadcrumbs. Spread half the kale in one layer. Top with the meat and then the cheese. Cover with the remaining kale and a sprinkling of breadcrumbs and hot paprika.

7. Preheat the oven to 375° F.

8. To make the topping: Combine the ingredients, beating well. Spoon the topping down the insides of the dish and just a little over the top. Let settle about 10 minutes. Bake, uncovered, 25 minutes, or until the topping is set and lightly browned. Remove from the heat, let settle 5 minutes, then cut in large squares and serve.

Inspired by a recipe in The Balkan Cookbook, *by Radojko Mrljes*

"Split Tummies" of Stuffed Eggplants

A casserole of "split tummies," as they're known in Aleppo and Turkey, makes a light and satisfying entree. Small, tender eggplants, stuffed with ground meat, are seasoned with traditional eastern Mediterranean flavorings—cinnamon, allspice, nutmeg, cloves, and pine nuts. The stuffed vegetables are then baked on a bed of chopped peppers and onions, and covered with rounds of sliced cherry tomatoes.

Please don't forego frying eggplants because you're worried they'll be too heavy. With the method of frying described below, the eggplants steam and fry at the same time, absorbing very little oil while developing a wonderful creamy-sweet texture and taste.

You can prepare the sauce, meat filling, and eggplants the day before, then assemble the parts just before baking. This dish is usually served with a pilaf of bulgur, but you can substitute a loaf of crusty bread to mop up the delicious pan juices.

Serves 4

1. To make the filling: Heat the oil in a large skillet and brown the pine nuts in the heated oil. Remove the pine nuts to drain. Add the meat and continue to cook until the meat is brown and crumbled, 1 to 2 minutes. Add the grated onion and 2 tablespoons water. Increase the heat to medium and sauté 2 minutes longer. Then add the spices, tomato paste, parsley, and salt and pepper. Remove from the heat. Allow to cool.

2. Remove three 1/2-inch strips of peel lengthwise from the eggplants, leaving 1-inch stripes of flesh. Heat 1 1/2 tablespoons olive oil in a medium-sized skillet over moderate heat. Place the eggplants in the skillet, cover tightly, and cook until the flesh is golden brown on all sides and all parts of the eggplant are tender, about 12 minutes. Cool on racks.

3. Discard the oil in the skillet. Add 1 tablespoon fresh oil, the chopped onion, bay leaf, garlic, chili, and bell pepper. Cook, uncovered, 5 minutes, stirring. Add the tomato paste dissolved in water, and cook 1 minute longer. Season with additional salt and pepper, and sugar.

4. Press open one of the striped sides of each eggplant. Spread equal amounts of the meat filling in each cavity.

5. Preheat the oven to 375° F.

FILLING

1 1/2 tablespoons olive oil
1/4 cup pine nuts
6 ounces lean ground beef, lamb, or turkey
1 small onion, grated
3/4 teaspoon ground allspice
1/8 teaspoon ground cinnamon
Pinch of ground cloves
Pinch of grated nutmeg
1 teaspoon tomato paste
1/4 cup chopped parsley
Salt and freshly ground black pepper to taste

12 Italian eggplants (about 2 pounds total weight), each approximately 4 1/2 inches long
2 1/2 tablespoons olive oil
1 cup chopped onion
1 small bay leaf
2 teaspoons peeled, minced garlic
2 teaspoons finely minced green chili or more to taste
1 small green bell pepper, cored, seeded, and minced, about 1/2 cup
2 teaspoons tomato paste, dissolved in 1/2 cup water
Salt
Freshly ground black pepper
Pinch of sugar
1 to 2 ripe tomatoes, seeded and thinly sliced
2 tablespoons chopped parsley

6. Line a 12-inch ovenproof serving dish with the vegetable sauce. Arrange the eggplants on top, with a layer of tomato slices over all. Cover with foil and bake for 45 minutes. Uncover and continue baking 15 minutes longer. Serve warm with a sprinkling of the chopped parsley. (The dish can be prepared ahead and reheated until just warm.)

With thanks to Amal Al-Jabri for sharing this recipe for Karniyarik

XIV
Desserts

NOAH'S PUDDING

৵৹

Before I even tasted this dish, I was sure I would hate it. I couldn't imagine a dessert made of white beans, chickpeas, husked wheat berries, and every conceivable type of dried fruit all mixed together and scented with rose water. And when I saw it, I was sure that I was right, because it was so unattractive. I was wrong. The dish is really good and, when decorated with nuts and pomegranate seeds, it can even be called "handsome."

Prepared by Armenians for Christmas and by Arabs to honor the martyrdom of a saint, the dessert is based on an ancient tale about Noah and the Ark. According to the tale, Noah, on sighting land, made a dish using all the stores he had left on board. This dish has come to symbolize an act of thanksgiving.

Serves 8

1. Soak the chickpeas and white beans in water overnight. Separately place the pistachios and almonds in a bowl, cover with water, and let stand overnight.

2. The following day, drain the beans, chickpeas, pistachios, and almonds. Peel the chickpeas. Working in batches, loosely wrap the soaked chickpeas in a terry-cloth towel. Use a rolling pin to gently pound and roll them so that their skins loosen. Then rub the chickpeas between your fingers and remove the skins. Use a knife to halve the almonds and slip off the peel. Rub the skins off the pistachios. Roughly chop the nuts and set aside.

3. Rinse the wheat berries and drain. Place the wheat berries, chickpeas, and white

¼ cup dry chickpeas, soaked overnight
¼ cup dry white beans, soaked overnight
⅓ cup pistachios, shelled and unsalted
⅓ cup almonds, shelled but with the skin on
¾ cup husked whole wheat berries
8 dried apricots
⅓ cup yellow raisins
4 dried figs
½ cup plus I tablespoon sugar
⅓ cup hazelnuts, peeled and coarsely chopped
⅓ cup walnuts, shelled, soaked in hot water for 10 minutes, drained and coarsely chopped
2 teaspoons rose water or more to taste
⅓ cup pomegranate seeds

continued

beans in a 3-quart saucepan. Add 2 quarts water and bring to a boil; skim carefully, then lower the heat and cook at a simmer until tender, about 1¼ hours.

4. Meanwhile, soak the apricots, raisins, and figs in hot water until soft, about 10 minutes. Slice the apricots and figs into bite-size pieces. Add the drained fruits to the contents in the saucepan and simmer another 10 minutes. Stir in the sugar and all the nuts. Simmer until thick, about 2 minutes. Stir in the rose water. Spoon into a large, wide serving dish and, when cool, scatter pomegranate seeds on top. Serve cold the following day.

RICE PUDDING

When I visited Syria and met that country's best-known cookbook author, Lamya Al-Jabri, we naturally exchanged books. Since hers was in Arabic, I couldn't read it. But when I got home, I found an exchange student to translate some of the recipes. When the young man read me this rice pudding recipe, with its instructions to dip three bay leaves into boiling milk for a moment, I was immediately intrigued.

"Oh, that's very common," my translator said. "My mother always does that. It transforms the taste of boiled milk from something not so good to something very nice."

That night I tried it. He was right; the trick really worked. Here is my version of Lamya Al-Jabri's recipe.

Makes about 2²/₃ cups, serving 6

1. Wash the rice in several changes of water. Place it and ¾ cup water in a saucepan and let soak 1 hour. Bring to a boil and cook until all the water is absorbed, about 10 minutes.

2. Meanwhile, blend the cornstarch with 2 tablespoons cold water until smooth. Combine the milk and cornstarch in a deep saucepan; bring to a boil, add the bay leaves and cook 1 minute; remove the leaves. Reduce the heat; add the rice and cook about 20 minutes. Stir in the sugar and gum arabic and cook, stirring often, until the mixture thickly coats a wooden spoon, about 20 minutes. Stir in the orange flower water. Remove from the heat and pour into 8 individual serving dishes (the pudding will continue to thicken as it cools). Garnish with the pistachios.

⅓ cup short-grain or pearl rice
½ tablespoon cornstarch
3 cups milk
3 imported bay leaves
⅛ cup sugar
1 small gum arabic crystal (mastic), crushed to a powder with 1 teaspoon sugar
¼ teaspoon orange flower water
2 tablespoons unsalted pistachios, peeled, crushed, and sieved for garnish

POACHED APRICOTS

Try to use Turkish apricots for this dish; they have the best taste. Cook them very slowly so that they swell up evenly with the sweet cooking juices while their skins remain smooth and silken. Apricots cooked this way, then stuffed with a spoonful of *kaymak*, whipped cream, or thick yogurt are truly delicious.

Serves 6

½ pound dried apricots, preferably Turkish

2 cups water

¼ cup sugar

3 cardamom pods, crushed and seeded

1 teaspoon fresh lemon juice

12"-by-12"-sheet of parchment paper

1 cup imitation *kaymak* (page 387) or very thick yogurt

About 28 unsalted almonds, blanched and peeled, or
   3 tablespoons finely chopped peeled and unsalted
   pistachios

1. Wash the apricots and soak in 2 cups water overnight.

2. Preheat the oven to 300° F.

3. Pour the apricot-soaking liquid into a 1-quart nonreactive, ovenproof saucepan. Add the sugar, cardamom, and lemon juice; bring to a boil. Add the apricots. Moisten and crumble a small sheet of parchment and spread over the apricots. Cover the saucepan and set in the oven 1½ hours. Remove the pan from the oven and allow the apricots to cool in the syrup. Chill well.

4. Just before serving, lift out the apricots to drain. Carefully open each one and stuff with imitation *kaymak* or thick yogurt. Place approximately 4 apricots on each serving dish, spoon over a few teaspoons syrup, and garnish with a blanched almond or a pinch of the pistachios.

NOTES TO THE COOK: If using sour apricots, double the amount of sugar.

CHERRY BREAD PUDDING

Many eastern Mediterranean desserts are too sweet for my taste. Not this Istanbul favorite, made with stale dense country bread, cherries, and a little sugar. Though the recipe was originally made with sour cherries, I get excellent results with ordinary sweet cherries and less sugar.

Serve with imitation *kaymak* (page 387) or a bowl of lightly sweetened yogurt.

Serves 4 to 6

Complete steps 1 and 2 early in the day. Complete step 3 at least 4 hours before serving.

1. Wash and pit the cherries. Place in a nonreactive saucepan; sprinkle with the sugar and allow to stand 30 minutes, stirring often.

2. Add ⅔ cup water to the cherries and bring to a boil. Reduce the heat and cook gently 10 to 15 minutes. Remove from the heat to cool. Add lemon juice.

1½ pounds cherries

⅓ cup sugar

⅔ cup water

Juice of ½ lemon or more to taste

8 slices trimmed stale bread, each slice about ⅔-inch thick, preferably coarse country-style bread or a dense French bread

2 tablespoons butter, melted

Confectioners' sugar

3. Lightly butter a heatproof shallow serving dish (I use a 9-inch oval gratin pan). Brush one side of each bread slice with butter and place, buttered side up, in the serving dish, slightly overlapping, in one layer. Set under a broiler to lightly toast the bread. Allow to cool completely.

4. Ladle the cold cherry juices over the cool bread. Scatter the cherries on top and bring to a boil over medium heat. Cover with foil and cook 5 minutes. Remove from the heat and allow to cool in the pan.

5. Serve at room temperature, sprinkled with confectioners' sugar.

With thanks to Chef Ismail Demir for sharing this recipe

HALVAH OF THE POOR SHEPHERD

In Macedonia, I met many women willing to share their family recipes. One was Anastasia. She lived in a small suburb outside the coastal town of Kavalla, in the eastern part of the province. A tall, thin, bespectacled, chain-smoking woman, she tested my sincerity over sweets and thick coffee, then leaned forward and revealed a favorite recipe, which, she informed me breathlessly, she had *never* given to anyone else!

In rasping tones she imparted her father's formula for *Sondourme,* halvah of the poor shepherd, a dish of very fresh, rich sheep's-milk cheese stirred slowly with flour and sugar over a low fire until transformed into a pink mass. It takes 45 minutes to create the "ambrosia," she whispered, and then added, "You eat it with a spoon."

Between cooks, one recipe is never enough. Once Anastasia had made the commitment to share, she had to tell me more. She described how she used a certain type of wild vine leaf, called *russiko* and found in the Pangio Mountains along the Bulgarian border, as part of her leavening when making bread, to ensure its freshness for 2 weeks. And she shared some pharmaceutical lore as well: "After the rains, the old men of the village catch a certain kind of lizard and, after drying it, give a piece to a woman who can't bear children." Anastasia's eyes sparkled. "It always works!" A deep sigh. "Alas, people who know such things are dying, and soon all the old wisdom will be lost."

Here is an adapted version of her father's halvah recipe, with whole milk ricotta.

Serves 4

15 ounces whole-milk ricotta

I tablespoon flour

4½ tablespoons granulated sugar

I. Choose a medium, heavy, nonstick skillet. Set it over medium heat, add the ricotta, and crush it with a wooden spoon until the cheese begins to boil. Immediately add the flour and 4 tablespoons of the sugar.

2. Continue to cook, stirring, until the cheese "mounts" the spoon, about 12 minutes. Remove from the heat, tilt the pan to a slight angle, and turn the cheese out onto a serving plate. (The halvah should have an oval shape.) Sprinkle with the remaining ½ tablespoon sugar. Let stand 5 minutes before serving. Use a thin-bladed knive to cut it into slices.

SYRIAN "CHEESE RAGS"

This is an Aleppine version of the previous recipe, made with sheep's-milk cheese and semolina, which will also work well with a moist, top-quality ball of unsalted fresh mozzarella. It takes less then 20 minutes to prepare. Please don't be put off by the look. The dish is supposed to look like a mess of cleaning rags but it tastes truly delicious.

Serves 4

1. Dip a thin-bladed knife into hot water and thinly slice the cheese. Pour the sugar syrup onto a clean baking sheet and set aside

2. Place the cheese slices in a small, heavy saucepan with 3 tablespoons water. Bring to a boil over medium-high heat, stirring constantly with a wooden spoon until softened, about 2 minutes. Stir in the semolina and beat vigorously to avoid sticking. When the mixture comes away from the sides of the pan, immediately pour the hot semolina-cheese mixture over the cold syrup.

6 ounces moist unsalted mozzarella, freshly made or vacuum-packed, chilled
½ cup cool sugar syrup (page 386)
2 tablespoons semolina #1 (page 384)

3. Dampen the palm of one of your hands and rapidly squash the mixture into the syrup. Then flatten it into a paper-thin sheet to cover the bottom of the tray. Flip the semolina-cheese dough to moisten the second side with sugar syrup. Return the dough to the original side and fold twice into a square, pressing more syrup into the dough as you work. Flatten the square into a thin sheet, while continuing to press in the remaining syrup. The dough should now resemble a thin cloth. Tear the dough into strips and place on individual serving dishes. Serve plain or with imitation *kaymak* (page 387). Delicious while still warm.

NOTES TO THE COOK: If the cheese has been salted, cut it in thin slices and soak in water to cover 1 hour, changing the water often.

Adapted from Lamya Al-Jabri's recipe for Helwaat El-Jibni *in her* Delicious, Good-Tasting

YOGURT CAKE

I first tasted this lovely home dessert, called *hareeseh*, in Amman, but it could have been made almost anywhere in the region. The special touch that makes this version unique is the type of fat used to brush the baking pan: sesame paste (tahini), which imbues the cake with a delicious aroma.

Makes 16 pieces

4 teaspoons tahini
1 cup plain, low-fat yogurt
⅔ teaspoon baking soda
1½ cups (8 ounces) semolina #1 (page 384)
5 tablespoons sugar
4 tablespoons butter, melted and slightly cooled
12 pine nuts
½ cup cool sugar syrup (page 386)

1. Preheat the oven to 350° F. Smear the tahini in an 8-inch square or round metal baking pan and set aside.

2. In a small bowl, combine the yogurt and baking soda and let stand 15 minutes.

3. In a medium bowl, combine the semolina and sugar; mix well. Add the butter to the yogurt and pour over the semolina mixture; mix to a stiff, well-blended dough. Spread evenly in the prepared cake pan. Do not pat down. With a thin-bladed knife, cut dough into diamond shapes and place a pine nut in the center of each portion. Bake 40 minutes or until the surface is golden and the edges are just beginning to brown.

4. Remove from the oven, immediately run a knife along the lines, and pour the syrup

over the hot cake. Return to the oven to bake 3 to 4 minutes. Serve warm or cold, with imitation *kaymak* if desired (page 387).

NOTES TO THE COOK: The cake will keep at room temperature up to a week.

With thanks to Mrs. Soudijah Hammudes for sharing this recipe

BAKLAVA, GAZIANTEP STYLE

In the court kitchen of the Ottomans, pastry making reached extraordinary heights. Baklava is probably the most famous example. In every region the Turks occupied during Ottoman times (Georgia, Tunisia, Greece, Syria, and Slavic Macedonia), one will find some version of this dish.

Gaziantep continues the tradition of great baklava. To Turkish gastronomes, it is a kind of mecca. When I visited Gaziantep, I was introduced to one of the finest baklava makers in the city, Burhan Çadǧas. There must have been twenty men in his bakery, busy rolling out paper-thin pastry leaves in a total cornstarch atmosphere. When I examine my photographs, it looks as if I was in a blizzard!

When I asked Mr. Cadgas what made his baklava superior to all others, he gave me a few pointers. I don't pretend that my recipe will give you his results, but I have incorporated some of his techniques, which yield a subtle and unique baklava. I recommend that you purchase the thinnest available phyllo, (which in America comes in two sizes only, so this will not be difficult).

I learned the criteria for great baklava: it must be crisp, light, and fluffy on top; it must have a moist, nutty filling and a syrupy thin bottom crust; perhaps most important, it must balance the taste of nuts, butter, and sugar; and, of course, it must be sweet.

continued

Here are five special things Mr. Çadğas does to make his wonderful baklava:

1. After layering all the leaves and filling, he cuts right down to the bottom so that each portion will be separate. At this point he also pours a good deal of clarified butter over the top and lets the baklava stand to absorb the butter.

2. After baking, when the baklava has slightly cooled, he turns the whole pan on its side so that the excess butter can drip out. This procedure removes the excess, but leaves behind the taste of butter. And since baklava is served at room temperature, it doesn't feel heavy in the mouth. (I use less butter in my adaptation, so this step is omitted below.)

3. He reheats the bottom of his baked baklava over a flat griddle, then shakes it to make sure every portion moves separately within the pan as the top cools.

4. He heats the syrup almost to the boiling point. Then, with a long ladle, he adds the hot syrup to the heated tray, pouring the hot syrup along the slashed lines. This makes each portion "jump" out of the pan. It looks almost like a dance. As a result, each portion receives a thin coating of sugar syrup, but the top stays crunchy and fluffy. (Note: If you do try this, please be careful; boiling sugar syrup can create serious burns.) He then dribbles a little of the hot syrup over the cool top.

5. After a short rest, he tilts the pan on its side, draining off the excess syrup. (This step is optional. You can control the amount of sugar syrup you wish to use.)

The following is a lower-fat, easier home version of Mr. Çadğas's recipe. Though my baklava takes about 1½ hours to bake, the actual working time is about 20 minutes.

It's best to leave the baklava at room temperature, covered with foil, or in a tin or cardboard box overnight before serving. If you make the baklava with clarified butter, it will keep more than a week without refrigeration.

Makes about 48 pieces

1. Bring the milk to a boil in a small saucepan; gradually whisk in the semolina or farina and cook, stirring, until thick and smooth, 5 minutes. (Or cook the mixture in a I-quart Pyrex measuring cup in the microwave. Cook, uncovered, on high 5 minutes.) Remove from the heat; fold in the nuts and ¼ cup of the melted butter. If desired, add sugar to taste. Set aside to cool.

2. Spray a 14- or 16-inch round baking tray with the oil spray. Unroll the phyllo sheets; divide them into 2 parts, keeping one half under a damp towel to prevent them from drying out. Cover the entire bottom of the pan with 6 double sheets of phyllo, overhanging the tray edge. Spray the bottom and the extended leaves with the oil. Then take the remaining sheets and stack them over the bottom of the tray, spraying every second sheet. Spread the semolina-nut mixture in one even layer.

3. Fold in the overhanging phyllo sheets and spray with the oil. Cover the filling with the reserved phyllo, without extending over the sides, brushing every second sheet with the melted butter. Trim the pastry edges to fit neatly in the pan and butter the top layer. Reserve the remaining butter. Cover the tray with plastic wrap and refrigerate until well chilled, about 30 minutes.

4. Use a sharp knife to cut the baklava into 1¼-inch diamond-shaped pieces.

5. Preheat the oven to 375° F.

6. Bake until light golden brown, about 20 minutes. Reheat any reserved butter to boiling and spoon over the baklava. Reduce the oven heat to 300° F. and continue baking until deeply golden but not brown, about I hour.

7. Remove and allow the baklava to cool 10 minutes. Tilt the tray so that it is propped up in a slanted position against a wall. (This allows the excess butter to flow into the bottom of the tray.) Remove one small serving portion at the bottom of the tray. Let the butter drain 30 minutes.

2 cups milk

5 tablespoons semolina or regular (not quick-cooking) farina

I pound unsalted shelled pistachios or walnuts, pulsed to a medium-fine grind in a food processor

I cup clarified butter (page 385), melted

3 to 4 tablespoons sugar if the nuts are bitter-tasting (optional)

Butter-flavored canola oil spray

I pound thin phyllo sheets (Omega or Krinos #4)

SUGAR SYRUP

2¼ scant cups sugar

1½ cups water

2 teaspoons fresh lemon juice

1½ teaspoons orange flower water (optional)

continued

8. To make the sugar syrup: Combine the sugar and water in a small saucepan. Bring the mixture to a boil and boil slowly 5 minutes. Reduce the heat, cover, and cook at a simmer 10 minutes. Add the lemon juice and cook a few minutes longer. Add the orange flower water, if desired. Keep hot.

9. Run a sharp knife along the scored lines of the baklava to loosen each portion. Set the tray on a heated *comal*, griddle, or flame tamer set on top of the stove and heat the bottom of the tray. Carefully and gradually ladle the hot syrup along the cut lines of the baklava. Allow the syrup to sizzle and boil, then carefully shake the tray to make sure all the pieces are separate. Remove the tray from the heat. When the pieces have "settled", recut the baklava. Dribble some of the remaining syrup over the top. Set the pan aside to cool.

10. Optional step: To remove excess syrup, tilt the pan so that it is propped up in a slanted position against a wall. Remove one small piece at the bottom of the tray. Let the syrup drain at least 2 hours and spoon away any collected syrup. Let the baklava rest in the pan overnight before serving. Store loosely covered at room temperature.

NOTES TO THE COOK: If the phyllo begins to brown, cover it with a sheet of aluminum foil and reduce the oven temperature.

An ideal baklava pan is shallow and flat, with a slightly outward-turned rim to enable the butter and, later, the syrup to be easily poured out.

PISTACHIO- AND CHEESE-FILLED KÜNEFE

On the Mediterranean coast of Turkey, about 10 miles from the town of Antakya, is an idyllic and popular picnic area, known as the Grove of Daphne. There are waterfalls, feeding a network of canals, and a group of restaurants that serve this dessert, a local specialty using the shredded pastry dough available at most Middle Eastern groceries. It is a splendid confection that must be served warm and fresh from the oven.

Following it is a variation that is commonly prepared throughout the region—a combination of unsalted fresh cheeses.

Serves 8

1. Unravel the dough strands, chop into large clumps, and place in the work bowl of a food processor. Pulse 5 to 6 times to break up the clusters. With the machine running, add the melted butter and milk or water in a thin stream. Pulse just enough to break the strands into ½-inch lengths. The strands will be pale yellow and feel soft and damp to the touch. Butter a 10-inch cake pan that is at least 1 inch deep. Line the prepared pan with half the dough strands in an even layer.

2. Use the fine grating disk of a food processor to grate the mozzarella. Spread the mozzarella over the chopped pastry. Top with an even layer of the ricotta. Mix the pistachios with the confectioners' sugar and nutmeg and sprinkle evenly on top of the grated cheese, covering it completely. Spread the remaining dough in an even layer, patting it down firmly with moistened palms. (At this point the dish can be wrapped and refrigerated 3 to 4 hours.)

½ pound (½ package) shredded pastry dough (*kataifi*)
8 tablespoons unsalted butter, melted, plus 1 teaspoon for greasing the pan
1½ tablespoons milk or water

FILLING
¼ pound moist unsalted fresh mozzarella, chilled
12 ounces unsalted ricotta
⅛ pound unsalted shelled pistachios, blanched, skinned, dried, and finely chopped (about ½ cup)
2 tablespoons confectioners' sugar
⅛ teaspoon grated nutmeg

1 cup thin sugar syrup with rose water (page 386)
2 tablespoons unsalted grated pistachios for garnish

3. About 1 hour before serving, preheat the oven to 375° F.

4. Set the *künefe* in the oven to bake until golden brown, 45 minutes. Remove from the oven and let rest 5 minutes. Gently warm the sugar syrup.

5. Loosen the sides of the *künefe* with a knife. Invert onto a serving plate. (The bottom side will be brown and smooth.) Make crisscrossing lines with the point of a sharp, thin-bladed knife and pour over ⅔ cup warm sugar syrup. Scatter the grated pistachios on top. Serve warm and pass the remaining syrup for those who like their desserts extra-sweet.

VARIATION:

CHEESE-FILLED KÜNEFE

This wonderful *künefe*, which in Syria is called *kdaif*, is sweet, warm, and creamy, and it literally melts in the mouth.

Serves 8

½ pound moist unsalted fresh mozzarella, chilled
½ pound unsalted ricotta
¼ pound unsalted butter, melted
½ pound (½ package) shredded pastry dough *(kataifi)*
1 cup sugar syrup with rose water (page 386)

Shred the mozzarella, using the fine grating blade of a food processor. Crush the ricotta with a fork. Follow the directions in the preceding recipe. Serve hot.

NOTES TO THE COOK: This dessert can be prepared through step 2 of the previous recipe and frozen. Bake directly from the freezer, adding 10 minutes baking time.

SEMOLINA BUTTER COOKIES

These rich shortbread-type cookies, called *ghraybeh,* which means "to swoon" in Arabic, are tender and mouth-watering. They are the pride of many home cooks, and are similar to sugar-dusted Greek butter-almond cookies, except that they are made with semolina and are even more delicate. They will keep two weeks in a tin and improve with age.

Makes 24 to 30 cookies

1. Sift the semolina and the cake and all-purpose flour into a small bowl and reserve.

2. Beat the butter in a medium bowl at medium speed until white, light, and fluffy, at least 10 minutes. (The more you beat, the lighter the cookie.) Gradually sprinkle in the confectioners' sugar and the orange blossom water and beat 2 minutes. Remove the bowl from the mixer and with a rubber spatula gradually fold in the combined flours. The dough will be quite soft. Refrigerate, covered, 10 minutes.

3. Preheat the oven to 275° F.

4. Shape the dough into small diamond-shaped cakes about 1 inch to a side, and ½ inch high. Place on an ungreased baking sheet about ½ inch apart. Place an almond in the center of each cookie. Bake 35 to 40 minutes. The cookies should remain pale; do not overbake. Allow the cookies to cool on the baking sheet at least 1 hour. Store the cooled cookies in an airtight tin at least 1 day before serving.

I cup semolina #1 (page 384)
½ cup cake flour
½ cup all-purpose flour
I cup clarified butter, chilled
⅔ cup confectioners' sugar
¾ teaspoon orange blossom water (*mazahar*)
30 blanched almonds

DATE AND SEMOLINA CAKES WITH TWO VARIATIONS

These wonderful date and semolina cakes are one of my favorite desserts. They are very pretty, with circles and swirls imprinted into their tops, a result of shaping them in special wooden molds. These cakes age beautifully. Wait a few days, until they reach their peak. Since they are made with clarified butter, they needn't be refrigerated; a simple tin box will do.

Middle Eastern stores sell wooden *ma'moul* molds, in which these cakes are fashioned. There are two types: domed, which are used for nut fillings (see the variation below), and flat, used for date fillings.

To use a decorative *ma'moul* mold: Dust the mold with flour; press a piece of flattened dough into the mold; then place the filling in the center and close up, pinching the dough to seal. Turn the mold upside down; give a good knock on a firm work surface and the cake will slip out. Place decorated side up on a baking sheet.

Makes 12

DATE FILLING
⅔ cup dates, chopped
1½ tablespoons unsalted butter

SHELL
1½ cups semolina #1 (page 384)
1 teaspoon ground *mahlab**
⅓ cup clarified butter, boiling
⅓ cup hot milk
2 tablespoons flour

1. To make the filling: In a small saucepan, cook the dates with 1 tablespoon water and the butter over low heat until soft, about 5 minutes. Crush the dates into a fine, glossy paste. Transfer the dates to a work surface and divide into 12 equal parts. Cover and set aside.

2. To make the shell: In a mixing bowl, stir together the semolina and *mahlab*. Stir in the hot butter, milk, and flour; mix well after each addition. Knead with your hands until you have a smooth dough, 5 minutes. Wrap in plastic wrap and set aside, tightly covered, about 1 hour.

3. Preheat the oven to 300° F.

4. Knead the dough another 5 minutes, then divide into 12 balls. To shape the cakes without a mold: Lightly press a portion of the dough into a thin patty about ¼ inch thick. Place the date ball in the center and bring the sides up to seal completely. Press gently to form a flat-topped round cake. Decorate with the tines of a fork. Place on an ungreased baking sheet.

5. Bake on the lower oven rack 30 minutes. Transfer to upper rack and bake another 20 minutes. The cakes should barely color. Allow to cool on the baking sheet. (The cakes can be wrapped in plastic boxes and frozen for long storage.)

6. To serve, dust with confectioners' sugar and serve at room temperature.

With thanks to Barbara Thomas Isaac, author of Everyday Delights of Lebanese-Syrian Cookery, *who shared this recipe with me*

VARIATION WITH DATES AND WALNUTS:
Halve the dates and cook as directed in the previous recipe. In a bowl, combine the dates with ⅓ cup finely chopped, lightly toasted walnuts and a sprinkling of rose water; blend well and divide into 12 equal parts. Use either flat or rounded *ma'moul* molds.

VARIATION WITH WALNUTS:
Omit the dates. Combine 1 tablespoon water and ¼ teaspoon rose water. Mix ⅓ cup coarsely crushed walnuts, 2 tablespoons finely ground walnuts, 1½ tablespoons sugar, and a few drops of rose water. Blend well. Divide into 12 equal parts. Use the dome-shaped *ma'moul* molds.

---

* Black cherry kernels available at Middle Eastern groceries. Crush in a heavy mortar just before using.

SEMOLINA

Semolina is the pale golden flour made from the hard, endosperm portion of durum wheat, available in fine and coarse grinds in Middle Eastern, Italian, and health-food stores or from King Arthur Flour (see Appendix C).

Use semolina #1, which has a texture similar to the granulation of fine salt, for the recipes in this chapter. Be sure not to confuse this semolina with the finer durum flour used to make bread and pasta.

People are often confused about the differences between semolina and farina, another strain of hard wheat, sold in supermarkets as "regular cream of wheat." Although farina may be used interchangeably with semolina in some recipes, that is not always the case.

When semolina is cooked with water and baked, it turns hard, so eastern Mediterranean cooks use milk and oil or butter. Farina, on the other hand, always stays soft.

But for the Date and Semolina Cakes, Yogurt Cake, and Semolina Butter Cookies, either semolina or farina can be used. I prefer to use semolina; there is finer texture and greater lightness, and the sweets stay fresher for a longer time.

CLARIFIED BUTTER

Y̶ou will need clarified butter to make tender cakes and cookies and also baklava. Not only do these desserts improve with age, but they keep perfectly without refrigeration because the moisture has been removed from the butter. Cookies and cakes keep well for several weeks if stored in a tightly closed tin box.

The use of bulgur in clarifying butter is an Arab trick employed to absorb the milk solids and other debris while making it easier to retrieve the butter.

Makes 3¾ cups (1½ pounds)

Place the butter and bulgur in a small, heavy saucepan and set over very low heat. Allow the butter to melt slowly without stirring and without browning. Remove foam as it appears on the surface. When the butter is golden and clear, remove it from the heat and leave to cool. Carefully pour the butter through damp cheesecloth into clean glass jars. Discard the milky bulgur residue. Clarified butter will keep for several months in a cool cupboard or the refrigerator.

12 sticks (2½ pounds) unsalted butter, cut into small pieces
¼ cup coarse bulgur, rinsed and drained

SUGAR SYRUP

Makes 2 cups heavy syrup

3 cups sugar

1½ cups water

I tablespoon fresh lemon juice

I scant teaspoon rose water

Place the sugar and water in a heavy saucepan and bring to a boil, stirring to dissolve the sugar. Skim the surface, then add the lemon juice and cook at a simmer 10 minutes, or until the syrup feels very sticky. Add the rose water and remove from the heat to cool. (For a thinner syrup, add ½ cup water.) Will keep in the refrigerator for months.

IMITATION KAYMAK

Nothing can really compare with the ethereal creamy *kaymak* of Turkey and the Balkans, originally made from buffalo's milk or sheep's milk. Clotted cream and crème fraîche are similar, except that crème fraîche is not as rich or thick. *Kaymak*, nearly as thick as butter, is spread on bread or served to accompany such sweets as baklava, poached fruits, and cherry bread pudding.

The best *kaymak* is made on farms, then sold at village markets. Unpasteurized milk is simmered over low heat until a thick cream, called "the face of the milk," builds on the surface. This cream is skimmed off and stored in wooden or earthen crocks to mellow at least a day. If aged longer, *kaymak* will have a slightly fermented taste.

True *kaymak* is for those who really appreciate the work involved and revere such culinary treasures. I offer two imitations that work successfully: Substitute ½ cup drained yogurt beaten with ½ cup strained ricotta; or forget about calories and nutritional good sense, and use ½ cup Italian mascarpone blended with ¼ cup whipped heavy cream.

GEORGIAN CHURCHKHELA

In autumn, in Georgia, when walnuts are plump but still a little green, they are made into an unusual snack for nibbling. I offer this description as a curiosity, since these walnut-grape confections are really good only when prepared by experts.

First the walnuts are shelled, then threaded with a needle to form 2-foot-long necklaces. They are left to dry under the rafters where freshly harvested grapes are pressed, sieved, and boiled down to a thick syrup. The necklaces are then dipped into this syrup, drained, allowed to dry, then dipped again several more times, until the syrup coating is thick, translucent, and dry, without any cracks.

APPENDIX A: EASTERN MEDITERRANEAN PEPPER PASTES

~~~~~~

People don't usually think of the eastern Mediterranean as a region of hot pepper recipes. In fact, the areas that receive the most attention in this book—Georgia, southern Turkey, Macedonia, and Aleppo, Syria—have cuisines using red hot peppers.

Peppers did not reach the eastern Mediterranean via Spain from the New World, but came most probably from the Turks. They entered the eastern Mediterranean cuisines much earlier than they entered the cuisines of the rest of Europe. Amal Naj, in his estimable book *Peppers*, writes, "Eventually it would be the Turks who would bring wide attention to the pepper as an item of food in Europe. It started with the Turkish invasion of India. The Turks of the Ottoman Empire besieged the Portuguese colony of Diu, near Calicut, and brought back the 'Calicut' pepper, which eventually went north with Ottoman soldiers to their conquered territories."

The red peppers of the genus *Capsicum* grow so well on eastern and southern Mediterranean shores that there are cities that have grown famous because of their chilis: Nabeul in Tunisia, Maraş and Urfa in Turkey, Aleppo in Syria, and Mingrelia in Georgia. In Macedonia, hot chilis are so well liked you will find them, alongside salt and pepper, on the table, in the form of *bucovo*, a paprika, with a strong, earthy aroma. But not all the distinguished eastern Mediterranean peppers are hot. The sweet red bell peppers of Flórina, in Greek Macedonia, are considered the finest in the world—thick and fleshy, sweet and fresh-flavored, large and shimmering, simply roasted and dressed with olive oil and garlic. The Macedonian version of *stifado*, made with short ribs, onions, and a few heads of garlic, is thickened with a generous scoop of Macedonian "butter," a preserved blend of peppers, tomatoes, and garlic.

Peppers are used raw, pickled, fried, stewed, and roasted. Georgia, Aleppo, and southeastern Turkey all use a unique red-pepper base, a blend of pomegranate juice, walnuts, and chilis, made into an irresistible sauce.

On the following pages I offer recipes for homemade pepper pastes, each from a different area. The first two can be used interchangeably in nearly all the recipes in this book that call for a pepper paste.

There are many commercial pepper pastes on the market. One that I use frequently, imported from Turkey under the name *Aci Biber Sosu*, is available at many Middle Eastern groceries and mail-order outlets. However, if you make a pepper paste from scratch, you will be greatly rewarded. By carefully choosing your peppers, you can customize the flavor, heat, color, and aroma.

NOTE: ALWAYS WEAR RUBBER GLOVES WHEN HANDLING HOT PEPPERS.

TURKISH RED PEPPER PASTE

In late August, in southeastern Turkey, most cooks harvest and dry red peppers, and put up their red pepper paste for the year. A good paste is not just hot; it has a vibrant, delicious flavor.

In Turkey, both hot and sweet peppers are stemmed, seeded, and pushed through a food chopper, then tossed with salt and spread out on large shallow pans to dry under a hot sun 5 to 7 days. Since I live in New England, where there are rarely that many hot days in a row, I have adapted the recipe, drying the peppers in a very slow oven—a process that can take from 5 to 6 hours, with occasional stirring.

Makes 2 cups

> 2 pounds mildly hot red chilis
> 2 pounds sweet red bell peppers
> Coarse salt
> 2 12-by-17 inch-sheets of parchment paper
> 1¼ teaspoons sugar
> 3 tablespoons olive oil

1. Wash the peppers; halve lengthwise, seed, and remove the membranes. Coarsely grind in a food processor (or using a food grinder), to yield about 10 cups. Toss with 3 tablespoons coarse salt and spread out on two parchment-lined baking sheets.

2. Preheat the oven to 175° F. Place the trays in the oven and allow the peppers to dry, about 6 hours. You will have about 2 cups.

3. Place half the peppers in a double thickness of cheesecloth and squeeze hard to emit excess moisture. Repeat with the remaining peppers.

4. In a food processor, blend the peppers with the sugar and half the oil. Add coarse salt to taste; the pepper paste should taste slightly salty. Pack into two dry, small glass jars. Top with the remaining olive oil, close tightly, and refrigerate.

NOTES TO THE COOK: Let the pepper paste mature for about a week before using. To avoid mold, always keep the paste covered with oil. If mold develops, simply remove it and discard; the remainder of the paste will still be good.

To store in the freezer: Individually wrap one-tablespoon dollops of paste in plastic. Place all in a freezer bag, press out air, and store in the freezer.

QUICK RED PEPPER PASTE

Makes ⅔ to ¾ cup

> 2 (1¼ pounds) fleshy red bell peppers, stemmed, cored, and cut up
> 1 small hot chili stemmed, cored, and seeded
> Pinch of sugar
> ¼ teaspoon salt
> 2 teaspoons olive oil

Grind the peppers and chili with 2 tablespoons water, the sugar, and salt in the work bowl of a food processor until pureed. Transfer to a saucepan and cook over medium heat, stirring often, until reduced to a jamlike consistency. (Can be reduced in a 2-quart Pyrex bowl in the microwave.) Store, covered with the oil, up to 3 or 4 days. To freeze, divide into 5 parts, wrap in plastic, and store in an airtight container in the freezer.

HOT RED PEPPER AND HERB PASTE, ABKHAZIA STYLE

The blending of ground fresh peppers with herbs and spices is common along the coast of the Black Sea, where the hottest red and green chilis are made into fresh, chunky sauce relishes. All Georgians make pepper pastes in huge quantities, then bottle them to use throughout the year. But this paste *(adzhika)* and the next are meant to be eaten within a few days of being made.

The first paste is from Abkhazia, a small Moslem enclave on the Black Sea. Make the paste at least one day in advance so that the flavors can mellow. It will keep up to a week in a tightly closed container in the refrigerator. Try it with a slice of creamy imported feta and some black bread.

Makes ¾ cup

1 clove garlic, peeled
½ cup lovage or celery leaves
⅓ packed cup coriander
2 tablespoons summer savory
2 sprigs fresh basil
1 teaspoon ground fenugreek
1 teaspoon ground coriander seeds
2 long thin red chilis, stemmed, seeded, and cut up

1 red bell pepper, stemmed, seeded, and cut up
½ teaspoon salt
Pinch of sugar
½ teaspoon mild vinegar or more to taste

1. In a food processor or food grinder, combine all the fresh and dried herbs; blend well. Add the peppers and grind again so that everything is well mixed.

2. Place in several sheets of cheesecloth and wrap up to express juices. Then fold in just enough liquid to obtain a spreadable paste. Season with the salt, sugar, and vinegar. Place in a clean, dry jar and leave until the following day before serving.

GEORGIAN GREEN PEPPER AND HERB PASTE

This second Georgian pepper paste, not as hot as the previous recipe, is from the Black Sea region called Samegrelo. It was there that I learned how to flavor a roast suckling pig, Georgian style, by rubbing this pungent preparation of ground green chilis and fresh herbs into the flesh when the pig is almost fully cooked and its skin is just beginning to crisp. The result is a pig with an amazing crackling crust, extraordinarily moist flesh, and an intensely fragrant, achingly hot flavor.

This fresh paste will benefit from a night's rest, and may be kept for 3 days in the refrigerator. Serve with pork or lamb kabobs, or add to the spinach pâté on page 176.

Makes 1 cup

5 thin green chilis

1 large green bell pepper, cored, seeded, and
   cut into strips

5 plump cloves garlic, peeled

¼ cup packed coriander

¼ cup packed fresh flat-leaf parsley

¼ cup packed fresh lovage

2 tablespoons slivered basil

2 tablespoons slivered mint

1 teaspoon fine salt

2 tablespoons mild vinegar

1. Trim away the stems of the chilis, but leave most of the seeds. Cut each chili into 4 or 5 pieces. Place the chilis, seeds, the green bell pepper, and the garlic in a food processor and pulse until well chopped, about 10 times. Scrape into a mixing bowl.

2. In the same work bowl, pulse the herbs ten times and add to the peppers; mix well. Stir in the salt and vinegar. Cover and refrigerate at least 4 to 5 hours (better, overnight).

MACEDONIAN "BUTTER"

The best time to make this is in late summer, when the tomatoes are ripe and fresh, and flavorful red peppers become available. Out of season, you can substitute imported canned tomatoes and Florida red bell peppers.

Makes about 1½ cups

4 pounds ripe tomatoes, peeled, seeded, and
   chopped, or 1 quart container Pomi
   crushed tomatoes imported from Italy

3 tablespoons olive oil, plus more for sealing

½ tablespoon salt

6 sweet red bell peppers

3 to 6 hot red chilis, depending upon their
   degree of hotness

2 cloves garlic, peeled and chopped

1. In a large cast-iron skillet, fry the tomatoes in 2 tablespoons of the oil, mashing and turning them with a wooden spoon as they cook down, about 1 hour. Add the salt.

2. Meanwhile, peel, seed, and coarsely chop all the peppers. In a separate frying pan, heat the remaining tablespoon oil and fry the peppers until they are soft and pastelike, about 10 minutes. Add the peppers and the garlic to the reduced tomatoes and continue to cook, stirring constantly, until all the liquid has evaporated and the mass starts to fry in the released oil. Ladle into a glass jar, cover, and refrigerate.

Making Pepper Flakes

If you live in a part of the country where there is a hot sun, you can dry thin-fleshed peppers—red, green, hot, mild, or sweet—until they become sufficiently brittle to be crumbled into pepper flakes. (Thick-fleshed peppers are better candidates for pepper pastes.)

If green peppers are hung individually by their stems on a line in a sunny window, they will turn red in about 2 weeks. I then dry them further in a slow oven, then crumble them to use in cooking.

Dried red chilis can be stemmed, lightly toasted, and ground to a coarse powder in a spice mill, or soaked and pureed.

APPENDIX B:
HOME-PREPARED SPICE MIXTURES

TURKISH *BAHARAT*

*B*aharat is a mixture of several spices and dried herbs used by Turkish cooks to season meat dishes and vegetable stuffings.

Makes 2 tablespoons

A handful of sprigs of summer savory or 1½
    teaspoons dried winter savory
1 tablespoon pickling spice
½ teaspoon ground cinnamon
½ teaspoon freshly grated nutmeg
½ teaspoon crumbled dried mint leaves
½ teaspoon ground cumin
1 teaspoon freshly ground black pepper

1. Dry the summer savory in a low oven or in the microwave. Crumble and measure to make 2 teaspoons.

2. Combine all the ingredients in a spice mill and grind to a powder. Store tightly covered. This spice mixture will keep fresh for up to 3 months.

SYRIAN MIXED SPICES
NUMBER I

*Y*ou can buy this all-purpose mixture of all-spice, cinnamon, cloves, and other spices at Arab groceries. Or you can make your own, as follows. This mixture is especially good in Stuffed Chicken (page 323) and fillings for Kibbeh.

Makes about ⅓ cup

2 tablespoons pickling spice
2 tablespoons whole allspice berries
1 tablespoon ground cinnamon
½ tablespoon whole cloves
1 tablespoon whole black peppercorns
½ whole nutmeg

Combine all the ingredients in an electric spice grinder or blender and work them until finely ground. Strain through a coarse strainer and store in a tightly covered jar. The mixture will keep up to 3 months.

SYRIAN MIXED SPICES NUMBER 2

This spicy mixture is especially good for seasoning meat pies, *köfte*, and stews.

Makes about 2 tablespoons

1 tablespoon Near East or Aleppo pepper (page 395) or substitute 2 teaspoons Hungarian paprika and 1 teaspoon hot Hungarian paprika
1 teaspoon freshly ground black pepper
½ teaspoon ground allspice
¼ teaspoon ground cinnamon
¼ teaspoon ground coriander seeds
¼ teaspoon ground cloves
¼ teaspoon ground cumin
Salt

Mix all the ingredients well and place in a small jar. Add a little salt to keep the mixture fresh and free of bugs. Close tightly and store up to 3 months.

GEORGIAN KHMELI-SUNELI

The moment you enter a Georgian kitchen, you will smell a variety of spices. The most typical is crushed sweet trefoil fenugreek husks and leaves. When these are combined with marigold petals, coriander, summery savory, dried basil, hot paprika, and smaller amounts of other ingredients, the dry spice mixture is called *khmeli-suneli*, reminiscent of Indian *garam masala*. Every good cook has her treasured formula. Georgian cooks warm their spices before using, just as Indians do.

The following recipe is an all-purpose mix, good in stews and soups, and as a marinade for meat.

Makes 2 tablespoons

1 tablespoon ground coriander seeds
2 teaspoons crumbled dried fenugreek leaves (*kasoor methi* in Indian shops; or see page 396)
½ teaspoon ground fenugreek
1 teaspoon dried marigold petals (see page 398)
⅛ teaspoon ground cloves
½ teaspoon dried mint
⅛ teaspoon ground cinnamon
½ teaspoon sweet paprika
¼ teaspoon freshly ground black pepper
1 teaspoon dried savory
¾ teaspoon dried basil
¼ teaspoon sugar

Grind the herbs and spices. Sieve and store in a tightly closed jar. Keeps up to 3 months.

SVANETI SALT

The Svaneti region of Georgia, 2,200 meters above sea level, has the highest mountains in Europe. Here the people, called Svans, value salt. In fact, in olden times a quart measure of salt was worth an entire cow. Because salt was so valuable, it couldn't be wasted, and it was stretched by being combined with other ingredients. The mixture would have remained localized if people from other parts of Georgia hadn't started visiting the area on vacations. Now Svaneti salt has become a popular seasoning also at sea level in Georgia, where it is offered in bowls to be sprinkled on salads, vegetable dishes, potatoes, and meats.

Makes ½ cup

1½ teaspoons peeled, crushed garlic

2 teaspoons ground caraway

1½ teaspoons ground coriander seeds

3 tablespoons coarse salt

½ teaspoon freshly ground black pepper

½ teaspoon ground fenugreek

Pinches of cayenne

Mix and serve.

APPENDIX C: STOCKING THE EASTERN MEDITERRANEAN LARDER

The successful execution of a recipe depends on the use of quality ingredients. A few years ago, many of the recipes in this book could not have been made in America—the ingredients were simply not available. Today it is easy to find the ingredients you need, either at local ethnic stores or from reliable mail-order sources.

When I moved out of Manhattan, I was concerned about finding a source for good eastern Mediterranean products. I got out my local telephone book and called a Greek Orthodox church in a neighboring town. The priest was happy to tell me where his parishioners shopped, which turned out to be a large, roomy store offering everything I needed: spices, dried herbs, grains, pulses, hard-to-find pepper pastes, pomegranate molasses, and more. On one visit I was able to purchase most of what I would use in a year. This is pretty much how an eastern Mediterranean home cook stocks her larder, keeping quantities of ingredients with a long shelf life on hand, to be combined with fresh seasonal produce as it becomes available.

SPICES AND HERBS

The following spices and aromatics are best purchased in an ethnic grocery or specialty store: Aleppo pepper (or Near East pepper); allspice; caraway; coriander seeds; cumin; fenugreek, ground and leaves; *mahleb*, mastic, and Mediterranean oregano; mint leaves, dried; paprika, sweet and hot; safflower threads and marigold petals; *za'atar*, *za'atar* blend, and sumac.

ALEPPO PEPPER OR NEAR EAST PEPPER

In the spice bazaars of southern Syria and southeastern Turkey, there are literally dozens of different ground red peppers displayed in open burlap sacks. Some, dark and intensely aromatic, are from Urfa, still others come from other towns famous for their peppers; some are aged, and others have a great number of seeds. In Turkey, the mildly hot, very aromatic bright red pepper of Maraş is the most coveted, because of its berrylike flavor.

Aleppo pepper is similar. Coarse, gritty, dark red, earthy, and robust, it contains oils that are released when it is heated or finely ground. Kept in the refrigerator, it will hold for a long time. Its warm, rich flavor is unique and famous throughout the Middle East.

I definitely recommend that you search for Aleppo pepper or the one from Maraş. Sometimes they are sold under the name "Near East Pepper." Both are excellent, the Maraş being slightly hotter than the one from Aleppo. If you can't find either, a combination of 3 parts sweet Hungarian paprika and 1 part ground, flavorful, mildly hot red pepper flakes will make an acceptable substitute.

Mail Order: Dean and DeLuca, Kalustyan, Oriental Pastry and Grocery, and Shallah's Middle Eastern Importing Company.

ALLSPICE, CARAWAY, CORIANDER SEEDS, CUMIN

This may surprise you: I recommend buying these spices finely ground. Of course, spices keep best when purchased whole, but if you buy pre-ground spices in small amounts, you will save a lot of time. Also, these particular spices do not grind finely enough in home electric spice mills to work effectively; they will keep up to 6 months, stored in a tightly closed jar kept in a dark cupboard.

Allspice is used in combination with other spices, for stuffing kibbeh and vegetables, and also in meat stews.

Caraway is an important spice for flavoring Georgian dishes.

Coriander seeds are used from Tripoli to Tbilisi, to flavor vegetable and meat dishes.

Cumin sold in Middle Eastern stores has a stronger flavor than the supermarket variety. When you cook with it, you will see how the Near Eastern variety "holds" its aroma in long-simmered dishes.

Mail Order: Dean and DeLuca, Kalustyan, Oriental Pastry and Grocery, G. B. Ratto and Company, Shallah's Middle Eastern Importing Company, The Spice House, and Sultan's Delight

FENUGREEK

Almost impossible to grind at home, fenugreek is an important flavoring in Georgian cooking. The dried leaves of sweet trefoil fenugreek (called *utskho suneli* in Georgia) can be replaced by *kasoor methi*, found in Indian stores.

Mail Order for Seeds: Dean and DeLuca, Kalustyan, Oriental Pastry and Grocery, G. B. Ratto and Company, Shallah's Middle Eastern Importing Company, The Spice House, and Sultan's Delight

Mail Order for Fenugreek Leaves: Kalustyan

Fereekeh. See Bulgur, under Miscellany

HERBS

Fresh-cut sorrel, Lebanese mint, lovage, nettles, summer savory, or purslane is sold by the quarter pound.

Lebanese or Egyptian mint, savories, nettles, and purple basil are available in small pots.

Mail Order for Cut Herbs: Fox Hill Farm
Mail Order for Live Plants: Fox Hill Farm and Well-Sweep Herb Farm

MAHLEB AND MASTIC

Mahleb is the core of the sour cherry pit and provides a delicious aroma to breads and cakes. Crush it just before using for best aroma and flavor.

Mastic, imported from Greece, is used for rice pudding. Crush it with a teaspoon of granulated sugar just before using.

Mail Order: Kalustyan, Oriental Pastry and Grocery, Shallah's Middle Eastern Importing Company, and Sultan's Delight

MARIGOLD PETALS

See page 398

MEDITERRANEAN OREGANO

Mediterranean oregano is used by eastern Mediterranean cooks to marinate meats or fish before grilling, and to sprinkle over olives, cheese, and salads. It is available on dried stems in plastic bags at Middle Eastern stores. The quality of imported Mediterranean oregano varies, so ask to rub a little between your fingertips. If it isn't intensely aromatic and pungent, I suggest buying it in jars packed by Peloponnese or sold in bulk by The Spice House. Please don't substitute fresh oregano; this is one herb that is best dried and crumbled just before using.

Mail Order: Dean and DeLuca, Kalustyan, Oriental Pastry and Grocery, Peloponnese, G. B. Ratto and Company, Shallah's Middle Eastern Importing Company, The Spice House, and Sultan's Delight

Mail Order for Oregano Dried on Stalks and Gathered in Bunches: G. B. Ratto and Company

MINT LEAVES, DRIED

Even when fresh mint is available, the dried leaves are preferred for certain dishes. They impart a special flavor to salads, stews, soups, and stuffings. In some of the Turkish recipes, dried mint is heated along with black pepper in a little oil or butter, then swirled in at the last minute. An exuberant and pungent aroma is released.

Purchase dried Egyptian spearmint at Middle Eastern stores, or dry out fresh spearmint leaves in a very low oven, or spread fresh leaves out on newspapers until dry and crumbly, then store in a tightly closed jar. Crush and sieve when ready to use. To make dried mint leaves quickly in the microwave: Loosely wrap fresh leaves in a paper towel; set at medium for 2 to 3 minutes; when cool, crumble and use at once. Do not store; leaves dried this quickly will turn moldy.

Mail Order: Dean and DeLuca, Kalustyan, Oriental Pastry and Grocery, G. B. Ratto and Company, Shallah's Middle Eastern Importing Company, The Spice House, and Sultan's Delight

SYRIAN MIXED SPICES

Mail Order: Kalustyan, Oriental Pastry and Grocery, Shallah's Middle Eastern Importing Company

NEAR EAST PEPPER

See Aleppo Pepper

NIGELLA SEEDS OR BLACK CARAWAY SEEDS

These are sprinkled on flat breads.

Mail Order: Kalustyan, G. B. Ratto and Company, Shallah's Middle Eastern Importing Company, and Sultan's Delight

PAPRIKA

Sweet and hot paprikas, imported from Hungary, are used in combination in Macedonian cooking, and as a substitute for Aleppo or Near East pepper in Middle Eastern and Turkish dishes. For long-time storage, pack in tightly closed jars and keep in the refrigerator.

Mail Order: Dean and DeLuca, Kalustyan, Oriental Pastry and Grocery, Paprikas Weiss, G. B. Ratto and Company, Shallah's Middle Eastern Importing Company, The Spice House, and Sultan's Delight

ROSEBUDS, DRIED

Mail Order: Aphrodisia

SAFFLOWER STIGMAS AND MARIGOLD PETALS

Safflower stigmas are used in Turkish and Arab cuisine to decorate some yogurt dishes.

In Georgia, the dried and ground petals of marigolds are an important flavoring in many dishes that also include walnuts, garlic, vinegar, red pepper, and onions. The petals imbue dishes with a slightly bitter, musky quality, and give them a golden-orange hue that makes them uniquely Georgian. When walnuts and vinegar are used together in Georgian sauces, the vinegar turns the walnuts an unsightly purplish black. But when marigold petals are also added, the color remains a golden beige.

The petals are also used in the spice mixture *Khmeli-Suneli* (page 393), as part of a trio with ground coriander and fenugreek.

If you want to grow your own marigolds, purchase seeds for gem marigold, which tastes good and not too bitter. Store the dried and finely ground petals in a tightly closed bottle.

Note: Neither safflower stigmas nor marigold petals should be confused with saffron or turmeric.

Safflower stigmas are called *haspir* in Turkish and *osfor* in Arabic.

Mail Order for Safflower Stigmas: Kalustyan, G. B. Ratto, Shallah's Middle Eastern Importing Company, and Sultan's Delight

Mail Order for Dried Marigold Petals: Aphrodisia

Mail Order for Gem Marigold Seeds: Cook's Garden

Mail Order for Gem Marigold Plants: Well-Sweep Herb Farm

SUMAC

Sumac is a nonpoisonous red berry that gives a distinctive, delicious, tangy-lemony flavor to chicken and onions (see *Musakhan,* page 319); grilled meats; yogurt sauces; pie stuffings; and the famous bread salad *fattoush* (page 140). In Turkey it is sprinkled over sliced onions and used as a garnish for kabobs. In the Kurdish lamb and eggplant stew (page 360), a half cup of sumac is soaked in water, strained, then used to impart a haunting, vivid magenta color to the dish. Neither vinegar, lemon juice, tamarind, or pomegranate juice can provide such a unique astringent flavor.

The quality of sumac can vary enormously. Try to buy it from a reputable grocer or mail-order source. Store ground sumac in your freezer.

Mail Order: Adriana's Bazaar, Dean and DeLuca, Kalustyan, Oriental Pastry and Grocery, Shallah's Middle Eastern Importing Company, and Sultan's Delight

ZA'ATAR AND *ZA'ATAR* BLEND

To clear up the confusion: Around the eastern Mediterranean, the word *za'atar* is used two different ways: to refer to a class of herbs and to refer to a spice blend of *za'atar* and sumac.

First, the herbs. There are several varieties, bearing various names in various eastern Mediterranean languages, and they are so prized for their fragrant savory-oregano-thyme aroma that they are often called the "king of herbs." None of the recipes in this book call for the rarely imported herb *za'atar;* substitutes are always given. If, however, you travel to the eastern Mediterranean, and visit some of its remarkable archeological sites, you may be approached by children offering to sell you bouquets of *za'atar* plants. There are so many different names and varieties, in so many different languages, that I offer only a few, for the true fanatic: *kekik* (Turkey); *throumbi* (Greece); *za'atar rumi* (Syria); *nadge* (Israel). If you purchase bouquets, dry them in your hotel room, then use after your return on meat and fish both before and after grilling. You will not be disappointed.

As for the spice blend *za'atar*, it is a mixture of sumac, sesame seeds, and one or more of the various *za'atar* herbs described above. It is part of a Middle Eastern breakfast dish of hot flat bread dipped in olive oil, then sprinkled with the mixture. See page 61 for *za'atar* bread. Imported za'atar blends are used on baked breads and salads, and sprinkled over kabobs. See page 61 for descriptions of Israeli, Jordanian, and Syrian types.

Mail Order for Live Plants: *za'atar (Thymbre spicata)*; its substitutes "barrel sweetener" or *thyba savory (Saturjea thymbra)*; oregano/hyssop *(Origanum syriacum)*; and summer savory: Well-Sweep Herb Farm

Mail Order for Dried Plain *Za'atar:* Shallah's Middle Eastern Importing Company

Mail Order for Israeli *Za'atar* Blend: Adriana's Bazaar

Mail Order for Jordanian and Syrian Blends: Kalustyan, Oriental Pastry and Grocery, and Shallah's Middle Eastern Importing Company

MISCELLANY

APRICOTS, DRIED TURKISH

Mail Order: Dean and DeLuca, Kalustyan, Oriental Pastry and Grocery, G. B. Ratto and Company, Shallah's Middle Eastern Importing Company, and Sultan's Delight

BEANS

Use Sweet White Runners for the hard-to-find Macedonian *gigantes.*

Use borlotti, bolita, cranberry, French horticultural, Jacob's Cattle, or Tongues of Fire for the Turkish *barbunya.*

For Georgian bean salads, use small red beans.

Mail Order: The Bean Bag

BULGUR AND FEREEKEH

Use fine-grain bulgur #1 and #2 for kibbeh, and coarse-grain bulgar #3 for cooking. *Fereekeh* is green wheat. See page 232 for more information.

Mail Order: Dean and DeLuca, Kalustyan, Oriental Pastry and Grocery, G. B. Ratto and Company, Sultan's Delight, and Shallah's Middle Eastern Importing Company

CHAPATI FLOUR

Mail Order: Kalustyan and Shallah's Middle Eastern Importing Company

CHEESES

All kinds of cheeses of the eastern Mediterranean are cooked inside breads; wrapped in phyllo or pastry dough; sliced and broiled; blended with all sorts of wild and cultivated greens inside pies; stuffed into peppers and broiled; battered and fried, then doused with vinegar; or simply fried, then served with lemon wedges or a hot red pepper sauce.

A good number of quality cheeses are produced in northern Greece, northern Turkey, and Georgia, which is not surprising, since it is these regions that produce the finest cheese pies and breads. The richest cheeses are made from the milk of buffalo and sheep. Recently a number of superior Greek cheeses have become available in U.S. markets, good for table eating or for cooking in pies. I encourage you to try Greek *manouri*, Cypriot *haloumi*, and the Indo-European brand's *akkawi*.

Green cheese: Several of the original Georgian, Syrian, and Turkish recipes in this book called for fresh cheese referred to as "green" or "virgin," a simple, unripened cheese made from fresh curds drained of whey. There are two such green or virgin cheeses used in eastern Mediterranean cooking. The first, with a mild flavor and dense texture, is something like farmer cheese or a Mexican *queso fresco*. The second, an unripened cheese that has gone through a secondary process, such as boiling and shaping, and thus has a smooth, buttery consistency is like unsalted fresh mozzarella.

Freshly made, unsalted mozzarella is becoming increasingly available. I see it in my supermarket, but not all the time. When I do see it I buy a lot, chill the cheeses, grate them in the food processor, then package them in 1-cup measures into small bags, from which I press out all the air. I store the grated cheese in a plastic container in the freezer, where it keeps for months. (The grating keeps the cheese from stringing when heated.)

Feta: When white fresh cheese is left to ripen in brine, it becomes more compact and mildly salty, and develops a tangy flavor. Such a cheese is called feta or *haloumi*.

Northern Greece and Bulgaria produce the tastiest, creamiest feta, made from quality sheep's milk. One of the most exciting new entries in the American market has been "barrel feta," imported from northern Greece. Its texture is creamy, and its taste is mellow.

To store feta: Make your own brine, with enough fresh water to cover and a spoonful of salt.

Some eastern Mediterranean cooks tell me that the debris at the bottom of a barrel of feta and the "bloom"-like creamy substance produced around a naturally made sheep's-milk feta are especially good in pies.

Mail Order for Sheep's-Milk Cheeses (including *Manouri*): Dean and DeLuca

Mail Order for Sheep's-Milk Cheese Log (packed fresh curds): Write Hollow Road Farms for the nearest supplier.

Mail Order for *Akkawi* Cheese: Write Indo-European Distributors.

COFFEE POT (BRIKI)

This is a long-handled, imported coffee pot. Its special shape insures perfect eastern Mediterranean coffee every time. Pots for 2 to 8 persons.

Mail Order: Kalustyan, G. B. Ratto and Company, and Sultan's Delight

CORNMEAL AND GRITS

Stone-ground quality cornmeal can be purchased at health food stores.

Mail Order for Cornmeal and Grits: Adam's Milling Company

Mail Order for Johnnycake Meal and Cornmeal: Gray's Grist Mill

CORERS OR REAMERS FOR ZUCCHINIS AND EGGPLANTS

Mail Order: Oriental Pastry and Grocery, Shallah's Middle Eastern Importing Company, and Sultan's Delight

FLOWERED WATERS

Years ago, I didn't much like imported Lebanese (as opposed to French) rose and orange flower scented waters, but the quality today is so much better that I feel confident recommending them.

Use a quick dash of orange flower water to perfume fresh pomegranate seeds. Use the same small amount of rose water to infuse ground pistachios for Baklava (page 375). Or use a tiny amount of the two together to flavor cheese for the Middle Eastern confection *kdaif* (see pages 379 and 380).

Mail Order: Kalustyan, Oriental Pastry and Grocery, Shallah's Middle Eastern Importing Company, and Sultan's Delight

FUL MDAMMES

Middle Eastern grocers sell these beans in ready-to-serve 20-ounce cans.

Mail Order: Kalustyan, Oriental Pastry and Grocery, Shallah Middle Eastern Importing Company, and Sultan's Delight

GRAPE OR WILD VINE LEAVES

In late fall, buckets of pickled grape leaves are available at Greek and Middle Eastern markets.

Otherwise, use jarred California grape leaves, which are extremely tender.

Wild vine leaves grow in almost every state and are well worth gathering.

HARDWOOD CHARCOAL

Call to order or for nearest outlet: Nature's Own Charwood 1-800-289-2427.

HONEY, CHESTNUT, OR PINE

Mail Order: Dean and DeLuca

LAMB

Here is a mail-order source for delicious lamb fed on grasses and natural grain, and free of antibiotics, chemicals, and hormones.

Mail Order: Jamison Farm

LENTILS

Unpeeled red lentils (*masoor*—whole) and cracked hulled red lentils.

Mail Order: Dean and DeLuca and Kalustyan

MA'MOUL MOLDS

Wooden molds for date cakes and walnut cakes.

Mail Order: Kalustyan, Shallah's Middle Eastern Importing Company, and Sultan's Delight

NUTS

Almonds: Ideally, almonds should be bought fresh, in the autumn. To check for firmness, cut one open; the interior should be creamy white. Remember, one rancid almond can ruin an entire dish, so avoid nuts with a grayish tinge. Buy whole almonds with the skin on. The skins not only protect the nuts from rancidity, they protect their delicate flavor.

To peel almonds: Place in cold water, bring to a boil, then turn off heat. Drain. When cool enough to handle, peel by squeezing one almond at a time out of its skin.

Freshly blanched almonds contribute greatly to sauces and stuffings, especially if they have been *very lightly* toasted, to bring up their flavor. If the only almonds available are whole blanched almonds, packaged in plastic, they may be a little dry. Soak them in water 10 minutes, then drain before using.

Hazelnuts: Hazelnuts grow abundantly in Turkey. Be sure to buy them fresh or vacuum packed; since they have a high oil content, they quickly become rancid.

I pass along the following trick for peeling hazelnuts from the famous pastry chef Jim Dodge in the anthology *Trucs of the Trade*, edited by Frank Ball and Arlene Feltman: "Place hazelnuts in a single layer on a cookie sheet and mist them with water. Bake in a preheated oven at 400° F. for five minutes. The small amount of water creates enough steam to loosen the skins so they slip right off the nuts."

Pine nuts, or pignolis: You find pine nuts in all kinds of eastern Mediterranean food—in pilafs, stuffed vegetables, meat fillings, kibbeh, and desserts. The best Mediterranean pine nuts are thin from end to end. Asian pine nuts are half the price, and may be substituted, but they really aren't as tasty.

To toast pine nuts, place on a lightly buttered or oiled baking sheet, then bake 10 minutes in a 300° F. oven, shaking the pan often, until lightly browned. Pack in the freezer to use as needed.

To make untoasted pine nuts extra creamy, soak them in water 15 minutes, then dry them out in a nonstick skillet set over a low flame for a few minutes, to open up their subtle resinous flavor.

Walnuts: In Georgia, walnuts are ubiquitous. Crushed, they are added to sauces, used to thicken soups and stews, to stuff eggplants, and to fill pastry. Walnut oil is frequently drizzled over vegetable pâtés. Whole walnuts are preserved, while still green, in a syrup to be eaten as a snack, while whole walnut kernels are left to dry and then candied directly on strings (page 387). Walnut leaves are used to wrap trout for roasting over coals. Finally, walnuts are used in at least a dozen Georgian sauces, some of which appear in this book.

Store all nuts in the refrigerator or freezer.

OLIVE OIL AND OTHER FATS

Olive oil is the great medium for Mediterranean cooking. The Mediterranean cook can do without butter if she must. She can even work without fat. But without olive oil she is lost. Olive oil is the backbone of the Mediterranean diet.

Middle Eastern stores offer the best buys in olive oil, especially if you purchase large cans. Light and heat place a strain on olive oil, so store your oil in a cool, dark place.

Around the Mediterranean, olive oil is used for deep frying because it preserves and protects the true taste of food, and because its smoking point is higher than that of almost any other polyunsaturated oil. Olive oil is also cost effective for deep frying, since you can use the oil several times, if you filter it. Try not to mix olive oil with other oils; different oils have different smoking points, and there is a possibility you may stress the non-olive oil, causing it to release unpleasant and possibly toxic elements.

In many regions of the eastern Mediterranean, butter, clarified butter, and sheep's-tail fat are used as cooking media, especially for meats and desserts. In this book I have retained the use of butter only in recipes for which it is absolutely required. Otherwise I have substituted olive oil or "butter-flavored" canola oil spray, a natural product. I never use sheep's-tail fat, and do not recommend it.

OREGANO PICKLE

Mail Order: Shallah's Middle Eastern Importing Company

PARCHMENT

Mail Order: G. B. Ratto and Company

PASTRY SHEETS

In Greek, they're called *fillo*; in Turkish, *yufka*; in Arabic *fila*; and in Abkhazian/Georgian, *penovani*. Whatever the name, they are the same wonderful sheets of pastry dough that bake up to shattering crisp, parchment-like leaves, making wonderful wrappings for all kinds of sweet and savory fillings.

Phyllo is made simply from flour, salt, and water, with an occasional dash of vinegar or soda water. Strudel dough contains fat and egg for greater strength. The two can be used interchangeably, if you make slight alterations in a recipe, taking into account the moisture and weight of the filling.

On the East Coast and in the Midwest, Apollo ultra-thin #4 phyllo has thinner sheets, while Apollo #7 has sheets of medium thick-

ness. On the West Coast, Omega is thin, and the Long Beach White Label is standard.

A note on handling commercial phyllo: Let stand at room temperature 2 hours before unfolding; keep the sheets from drying out by covering with plastic wrap or a damp towel and brushing each pastry sheet with melted butter and oil. If the phyllo is frozen, allow it to thaw in the refrigerator overnight.

True strudel leaves (4 sheets to the box) are available at Hungarian bakeries. They hold moisture, have good flavor, and are uniquely tender and crunchy.

Kataifi, a shredded pastry dough, is available at Middle Eastern groceries.

Mail Order for Strudel Leaves: Paprikas Weiss (winter months)
Mail Order for Kataifi: Sultan's Delight

PEPPER PASTE, TURKISH RED

See Appendix A, page 389, for a milder and more flavorful home made version.

Turkish hot pepper paste can be purchased in jars through mail order. If unavailable, the Indonesian pepper paste *sambal oelek* makes a respectable substitute.

Mail Order: Kalustyan, Oriental Pastry and Grocery, Shallah's Middle Eastern Importing Company

PIZZA PANS AND TERRA-COTTA PANS

Fourteen-inch-round regular and deep-dish Bakalon pans for Greek country pies and Middle Eastern desserts.

Terra-cotta pizza pans for Crackling Flat Bread (page 46).

Mail Order: The King Arthur Flour Baker's Catalogue

POMEGRANATE MOLASSES

Pomegranate molasses (called *nasrahab* in Georgian and *dibs rumman* in Arabic), is an essential eastern Mediterranean ingredient that may be purchased at Middle Eastern groceries or by mail order. A good-quality brand is Cortas, imported from Lebanon. Pomegranate molasses has a wonderful flavor and a heady aroma, and its thickness and dark color make food look very appealing. It keeps almost indefinitely in the refrigerator.

The uses for this thick, tangy, piquant syrup are many. It blends well with walnuts, adds a tart and pungent flavor to beans, sharpens the taste of poultry, gives a clean, tart taste to fish, gives an astringent edge to salads and vegetables, and is a great tenderizer for lamb and pork. It can also be diluted and used for sharp drinks and tart sorbets.

A few years ago, when I heard the Syrian army had bombed the Lebanese factory that produced my favorite pomegranate molasses, I immediately ordered a case. I didn't want to be without this wonderful flavoring.

Pomegranate molasses should not be confused with grenadine syrup, which is made from the same base but has other flavorings added.

HOMEMADE POMEGRANATE MOLASSES

Makes I pint; I tablespoon molasses is equal to about 1/2 cup juice

Buy the largest, reddest pomegranates. Check that the blossom end is just a little soft when pressed with the thumb. You will need about 2 dozen to make 6 cups juice. Or substitute bottled pomegranate juice.

I. Wash the pomegranates. Roll them around until they soften, then break up the pomegranates under water to keep juice from spurting. Give a good bang with the back of a knife to loosen the seeds of each section.

2. To squeeze out the juice: Wrap a handful of seeds in cheesecloth, then use your hands to squeeze into a bowl to obtain the rich, shiny liquid. Repeat with the remaining seeds. (Do not use a juicer. Pomegranate juice stains are difficult to remove, and the bitter, tannic white part of the fruit gets mixed in and mars the flavor.)

3. Place 6 cups fresh or bottled pomegranate juice, I cup sugar, and I cup lemon juice in an enameled saucepan and slowly reduce by boiling to 2 cups. Cool, bottle, and keep refrigerated.

NOTES TO THE COOK: In the fall, buy extra pomegranates, remove their seeds as directed above, then store in plastic containers in the freezer. They keep up to a year. Use on Georgian salads, in the Gaziantep Cracked Green Olive and Walnut Salad (page 148), or as a simple dessert, sprinkled with orange flower water.

Mail Order: Dean and DeLuca, Kalustyan, Oriental Pastry and Grocery, G. B. Ratto and Company, Shallah's Middle Eastern Importing Company, and Sultan's Delight

SEMOLINA

Mail Order: Dean and DeLuca, Kalustyan, The King Arthur Flour Baker's Catalogue, Oriental Pastry and Grocery, G. B. Ratto and Company, and Shallah's Middle Eastern Importing Company

SHEEP'S-MILK YOGURT

Write Hollow Road Farms for the nearest supplier.

TAHINI (SESAME SEED) PASTE

Imported, smooth, camel-colored paste is milder than the domestic Sahadi brand. Try both and use the one you like best.

The oil at the top of the jar should always be stirred in before using. From time to time set the jar upside down so the oil can penetrate the paste. A well-closed jar, stored in the cupboard, will keep indefinitely.

TOMATO PASTE

It was only when I started to work on this book that I came fully to appreciate tomato paste—the way it can create deep, rich, nonacidic sauces. The secret, I learned, is twofold: to use this paste in only small amounts, and to revitalize it before use.

Some cooks sizzle tomato paste in olive oil until it glistens, making it lively, light, and aromatic. Whenever one of my recipes calls for canned tomato paste, you will find this instruction added.

Not all tomato pastes are the same. Some, in fact, are outright nasty. I personally like the Contadina brand. You can make your own with crushed ripe tomatoes. Simply add salt (about 1 teaspoon per pound) and cook the tomatoes slowly until they have lost most of their moisture, stirring toward the end to avoid burning. Pack the paste in small dollops as described below and store in freezer.

After opening a can of tomato paste, tear off about a dozen 12-inch square sheets of cellophane wrap and drop dollops of paste on each sheet. Wrap each individually into airtight packets, place the whole lot in a freezer bag, and store in the freezer. Use as needed. Frozen tomato paste will keep a long time.

WILD GREENS

Seeds for amaranth, arugula, orach, purslane, and mixed chicories called *misticanza*.

Mail Order: Johnny's Selected Seeds and Cook's Garden
Mail Order for Mixed Chicories: Cook's Garden

WHEAT BERRIES, HULLED

Mail Order: Kalustyan, Oriental Pastry and Grocery, Shallah's Middle Eastern Importing Company

MAIL-ORDER ADDRESSES

To the best of my knowledge, all the mail-order sources listed here are reliable.

Starter Pack

Dean and DeLuca, the fine gourmet grocery in New York, will mail a special starter pack to readers of this book. Call (800) 221-7714 and ask for the "Paula Wolfert Eastern Mediterranean Starter Pack." It will be sent via UPS and will contain the following ingredients, which may not be available in your area:

I jar pomegranate molasses
I pound green wheat (fereekeh or frik)
¼ pound ground sumac
¼ pound Near East or Aleppo pepper
I pound fine bulgur
I pound coarse bulgur
3 ounces Mediterranean oregano
I pound black lentils (whole red lentils) with skin on

Adams Milling Company, Route 6, P. O. Box 148A, Napier Field Station, Dolthan, AL 36303. (205) 983-4233

Adriana's Bazaar, 2152 Broadway, New York, NY 10023. (212) 877-5757

Aphrodisia Products, Inc., 282 Bleecker Street, New York, NY 10014. (212) 989-6440

The Bean Bag, 818 Jefferson Street, Oakland, CA 94607. (800) 845-BEAN

Cook's Garden, P. O. Box 535, Londonderry, VT 05148. (802) 824-3400; (802) 824-3027, fax

Dean and DeLuca, 560 Broadway, New York, NY 10012. (800) 221-7714 or (212) 431-1691

Fox Hill Farm, 443 W. Michigan Avenue, P. O. Box 9, Parma, MI 49269-0009. (517) 531-3179

Gray's Grist Mill, P. O. Box 422, Adamsville, RI 02801. (509) 636-6075

Hollow Road Farms, Stuyvesant, NY 12173. (518) 758-7214

Indo-European Distributors, 1000 Airway, Glendale, CA 91201. (818) 247-2000

Jamison Farm, 171 Jamison Lane, Latrobe, PA 15650-9419. (800) 237-LAMB

Johnny's Selected Seeds, Foss Hill Road, Albion, ME 04910-9731. (207) 437-4301

Kalustyan, 123 Lexington Avenue, New York, NY 10016. (212) 685-3416

The King Arthur Flour Baker's Catalogue, P. O. Box 876, Norwich, VT 05055. (800) 827-6836

Mo' Hotta Mo' Betta, P. O. Box 4136, San Luis Obispo, CA 93403. (800) 462-3220

Oriental Pastry and Grocery, 170–172 Atlantic Avenue, Brooklyn, NY 11201. (718) 875-7687

Paprikas Weiss, 1572 Second Avenue, New York, NY 10028. (212) 288-6117

People's Woods, 55 Mill Street, Cumberland, RI 02864. (800) 729-5800

Peloponnese, 6500 Hollis Street, Suite #10, Emeryville, CA 94608. (510) 547-7356

G. B. Ratto and Company, 821 Washington Street, Oakland, CA 94607. (800) 228-3515 in California; (800) 324-3483 in continental U.S.

Shallah's Middle Eastern Importing Company, 290 White Street, Danbury, CT 06810. (203) 743-4181

The Spice House Ltd, P. O. Box 1633, Milwaukee, WI 53201. (414) 768-8799

Sultan's Delight, P. O. Box 253, Staten Island, NY 10314. (718) 720-1557

Well-Sweep Herb Farm, 317 Mount Bethel Road, Port Murray, NJ 07865. (908) 852-5390

APPENDIX D: YOGURT

Although the healthful benefits of yogurt have been known around the eastern Mediterranean for thousands of years, they were not known in Western Europe. Except, that is, for a brief moment in the sixteenth century. Here is the intriguing story, as recounted by Maguelonne Toussaint-Samat in her fascinating *History of Food*:

> François I was suffering from what would now be diagnosed as severe depression. The doctors could do nothing for his listlessness and neurasthenia until the Ambassador to the Sublime Porte disclosed that there was a Jewish doctor in Constantinople who made a brew of fermented sheep's milk of which people spoke in glowing terms, even at the Sultan's court. The King sent for the doctor, who refused to travel except on foot; he walked through the whole of southern Europe, followed by his flock [of sheep]. When he finally arrived before François I, the latter's apathy had given way to a certain impatience, but he still did not feel well. After several weeks of sheep's milk yogurt, the King was cured. The sheep, however, had not recovered from their long walk and caught cold in the air of Paris. Every last one of them died, and the doctor left again, refusing to stay despite the King's offers. He went home, taking the secret of his brew with him. The health of François continued to improve, which was the point of the exercise, and yogurt was forgotten for nearly four centuries.

In the eastern Mediterranean, yogurt (called *laban* in the Middle East; *rayeb* in the Magreb; *matsoni* in Georgia and Armenia; *yogurt* in Turkey; and *yaourti* in Greece) is used to leaven dough and cakes; to enrich soups and sauces; as a foundation for dips and salads; as an accompaniment to pilafs, stuffed vegetables, and meat pies; as a poaching medium for meatballs and kibbeh; as a tenderizing marinade for meats and poultry; and as a substitute for butter in stuffings.

In Thrace and Macedonia, yogurt and eggs are beaten and spread over roasting meat and layered vegetables (see Balkan Moussaka with Fried Kale, page 362), to create a soft, golden-brown crust. In Turkey the famous stuffed pastas, *manti*, are covered with yogurt sauce, while in Syria and Lebanon kibbeh balls are poached in it, as are stuffed dumplings.*

In the Arab world, yogurt is perfumed with dried mint or gently fried garlic and fresh coriander, to be used as a topping for stuffed eggplant and chickpeas. In the Greek islands, yogurt appears in the ubiquitous cucumber and garlic salad, *tzatziki* (page 29).

In southeastern Turkey, where large amounts of yogurt are added to soups, very thick drained yogurt is used. It is so thick, in fact, that it must be thinned with milk before being beaten with a stabilizer, such as an egg. This procedure also removes some of the sour flavor. When yogurt treated this way is gently heated, it is extra creamy.

*See Lamb Dumplings and Kibbeh in Yogurt Sauce in my book *Mediterranean Cooking*.

You won't find hot yogurt soups in Greece, but you will everywhere else in the eastern Mediterranean. As far away as Georgia, cooks prepare yogurt soups year-round. (See pages 124–130.)

In many parts of the eastern Mediterranean, the most prized yogurt is made from buffalo's or sheep's milk, because of its high butterfat content. (Delicious sheep's-milk yogurt is now being made in New York State. It makes the best cucumber, garlic, and mint salad; see page 29.) Home cooks, when making yogurt, often stir some powdered milk into the cow's milk to simulate this richness.

In the Middle East, yogurt is sold in two ways, regular and drained. The latter is called *labne* in the Arab countries, *süzme yogurt* in Turkey, *khacho* in Georgia, and *stranguismeno* in Greece.

You can buy commercially prepared drained yogurt under the name *labne* in some Middle Eastern markets. Beware of brands in which heavy cream has been added.

HOMEMADE YOGURT

Although commercial yogurt is good, I use so much that it is more economical for me to make it at home. This is not at all difficult, and the yogurt lasts about 1 week before turning tangy, at which point it is not so good to eat but ideal for use in soups and sauces.

Makes 4 pints

2 quarts low-fat milk
3 heaping tablespoons plain low-fat yogurt with active cultures or 1 packet Bulgarian dried culture, available at health-food stores

1. In a heavy-bottomed saucepan or casserole, bring the milk to the boil, let it simmer for 2 minutes, and remove from the heat. Allow the milk to cool to about 110° F.

2. In a small bowl, combine the yogurt or culture with some of the warm milk and stir until smooth; stir back into the remaining milk. Divide among 4 pint jars. Set jars on kitchen toweling in the warmest part of the kitchen. Cover each with plastic wrap and more toweling. Yogurt will jell from 4 to 12 hours for a sweet flavor. (This depends upon how and where you let the yogurt incubate.) After it jells, stop the fermentation by placing the jars, loosely covered, in the refrigerator. Chill overnight; the yogurt will continue to thicken.

NOTES TO THE COOK: The flavor of yogurt—tart and strong or mild and sweet—depends on how fast the yogurt jells. "The quicker the sweeter" is a good rule, which is why you will often see cooks filling a number of small jars rather than one large one. If you can keep the temperature of incubation at 100° F., the culture will jell within 6 hours. If the yogurt is left to incubate at a lower temperature, it can take as long as 24 hours for the curds to set, in which case the yogurt will be very tart.

When buying yogurt to use as a starter, check for brands that include *Lactobacillus acidophilus*, especially healthful bacteria. Always save 3 or 4 tablespoons of your homemade yogurt to start up another batch.

You can use whole milk or reconstituted milk or any combination to make your own yogurt. I used low-fat milk to make the yogurt for most of the recipes in this book.

Draining Yogurt

Yogurt, whether homemade or all-natural lowfat commercial, consists of a delicate balance between curds and whey. Yogurt thins out when vigorously stirred, breaks down when heated without a stabilizer, and "weeps" when salty foods are added. For cooking purposes, I always drain low-fat yogurt to obtain a thicker consistency: Place lightly salted yogurt in a sieve lined with cheesecloth and leave it to drip 30 minutes to 24 hours. (You can substitute nonfat yogurt, but the resulting texture is a little chalky.)

Within an hour from the time you begin to drain it, your yogurt will lose about 20 percent of its liquid, acquiring the consistency of light whipped cream. This is about right for use in salads. Within several hours, your yogurt will lose almost half its volume and acquire the consistency of sour cream. In this form it is perfect for dips, sauces, and soups, for thickening vegetable purees, as a basting medium for fish, poultry, and meats, as an accompaniment to rice and bulgur pilafs and stuffed vegetables, or as a substitute for butter in meat fillings.

If you want your yogurt to obtain the very thick texture of cream cheese, allow it to drain even longer, after stirring in a few more pinches of fine salt.

Whenever you are draining yogurt, save the whey for cooking vegetables or for using as a drink. It's reputed to be good for the kidneys.

Drained yogurt, lightly salted, keeps longer in the refrigerator than commercial or homemade yogurt. Cover and store in plastic or glass containers and keep refrigerated for up to 2 weeks or until needed.

Goat's milk yogurt, available in fine food stores and health-food stores, has a tangier flavor than cow's-milk yogurt. You can use it drained for dips and salads.

Sheep's milk yogurt, which is naturally rich and dense, needs less draining for dips and salads.

ICED YOGURT DRINK

Iced yogurt drink is called *ayran* in Turkish, *lben shrab* in Arabic, and *tahn* in Armenian.

It goes well with many of the dishes of the eastern Mediterranean, cooling the body, soothing the stomach, and quenching thirst. The drink is made by whipping together thick yogurt and icy water.

Remember, there is a difference between the two popular fermented milk drinks of the eastern Mediterranean: *Ayran*, described above, and *lben*, a type of buttermilk, which is made by fermenting milk as if for yogurt, then churning it to remove the butterfat.

Serves 2

½ cup all-natural plain yogurt, drained to
    ¼ cup (see page 409)
8 ounces cold water
Pinch of salt or sugar
Ice cubes

Combine the yogurt, water, and seasoning in a blender jar and blend until foamy. Serve chilled with ice cubes.

YOGURT CHEESE BALLS PACKED IN OLIVE OIL

This dish is called *labne bi zeit* in Lebanon. Very thick yogurt can be drained even further, to a fetalike consistency, then rolled into cheese balls to be preserved in olive oil. Served with a fresh drizzle of olive oil, a pinch of herbs, and a squeeze of lemon, these balls make a typical Middle Eastern breakfast, accompanied by hot fresh flat bread, fresh tomatoes, olives, cucumbers, and all sorts of other fresh and pickled fruits and vegetables.

You can use these freshly made balls instead of feta in pies and pastries. Or crush them with a fork, blend with minced scallions, green chilis, and parsley, and use to fill phyllo pastries or bread dough triangles.

If the cheese balls are properly prepared, they will last a few weeks in a cool place and longer in the refrigerator. In the Middle East they are likely to be made with goat's milk, which has a sharp flavor and is better for long-term storage. Goat's-milk yogurt cheese balls will keep up to 6 months before turning acrid and breaking apart. You can buy these very pungent goat's-milk balls packed in olive oil at some Middle Eastern groceries.

Makes ¾ cup fresh fetalike cheese, to make 24 1-inch balls

2 cups well-drained, low-fat plain yogurt
1 teaspoon salt
½ teaspoon Near East or Aleppo pepper,
    (page 395) or ¼ teaspoon hot paprika and
    ¼ teaspoon sweet paprika
Olive oil
Small dried red chilis

1. Mix the yogurt and salt and dump into a triple layer of clean cheesecloth and tie up into a sack. Suspend the sack over a kitchen faucet with a bowl below to catch the drip. Allow it to

hang 24 hours. (See below for preserving this yogurt cheese.) A good tip is to scrape the outside of the cheesecloth once or twice to facilitate draining.

2. Crumble the cheese onto a paper towel and refrigerate until firm and dry to the touch. With oiled palms roll into 1-inch balls and dust with Near East pepper or a mixture of sweet and hot paprika. Cover with plastic wrap and refrigerate. The balls will stay fresh for a few days. For longer storage, let them dry another day on paper toweling, then place in a glass jar and completely cover with olive oil. Add a few small dried red chilis. Keep the jar in a cool place or refrigerate. Return the jar to room temperature before serving.

Another Kind of Yogurt Cheese

There is an extremely salty type of yogurt cheese, called *cökolek,* which was traditionally churned in a goatskin or sheepskin bag. Today, in rural Turkey the cheese is made in the home in an electric churner marketed expressly for this purpose. I saw this machine in operation when I was visiting a farmhouse on the Black Sea coast, a few miles from Bolu, a town famous for its good cooking. Here I observed the mother of a friend place a canister of chilled undrained yogurt in the machine, which shook it slowly enough to separate the butterfat from the liquid. After setting the butterfat aside, the woman salted the defatted yogurt, which was little more than whey, boiled it down to a concentrate, then dumped it into a thin piece of cloth suspended over a pan. The residue caught in the cloth was *cökelek,* which she left to dry.

She offered me a taste of an earlier batch, which she tossed with hot red pepper and bitter herbs.

The same cheese is made in the Middle East, where it is pressed into cakes and dried in the sun. The result is called *jameed,* used in the famous Bedouin dish called *mensaf.* Both *cökolek* and *jameed* are definitely acquired tastes!

BIBLIOGRAPHY

Abdy, Emilie, editor. *Cookin' Good with Sitto*, second edition. West Paterson, N.J.: Saint Ann's Melkite Catholic Church, 1982.

Aldeen, Batool Sharaf. *Fan Altabkh* (The Art of Cooking). Beirut: Modern Bookshop, 1984 (in Arabic).

Alexiadou, Vefa. *Greek Cuisine*. Salonika: Alexiadou, 1989.

————. *Greek Pastries and Desserts*. Salonika: Alexiadou, 1991.

Algar, Ayla. *Classical Turkish Cooking*. New York: HarperCollins, 1991.

Al-Jabri, Lamya. *Shahiyya Tayyiba* (Delicious, Good-Tasting). Damascus: Tlas, n. d. (in Arabic).

Andrews, Jean. *Peppers*. Austin: University of Texas Press, 1984.

Anthony, Dawn, Elaine, and Selma. *Lebanese Cookbook*. Sydney: Lansdowne Press, 1986.

Antreassian, Alice. *Armenian Cooking Today*. New York: St. Vartan Press, 1977.

Antreassian, Alice, and Marian Jebejian, *Classic Armenian Recipes*. New York: Ashod Press, 1981.

Aoun, Fayez. *280 Recettes de cuisine familiale libanaise*. Paris: Jacques Grancher, 1980.

Baghadady, Nadeen, and Hamdy Zamzam. *Atbaq Shaheh* (Delicious Dishes). Damascus: Dar Aliman, 1986 (in Arabic).

Ball, Frank and Arlene Feltman, editors. *Trucs of the Trade*. New York: HarperPerennial, 1992.

Benghiat, Suzy. *Middle Eastern Cooking*. New York: Harmony Books, 1984.

Bezjian, Alice. *The Complete Armenian Cookbook*. Fairlawn, N.J.: Rosekeer Press, 1987.

Blanch, Lesley. *From Wilder Shores: The Tables of My Travels*. London: John Murray, 1989.

Boulos-Guillaume, Nouhad. *La Cuisine libanaise naturelle*. Paris: Edifra/Ediframo, 1988.

Burum, Linda. "Pulling Strings: Cheese from the East," *Los Angeles Times*, January 28, 1993.

Corey, Helen. *Food from Biblical Lands*. Terre Haute, IN Char Lyn Publishing, 1989.

Davidson, Alan. *Mediterranean Seafood*. London: Penguin Books, Ltd., 1972.

Dictionario biologia. Tbilisi: Menabde, 1965.

Durrell, Lawrence. *Spirit of Place*. New York: Dutton, 1969.

Eren, Neset. *The Delights of Turkish Cooking*. Istanbul: Redhouse Yavinevi, 1988.

Facciola, Stephen. *Cornucopia: A Source Book of Edible Plants*. Vista, Calif.: Kampong, 1990.

Field, Carol. *The Italian Baker*. New York: Harper & Row, 1985.

Gray, Patience. *Honey from a Weed.* New York: Harper & Row, 1985.

Food and Agricultural Organization of the United Nations (FAO). *Traditional Foods in the Near East.* Rome: FAO Food and Nutrition Paper No. 50, 1991.

Halici, Nevin. *Güney Doğu Anadolu Bölgesi Yemerkleri* (Southeastern Anatolian Regional Cooking). Konya: 1991 (in Turkish).

————. *Türk Mutfagi* (Turkish Kitchen). Ankara: Guven Matbaasi, 1990 (in Turkish).

————. *Nevin Halici's Turkish Cookbook.* London: Dorling Kindersley, 1989.

Haroutunian, Arto der. *Middle Eastern Cookery.* London: Pan Books, 1984.

Isaac, Barbara Thomas. *Everyday Delights of Lebanese-Syrian Cookery.* Harper Woods, Mich.: Woodmont Publishing, 1977.

Kalcas, Evelyn Lyle. *Foods from the Fields.* Izmir: Bilgehan Matbeasi Bornova, 1984.

Karaoglan, Aida. *Food for the Vegetarian.* New York: Interlink, 1988.

Kochilas, Diane. *The Food and Wine of Greece.* New York: St. Martin's Press, 1990.

Kremezi, Aglaia. *The Foods of Greece.* New York: Stewart, Tabori & Chang, 1993.

Kummer, Korby. "Friendly Beans." *The Atlantic Monthly,* April 1992.

Ladies' Auxiliary "Mara Buneva" of the Macedonian Patriotic Organization. *Traditional Macedonian Recipes,* revised edition. Toronto: 1984.

Lassalle, George. *East of Orphanides.* London: Kyle Cathie, 1991.

Leyel, C. F., and Olga Hartley. *The Gentle Art of Cookery.* London, 1925. Revised edition, Chatto & Windus, 1983.

Lomidze, Tamara. *Kulinaris Khelovneba da Kartuli Kerdzebis Samazareulo* (The Culinary Art of the Georgian Kitchen.) Tbilisi: 1991.

Mallos, Tess. *The Complete Middle East Cookbook.* Sidney: Lansdowne Press, 1979.

Man, Rosamund. *The Complete Mezze Table.* London: Ebury Press, 1986.

Margvelashvili, Julianne. *The Classic Cuisine of Soviet Georgia,* New York: Prentice Hall Press, 1991.

Miller, Joni. *True Grits.* New York: Workman, 1990.

Mouzannar, Ibrahim. *La Cuisine libanaise.* Beirut: Librairie du Liban, 1983.

Mrljes, Radojko. *The Balkan Cookbook.* Belgrade: Jugoslovenska Knjiga, 1987.

Naj, Amal. *Peppers.* New York: Alfred Knopf, 1992.

Pape-Gegelaschvili/Dschanelidze, Nikolos. *Georgisches Kochbuch.* Izehohe, Germany: 1970.

Phillips, Roger. *Wild Food.* Boston: Little, Brown, 1986.

Qudaama, Ahmed. *Qamoos al Tabakh al Saheih* (Encyclopedia of Correct Cooking). Beirut: Dar An-Nafaes, 1980.

Ramazanoğlü, Gülseren. *Turkish Cooking.* Istanbul: Ramazanoğlü Publications, 1992.

Roden, Claudia. *A Book of Middle Eastern Food.* London: Thomas Nelson, 1968.

————. *A New Book of Middle Eastern Food.* London: Penguin, 1988.

Salaman, Rena. *Greek Food.* London: Fontana, 1983.

Sasson, Grace. *Kosher Syrian Cooking.* New York: 1958.

Şavkay, Tuğrul. "A Taste of Turkey," unpublished manuscript. Istanbul, 1992.

Simopoulous, Artemis. "Common Purslane: A Source of Omega-3 Fatty Acids and Antioxidants." *New England Journal of Medicine,* March 15, 1986.

Steingarten, Jeffrey. "Pain au Levain Naturel." *Vogue,* November 1990.

Toussaint-Samat, Maguelonne. *History of Food.* Cambridge, Mass.: Blackwell Publishers, 1992.

Natro Naradotes Ellinikes Eientages (Traditional Greek Recipes), 6 volumes. Athens: Fytrakis, n.d.

Waines, David. *In a Caliph's Kitchen.* London: Riad El-Rayyes Books, 1989.

Weiss-Armush, Anne-Marie. *Arabian Cuisine.* Beirut: Dar An-Nafaes, 1984.

Wolfert, Paula. *Couscous and Other Good Food from Morocco.* New York: HarperPerennial, 1973.

————. *Mediterranean Cooking,* revised edition. New York: HarperPerennial, 1994.

————. *Paula Wolfert's World of Food.* New York: Harper & Row, 1988.

Yassine, Sima Osman, and Sadouf Kamal. *Middle Eastern Cuisine.* Beirut: Dar El-Ilm Lil-Malayin, 1984.

INDEX

Sauce, (*cont.*)

    Swiss chard and walnut, green kibbeh with, 282

    tahini

        about, 21

        fish smothered in, 299

        pepper fish in, 300

    tomato

        cumin-flavored, fish poached in, 297

        eggplant trotters steamed in, 202

        in Nevin Halici's mixed vegetables with two sauces, 196

        pomegranate-, stuffed eggplants with, 216

    walnut and fresh coriander, baked fish fillets with, 296

    yogurt

        cinnamon-flavored, Adzharian-style green beans with, 195

        cucumber, garlic, and, 29

        garlic-, 27

        garlic-, in Nevin Halici's mixed vegetables with two sauces, 196

        Turkish dumplings with (*manti*), 101

Savory, summer

    Damascus summer salad with purslane and, 134

    salad, with pomegranate, fresh summer, 145

Savory pies and pastries

    all-purpose dough with yeast for, 57

    beef pie in the style of Svaneti, Georgian, 64

    börek

        Damascus-style, in a tray, 93

        eggplant, Pandeli's, 96

    cheese bread pie, Georgian home-style, 66

    homemade pastry dough with olive oil for, 73

    northern Greek pies

        cheese pitta, Kiki's, 86

        cheeses for, 77

        dandelion, Swiss chard, and cheese pie, 75

        Epirote sorrel, spinach, and cheese pie, 80

        gathering, cleaning, and preparing greens for, 82

        late-summer pitta with mixed greens, 78

        leek, spinach, and cheese pie in a cornmeal crust, 89

        leek and walnut rolls, Macedonian, 84

        Macedonian phyllo dough for, 69

        nettle and cheese pie, Macedonian, 83

        pickled cabbage pie, 91

        wild and cultivated greens for, 79

        yogurt and fresh herbs wrapped in grape leaves, 87

    spicy Eastern Mediterranean pizza with meat, 58

    Swiss chard and tahini beureks, Mrs. Bezjian's, 62

    za'atar pie, 61

Scallion(s)

    black-eyed peas with walnuts and parsley, 182

    black olive salad, Macedonian, 151

    mung bean and pomegranate salad, 180

Semolina

    about, 384

    butter cookies, 381

    sources for, 405

Shallots, *köfte* with, 341

Shish kabab, about, 330

Shredded beets with thick yogurt, 30

Skewered swordfish, 307

Slow-grilled eggplants, 205

Small brown beans (*ful*), 254

Smoky eggplant-yogurt foam with lamb crisps, 207

Sorrel

    and creamy giant white beans casserole, 257

    spinach, and cheese pie, Epirote, 80

Soup, 106–31

    beef, Georgian spicy and sour, 117

    green cream, Macedonian, 122

    lentil

        black, speckled with wheat berries and tarragon, 114

        red, Kurdish hot and spicy, 111

        red, with caramelized onions, from Aleppo, 113

        red bean and hot pepper, from Dagestan, 120

        sour, Anatolian, 108

        white, with fresh herbs, Georgian, 116

Sour plum sauce, Georgian, 32

Sour soup, Anatolian, 108

Spice(s)

    about, 395–99

    Georgian, *badza* with, 316

    home-prepared mixtures of

        Georgian *khmeli-suneli*, 393

        Svaneti salt, 393

        Syrian mixed spices number 1, 392

        Syrian mixed spices number 2, 393

        Turkish *baharat*, 392

    red beans, and cheese, 172

drink, iced, 411
-eggplant foam, smoky, with
    lamb crisps, 207
and fresh herbs wrapped in grape
    leaves, 87
homemade, 409
and lemon marinade, chicken
    broiled with, 313
sauce
    cinnamon-flavored,
        Adzharian-style green beans
        with, 195
    cucumber, garlic, and, 29
    garlic-, 27

garlic-, in Nevin Halici's
    mixed vegetables with two
    sauces, 196
Turkish dumplings with
    (manti), 101
sheep's milk
    about, 409
    sources for, 405
soup
    about, 124–25
    leek and, with mint, 129
    potatoes and, with safflower
        swirls, 126
    spring peas and, 127

wheat berry and, with
    pistachios, 128
stuffed eggplants with, 218
tahini with, 23

Za'atar and za'atar blend, 398–99
Za'atar pie, 61
Zucchini(s)
    corers or reamers for, sources for,
        401
    stuffed with bulgur, tomatoes,
        and hot pepper, 220